The Making of Grand Paris

Urban and Industrial Environments
Series editor: Robert Gottlieb, Henry R. Luce Professor of Urban and Environmental Policy, Occidental College

For a complete list of books published in this series, please see the back of the book.

The Making of Grand Paris

Metropolitan Urbanism in the Twenty-First Century

Theresa Enright

The MIT Press
Cambridge, Massachusetts
London, England

© 2016 Massachusetts Institute of Technology

All rights reserved. No part of this book may be reproduced in any form by any electronic or mechanical means (including photocopying, recording, or information storage and retrieval) without permission in writing from the publisher.

This book was set in Stone Sans and Stone Serif by Toppan Best-set Premedia Limited.

Library of Congress Cataloging-in-Publication Data

Names: Enright, Theresa, author.
Title: The making of grand Paris : metropolitan urbanism in the twenty-first century / Theresa Enright.
Description: Cambridge, MA : MIT Press, 2016. | Series: Urban and industrial environments | Includes bibliographical references and index.
Identifiers: LCCN 2016000959 | ISBN 9780262034692 (hardcover : alk. paper) ISBN 9780262549226 (paperback)
Subjects: LCSH: City planning—France—Paris. | Cities and towns—France—Paris. | Cities and towns—Growth.
Classification: LCC HT169.F72 E57 2016 | DDC 307.1/2160944361—dc23 LC record available at https://lccn.loc.gov/2016000959

Contents

Acknowledgments   vii

Introduction   1

Part I: Envisioning the Unified City

1 Paris and/Is Its Suburb   31

2 The Shared Dream of Grand Pari(s)   65

Part II: Connecting the Networked City

3 Transit Debates and the Contested Regime of Metromobility   97

4 The Mobilizing Myths of the Grand Paris Express   125

Part III: Governing the Competitive City

5 A Thousand Layers of Governance   159

6 Metropolitan Governance and Global City Productivism   191

Conclusion: Grand Urbanism in Perspective   221

Notes   241
References   261
Index   289

Acknowledgments

Learning, writing, and producing knowledge are all collective processes. This book is a shared endeavor, and I thank all who have contributed along the way.

At the University of California, Santa Cruz, where this project first emerged, special thanks go to Dean Mathiowetz, Miriam Greenberg, and Robert Meister. They showed exceptional care and attention in facilitating the early stages of research and writing, and each had a great influence on the development of the ideas and arguments presented here. Their mentorship and unwavering support are much appreciated. Thanks also to the Politics Department of the University of California, Santa Cruz, for its commitment to interdisciplinary social science work, and to the Urban Studies Research Cluster and the Center for Cultural Studies for the vibrant scholarly community and countless provocations.

At the University of Toronto I am grateful to my colleagues in the Department of Political Science, especially Richard Stren, Patricia McCarney, Louis Pauly, and Peggy Kohn. Not only did they provide crucial guidance throughout the writing process but together they have also created a stimulating and exciting environment in which to think about urban and spatial politics. Acknowledgments also extend to the Center for Ethics and to the Law, Urbanity, and Justice Research Group where some of the ideas for the book were workshopped.

A number of other friends, colleagues, reviewers, students, and interlocutors have contributed to the making of this text by reading drafts, offering critical commentary, pointing me in new directions, and more generally offering good advice and moral support. Many thanks to Gopal Balakrishnan, Alexander Hirsch, David Hoy, Stefan Kipfer, Jan Kotowski, Alan Mabin, Sarah Mak, Eleonora Pasotti, Guillaume Poiret, Sarah Romano, Jasmine

Syedullah, Megan Thomas, Immanuel Wallerstein, and Dan Wirls. I received valuable feedback from a variety of audiences to which I presented parts of this research. The ideas presented here were enriched by discussions held at the Association of American Geographers Annual Meeting in 2011 and 2012, the Western Political Science Association Annual Meeting in 2012, the University of Minnesota's Department of Geography, Environment, and Society in 2012, the Suburban Revolution Conference at York University in 2013, and the International Studies Association in 2014. This work would also not have been possible without the many formal and informal encounters and conversations with the inhabitants of Grand Paris—I thank everyone who took the time to speak with me about the making of the city. At the MIT Press I am indebted to Beth Clevenger, Miranda Martin, Deborah Cantor-Adams, and Marjorie Pannell for facilitating the editing and production of the book. Closer to home, I am sincerely grateful to my family, and especially my parents, Wayne and Rosemary Enright, who provided encouragement and generosity throughout the time of the book's writing. Donald Kingsbury has been a constant support in this book as in life. I am incredibly grateful for his brilliance, love, and partnership.

I am grateful to several publishers for permission to reprint in modified form a number of previously published works. These include (all by Theresa Enright) "Illuminating the Path to Grand Pari(s): Architecture and Urban Transformation in an Era of Neoliberalization," *Antipode* 46, no. 2 (2014): 382–403; "Mass Transportation in the Neoliberal City: The Mobilizing Myths of the Grand Paris Express" *Environment and Planning A* 45, no. 4 (2013): 797–813 (Pion Ltd., London, http://www.pion.co.uk, http://www.envplan.com); "Contesting the Networked Metropolis: The Grand Paris Regime of Metromobility," in *Transport, Mobility, and the Production of Urban Space,* edited by Julie Cidell and David Prytherch (New York: Routledge, 2015); and "Coordinating the Competitive Parisian Metropolis" *Flux* 2, no. 101–102 (2015): 57–68.

Introduction

Grand Paris: what will be the face of the future Île-de-France metropolis?
—François Fillon, Prime Minister of France, 2009

Quite simply, Grand Paris is the face of tomorrow's France.
—Maurice Leroy, French Minister of Cities, 2010

The Ambition of Grand Paris

In April 2009, in the wake of the global economic crisis, and with metropolitan Paris still reeling from the aftermath of the 2005 *banlieue* (suburban) uprisings, the beleaguered French president Nicolas Sarkozy stood at a dais in the majestic Cité de l'Architecture et du Patrimoine (Museum of Architecture and Heritage) in central Paris to share his vision for urban revitalization.

How is a city to be remade? The civic link? The social link? Solidarity and citizenship? How are these achieved for great metropolises such that they become once again sites of progress, prosperity and partnership? How does one invent the sustainable city? The post-Kyoto city? ... This is perhaps the greatest challenge to politics of the twenty-first century. France has decided to take up this challenge. France has decided to give an example. This is the ambition of Grand Paris. (Sarkozy 2009)[1]

With this proclamation, Sarkozy inaugurated the first stage of a multifaceted venture to address the economic, political, and social challenges facing Paris and France. This venture seeks to bring about a new Paris, a Paris for the new century, a larger, better, "Grand" Paris.

The Grand Paris project, first announced in 2007, aims to radically redefine Paris and how it functions. Undertaken through the coordination of the French state, the City of Paris, the Regional Council of the

Île-de-France, and the Île-de-France Mayoral Association, but including many other municipal leaders, civil society groups, think tanks, bureaucracies, and the inhabitants of Paris more generally, the project is a concerted effort to create a new city. Grand Paris comprises several specific policy initiatives, laws, and institutions: a high-profile architectural consultation and exhibition on the future of the region, the Great Wager (Grand Pari(s)) of Parisian Agglomeration; the 2010 Grand Paris Act, which provided the legal framework for redevelopment; a new mass transportation network, the Grand Paris Express (GPE); a special-purpose agency to oversee the construction of the transportation network, the Society of Grand Paris (SGP); an organization tasked with the development of an innovation cluster southeast of the city, the Public Authority of Paris-Saclay (EPPS); a permanent architectural studio to reflect on questions of urban design, the International Workshop of Grand Paris (AIGP); a new administrative body, the Métropole du Grand Paris (MGP); targets for housing and city greening; and designs for hundreds of site-specific works. More than a single redevelopment plan, however, Grand Paris represents a new political vision for Paris and a new paradigm for urbanism.

The various elements of Grand Paris aim to redefine the city for the twenty-first century by expanding Paris well beyond its historic core and creating a polycentric and networked urban region competitive in the global marketplace. Chief among the virtues of the Grand Paris paradigm is the creation of a world-class environment for business paired with social responsibility, civic engagement, and environmental sustainability. The imagined city of Grand Paris is integrated, accessible, dense, mixed use, and intelligent. It incorporates the latest technological and informational innovations into its networked infrastructures, which are designed to meet the needs of both international investors and city dwellers. In typical French fashion, Grand Paris also claims to be aesthetically pleasing and historically aware, attuned to the beauty and poetry of modern collective life. Grand Paris fosters cultural services and sites, as well as public spaces that optimize the ineffable joys of urban encounters. Furthermore, proponents of the plan celebrate its democratic ethos of utilizing innovative governance arrangements and participatory planning at each stage of the design process, thus ensuring accountability and partnership between various stakeholders in the Parisian metropolis.[2] The Grand Paris paradigm is being heralded both in France and internationally as a model for future urban developments. Indeed, city boosters are actively exporting it, and reform- and growth-minded urban planners and politicians throughout the world are carefully studying its inner workings.

The ambitious vision of Grand Paris raises important questions for the city of Paris and for global metropolitan futures more generally. These include: How do we define and delimit the contemporary metropolis? How can "greater" urban areas be effectively managed and integrated into the fabric of the city? In light of the complex interdependence brought about by globalization, how can cities effectively plan in the twenty-first century? What actors, institutions, ideas, and structures are involved in the making of a city? What is the relationship of urban spatial organization to social, economic, and political life? How can the pressure to be competitive in a global marketplace be balanced with the needs of daily inhabitation? How can global city regions be built in democratic and socially just ways?

This book seeks responses to these questions through a critical analysis of the important undertaking of Grand Paris. It situates the Grand Paris initiative within a history of modern urban planning in France and within the global processes of twenty-first-century urbanization in order to understand the meaning of Paris's restructuring. Focusing on the initial stages of the project's formulation, roughly from 2007 to 2014, this book analyzes the terms in which the initiative was framed and described, the conditions underpinning its conception, the means of inventing this future, and the potential implications of its implementation. Attending to the complex interactions of ideas, actors, and institutions that together are reconfiguring Paris and to the normative values that are constituted through this activity, it traces a response to Sarkozy's provocative question, *How is a city to be remade?*

In so doing, it shows how the future city of Grand Paris is an important site of conflicting aspirations and plans where the organizing principles of contemporary collective life are being reworked. Moreover, it finds that there are internal contradictions between the hegemonic tenets of urbanism that are guiding the project. The twinned goals of, variously, economic growth and equality, state productivism and democracy, competition and social cohesion cannot be reconciled, and by resting on the first term in each pair, Grand Paris is poised to renege on its formidable promise. To suggest that this project is delusional and self-defeating is thus to be at odds with the prevailing views of what makes a livable city, and with the best practices of urban design in the twenty-first century.

I contend that while Grand Paris purports to create equality and balance across a region plagued by inequality and social division, in orienting the city around economic growth, competition, and private investment, the initiative cannot but reproduce the social and spatial hierarchies it sets out to address. I demonstrate how large public expenditures, particularly on the new Grand Paris Express mass transit system, are not undertaken for the purpose of social service but to increase the economic attractiveness of the region and to promote speculation in suburban real estate markets. This state-led plan to orient the city around what Andy Merrifield (2014, 5) calls the "financial real-estate complex" is supported by an emerging regime of megaproject-based governance and is ideologically legitimated through an artful combining of the neoliberal political rationalities of competition and economic growth with the republican cant of state providence and social cohesion. The political consequences of a property regime and institutional framework that support rent production over inhabitation are dire. Through Grand Paris, the built environment is being redeveloped according to the powerful interests of local and transnational elites, while social polarization persists and may indeed worsen. This is especially troubling as what is happening in Paris is indicative of an emerging form of grand urbanism that is revealing itself in large metropolitan regions globally.

The Invention of Grand Paris

The Making of Grand Paris explores how imagined city futures become materialized in the built environment, how distributions of people, places, and functions are tied to policy initiatives, and the implications of these dynamics for social equality and democracy. To achieve this, the book focuses on three interlinked sites through which Grand Paris is being invented: (1) practices of metropolitan representation, (2) infrastructures of transportation, and (3) structures of governance. Corresponding to the imaginative, the economic, and the institutional aspects of Grand Paris, the intertwined sections specify three primary perspectives from which to understand emerging spatial forms of citizenship, production, and statehood.

What I call "grand urbanism" refers to a distinctive mode of metropolitanization that relies on state-led megaprojects that channel regional space for productive purposes in a financialized economy. If grand urbanism is a response to political problems of urban size and bigness, it frames its solutions in terms of market optimization. Grand urbanism is proliferating in urban practices around the world, but is at its apex in Grand Paris, with architects, politicians, planners, corporate elites, and technocratic experts aligning their resources to make greater Paris competitive in an economy of global city rent production.

Following the work of critical geographers on the urbanization of capital (Brenner and Theodore 2002a, 2002b; Harvey 1985, 1989; Lefebvre 1991; Peck and Tickell 2002), I show how the making of Grand Paris aims to increase capacities for regional accumulation and to adjust urban social relations and the structure of the state to the mandates of a capitalism in the twenty-first century. The Grand Paris process of metropolitanization can thus be seen as a particular variant of capitalist urbanization tied to an era of a consolidated information economy (Amin 1995; Hardt and Negri 2001; Sassen 2001), generalized gentrification (Smith 2002), real estate proliferation (Haila 1988; Lefebvre 2003), and the financialization of space (French, Layshon, and Wainwright 2011; Pike and Pollard 2010; Weber 2002, 2010).[3]

Yet in considering how the logics of capitalism work "on the ground," it also acknowledges that there is no direct and deterministic formula for how space is being produced. Urbanization is shaped by contingent politics (or, as regulation theorists have pointed out, by a dynamic *mode of regulation* that secures and normalizes particular relations of accumulation) (Boyer 1990; Jessop 1990; Lipietz 1987). Grand Paris is not the product of a seamless process whereby spatial economies and state structures are rescaled according to an abstract functionalist imperative. Rather it comprises a set of negotiations, contradictions, conflicts, experiments, and compromises among diverse institutions, organizations, and individuals. Assessing the political economy of Grand Paris thus also involves analyzing the complex activities, practices, beliefs, and behaviors through which power relations materialize in the built environment and in speaking subjects. The state—composed of people, parties, and government bodies—is crucial to this story of Grand Paris, as are private governance arrangements. What I emphasize throughout is that the Grand Paris initiative is never a simple personal, institutional, class, or partisan struggle for power but is always thoroughly embedded in a historical and cultural context where these overlap in myriad dynamic configurations.

The interaction of capital accumulation processes with public and private regulation and planning defines the field of forces that are shaping metropolitanization through grand urbanism. Three main critical approaches that seek to understand the political economy of urban change act as touchstones for the discussion of Grand Paris: (1) literature identifying the global/world city as a significant node in the financial economy, as an extended urban form, and as a planning ideal (Brenner and Keil 2006; Massey 2007; Sassen 2001); (2) Colin McFarlane and Jonathan Rutherford's (2008) notion of "political infrastructure" which explains how networks such as transit systems are key sociotechnical institutions involved in the production of the contemporary city; and (3) Neil Brenner's (2004) conceptualization of state rescaling as a framework for analyzing the shifting practices of governance and territoriality in a neoliberal climate. Each of these approaches, which are elaborated and assessed in the context of relevant chapters, suggests a dynamic interplay between accumulation dynamics and glocal politics in the processes of urbanization. Together these literatures offer a fruitful ground from which to theorize the ongoing transformation of the Paris region, and to assess the role of planning and policy making in the construction of new urban futures.

To account for the changing practices of French urbanism, the analysis presented in this book thus looks beyond the surface of personal politics or policy prescriptions (Jessop 2002). Instead it considers the more subtle rationalities of architecture, planning, and politics that shape how power is exercised, relatively independent of who governs (Flyvbjerg 1998). This book is an analysis of policy, but it is not strictly concerned with positivistic evaluation (measuring the "success" or "failure" of formal plans and procedures) or with prescribing remedies and alternatives. Rather, the work offers an immanent critical analysis of the discourses, the "web of relations and practices" (Rose and Miller 2008, 6), that define this planning moment—how Grand Paris is framed, according to what assumptions, and to what ends.[4] Using evidence from policy documents, spatial designs, plans, maps, categories, laws, names, statistics, speeches, and statements, the analysis traces the articulation of a metropolitan world and worldview. It aims to explain how and why in the first fifteen years of the twenty-first century the Parisian metropolis came into being as the central target of French urban politics and planning. This effort requires deconstructing the texts of Grand Paris and situating the initiative historically within the inheritance of French urbanism and within a contemporary constellation of more-than-local political and economic relations.

What Makes a City *Grand*?

Grand Paris is thus both a paradigm for urbanism and urban planning and a projected object (the urban environment) that is in the midst of being made. It is also, as the pun on the French word *"pari"* suggests, a "great wager" (or bet) on a future whose terms are in constant negotiation and whose outcome is unknown and unknowable. Depending on its iteration, Grand Paris suggests a shared dream, an official plan, a bounded territorial unit, a metropolitan ideal, a cartographic representation, a network of flows, an administrative body, an imperial feat of social engineering, a mode of thought, an ideology, a manifesto, a utopian vision for the future, or a nightmare. Identifying the precise dimensions of Grand Paris and differentiating the emerging form of urbanism from the multiplicitous practices and policies of urban planning today is difficult if not impossible. The stakes of these definitions are great, however, for in naming the metropolis, one summons it into being, sets the conditions for how it is known, and delimits its horizons of transformation.

Even the use of the name "Grand Paris," for example, is a calculated tactic in a much larger political struggle over who should direct the city's future. "Grand Paris" would typically be rendered in English as the "Greater Paris Region," yet the concept carries with it multiple ideas that undercut this simple translation. Although as late as 2006 the term was more likely associated with socially oriented local partnerships, today this appellation is associated with national spatial planning. "Grand Paris" implies annexation and is used to secure the symbolic dominance of Paris over its suburbs and to refuse the governing authority of the Île-de-France region ("Paris" here is the key nomenclature). "Grand Paris" can also be usefully contrasted with the designation "Paris Métropole" preferred by former mayor of Paris Bertrand Delanoë and the grassroots group of local representatives that joined their municipalities together under this name. Opposing the hegemony of Paris suggested by Grand Paris, Paris Métropole conveys instead the composite nature of the metropolis, suggesting not just an expanded

Paris but the cooperation and interdependence of a complex unit. While attuned to the conflicts over naming, I use the term "Grand Paris" throughout the book not merely with reference to Sarkozy's initiative but to invoke the many varied imaginaries of the metropolis animated by the 2007 venture. Part of the task of this analysis is to unpack the diverse iterations of metropolitanization brought together under this name.

As an amalgam of ideas, guidelines, procedures, and expertise, Grand Paris thus extends well beyond the personality of Sarkozy or any individual. Nevertheless, with his initial vision, Sarkozy crystallized certain priorities that have been difficult to undo. Indeed, the dominant expression of Grand Paris was most directly and succinctly established in Sarkozy's 2009 speech to inaugurate the Grand Pari(s) architectural consultation. This speech outlines the project rationale, and it is this version of Grand Paris that set the tone for subsequent discussions (and continues to be implemented in policies even after Sarkozy's presidential succession by his Socialist Party rival, François Hollande, in May 2012).[5] Taking up the various connotations of the word "grand," Sarkozy identified at least four main axes around which the discourses of Grand Paris are organized.

A Post(sub)urban Network

The city must not exclude but unite. ... The city is a whole. ... Grand Paris will cease to be an agglomeration to become a city *where one no longer speaks of the banlieues*.
—Nicolas Sarkozy, 2009 (emphasis added)

The primary aim of Grand Paris is to restructure relations between the city proper and its surroundings. Currently, the city of Paris has a population of just over two million inhabitants and covers an area of 105 square kilometers, but the surrounding Île-de-France administrative region has 11.9 million inhabitants (governed by eight departments and 1,281 local communes) and covers an area of 12,012 square kilometers (see figure 0.1). The French National Institute for Statistics and Economic Research (Institut National de la Statistique et des Études Économiques, INSEE) defines the urban area (*aire urbaine*) of Paris even more broadly, for a total of 12.2 million inhabitants and an area of 17,174 square kilometers. None of these fixed official designations, however, captures the ensemble of relations that defines the metropolis as a form of urbanity and citizenship, public action and decision, social interaction and communication. Indeed, one of the main

Administrative boundaries of the Île-de-France. *Source:* IAU Île-de-France, 2015.

challenges that Grand Paris faces is that there is no identifiable spatial form, political structure, or representational apparatus adequate to the contemporary metropolis (Chemetov et al. 2003; Fourcaut, Bellanger, and Flonneau 2007; Gilli 2008b; Offner and Gilli 2010; Panerai 2008). Where does Paris end and other non-Parisian spaces begin?

Redefining Grand Paris as a united metropolitan region represents an effort to capture and express the flux of urban relations that defy administrative limits and settlement types. It aims to give greater definition to the contours of the existing metropolis that are blurring the traditional distinctions between urban, suburban, global, local, regional, and national scales. As an exemplary global city region (Scott et al. 2001), Paris is no longer (and likely never was) adequately depicted as a bounded territorial unit. Paris is better understood as one example of a what Edward Soja (2005) describes as "the new and still unsettled forms of polynucleated, complexly networked, multi-cultural, and polyglot regional urban systems" that are coming to define urban spatial forms today.

More than an epistemological project to understand contemporary urbanization, Grand Paris also exemplifies a pragmatic attempt to govern metropolitan bigness and to manage and plan for the new morphologies of the urban age. Absolutely central to this task is urbanizing and retrofitting twentieth-century postwar suburbia, what Ellen Dunham-Jones and June Williamson (2009, v) call the architectural, engineering, and governance "project for this century." Some of the broad challenges facing large complex urban systems include the difficulties of forging metropolitan identities, providing services and infrastructures to rapidly growing territories, promoting prosperous regional economies, and creating democratic institutions responsive to the needs of to emerging polities. Notably, without effective governance at the metropolitan level, it is difficult to address these concerns and to manage interterritorial issues such as transportation, housing, welfare, and employment distribution.

While growing conurbations around the world are faced with disjunctions between economic, administrative, territorial, and social definitions of the city, in Paris these misalignments take on a particular form. They are indelibly marked by centralized patterns of urbanization that have long structured the region and by deep historical divisions between Paris and its *banlieues*, or suburbs.[6] Imbued with a richly mythologized past, Paris is seen as a vital center of modern urban life, whereas the *banlieues* have long been seen as empty and dangerous hinterlands and stigmatized as places of savagery, disorder, lawlessness, and poverty. In this core-periphery model, the *banlieues* do not qualify as urban spaces proper but are always external and inferior (infra-urban) to the city. The area surrounding Paris is extremely varied, but in general, between Paris and its *banlieues*, and between the bourgeois west and the working-class east of the metropolitan region, there remain great asymmetries in power, wealth, income, unemployment, social service provision, and demographic makeup (Balibar 2007; Dikeç 2007a; Fourcaut, Bellanger, and Flonneau 2007; Wacquant 2008). In particular, mobility and access to public transport within the suburbs are extremely limited when compared with the urban core. Paris is also overrepresented in regional governance with central city issues (and those of the national capital) often dominating the regional agenda at the expense of suburban concerns. The suburban riots that erupted in the northeastern municipality of Clichy-sous-Bois in November 2005 made visible these overlapping geographies of exclusion, discrimination, and marginality (Dikeç 2007b) and signaled the urgent need for Paris to confront its suburban crisis.

The prime objective of Grand Paris is to tear down the walls separating the core and periphery and to finally integrate the metropolis. There is a political and economic mandate to recast metropolitan Paris as an inclusive (*solidaire*) and globally competitive region and to create a regional geography appropriate to the networked realities of the twenty-first century. The metropolitanization of Grand Paris is thus both intensive and extensive. It seeks to rescue the body politic from its fragmented state through the creation of more harmonious forms of collective urban life, through physical infrastructures of mass mobility, and through expanding the city administratively into the inner suburbs. Essential to this task is a rearticulation of urban centrality and the creation of a multipolar assemblage that incorporates the *banlieues* as constitutive parts of Paris. Sarkozy asserted this through his ominous promise that in Grand Paris, one "no longer speaks of the *banlieue*," but only a unified *ville-monde*.

A Model Global City

Paris is a world city [*ville-monde*] whose name has significance for all men on earth. ... Paris is a global city [*ville-monde*] and a global economy. It is not only the capital of France. It is also the rival of London, New York, Tokyo and Shanghai. It takes part

in a large network of planetary exchanges and communications. It is destined to be at the forefront of civilization and the global economy. But it can lose its rank if we are not careful.
—Nicolas Sarkozy, 2009

Grand Paris is not merely an attempt to rethink the ways in which Paris's urban fabric extends beyond its municipal boundaries into the surrounding periphery but, for Sarkozy (2009), the grandness is also "a matter of [global] perspective." Insofar as it is constituted through complex transnational relations and is influential far beyond its official borders, Paris, like Doreen Massey's (2007, 13) London, is a "world city" with a "vast geography of dependencies, relations and effects." To transform Paris is thus to transform social, political, familial, financial, and trade engagements that span the globe.

The de facto world importance of Paris is accentuated by a long-standing myth that places Paris at the center of modernity (Baudelaire 2010; Benjamin 2002; Buck-Morss 1991; Harvey 2003) and the "capital of the world" (Higonnet 2009). Indeed, the symbolic import of Paris means that it frequently serves as an urban ideal to which all cities should aspire. As such, Paris is in a universal and universalizing position, treated as a proxy for the diverse experiences of urbanization and modernization the world over. Proponents of Grand Paris are quick to reiterate this fantasy of exceptionalism and avant-gardism and to claim, without irony or reservation, that the project of Grand Paris stands in for the future of cities more generally (see especially Blanc 2010).

The significance of Paris as a *ville-monde* goes beyond its planetary connections and symbolic distinction. As Sarkozy makes clear, to be a global city is also to be as Saskia Sassen (2001) defined it, a command-and-control center of the global economy. Even though Paris is not in fact one of Sassen's three financial powerhouses, in terms of its economic weight and productive profile the Greater Paris region exhibits many global city features. Paris is generally included in the "alpha" group of global and world cities, fourth behind London, New York, and Tokyo (Beaverstock, Smith, and Taylor 1999; Derudder and Witlox 2008). The Île-de-France is the European Union's wealthiest regional economy, with a GDP in 2009 estimated at €552 billion (INSEE 2010b). It is ranked second in the world in terms of the number of Fortune 500 companies headquartered within its borders (*CNNMoney* 2010), third in the world in terms of global influence (A.T. Kearney 2014), and seventh in the world in terms of commercial competitiveness (MasterCard 2008). Paris is a powerful node in the new spatial economy of financial globalization.

Paris is undeniably influential the world over, but maintaining this influence and, by extension, its global city reputation and status requires constant renovation and innovation. Not only must Paris keep productivity high and resident corporations happy, but the competitive nature of the global cities marketplace also impels Paris to perpetually improve its growth rate and attractiveness for investment.[7] In order not to "lose its rank," Grand Paris must adjust its rather diverse regional economy more exclusively toward the most productive sectors and expand the scale of command operations. Reconfiguring the suburbs is one way to promote new clusters of high-value industry, revive underperforming territories, and achieve the diffuse, multinodal organization so emblematic of more prosperous global cities.

Following what Jennifer Robinson (2002) calls the "regulative fiction" of the development model of the global city, Grand Paris has tied its economic development strategy to the creation of a network of suburban excellence poles, or hubs (a network of "hubburbs"). It aims to grow these poles around a variety of advanced producer services, building in particular its FIRE (financial, insurance, real estate), tourism (culture, leisure, recreation, commerce), and information (especially technology, research, and higher education) industries. These hubburbs are to be physically connected to one another and to the world at large through an improved high-tech infrastructure (e.g., by metro and European rail and airports). They are also connected socially to global professional, communication, and financial networks.

A *Très Grand Projet*
This is the first time in the world that a reflection of this amplitude has been undertaken on the phenomenon of the great modern metropolis. The work accomplished is without precedent in its profundity and audacity.
—Nicolas Sarkozy, 2009

The appellation "grand" is also a measure of magnitude. As an exemplary *grand projet,* Grand Paris is a wholesale redesign of the city, and the project most provocatively suggests that the reorganization of space and the built environment is crucial to social and political life. While most recent presidents have bestowed on the city of Paris a parting gift in the form of a single architectural monument or project (e.g., the eponymous Centre Pompidou and Bibliothèque Nationale de France François Mitterrand), Sarkozy went even bigger, and aimed to transform the entirety of Paris. Guided by the central state, Grand Paris demonstrates the importance of cities to national works. It is a *grand projet* taken to hyperbolic extremes.[8]

This pharaonic project cannot be considered divorced from the massive overhauls in space that preceded it—in particular, those brought about by Georges Eugène (Baron) Haussmann's notorious Second Empire reforms and the massive modernization and reconstruction efforts after World War II. Like those earlier civilizational projects, Grand Paris involves struggles over the meaning and management of collective life and an attempt to refashion economic and social relations on a vast scale. In Grand Paris, megaprojects are set to be the drivers of regional transformation. They leverage territory into productive global circuits; they arrange populations and localities in relation to one another; and they entrench the ideals of smart technology, scientific innovation, monumentalism, and spatial mastery. Large-scale projects are thus crucial technologies governing the metropolis.

The use of the metro in urban regional development (what I call throughout "metromobility") and the corollary shift from urban planning to project management are indicative of a new global culture of megaproject-driven urbanism (see also Flyvbjerg, Bruzelius, and Rothengatter 2003; Jones and Moreno-Carranco 2007; Swyngedouw, Moulaert, and Rodriguez 2002). The almost €30 billion, 200 km Grand Paris Express mass transit network is the keystone of the monumental metropolitan transformation. The GPE and the local urban development projects that are planned around each new metro station are poised to radically reconfigure urban space and urban life. The cost and length of the network is unprecedented and represents a highly significant investment of public funds and expertise.

The megaproject-driven metropolitanization of Grand Paris is also actively transforming regional governance arrangements. The extensive state (national level) involvement in Grand Paris certainly reflects a republic tradition of intervention and a centralized dirigiste administrative model, but this more traditional statism has also been adapted to a global climate in which local entrepreneurialism reigns supreme (Harvey 1989). As the initiative progressed it became clear that Sarkozy was not in fact a "prince and architect" who could coordinate space at his will. Rather, the making of Grand Paris, and in particular the coordination of the Grand Paris Express, involved negotiation and compromise on the part of many different agents. Sarkozy's Grand Paris vision merely provided a map for regional growth poles, and the Grand Paris Express coordinates a vast array of governing actors and institutions, from global experts to bureaucrats to private developers and corporations. In the twenty-first century the *grand projet* is built through a heady mix of state and nonstate forces.

A Better Future
Grand Paris is France after the crisis. It is France that exits the crisis stronger, more beautiful, more competitive, and I hope, happier.
—Nicolas Sarkozy, 2009

The fourth meaning of grand in Sarkozy's narrative of Grand Paris is evaluative, and invokes the modernizing tropes of progress and improvement. Building a new Paris is ultimately about making things better. The revival of Paris is set against a national atmosphere of stagnation and degradation and a deep "national anxiety" over the inexorable decline of power and influence of France's culture and economy (Subra 2012). This anxiety for lost glory and lost empire, what Paul Gilroy (2005) in the case of the UK describes as "melancholia," is intensified in the contemporary climate of heightened global economic competition and sustained worldwide financial crisis.[9] This national situation is compounded by concerns over the diminishing vitality of Paris. In recent years representations of *"le grand corps malade"* (the sick body) of the Île-de-France have flourished (Leloup and Bertone 2009). There have been concerns over the continued *banlieue* unrest, controversies over the "museumification" of the historic city (Rehberg and Ricupero 2008) and the banalization of gentrification (Hussey 2007), and a rising middle-class fear of supposedly "non-French" immigrant populations invading the city (Badiou 2009; Revel 2008; Rey 1996).

As justification for Grand Paris, this national and local decline is explained in primarily economic terms. According to Sarkozy, Paris is stagnating in a socialist state and is losing its global status of beauty and innovation that ushered it to the fore of the modern twentieth century. Christian Blanc (2009), a key proponent of Grand Paris, echoes this sentiment, blaming the postwar redistribution efforts for creating a "deficit in dynamism" for the capital region and arguing that "reduction is omnipresent, it threatens to reduce the last aspirations for global competitiveness." Sarkozy sought through the Grand Paris initiative to restore to Paris the values of the ideal city (*"le Vrai, le Beau, le Grand,"* or "truth, beauty, greatness") so that Paris may become an economic, political, and cultural leader (once again). With economic prosperity and renewed republican social bonds, the illnesses of the polity can apparently be healed.

To solve the problems of decay and obsolescence and to ensure that the region of Paris is as economically productive as possible, progress is tied inextricably to growth. In the words of Blanc (2010, 137), "One can try to become a world-city without being based on economic growth. One can also swim with weights on one's feet."[10] The focus of Grand Paris is on maximizing the capacities of the city as an engine of production through new developments in areas that are not yet meeting their full potential and through a directed shift in the economy toward advanced producer services. As the SGP (2012) stated, "Grand Paris also answers the needs of a global city. … It will have a considerable impact on business activities in the Ile-de-France area, the key growth driver in France." In particular, the creation of strategic sites of enterprise in the peripheries of Paris is expected to alter real estate markets, the most important sector of surplus value in contemporary cities. One of the distinguishing features of Grand Paris is its explicit orientation of planning toward the production of metropolitan rent. Closing the gap between current and potential land values, improvement here relies on the valorization of the city by capital and the appropriation of territory by the dominant social classes. Transformations to improve attractiveness and improve the *rentabilité* (rentability) of suburban space are tied to quality-of-life concerns only secondarily, with environmental well-being and livable places pursued as resources to be mobilized to underwrite the agenda of global city creation. The narrative of decay and obsolescence of metropolitan Paris thus sets the parameters for gentrifying reform.

Neoliberalism and the Global City

The Making of Grand Paris considers how the fourfold promise of regional unity, globality, monumentality, and progress is embedded into a competitive form of French metropolitan urbanism. It claims that urbanization in Paris, which until recently was directed by universal social welfare objectives, has now been firmly reoriented to more neoliberal planning and political priorities in pursuit of the global city. To the extent that social welfare objectives are maintained—and it is important to recognize that this is the case—these objectives are reframed in ways that are marketable and commodifiable.

Broadly, this book understands neoliberalism as a regime of capital accumulation that shifts production away from manufacturing and toward information, service, tourist, cultural, and FIRE industries (Amin 1995; Sassen 2001), as a "political rationality" of governance that permeates all aspects of life with the logic of market optimization (Brown 2003; Dikeç 2007a; Peck 2010; Rose 1999), and as a project to cement elite power by reconstituting wealth in the hands of a "transnational capitalist class" (Harvey 2005; Sklair 2005). Also important for the purposes of the present analysis is the extent to which processes of neoliberalism are articulated spatially (Peck and Tickell 2002), in particular through urban planning and development (Brenner and Theodore 2002b; Davis and Monk 2008; Swyngedouw, Moulaert, and Rodriguez 2002). Grand Paris achieves these features by entrenching technocratic spatial strategies aimed at maximizing urban value.

A path-dependent process, the neoliberalization of urbanism evident in Grand Paris builds on a number of glocal dynamics. Over the past thirty years, there has been a marked shift in France from nationally organized territorial management and policies of redistribution to management based on priority urban areas and policies fostering entrepreneurialism and interurban competition (Brenner 2004). Like much of the liberal democratic world, since the 1970s at the national level France has experienced a shift in economic production away from industry and toward information and advanced service sectors. The adoption of the shared euro currency in 1999 lessened the grip of the state over macroeconomic policies, and since the 1990s, the successive right-leaning governments of Chirac and Sarkozy instituted cuts to social services, and advanced business-friendly policies, and corporate tax breaks. This was accompanied by an emphasis on project-based economic growth (Pinson 2009), an increased importance of infrastructural and real estate sectors (Lorrain 2002), the privatization and financialization of city space (Baraud-Serfaty 2011; Renard 2008), and new regimes of security and penality, especially in suburban areas (Dikeç 2006, 2007a; Wacquant 2008). While reforms are felt in diverse ways across the country, Paris has been one of the primary sites where neoliberal governance has emerged in France, and it is through the production of this city space that competition, efficiency, and security have taken hold as important values of collective life.

While the process of what Bruno Jobert and Bruno Théret (quoted in Dikeç 2007a, 24–28) call "neoliberalism *à la française*" has been slow-moving and tempered by the social democratic norms of republicanism, Grand Paris aims to intensify and quicken the pace of reform, fully subsuming concerns of social welfare and justice into those of competition and economic growth (Blanc 2009; République Française 2009).[11] The Grand Paris reforms thus contrast starkly with the situation in France less than a decade ago. Mustafa Dikeç (2007a, 174) describes urban policy before Grand Paris as follows:

Despite brief periods of experimentation with neoliberal ideas, French urban policy has not sought to institutionalize inter-urban competition and to encourage a growth-first competitive logic as an overriding goal. Economic growth and competition have not replaced social issues as primary objectives; urban policy is a social not an economic development policy.

If the influence of neoliberalism on French urban policy was until 2007 "only partial," then Grand Paris is a very directed and self-conscious attempt to bring to the fore the latent neoliberal forces within urban policy and to reverse the ordering of social and economic priorities.

Today, the language of balance and solidarity persists, but attractiveness, competitiveness, and economic growth are the overriding concerns of urban development, and even the socialist, communist, and green parties consent to these terms. These are the basic tenets of each of the new policy and planning initiatives under the umbrella of Grand Paris and the goals that are most directly and fully operationalized. Today, the social aims of collective consumption and livability are either vaguely tagged on to economic policies or are themselves brought into a logic whereby use values ("sustainability" or "quality of life") become place-marketing assets to be sold to the world. The neoliberal utopia of Grand Paris was explained clearly by Maurice Leroy, minister of cities, at a speech given to potential investors in London in 2011:

> Grand Paris is ... an economic ambition served by a political will at the head of the State, that of Nicolas Sarkozy, that wants to strengthen the place of Paris in the growing competition to which large metropolises must surrender. ... We lead this competition with an entrepreneurial spirit and with companies. ... We bet on the future as you bet on the future of your companies.

Not only does the speculative wager of Grand Paris equate the city with a corporate enterprise, but it represents a solid shift away from the welfare state and from governing according to collective needs to governing according to risk and insecurity (Beck 1992; Callon, Barthe, and Lascoumes 2001). It also removes accountability from the practice of planning, "surrendering" the future of the city to the vagaries of the marketplace. According to this logic there is no alternative beyond the benevolent yet privatized global city.

Even in the aftermath of the 2008 global financial crisis and the ongoing sovereign debt crises reverberating across Europe it is growth (paired uneasily with austerity) that guides Grand Paris. Haussmannesque, the revitalization effort subsidizes private development during a recession through debt-financed state projects. While other countries in Europe implement austerity programs in the face of financial hardship, France continues to officially eschew programs of *rigeur* (a more benevolent term for austerity), opting instead for large-scale infrastructural programs to stimulate the economy.[12] In other words, through a state-backed productivism, Grand Paris explicitly redirects money from public ventures into private hands in the name of, but also with a priority over, collective welfare.

Among Western European and North American commentators, France is often singled out for being an exceptional social democracy. As such the very notion of neoliberalism *à la française* seems to be a contradiction in terms. Certainly a simplistic reading of urban planning's changing aims in terms of a single neoliberal dogma would be misleading. It is my contention that France's unique political culture and institutional landscape matter greatly. Yet what I argue is that it is through, not despite France's republican ideals, welfare policies, and centralized governing that Grand Paris is able to achieve its dynamic of competitive territorial optimization and hence, metropolitan neoliberalization.

Grand Urbanism

In this book I develop the more general concept of grand urbanism to capture the large-scale plans of growth-maximizing urbanization in which the overarching goals of metropolitan redevelopment are tethered to valorizing regional land, upgrading suburban amenities, and providing the conditions for future private investment. This framework of metropolitan planning and policy making is especially evident in Grand Paris but is illustrative of similar practices in other globalizing city regions around the world. Grand urbanism is a particular manner of governing bigness that relies on the use of megaprojects to restructure metropolitan political, economic, and social relations in pursuit of speculative growth and generalized gentrification.

Grand urbanism responds to the purported needs of vast metropolitan areas undergoing rapid transformations. Over the past forty years, extensive and intensive global flows have overhauled traditional administrative structures and land-use patterns in cities around the world. In place of relatively bounded subnational units with clear city and noncity frontiers are new urban arrangements that are at once limitless and fragmented (Brenner and Schmid 2014; Marcuse and Van Kempen 2000). The sheer scale of new urban regions and the immense transformations in everyday life resulting from globalization are accompanied by a series of urgent and ongoing challenges, among them uneven patters of development leading to increasing social polarization, new densities creating service and infrastructural needs, territorial interdependence undermining fixed governance arrangements, and periodic crises of accumulation. As "greater" regions bypass both nations and municipalities as the essential sites of organizing social, political, and economic relations, new planning paradigms and apparatuses are required to connect, govern, manage, and regulate the welter and flux of urban life and to ensure continued capitalist growth. One response has been to revive a modernist agenda of big vision, big plans, and big government, but with a decidedly postmodern twist. Grand urbanism employs techniques of large-scale planning to address the immense challenges of the contemporary metropolitan age, but unlike its twentieth century predecessors, it is a paradigm that is essentially speculative, flexible, and collaborative.

I borrow the term "grand urbanism" from a 2013 special issue of the Dutch urban and architectural magazine *MONU* dedicated what the editors labeled "Greater Urbanism."[13] Drawing on the Paris example, but with reference as well to metropolitan planning in Moscow, Athens, Detroit, Toronto, Singapore, La Paz, and Helsinki, the issue sets an agenda for thinking about the challenges of planning and politics in expanding urban regions in the twenty-first century. *MONU* editor Bernd Upmeyer (2013, 1) sets up the issue as follows:

> It appears that cities of today, and especially big cities, all around the world, are all struggling with similar problems, as they all have developed huge territories—their metropolitan or "greater" areas—during the twentieth century that cannot be properly understood by anyone in terms of their form, but that now need to be recognized as something that truly exists, because it is a form that is in perpetual transformation and without limits. In such unlimited spaces infrastructure plays without a doubt a crucial role in constructing a connected geography and reconfiguring new urban morphologies.

Building on the morphological analysis offered in *MONU* and the empirical details of Grand Paris, I consider grand urbanism to be defined by six interconnected features: (1) a political economy of the large global city; (2) a polycentric metropolitan form; (3) an emphasis on infrastructure megaprojects, especially those concerning transport; (4) a strong central state managing ambitious territorial restructuring; (5) consensual and collaborative governance; and (6) urban planning geared toward market optimization.

In many ways, grand urbanism refers to how cities, regions, and municipalities react on the ground to the transformations in space and society brought about by globalization. Whereas Sassen's (2001) analysis is useful for demonstrating the rise of a global command network and the reorganization of cities' internal space economies away from central business districts to more multimodal webs, an analysis of grand urbanism emphasizes how these changes were mitigated, facilitated, and responded to by planning and policy making at various scales. In addition, grand urbanism does not merely consider the compact global "city" as such, but a larger set of metropolitan relations (closer to what Sassen 2001, 351–351, calls the "global city-region"). Moreover, rather than focusing exclusively on advanced producer services, grand urbanism pursues a more expansive idea of world importance and global influence, seeking to bring the many regional and global connections that constitute the urban fabric to the forefront of planning and policy making.

In pursuit of the prosperity promised by the global city and in order to entice the investment and talent necessary to keep cities competitive, grand urbanism uses the now well-established techniques of "new urban politics" (Cox 1993; MacLeod and Jones 2011), such as growth coalitions, public-private partnerships, and megaprojects, and reworks them at a metropolitan scale. Urbanization and gentrification under grand urbanism become the key modes of political and economic production (see especially Smith 2002). Indeed, grand urbanism has an inescapable speculative character tied to land and territory. It is not merely about imagining the future of the urban region as a global powerhouse, it is also about leveraging this future into financialized property markets. The production and distribution of attractive urban futures is a crucial strategy undertaken by governments seeking to attract global capital and to mobilize national and local territory into global circuits of exchange. Grand urbanism thus transforms how design and architectural vision are instrumentalized within grand schemes and local contractual projects.

With the economic, spatial, and population growth associated with this sort of global city production, come new demands for social reproduction as well. Grand urbanism thus also identifies large-scale strategies to deal with the social consequences of becoming metropolitan. When cities grow in size and complexity, so too do their problems. As Kantor and coauthors (2012, 3) note, the challenges in global city regions are "vast, varied and constantly changing." Global city regions require extensive and broadly distributed facilities of transportation, education, health, housing, and leisure. To manage the unequal way that benefits are distributed under financial capitalism and to defuse social antagonisms caused by this, they also require diverse and stable employment opportunities, environmental protections, social services, and democratic institutions. Major cities around the world are developing experimental policies to address these challenges resulting from globalization and metropolitanization.

Infrastructures, and particularly megaprojects of mobility, are exemplary features of grand urbanism that respond both the changing size of large urban regions and to the contradictions inherent in capitalist urbanization. Infrastructure in the contemporary metropolis is thus crucial to "governing and controlling urban change" (McFarlane and Rutherford 2008, 364). Creating new scales for populations and functions, organizing multiple administrations and stakeholders, coordinating different planning apparatuses (especially transit and land use), anchoring investment in priority sites, and creating a networked topology of connection and flow, infrastructure is at the heart of grand urbanism's strategic functions. Large-scale transport projects are particularly salient for cleaning up faltering urban reputations ("rebranding"), selling the amenities associated with a global city, soliciting public support for finance and technology, and entrenching a paradigm of multipolar growth. They also provide physical supports of connection between populations and localities. In other words, infrastructures of mobility are fundamental to social equity insofar as they are tangible bearers of access and movement, yet they also redistribute public funds to private enterprise and work to bolster the uneven urbanization patterns that they are otherwise meant to address. This tension is one of the central features of grand urbanism.

Infrastructural provision is also instrumental in recasting relationships of power and authority. The difficulty of organizing metropolitan infrastructure is exemplary of the cross-territorial problems of large metropolises, and like many problems of interdependence, regional transportation needs are poorly met through the workings of the free market and antiquated government institutions. New tools are needed to coordinate collective action at the metropolitan scale. Grand urbanism initiates a process of state rescaling whereby the greater urban region becomes the key site and stake of political intervention. Due to the scale and scope of metropolitan endeavors, the state remains an important force in creating a new knowledge of the urban, coordinating the social and economic arrangements of the city, and forging new tools of political management at the metropolitan scale. At the same time, however, subnational, private, and other nonstate influences are involved in governance and project delivery in myriad ways.

Indeed, grand urbanism denotes a more limited type of governance built on multiple and overlapping forms of authority and non-sovereign relationships within the state and between public and private actors. Under grand urbanism, national states are invaluable for their ability to organize territory and overcome interinstitutional conflicts and blockages. Yet in order to arrange collective action at the metropolitan scale, they must also abrogate certain responsibilities vertically to other levels of government and horizontally to the private sector. In addition to multinational corporations, private speculative developers, and business associations that drive the creation of the global city, the work of intellectual and cultural producers such as architects (themselves multinational corporations and embedded in financial and real estate markets) is crucial for a comprehensive yet fragmented mode of project-led territorial reform.

In summary, in its empirical focus, the analysis of the grand urbanism of Grand Paris makes two main contributions. It brings to light a recent history of territorial planning and policy making that has thus far been neglected in the Anglo-American world. *The Making of Grand Paris* adds an essential third chapter to existing narratives of Second Empire and postwar overhauls of Parisian space. It also demonstrates the particular workings of French urban neoliberalism and shows how neoliberal strategies and tactics, which until now have been only an undercurrent of policy making, have through Grand Paris become a broad common sense. In looking at how various stakeholders create spaces and norms for metropolitan gentrification (bound up in notions of solidarity and state providence), it thus unsettles typical understandings of French social democratic exceptionalism.

Through the conceptual framework of grand urbanism, the present analysis of Grand Paris also offers three theoretical lessons on the changing nature of urbanism and the construction of global cities today. In this sense, the single case study can be used to understand more general patterns of contemporary metropolitan transformation. First, it opens up global city analysis from the central business districts to suburban terrains. Grand urbanism concerns global suburbs as crucial territories of the contemporary capitalist economy and horizons of urban life. Second, it highlights transportation and especially metro systems as key coordinating apparatuses of a financialized urbanization processes. Networked infrastructures materialize the urban form of the polycentric metropolis and support its neoliberal priorities. Third, a focus on grand urbanism accounts for the role of the nation-state in directing urbanization processes. The framework of grand urbanism gives empirical and conceptual depth to notions of state rescaling, revealing the metropolis as a shifting ground for territorial policies. These three insights extend well beyond the case at hand. Grand Paris is thus offered here as a reference point in the increasingly important research areas of global urban studies and of comparative urban planning, politics, and policy-making.

Organization of the Book

This book is divided into three substantive sections: Part I, "Envisioning the Unified City," Part II, "Connecting the Networked City," and Part III, "Governing the Competitive City." Each section addresses a prominent aspect of the overall Grand Paris plan, and taken together, these discursive terrains afford entry into the broad workings of the Grand Paris initiative. Though not exhaustive of the urban fabric, this triangulation—design, mobility, and governance—enables the high stakes of the Grand Paris project to become most clear and focuses attention on the dynamics of redevelopment in a broad context that necessarily interweaves the cultural, economic, and political lives of Paris.

Through this framework, I demonstrate how policy problems—of metropolitan identity, of mobility, and of autonomy and legitimacy—are created in ways that imply the solution of a global city metropolis. Each part highlights productive conflicts over the metropolis whereby different urban meanings confront one another, and a rationalizing consensus whereby controversial aspects are rendered into the technical and objective terms of grand urbanism. In each of the three policy terrains, I trace how the trajectory of the future city is being shaped by complex nets of power and knowledge comprising interactions between global economic forces, local and national political cultures, urban planners, ordinary citizens, and transnational financial, corporate, and intellectual elites.

In Part I, "Envisioning the Unified City," I show how international starchitects, as consultants to the Grand Paris project, were key producers of urban know-how and urban practices. I argue in chapters 1 and 2 that the design spectacle of an architectural competition and public exhibition acts as a distraction from tense regional politics, and that the knowledge produced and disseminated by these architectural experts is important for interpreting and therefore for creating a new metropolitan reality.

The architectural consultation is primarily used by the state to give a sense of imagined solidarity to the fractured metropolitan populace, to legitimize a massive overhaul of regional space, and to valorize the global city ideal. It thus works as an essential apology to garner civil society's support for the subsequently announced material and institutional changes to metropolitan Paris.

Part II, "Connecting the Networked City," assesses the relationship between metropolitanization and the construction of a new metro network. Chapter 3, for example, examines the public debates held in 2010 and 2011 on two competing routes for the metro. It traces how a single vision for metromobility and the city emerged through participatory planning and how a plethora of incommensurable viewpoints were tenuously reconciled into an agreement on the global city ideal. Chapter 4 examines more closely how the Grand Paris Express orders the peripheries into a functional network of high-value industries and sites and promotes real estate development in underutilized suburban areas. In particular, it looks at the use of contrats du devéloppement territorial (CDTs, Territorial Development Contracts) as a mechanism for catalyzing development and raising land values around new transit stations. With uneven development as the very pillar of urbanization, low-income populations, and nonprofit-oriented spaces such as parks, community centers, and health facilities are poised to be made inaccessible and risk being further peripheralized as megamalls, sports stadiums, leisure complexes, and high-end residential units come to occupy targeted territories.

Finally, Part III, "Governing the Competitive City," analyzes how the neoliberalization of Paris requires a stable entity to coordinate production and reproduction. Accompanying the imaginative and infrastructural plans, one of the guiding threads of Grand Paris is to agglomerate the city politically and to streamline governance of the more than 1,200 communes, as well as eight departments and dozens of intermunicipal establishments that make up the institutional landscape of the Île-de-France region. In chapters 5 and 6 I look at how Grand Paris restructures state relations and political forces in the region by securing collective action at the level of the metropolis and through pursuing a global city "state mode of production" (Lefebvre 1978). While the nation-state's ability to organize territory on a large scale remains especially salient, governance—the management and regulation of people and functions—is being pluralized and sovereignty ceded to supranational and subnational levels. Through CDTs, public-private partnerships, and real estate investment trusts, authority is made polymorphic, consensual, participatory, and contractual, and spatial policies are increasingly oriented toward private concerns. This form of state productivism marks a significant shift in public policy from welfare to market goals, and in planning from comprehensive regional schemes to speculative "wagers" (*paris*) on the future.

I Envisioning the Unified City

1   Paris and/Is Its Suburb

The most significant aspect of the metropolis lies in this functional magnitude beyond its actual physical boundaries and this effectiveness reacts upon the latter and gives it life, weight, importance and responsibility. ... A city consists first in the totality of its effects that extend beyond its immediacy.
—Georg Simmel, 1903

And if Paris had emptied, if it was no more than a ghost town, didn't that mean the true centre was now "all around"?
—François Maspero, 1994

A Vision of the Future

Perhaps more so than any other city, Paris has been the subject of countless artistic, architectural, academic, and technical works that have both reflected and produced its unique urban iconography and identity. Grand Paris, however, is far less mediated, and there remains a notable gap in thought and a deficit of representations beyond official city limits.[1] Without a language or a symbolic framework with which to signify Paris as a broad and diverse region, its politics of space remain caught in an anachronistic trap whereby the historic center stands in for the metropolitan reality. Although the greater Paris region has changed dramatically over the past thirty years, its tools of representation remain bound to an outdated and insular urban form. There is a mismatch between how Paris is imagined and its prevailing economic and social realities. The various initiatives of Grand Paris are crucial to bringing the image of the greater metropolitan area into focus.

In the twenty-first century, the physical, economic, and political limits of cities around the world have been radically called into question. Not only are traditional urban mappings and concepts disrupted by new global flows and interdependencies but dichotomies such as urban and rural, downtown and suburb, city and nature, or center and periphery no longer convincingly describe regional dynamics. New patterns of concentration and dispersion have led to wide-ranging territorial transformations (Lefebvre 2003; see also Brenner and Schmid 2014). As cities grow in size and develop thick relational connections, our epistemological frameworks become unable to capture the scale and diversity of urban processes. The contemporary urban fabric is woven into local, regional, and transnational circuits in complex ways. A crucial aspect of contemporary urbanism is to make sense of the rapidly shifting dynamics of the metropolis. The fundamental crisis of representation facing Paris thus reflects both the city's particular conditions of change and general global trends.

In the first years of the twenty-first century a critical mass of citizens, academics, architects, and politicians expressed in various ways the shared belief that existing conceptual apparatuses for understanding or building Paris were no longer working. In particular, the long-standing distinction between the central city and the peripheral suburb was inadequate to describe the reality of the urban region and, moreover, placed limits on economic growth, social cohesion, and effective governance. The first task of Grand Paris was thus to provide a strategic vision to frame the city's future. The architectural consultation of Grand Pari(s) accomplished this by providing an innovative iconography to an emergent metropolitan society, situating it within the local and national imagination and within the space of the global economy. This representational horizon was the necessary precondition for the specific redevelopment and restructuring initiatives through which Grand Paris is taking shape.

Planning the contemporary metropolis is not merely a technical exercise, it is also a practice of visualization, exploration, discovery, and philosophy (Viganò 2012). It is as much an activity of imagination and thought as it is an intervention of construction. The making of Grand Paris requires not just master programmatic agendas and design blueprints but a new way of conceptualizing the nature of the contemporary metropolis and its future. Through Grand Paris, a range of strategies, projects, designs, visions, dreams, maps, and images brings to mind the future urban region, and these representations are concretized through material structures and institutions. This is guided both by the central state and by local stakeholders who desire to make the city accessible to local inhabitants and external spectators (and speculators). Owing to their position within apparatuses of urban knowledge production, urban architects have a special purview to guide and frame this design process.

In general, grand urbanism proceeds by first creating and nurturing a metropolitan identity that can serve as the basis of large-scale redevelopment. The program of a 2013 conference organized by the City of Paris sums up the stakes of providing the metropolis with an appropriate representation as follows:

> The question of metropolitan identity is a theme given scant consideration in academic work and government policies. Considered the result of a process that leads to a sense of belonging and to a territory and to the idea of a collectively built future, it represents the construction of a specific but not exclusive citizenship. A metropolitan identity is essential because it contributes to the legitimacy of the metro area and thus to the production and the efficiency of policies designed to deal with the problems and challenges encountered at this level. (Mairie de Paris 2013)

Grand Paris and related metropolitan initiatives seek to create a common identity and a common orientation for action at the urban regional scale. A comprehensive urban vision connects populations, territories, sectors, and activities usually considered in isolation. New visions also have a mobilizing function. A shared consensus on what constitutes urban society can bring disparate actors together around collective goals and can orient their activities toward addressing common concerns. The emerging imaginary of Grand Paris thus does not mirror the objective conditions or precise facticity of the world, but it is an interpretive framework for defining what is desirable and what is possible in relation to the observable and the experiential.

Urban visions, exemplified in the designs of the Grand Pari(s) architectural consultation, are part of the Grand Paris strategy to rethink the metropolitan area and the objectives of policy making and planning in line with a growth-maximizing neoliberal logic. In particular, these representations are crucial to justifying the competitive political economy of the global city. In his analysis of nineteenth-century impressionist paintings, T. J. Clark (1984) showed how artistic works, as capitalist reimaginings, reflect and give form to a new "framing" of modernity, instrumental in reshaping Paris. In a similar way today, the architectural designs and spatial projects of Grand Paris reflect a new reality of the financialized global city and its property relations and accumulation dynamics. In particular, the architectural consultation that launched the Grand Paris initiative attempted to conceive of the city in terms of an expansive, flexible space of flows. By confirming the image and identity of such a global city region, the architects and designers thus became crucial enablers of collective action by government, business, and citizenry at the scale of Grand Paris.

In what follows I outline how Grand Paris creates a recognizable image of the metropolis. The chapter begins with a brief history of the relationship between Paris and its outside. This is followed by an examination of how this relationship is reconfigured through global restructurings. I then show how the Grand Pari(s) architectural consultation accumulated and animated discourses of the metropolis. I argue that this consultation was a concerted effort of state-sponsored imagineering of a new political, economic, and social community.

Paris of City Walls

The urban historian Eric Hazan (2010, 16) suggests that the most effective way to tell the story of Paris is not through a chronology of successive reigns or republics or as an epic narrative of heroic men but through "the time of city walls." For Hazan, changes in the built form of the city and its physical borders have always marked significant milestones and suggested profound revolutions in urban living. "Whenever Paris advanced from one boundary to the next," he writes, "this signaled a time of changes in technology, society and politics. It was as if the emergence of a new epoch led both to the obsolescence of the old walls and to transformations in the city's life" (13). At periodic intervals, the city would expand beyond its former limits and define a new set of urban boundaries. The defining element in the history of city walls is the changing relationship between Paris and its *banlieue*.

Accentuated by its role as national capital, Paris has traditionally maintained clear borders between the city proper and the excluded outside, or *banlieue*. From the first Gallo-Roman wall erected on the Île de la Cité in the third century, through the successive ring walls of Philippe Auguste (1213),

Charles V (1383), Louis XIII (1636), Farmer's General (1818), and Thiers (1844), to the construction of the *boulevard périphérique* ring road that now encircles the city (completed in 1978), planners and policy makers have attempted to enclose the municipality for purposes of security, governance, and communication. City walls were deemed necessary for the defense of territory, for the demarcation of administrative boundaries, and for the management of flows in and out of the city. For centuries, growth and change in Paris have followed a standard pattern of centrifugal urbanization: the city expands, incorporates its immediate suburbs, and builds a new wall at an ever greater distance from the historic core. While the walls themselves change location, the logic of enclosure remains the same, and, like the rings of a redwood, the concentric walls around Paris can be read as indicators of the shape and health of the city over time. "Paris keeps the trace of these successive states and its plan reveals the nesting of scales which mark almost twenty centuries of growth" (Panerai 2008, 47). Walking through the city today, one still encounters these walls in passing from the inner to outer arrondissements or, most dramatically, traversing one of the dozen or so city gates along the *périphérique*.

Although the time of city walls predates industrialization, this growth dynamic takes on a particular form in the capitalist city. The two sides of this expansionary/exclusionary process reveal a dialectic of uneven development (Smith 2002) whereby peripheral space is periodically opened up for urbanization through a variety of symbolic, administrative, economic, and social means. In the modern era, the transformation of city walls is shaped in essential ways by changes in the scale and function of accumulation (Hazan 2010). Capital's ceaseless quest for new territories of extraction, consumption, and investment is a powerful driver of urban growth and change. The modern history of city walls in Paris is thus fundamentally a history of capitalist urbanization that is situationally influenced by political conflicts over belonging, social and spatial solidarity, land use, resource distribution, political legitimacy, and the values of urban life.

Although always porous, Paris's city walls fundamentally establish a framework of a valuable core separated from a negligible periphery. Its walls entrench uneven material and symbolic relations between a small and elite city *intra-muros* (between the walls) and the peripheral suburban, exurban, and rural territories *outré-muros* (outside the walls). This structure is then replicated in powerful civic identities. As a result, Paris has a center that is clearly delineated and recognizable to all those within and without the walls. The metropolis as a broader economic, political, cultural, and sociological entity, however, is vaguely defined, eternally contested, and largely unrepresentable.

Grand Paris is a novel paradigm for urbanism in France in that it aims to do away once and for all with the walls around Paris and with the monocentric arrangements they enact. Suggesting a more multiform and interdependent urban fabric than can be captured through periodically expanded borders, Grand Paris redefines the city as a fundamentally excessive entity, not merely as a larger though still fixed territory but as a relational complex, always defined by sites and scales beyond its immediate vicinity. Challenging hegemonic spatial arrangements as well as traditional understandings of urbanization as such, Grand Paris repudiates the concentric city model. In place of a city divided from its *banlieue* (*Paris et sa banlieue*), it insists instead that Paris is its *banlieue* (*Paris est sa banlieue*).

Grand Paris appears to signify a break with existing regional relations of an insulated city and surrounding hinterland. Yet if we look deeper into the "time of city walls," it is also possible to understand the making of Grand Paris as the outcome of a much longer contingent process of metropolitanization. Indeed, "Grand Paris" was hardly invented by Sarkozy: there have been efforts for at least a century to recognize the city and its suburbs as an integral unit and to blur the distinctions between city and suburb in terms of powers, services, and economy. This counterpart to the time of city walls suggests that the creative destruction of borders is driven by ongoing deliberations on the very nature of the inside-outside relationship. Seen in a different light, the history of urbanism in modern Paris can be expressed as a struggle between asserting the autonomy of the center and recognizing the excessive qualities of the city.

Heuristically, we can situate today's Grand Paris as the third major moment in a modernizing project of metropolitanization begun during the Second Empire (1853–1870) and reinvigorated in the post–World War II era (1945–1975). In each of these eras, large-scale spatial transformations were achieved through resignifying urban space and investing in the built environment on the urban frontier. The annexation of suburban territory involved symbolic, physical, political, and economic expansion and a reconfiguration of social relations. In particular (and relevant to the analysis of Grand Paris), aggrandizing in each of these moments of metropolitan urbanism was a means of integrating the region, promoting real estate speculation, and overcoming political stalemates and class struggles.

A political history of metropolitan urbanism in Paris reveals how the questions of walls, borders, and metropolitan space are bound up with questions of property, collectivity, and the state (Phillips 1987). It also demonstrates the extent to which urban planning is a modernizing exercise to make society "legible" to inhabitants, policy makers, and investors (Scott 1998). Although other technical and aesthetic urban practices have contributed to metropolitan transformation, urbanism and architecture have led these efforts, not merely as technical professions but as ideological sites of knowledge production. Urbanism is an inextricably political practice that reflects and refracts contests over the nature of land and property and quintessentially shapes the social institutions that govern these (Phillips 1987, 3).

Sarkozy's project is most often compared to the reforms of Baron Haussmann, prefect of the Seine department, which were conducted over a period from 1853 to 1870. Haussmann's vast growth and renovation program, commissioned under Napoléon III, was based on a model of opening the crowded, diseased, and crime-ridden working-class quarters of the city and replacing them with more spacious and rational settlements. Large-scale renovations included annexing eight peripheral villages or arrondissements to bring the total in Paris to the present-day twenty, and constructing the iconic wide boulevards (e.g., Magenta, Malesherbes, Saint-Germain) that extend outward from several central axes. The massive overhauls in space aimed to unify the design of the expanded city through strict regulations with respect to road width and building height and appearance. In a time of economic and political crisis, public works of infrastructure (sewers, fountains, parks, and especially roadways) also provided a venue for Napoléon III to channel surplus capital into the built environment and into the secondary circuit of real estate, thus keeping the economy fluid during a recession and workers relatively pacified during a Europe-wide revolutionary moment (Harvey 2003). Innovations in credit, debt, and expropriation tools further facilitated speculative development in the new territories of Paris (Benjamin 2002; Harvey 2003; Hazan 2010), and through these arrangements of state-sponsored real estate promotion and gentrification, finance became thoroughly embedded in the urban experience (Merrifield 2014, 36).

Haussmann's projects were exorbitantly expensive (Ferry 1868), and for the lower classes they also came at a high social and political cost. *Gens aises* (wealthy inhabitants) were ensured space in the newly refurbished bourgeois city, but the poor and the working classes were pushed forcibly, and by lack of affordable housing, toward restructured edge spaces. The new streets were weapons of class war in two senses: in gentrifying Paris they secured bourgeois occupation of the central city, and they also militarized space, enabling French armies a clear path through the city in the event of popular unrest and barricades. As Andy Merrifield (2014, 37) sums it up, Haussmann's expansion of Paris "was concurrently profitable and pragmatic, aesthetically edifying yet militarily convenient."

From a working-class perspective, Haussmann "bludgeoned the city into modernity" (Harvey 2003, 3). Indeed, the aggressive appropriation of Paris by the bourgeoisie was one of the main targets of the Paris Commune of 1871.[2] Haussmann's transformation of Paris and its aftermath thus highlight a battle between the individualized property and security regimes of grandiose state-led urban planning and those competing regimes of solidarity, regional equality, self-management, and wealth distribution. This battle is at the heart of the dynamic of metropolitan urbanism.

Although the political topologies of capitalist urbanization established by Haussmann were remarkably resilient, in the early twentieth century, conflicts within urbanism and town planning over institutions of property, liberties, and communal well-being shifted in favor of more socialist principles. In 1909 the Seine prefect, Justin de Selves, commissioned the first official work using the appellation "Grand Paris." At the time, Paris had just laid the first tracks for the Métropolitain urban railway (the metro) through Paris, and the built infrastructure continued to define the social and spatial organization of the city. A wealthy center benefited from modernizing efforts, while a working-class periphery was largely excluded from these gains. Prefiguring debates that would be repeated a century later, there was heated disagreement between Selves (alongside the left-leaning municipal council) and the right-leaning state over whether urban services should be pursued in order to improve quality of life for all, or to enhance Paris's elite international reputation and connections. Selves's designs for Grand Paris sided with the former. They aim for an equitable distribution of amenities throughout regional space, improved circulation throughout all of Paris, and improved leisure space of parks and public facilities in the near periphery. However, the project was largely ignored, overshadowed by the exigencies of World War I.

In the 1920s, however, socialist municipal officials revived this effort and pushed for an officially recognized regional unit akin to Grand Paris in order to organize services, claiming an "effective solidarity" between the capital and the *banlieue* (Subra 2009, 15–17). Without legal definition, it was thought, there would be no way to formalize the equal footing of Paris and its environs. The central state, however, did not want to upset the existing balance of forces in the region, which were stalemated between privatized and collective controls over space (Phillips 1987). This initial proposal, though unsuccessful, was followed by a series of similar plans to combat the centralization of the city in 1921 and again in 1928, when a superior committee for development of the region was created with the purpose to deal with regional affairs from a uniquely metropolitan perspective.

Grand Paris in the early part of the twentieth century was thus understood as the collective life of the city bound together by a common fate. The geographer Albert Demangeon in 1932 described Grand Paris as the "geographical unit defined by the solidarity of problems which it poses" (in Blanc 2010, 72). The Prost Plan of 1934 (named after the architect and planner Henri Prost) established a new paradigm of "regional planning" that sought to address common problems and direct the common fate on the basis of regional unity and planning on a scale outside of individual communes. More specifically, the plan introduced a scheme of functional planning at a regional scale that would coordinate 656 communes that composed the greater city. It proposed better transportation between Paris and the *banlieue*, more free public space, affordable housing, and the protection of notable cultural and heritage sites. Above all, however, the plan was primarily concerned with coordinating institutions in order to provide services and infrastructure to working-class neighborhoods outside the city. The Prost Plan was approved in 1939; however, it too went unachieved because of World War II.

While Grand Paris for the first half of the twentieth century was largely a socialist project, Haussmann's priorities of private property and authoritarian order returned again after World War II. In the postwar era of reconstruction the suburbs of Paris became key frontiers for prospective growth, and the French state sought to modernize and dynamize the region through integrating municipalities and opening peripheral land to new settlement and economic activity.[3] The practice of urbanism grew rapidly apace with demographic expansion, and processes of change were controlled by a series of new urban and regional policy instruments. Most notable among these were the DATAR (Delegation for Regional Development and Territorial Planning), which established national strategies to distribute settlement, infrastructure, and manufacturing activities, and the PADOG (Plan for the Development and General Organization of the Paris Region), which was a local plan to address the need for adequate housing and the renovation of the shantytowns (*bidonvilles*) that still circled the city and lacked fresh water, sanitation, and heating. The goals of integrating Paris with its inner and outer suburbs (the *petit* and *grand couronne*, respectively) and preventing sprawl and rural encroachment were later absorbed into the more modernist and technocratic zoning regimes of Fordist industrial and social policy (Merlin 1991, 2003).

Although planning during this time was centrally mandated in pursuit of growth, it too retained a strong social focus. The broader suburbanization of France, driven by manufacturing in the post–World War II era, was concerned with how to invest industrial surplus in new territorial arrangements, ostensibly to enhance the public good. Postwar urbanism in Paris sought to organize and rationalize the rapidly growing urban areas outside the city and to distribute the fruits of reconstruction, such as roads, schools, energy, and communications—modern city infrastructures—more generally across metropolitan territory. This embedded liberalism of planned economic growth and managed prosperity was marked in urban planning efforts. The conflicts of private property and statist regulatory authority came to define the planned capitalism of the era and played out in conceptions of Grand Paris as a site of balanced polycentric growth (Phillips 1987).

Paul Delouvrier, a bureaucrat who had previously carried out planning projects in colonized Algeria and who was appointed delegate general for the Paris region in 1961, later becoming prefect in charge of regional development, was largely in charge of reconciling these quarrels through a new urban planning paradigm. Delouvrier was known as "de Gaulle's Haussmann," and in this role he elaborated an ambitious new plan for urbanism and management of the capital region. In 1961 he proclaimed his intention in a plan to bring order to an anarchic Parisian region through the creation of highly functional satellite *villes nouvelles* (New Towns) on the perimeter of the city (Giacone 2010). Distinguished from the *grands ensembles,* prefab residential estates constructed quickly across the region in the 1950s in response to a pressing housing crisis, these New Towns—including Cergy-Pontoise, Saint-Quentin-en-Yvelines, Évry, Marne-la-Vallée, and Melun-Sénart—were to be largely self-sufficient communities created with the priorities of meeting housing needs and building neighborhoods with all the amenities of modern French life. The New Towns were articulated more fully in Delouvrier's Schema directeur d'aménagement et d'urbanisme de la région de Paris (Master Plan of Urban Development) of 1968, which envisioned the newly created region of Île-de-France connected both by a network of highways and by the RER (Regional Express Network) rail extensions. Delouvrier's emphasis on satellite developments was meant to demagnetize the center of Paris and achieve a truly polycentric foundation for future growth that at the same time would maintain significant regional green space.

Following in the footsteps of Haussmann, and prefiguring the leadership of Sarkozy and Blanc, Delouvrier was chosen not for his knowledge of urbanism necessarily but also for his acumen in financial planning. His development plan aimed not only to provide housing outside the current perimeter of the city but, more important, to permit mobility throughout the region and to promote the unification of markets across the city. The 1968 master plan, with its new towns and satellite arrangements, thus posed the question of a radically new scale for the capital. Delouvrier's growth-oriented regional policy involved public investments in infrastructure to expand the city outward and, in so doing, raise suburban property values (Giacone 2010; Merlin 1991; Subra 2009).

Delouvrier's projects expanded the city territorially, but they also established new geographies of control over planning. His plans, for example, were also used politically to consolidate state (here Gaullist) power in the Paris region and to deny local (particularly Communist and Socialist) autonomy over urbanism.[4] They also created new divisions of access to metropolitan space along the lines of class and race (Dikeç 2007a; Préteceille 1986, 2006; Wacquant 2008). With expanded regional urbanism and rising rents, this polycentric growth model gave rise in the 1970s and 1980s to a fracture between the working-class "red belt" of *grands ensembles* and high-rise towns in the inner suburbs and the middle- and upper-class *banlieue pavillonnaire,* composed of single-family low-rise homes extending in between and beyond the inner suburbs.

Although the essential division between the city of Paris and its suburban communities was marked, with these changes the city walls, which separated the "core" aspects of urbanity from its more peripheral features, could no longer be located with the administrative boundaries alone. A strong urban-suburban divide remained, but the logic of walling and the nature of Paris's boundaries began to shift. In the decades that followed, the urban-suburban border was even more radically called into question through processes of globalization.

From Walled to World City

The nonconcentric patterns of urbanization instigated by Delouvrier were intensified by macroeconomic changes in the global economy. Globalization from the 1970s onward brought about a new significance for the city region at the same time that it reorganized the internal power geographies and spatial relations of the Île-de-France. The institutional aspects of this—most notably a process of decentralization and a rearrangement of urban planning apparatuses—are examined more closely in chapters 5 and 6. What is significant in terms of the time of city walls and the imaginary of Grand Paris, however, is how Paris's rise to a global city transformed its relational geography and, as a result, called into question the capacity of urbanism to conceive of the metropolis as a coherent unit.

Urbanization from the 1970s on was marked by metropolitan expansion and by internal spatial and social restructuring, leading to fundamental changes in center-periphery relations. These transformations were largely driven by shifts in sectoral growth. In line with much of Western Europe, France's opening to global markets catalyzed a process of deindustrialization. The manufacturing sector that had traditionally defined the Paris region relocated elsewhere, at the same time that new tertiary economic activities began to concentrate in the Paris region. These shifts primarily registered in the reorganization of suburban territory.

Emblematic of the shifting regional economy from industry to service and tourism was the closing of the Renault factory in Île Seguin in March 1992 and the opening of Euro Disney in Marne-la-Vallée less than a month later (Ross 1996). La Défense, originally launched in 1959 as a purpose-built financial district at the western border of the city, also saw significant growth in the 1980s and 1990s. Through the guidance of the state-sponsored La Défense Public Development Authority (EPAD), the neighborhood began to welcome the headquarters of advanced service, management, and financial firms. Indeed, Paris became a global or world city—that is, a command hub in the global economic networks and an important node of labor, capital, and decision-making powers—through its suburbanization.

Overall, between 1970 and 2000 the city of Paris lost 300,000 jobs, while the inner suburbs absorbed 100,000 and the outer suburbs 700,000 (see Gilli 2005, 2014). As the core became more residential and focused on high-end political and economic functions, the peripheries saw diverse patterns of employment and population growth. In other words, at the same time that the historic core became more homogeneous, the suburbs came to exhibit diverse functions and characteristics. During the 1990s and 2000s, the greater regions of Paris increased their share of FIRE (financial, information, and real estate) industries, information and communications technologies, and research and development. Although these high-end sectors of the economy settled throughout the Île-de-France, their locations were by no means universal, and changes tended to be distributed unevenly, concentrating in loose clusters around the inner suburbs. The notion of the suburbs as hinterlands or dependent territories, in an inferior position to the central city, began to erode.

Today the city of Paris represents only a small fraction of the urbanized territory in the Île-de-France, whereas the greater Paris region hosts intricate networks of global financial, social, and cultural power. While the city of Paris retains important political and tertiary economic functions (national ministries, publishing houses, universities, headquarters of major enterprises and banking institutions, commercial spaces), in terms of demographics, employment, and productivity, the suburbs are "greater" than the urban core. La Défense, for example, is the principal business center in France and one of the most powerful financial districts in Europe. In addition, new poles of the economy, such as Plaine-Saint-Denis, have effectively captured investment (e.g., the Stade de France in 1998). Burgeoning research and technology clusters in Saclay, Évry, and Aubervilliers, and growing universities in Nanterre, Créteil, Villetaneuse, and Orsay, also suggest a shift in informational and intellectual activity outside the walls of Paris. In fact, the majority of university students in the Île-de-France today do not study in the storied classrooms of the left bank but on relatively new suburban campuses (Subra 2009). Even the largest commercial centers are located in the inner suburbs and not in the city of Paris proper. Greater Paris is, for all intents and purposes, a large and multipolar space with an international presence. Even if these other poles do not concentrate all of the urban activities that Paris does, and though the region of Île-de-France remains primarily agricultural and rural, the suburbs together have significant weight, forging what Philippe Subra (2009, 44) calls a system of "hierarchical polycentrism."

Hierarchical polycentrism is an apt description of the uneven spread of tertiary activities and the functional division of labor between various new hubs of the metropolis. Notably, it also suggests the marked territorial polarization and fragmentation that has accompanied urban restructuring under globalization. For Sassen and other theorists of these transformations, world city (or global city) formation is inextricable from the production of social and spatial inequalities. As they grow in size and influence and become nodes in the global reproduction of financial capitalism, global cities tend to bifurcate locally into "citadels and "ghettos" (Friedmann and Wolff 1982; Marcuse and Van Kempen 2000; Sassen 2001). The relationship between the beneficiaries and the disadvantaged of the global city defines the contours of Paris's most recent round of metropolitanization.

Complicating the narrative of Paris's expansion and development, from the 1970s on, the *banlieue,* once denoting suburban territory more generally, came to be associated primarily with the negative fallout of globalization. Simultaneous with the rise of the global city, deindustrialization, aggressive and racist policing, and declining social services, including public transportation, led to precarious conditions in many communities. As middle-class advancement and prosperity in Paris and across wealthy pockets of regional territory grew, so too did the misery associated with the declining *banlieues.* The *banlieue* now became shorthand for the declining housing projects of the postwar boom and the racialized and marginalized communities who lived there. The *banlieue* no longer symbolized merely the administrative limit of Paris's city boundaries but the more ephemeral limit of the new urban economic and social order.

Étienne Balibar (2007), for example, describes the "ghetto-ized" *banlieue* as the subordinate correlate of the global city. "We would have to speak of global banlieues, whose demographic composition and movements reflect the contradictions of globalization and their local projection." The *banlieue* thus is not merely the designation for any community which lies outside the *périphérique*, it is a designation for "advanced marginality" (Wacquant 2008), for the places disadvantaged by the contradictions of global city processes. The geography separating the global city region and global *banlieue* does not map concentrically; rather, these two worlds exist in more diffuse, overlapping, and fragmented relations.

Paradoxically, the polycentric paradigm of Delouvrier had backfired. Owing to the uneven nature of regional development, binary hierarchies in the city (Paris and its *banlieue*) persisted despite the great extent of suburbanization. In many ways, polycentric growth and development had actually entrenched the social and spatial divisions that Delouvrier was hoping to overcome. While the divides between Paris and its marginal suburbs were targeted through New Left urban policies under Mitterrand in the early 1980s, the distinction was strengthened in the 1990s and early 2000s through a pronounced retrenchment of planning aimed at security and property concerns.[5] Through this penal turn in urban policy, for example, the *banlieue* transformed in official and unofficial discourse from "'neighborhoods in danger' to 'dangerous neighborhoods'" (Dikeç 2007a, 93). The racialized "ghetto" image of the *banlieue* perpetuated by socialist planners in hopes of inspiring renewal merely reinforced the territorial stigma of low-income neighborhoods (Begag 2007; Wacquant 2007). The material and symbolic walls around the global city of Paris continued to rise in the twenty-first century as fear of the dangerous "badlands" grew (Dikeç 2007a; Roy 2006). Indeed, in 2002 the daily newspaper *Libération* listed the *banlieue* as one of the "major phobias" of French in the new millennium.

The unrest caused by the growing chasm between two sides of the global city (its winners and losers, productive and reproductive spaces), erupted with force in 2005 in the municipality of Clichy-Sous-Bois, where two youths were killed in an attempt to flee the police. The riots that ensued and the fires that spread across suburban territories throughout France illuminated the still existing divides between *petit* and *grand* Paris and the *"proximity of extremes"* of the urban frontier (Balibar 2007, 48). At once about the internal colonization of French territories, the lack of opportunities within deindustrialized neighborhoods, the breakdown of traditional class solidarities, the physical segregation of certain municipalities' populations, and the pervasive experience of civic disenfranchisement among youth (especially immigrant youth), the 2005 riots were caused by complex and overlapping geographies of exclusion (Dikeç 2007b). Whatever else their effects, the uprisings forcefully disrupted the divided city and opened up new ways of conceiving the common territory, common life, and common wealth of metropolitan Paris.

If the *banlieusards* who took to the streets in 2005 brought national and international attention to the need to destroy the walls of the greater Paris region and to incinerate the "apartheid" arrangements of urban space (Rogers Stirk Harbour + Partners, LSE and ARUP 2006), this call was also echoed across a range of urban planning, policy, and cultural spheres leading up to and following from the eruption. Indeed, new demands for a truly metropolitan identity—one that would be global, but also inclusive of and based in the experience of the *banlieue* not as "other" but as part of the city region—were evident in a wide range of discourses during the first decade of the new century.

As I discuss in chapter 5, in terms of governance, municipal officials in Paris and communes across the Île-de-France began a campaign for reform of the boundaries separating Paris from the suburbs as a way to address the disproportionate weight of Paris in regional affairs, and problems such as poverty, unemployment, economic development, and housing that could not be solved without cross-border coordination.[6] In similar fashion, local authorities and advocates also organized for the creation of new infrastructures that would better democratize access within the suburbs and equalize the regional territory (see chapters 3 and 4).

A precondition of these reforms, however, and one that finally made them successful, was a redefinition of the metropolis itself and its foundational concepts. One element in this process of identity formation was determining the precise nature of the Paris-*banlieue* relationship, which, despite the long history of regional planning and action, had largely remained a "black hole" (Paul Chemetov, in Fourcaut, Bellanger, and Flonneau 2007, 12). In 2002 the City of Paris and the Pavillon de l'Arsenal (a center for architecture and urbanism) consecrated an exhibition on the multiple processes (physical, historical, sociological) of metropolitan formation. This exhibition had the dual purpose of clarifying the structuring conditions of the Île-de-France and emphasizing the city's willingness to become a regional partner. To better understand the constitution of regional territory, the city, in conjunction with the Center for Twentieth-Century Social History, CNRS, and Paris 1, also organized a series of seminars, led by Annie Fourcaut. The proceedings, published as *Paris banlieues: Conflits et solidarités* (2007), shifted public debate over the metropolis by demonstrating a long history not of annexation and exclusion but of metropolitan urbanism.

The call for a renewed suburban understanding was echoed across various nonstate institutions as well. In 2005 a number of urbanists and architects picked up on this idea and launched an appeal for the establishment of a "Grand Paris" that would definitively solve the core-periphery divides in housing, transportation, employment, and poverty (Barré et al. 2005). Less formally, the demand for shared belonging for all in the metropolis and the revalorization of the periphery was heard in popular culture as well. Rapper Kery James's 2008 hit single "Banlieusard," for example, speaks of the grave structural impediments to *banlieue* prosperity but impels suburban residents to strive to overcome the barriers that divide the "two Frances." Jean-Paul Chapon's popular blog *Paris est sa banlieue* (http://parisbanlieue.blog.lemonde.fr) was also instrumental in recording the conflicts over how to represent and build the greater Paris region. With the tag line "Who's afraid of Grand Paris, or why is Paris stuck and ossified in the *périphérique* ramparts?," Chapon has since 2005 explored the question of city walls from a variety of perspectives. In particular, his frequent suburban "postcard" posts featuring photographs from the suburbs are striking insofar as they make visible the expansiveness and heterogeneity of the metropolis beyond the myopic tourist gaze. The *Bondy Blog* (http://bondyblog.fr) has also been active since 2005 in providing alternative media to the greater Paris region from an ex-centric perspective, focusing on issues of the metropolis from the vantage of the *banlieue* and the *banlieusard*.

A number of other media outlets have emerged at the scale of Grand Paris. The magazines *Megalopolis* (launched in 2010), *Objectif Grand Paris* (launched in 2012), and *Centralités* (launched in 2013) are particularly notable. In recent years, however, perhaps the most common way that inhabitants encounter the entity of "Grand Paris" is through the sections of the *Metronews* and *20 Minutes* (free daily newspapers handed out on Parisian transit) that bear this name. Certainly not all of these cultural representations have in mind the same metropolis or the same "Grand Paris," and the tensions between various iterations of the city are crucial, but what they all share is the act of putting Grand Paris into question and affirming the existence and importance of Paris beyond Paris.

The crisis of the *banlieue* is undoubtedly about material and social inequalities, but it is also about meanings and representation.[7] Insofar as the urban region of Paris is no longer defined by a single density of culture, power, recreation, research, commerce or citizenship, new representations are needed that capture its polycentric character and allow the *banlieue* to be thought as the central scale of the urban (Gilli 2008a). Here architecture and urbanism play a key role. Frédéric Gilli (2008b) calls attention to the extraordinary stakes of our understandings and significations of space, saying that "the real issues of Paris are not institutional but lie in our representation of Parisian space and in the place of democracy on the metropolitan scale." He continues, "The reflection on the heart of agglomeration and on the frontiers between the heart and the peripheral zones cannot content themselves with being anchored in practical problems because the reflection is equally an affair of symbols and representations." Attention to the form of the city and how it might be represented is crucial to understanding the history, contemporary daily life, and possible futures of Paris.

Today's discourses on metropolitan Paris speak to the sheer magnitude of growth of the metropolis and to the restructured relations between Paris and/as its outside, Paris and/as its suburb across a variety of fields. Locally, these discourses try to capture the complex array of relationships that structure the region beyond a simple core-periphery framework. As monocentric urbanism increasingly fails to account for the wide-ranging processes and patterns of expansion and restructuring in the Île-de-France, new representational tools are needed.

More generally, the discourses of metropolitan Paris also seek to grasp the large-scale transformations of space and social life that have been enacted through global urbanization over the past few decades. In this sense, Grand Paris partakes of more widespread theoretical reflections on the globally connected urban region. The ancient or medieval walled city might heuristically be treated as an autonomous closed unit, but the modern globalized metropolis always exists beyond itself. Marked by heterogeneity, flexibility, and mixity, this new cityscape confuses the boundaries of the urban and demands innovative ways of representing multiple and overlapping ecosystems, relationships, flows, interdependencies, and conjuncture beyond the physical boundaries of contiguous territories.[8] Grand Paris thus participates in a broader reflection on contemporary cities captured in such notions as the cybernetic network society (Castells 1996), the "rhizomatic" spatial ontology of global capitalism (Deleuze and Guattari 1987), the new lifeworlds of the "postmetropolis" (Soja 2000), the "edge city" frontiers of sprawling agglomerations (Garreau 1991), and the complex multifunctional mix of the "post-suburbs" (Phelps and Wood 2011).

Resolving the tension of Fordist imaginaries with post-Fordist realities requires innovative ways of comprehending and attending to metropolitan questions. Attempts to envision Paris's most recent breakthrough beyond its city walls are essential reflections on how the large metropolis is being rendered thinkable and visible, and to what effects.

Grand Paris to the Power of Ten

It was against this backdrop of a growing consensus on the existence of an urban region but uncertainty over its shape and trajectory that Sarkozy proposed an ambitious new vision for Grand Paris. In 2007, Sarkozy launched his regional development project not with an official master plan, infrastructural scheme, or legal decree, as one might expect, but with a speculative venture of creative design in the form of an architectural competition and consultation, Grand Pari(s): Consultation International sur l'Avenir de la Métropole Parisienne (Grand Pari(s): International Consultation on the Future of the Parisian Metropolis, or Grand Pari(s) for short).[9] Challenging ten international teams to "dream together" Paris of the twenty-first century, "without restriction" and "without taboo," Sarkozy (2009) acknowledged the radical potential of architecture to orient the city and its idiosyncratic ability to materially and symbolically modify the urban territory. The consultation recognized that the built environment is crucial to social and political life, and that architectural social imagineering can be an essential tool for rebuilding a polity beset by social fragmentation, economic decline, and political unrest.

The majority of the ten multidisciplinary international teams selected by Sarkozy (out of an initial forty-three contenders) were well-established

French architectural and urban design firms, but they varied considerably in political allegiance and professional experience. For Parisians, the most recognizable contenders notably included Jean Nouvel (of AJN—Jean Nouvel/AREP—Jean-Marie Duthilleul/Michel Cantal-Dupart) and Roland Castro (of Atelier Castro Denissof Casi). The French participants also included Atelier Christian de Portzamparc, l'AUC (of Djamel Klouche), Groupe Descartes (featuring Yves Lion), and Agence Grumbach & Associés. Internationally, the consultation was rounded out by the experimental Dutch collective MVRDV (under the supervision of Winy Maas), the German design firm LIN (with Finn Geipel and Giulia Andi), the Italian Studio 09 (of Bernardo Secchi and Paola Viganò), and the British firm of Rogers Stirk Harbour + Partners (partnered by Richard Rogers and Mike Davies).

Though headed by star architects, "among the most important of our time" (Sarkozy 2007), each design team was also explicitly interdisciplinary, and most included a selection of sociologists, architects, philosophers, engineers, and environmental scientists. In addition, prominent theorists of the late capitalist city, including Saskia Sassen, Manuel Castells, and Christian Lefèvre, were also engaged with the project in consultative roles on the Conseil Scientifique (Scientific Council), which ensured the complementarity of the ten designs and the quality of the final exhibition (Le Moniteur Architecture 2009). The administrative direction of the project, while headed by Sarkozy and the Office of the President, was also shared with the Ministry of Culture and Communication, the City of Paris, the Île-de-France Regional Council, and the Île-de-France Mayoral Association. Because of the broad range of collaborators and the theoretical focus of the exhibition, it was proclaimed that the "large scale perspective has nothing of a classical urban competition" and was instead to be a unique and genuinely collective venue for imagining the future of the city (Christine Albanel in Le Moniteur Architecture 2009, 9).

The consultation was to be the "research-and-development" (R&D) stage of the broader Grand Paris endeavor. It was thus deemed to be both a forum for thought and exchange, a guide for future policy decisions, and a venue to develop the metropolitan "product." During the initial phase of the consultation, from October 2007 to March 2009, the teams conducted research and workshopped ideas in a series of joint seminars. This phase was followed by an official public design exhibition from April 2009 to November 2009, installed at the newly established Museum of Architecture and

Heritage (Cité de l'Architecture et du Patrimoine). The financing of the consultation was shared by the Ministry of Culture and the City of Paris, which contributed €3 million and €400,000 respectively. Overall, each team was given a budget of €240,000 to cover the research and the material costs of the exposition (LeLoup and Bertone 2009).

The consultation was organized around two guiding themes: "The 21st Century Post-Kyoto Metropolis" and "The Prospective Diagnostics of Parisian Agglomeration." The first theme arose from the institutional and disciplinary attention to "green" cities. Signaling a concerted international commitment to a reduction of greenhouse gases, as well as new paradigm of ecology paired with a breakdown of the urban/rural divide, the post-Kyoto paradigm demands a rethinking of the role of urban centers in sustainable global development.[10] The post-Kyoto perspective also stresses the interdependence of nations and cities around the world and the mutual vulnerability of each to the actions of others. In this way, Grand Paris is understood not an insular space but as one that is always integrated into global networks of production and resource management.

Inquiry into the second theme, though, that of "Prospective Diagnostics of Parisian Agglomeration," is perhaps the central task of Grand Paris: how to analyze and plan the large global city. In French, *"agglomeration"* is a general term for the built-up area of a city or town. Unlike in English, it is a commonplace way of referring to an urban area. The theme "Prospective Diagnostics of Parisian Agglomeration" thus meant to chronicle the ways in which this clustering together of different parts had happened already within the Paris region, and to provide a model for the best mode of agglomerative processes in the future. Involving putting various parts of the Paris region together in a purported whole, this process has particular relevance to the activity of representation as a material and cultural practice and to the force of imaginative ventures in forging metropolitan solidarities.[11]

Taking up the challenge of creating an image and language of unification, the ten Grand Pari(s) design teams proposed many versions of Paris as an agglomerated global city (see table 1.1). A full summary of the ten designs can be found on the International Workshop of Grand Paris (AIGP) website (http://www.ateliergrandparis.fr/aigp/conseil/consultation2008.php). The architectural visions presented innovative ways to think about the global city metropolis, to map its connections, and to frame its

Table 1.1
Ten Visions of the Metropolis

Team Name	Exhibition Title	Primary Representation of Metropolitan Paris
Rogers Stirk Harbour + Partners/London School of Economics—ARUP	*Ten Principles for the Paris Metropolis* (*Dix principes pour Paris métropole*)	A single body composed of multiple integrated systems
Groupe Descartes	*Paris, Capital, Region, City, Cities* (*Paris, capital, region, ville, villes*)	A networked cluster of twenty sustainable cities
L'AUC	*Stimulated Grand Paris* (*Grand Paris stimulé*)	Multiple "scenarios" based on a polymorphic historical matrix
Atelier Christian de Portzamparc	*From Cyberspace to Physical Space—A Challenge for the Metropolis* (*Du cyberspace vers l'espace physique—Un défi pour la metropole*)	Three overlapping urban rhizomes
Agence Grumbach et Associés	*Seine Metropolis—Paris Rouen Le Havre* (*Seine Métropole—Paris Rouen Le Havre*)	Maritime space organized around the river Seine
AJN—Jean Nouvel/AREP—Jean-Marie Duthilleul/Michel Cantal-Dupart	*Birth and Rebirth of a Thousand and One Parisian Joys* (*Naissances et renaissances de mille et un bonheurs parisiens*)	A multipolar mobile network
Studio 09—Bernardo Secchi et Paola Viganò	*The Porous Post-Kyoto Metropolis* (*La métropole poreuse de l'après-Kyoto*)	A dense isotropic fabric
LIN—Finn Geipel + Giulia Andi	*Grand Paris, Light Metropolis* (*Grand Paris métropole douce*)	A cluster of micropolarities
Atelier Castro Denissof Casi	*Capital for Man/Capital for the World* (*Capitale pour l'homme/capital pour le monde*)	A decentered patchwork
MVRDV	*The Great Wager of Grand Paris: Smaller Paris (Capa-City), Intensification* (*Le grand pari du Grand Paris: Pari(s) plus petit (capa-city), l'intensification*)	A code-space of smart data

problems, and thus to set the parameters for potential solutions. The ten designs are briefly explored in the following section.

Rogers Stirk Harbour + Partners/London School of Economics—ARUP: *Ten Principles for the Paris Metropolis*

Pritzker Prize winner in 1997, the famed British architect Richard Rogers is best known in Paris for his work with Renzo Piano on the Centre Pompidou. In addition to his experience with site-specific works in Paris, Rogers also has experience with design at the metropolitan level, counseling, for example, former mayor of London Ken Livingstone on plans for Greater London. For the Grand Pari(s) consultation, Rogers partnered with Mike Davies and the London School of Economics (and their Deutsche Bank–sponsored Urban Age project) and with the international design and engineering firm ARUP.

Rogers and his team identified social inclusion, the built environment, and environmental sustainability as the three major axes along which cities must be planned today. Building on Rogers's already developed notion of urbanism as a balance of populations, resources, and environment to be achieved through efficient design (Rogers 1998), the team imagined the future Grand Paris as a compact and connected global city built with a small ecological footprint. To achieve this vision, they suggested a vast effort of regional renewal and the infusion of currently degraded suburban territories with amenities, parks, housing, and infrastructure. These interventions primarily aimed to intensify the functional polycentrism of the region (see figure 1.1).

Groupe Descartes: *Paris, Capital, Region, City, Cities*

Groupe Descartes gets its name from the research institute in Marne-la-Vallée where its participating academics and practitioners are located. The position of the team in Marne-la-Vallée, a former "New Town," was unique among the competitors and thus gave the team a particularly peripheral perspective on metropolitan affairs. Under the supervision of the French architect and urbanist Yves Lion (Grand Prix de l'Urbanisme in 2007), the team suggested that planning should capitalize on the underexploited territory of the Île-de-France and optimize the existing resources of the region, particularly those outside Paris proper (where they identified "derelict sites"

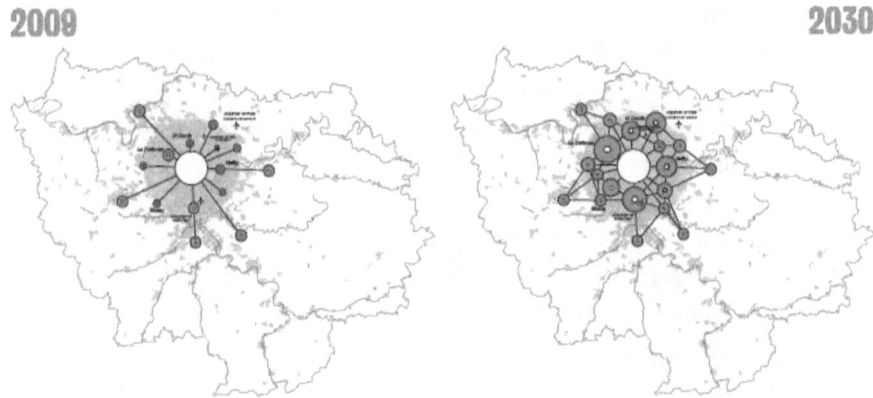

1. The center of Paris, the historic heart of the region, is so strong it continues to dominate the metropolis. In reality, this monocentric representation of the city does not reflect the change taking place in the metropolis—the population and economic growth is happening outside the center.

2. The polycentric urban model recognizes the importance of local centers, and it is a more exact representation of how the majority of the region's citizens live today. The vitality of the metropolis over the long term requires a rebalancing of the relationship between the center and the periphery. Polycenters will grow around the pre-existing centers, anchored to the hubs of enhanced transport infrastructure.

Figure 1.1
Intensifying the polycentric metropolis.

covering more than twice the surface area of Paris that could be effectively repurposed).

Like many of the teams, Groupe Descartes concluded that the geographic conditions of Paris overwhelmed the existing systems of infrastructure, particularly those of mobility. The central orientation of the group's Grand Paris design was to recast Paris as a networked space by renovating the systems of transit. To address the deficit in transportation options at the metropolitan scale and the automobile dependence of the *banlieue*, the team proposed a series of new urban pathways and public transportation axes. In particular, it suggested turning motorways into boulevards for public transportation and encouraging greater use of nonautomotive alternatives such as trains, trams, buses, and bicycles. According to Groupe Descartes, such an integrated multimodal approach would reduce commuting time, increase mobility, and maintain regional cohesion. Of note, the group also asserted that questions of mobility were integral to those of land use planning and residential availability and cost.

L'AUC: *Stimulated Grand Paris*

Critical of large-scale urban design, l'AUC (Ab urbe condita, "Since the founding of the city"), led by the youngest architect, Djamel Klouche, refused altogether to present a utopian design of a future Grand Paris. Klouche criticizes large-scale planning exercises for their violence and their founding on an imperial regime of visuality, and he rejects the demand for planners to impose totalizing and universalizing perspectives onto undeniably heterogeneous metropolitan spaces. He instead aims to map the city outside of conventional cartographic modes or blueprint designs. L'AUC contributed the following: "We propose neither a model, nor plan, nor images of an ideal post-Kyoto metropolis or of a future Grand Paris" (in Le Moniteur Architecture 2009, 82).

Rather than utilizing architecture's typical visualization tools of maps, charts, designs, and maquettes, then, l'AUC unilaterally resisted fabricating utopian images. To deal with the "crisis of representation," in the final public exhibition the group instead displayed a multivalent timeline that concentrated on eighteen territories selected to represent the diversity of the metropolis. This timeline or "matrix" revealed the palimpsest of coexisting particularities that define the city. Despite the promise to avoid prescription, l'AUC nevertheless did identify priorities and values toward which the planning of Grand Paris should be oriented. Above all, the group pursued the future city as a democratic and open commons to be built in the interest of all metropolitan inhabitants.

Atelier Christian de Portzamparc: *From Cyberspace to Physical Space— A Challenge for the Metropolis*

Christian de Portzamparc (also winner of the Pritzker Prize in 1994), in collaboration with a multidisciplinary research group from Université Paris XII at Créteil, defined Paris in terms of its networks of finance and information, or what the group called the incipient "cybermetropolis." De Portzamparc claimed that the now and future metropolis of Grand Paris, existing through a range of connections and relations beyond physical territory, fixed buildings, or social milieus, was fundamentally global and relational in nature. In this view, it is the dynamic between the relational and territorial (or virtual and material) metropolis that gives shape to Grand Paris. For De Portzamparc, "At this juncture, the virtual connection responds to the decline of our real space and our incapacity to master it. ... We must understand the new problem of the metropolis and its global dimensions. The metropolis is not merely a large city, it is a new anthropological phenomenon" (in Le Moniteur Architecture 2009, 104–105). To communicate and represent this new scalar phenomenon in the existing language and terms of cities and urbanity is, according to Atelier de Portzamparc, the most difficult task facing contemporary architects.

De Portzamparc depicted the shape and constitution of the new "a-spatial" metropolis of Paris through the figure of the rhizome (Atelier Christian de Portzamparc 2008). In particular, he described the organizational tissue of Grand Paris in terms of three interconnected multifunctional rhizomes: the South (Saclay/Orly), the Northeast (Creil/Disney), and the North (Paris/Roissy) (see figure 1.2). Each of these promises growth and propagation through new motors of innovation, dynamism, and creativity tied to research and financial sectors. The objective of de Portzamparc's intervention was to use robust networks of mass transportation to link these nascent nodes of density, magnetism, and exchange in more substantial and rational ways so that they might better attract hotels, headquarters, offices, and financial institutions and better innervate regional territory.

Agence Grumbach et Associés: *Seine Metropolis—Paris Rouen Le Havre*
Antoine Grumbach is a well-known French architect (also a winner of the Grand Prix de l'Urbanisme in 1992) whose critical environmental approach to design is inspired by the iconoclastic revolutions within the discipline of the 1960s. Grumbach used Grand Pari(s) as an opportunity to engage his more sustained reflections on a grand metropolis able to respond to the challenges of economic globalization and environmental sustainability in tandem. One of the most distinctive designs, Grumbach's Grand Paris was organized around the axis of the river Seine. Emphasizing that great international cities have highly developed port spaces, and taking a cue from Napoléon, who argued that Paris must have a link to the sea, Grumbach's design sought to overcome Paris's inland location by extending the city through Rouen to Le Havre and on to the English Channel. A naturally integrated maritime space, his "Seine Métropole" combined large-scale metropolitan thinking with a maritime leitmotif.

Grumbach stressed the need to do away with the concentric model of urban space in order to improve both the economic performance and social

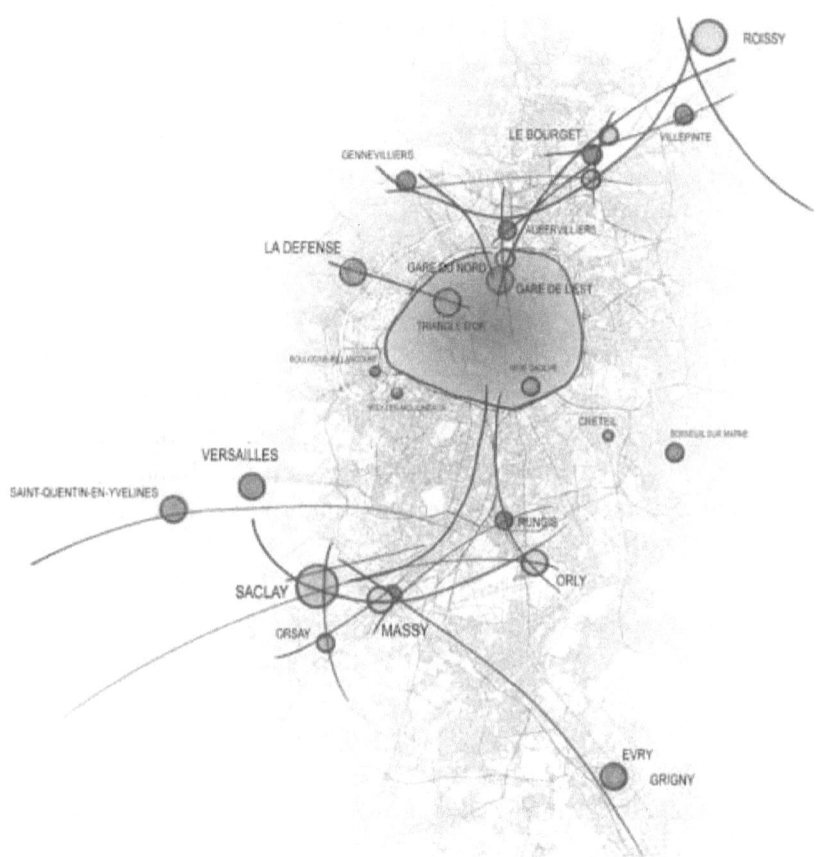

Figure 1.2
The Grand Paris rhizome.

organization of the metropolis. Against a weak image of Grand Paris, the Seine metropolis also defined regional space in a clear and recognizable way, addressing "the lack of identity of the Parisian agglomeration" (Antoine Grumbach et Associés 2009, 13). While the river offered a notable attribute around which to organize the city and served as a symbol for the ceaseless flow of metropolitan life, the surrounding river valley provided a littoral terrain for diverse projects of growth. Development of the metropolis would be based on industrial and agricultural development, the revitalization of abandoned river sites, waterfront renewal, and the construction of new rail and road networks braided along the banks of the river. The

Seine Metropolis thus promised solidarity among urban, agricultural, industrial, and rural spaces and between local and global economies.

AJN—Jean Nouvel/AREP—Jean-Marie Duthilleul/Michel Cantal-Dupart: *Births and Rebirths of a Thousand and One Parisian Joys*

Jean Nouvel (winner of the Pritzker Prize in 2008) is likely the best-known architect in France. His Institute du Monde Arabe, Fondation Cartier, and Musée du quai Branly, for example, are well-known Parisian monuments. Building on this legacy of specific *grands projets,* his team—a partnership with Michel Cantal-Dupart and Jean-Marie Duthilleul (of the SNCF)—proposed not a grand model or plan but practical interventions. Overall, Nouvel and his team wanted to transform the living conditions and the image of Paris through feasible, buildable projects (Le Moniteur Architecture 2009). These interventions were based on the ideas of mobility, mixity, and mutation (Nouvel, Cantal-Dupart, and Duthilleul 2008).

Most broadly, their plan involved building on and with the "existing city." Their projects aimed to intensify and diversify the various neighborhoods of Greater Paris through targeted infilling of green space, residence, commerce, and art. Based on the principle of "adding rather than replacing, densifying, building upward," the goal was not to tear down and start anew but to realize the hidden potential of given spaces and arrangements (Cité de l'Architecture et du Patrimoine 2009). Specific proposals included redeveloping brown fields, extending houses upward (in defiance of the thirty-two-meter limit within Paris), enlarging existing buildings, and transforming unifunctional into multifunctional sites. Nouvel and his team also suggested renovating *grands ensembles* and transforming their frequently isolated and alienating concrete towers into welcoming residential spaces with public spaces, gardens, leisure sites, artistic symbols, and transit connections. While projects would be found across the region, they would be concentrated around key links in the proposed transit network: fifteen priority local hubs and a dozen TGV nodes connected with the rest of continent.

Studio 09—Bernardo Secchi et Paola Viganò: *The Porous Post-Kyoto City*

Bernardo Secchi (1934–2014) and Paola Viganò headed the Italian firm Studio 09 (now Studio Paola Viganò). They are both architects of considerable professional and intellectual stature (Secchi won the Grand Prix de l'urbanisme, France's highest architectural honor, in 1994, while Viganò was awarded it in 2013). Known in Italy for their post-'68 critical urbanism and their meditations on the "new urban question" across European territories, Secchi and Viganò combined situated design practice with theoretical reflection on the nature of metropolitan form. Unlike some of the teams that felt the need to sideline philosophy for pragmatism, they pointedly used the Grand Pari(s) consultation as a mode of praxis, that is, as an opportunity to organically develop better conceptual tools and schemas based on empirical engagements with the rich complexities of a lived urban world (Studio 09 2009; see also Viganò 2012). Indeed, their work on Grand Pari(s) built on their individual and joint efforts to comprehend the contemporary urban condition through systemic municipal engagements in Bergmo, Brescia, Prato, and elsewhere. For Studio 09, then, design must emerge from and reflect a particular emerging social order. The rooted knowledge they produced in Grand Pari(s) formed the context in which specific projects could then take root (Le Moniteur Architecture 2009).

Studio 09 found Greater Paris to be fragmented and beset by environmental problems (of energy, water, and biodiversity), social inequality, and immobility. The team claimed that the unevenness of Paris was not simply felt along the core-periphery or northeastern/western divide but through a "kaleidoscope" of regional inequality (Secchi and Viganò 2010). In place of the existing territory, which was blocked and disconnected, Secchi and Viganò (2010) proposed a "porous, accessible, isotropic and permeable city." Based on the notion that town planning must open up the entire city, their designs aimed to help people get around the city with complete accessibility. Indeed, the principle of isotropy they presented poses a radical challenge to the uneven development and spatial hierarchies that currently define metropolitan life. Instead, the isotropic city suggests that the conditions in one part of the city must be identical to those in another part; isotropy fundamentally implies "the same conditions everywhere" (Secchi and Viganò 2010). Overall, their interventions were meant to equalize accessibility and the use of space, engender sustainability, and mobilize citizens in the improvement of their own lives.

LIN—Finn Geipel + Giulia Andi: *Grand Paris, Light Metropolis*
Based in Germany, the transdisciplinary team LIN is composed of researchers and practitioners from across Europe and North America. The team's

overarching theme for Grand Paris was the idea of *ville douce*, a "light" or "soft" city. The light city is not monumental and permanent but ephemeral and flexible. It is not arranged by a single density but by a loosely structured fabric built of microcenters, micropolarity, and micromobilities in an integrated system of diverse landscapes. It is not planned in its totality but through the ongoing construction of flexible and multifunctional spaces based on public and private partnerships. The soft and light Grand Paris is diverse, heterogeneous, simple, and streamlined. The task of urban planners and policy makers is to rebalance the composition of the metropolis to account for this lightness and to appreciate multiple polarities (Geipel, Andi, and Équipe LIN 2009, 42).

A number of other key principles guided the project, including those of "graduated mobility" and urban renewal. To realize the former, the team focused on the provision of diverse transit options (new rail, bus, and pedestrian networks) and on the construction of infrastructures of mobility that would improve connection, in the form of both large-scale projects linking major urban hubs (orbital ring metros) and lighter transport offerings based on alternative modalities (bicycle paths and walkways) in the in-between spaces of the metropolis (Geipel, Andi, and Équipe LIN 2009). Recognizing that the Île-de-France was not a blank slate but an existing territory, LIN focused on working with existing structures and on renovating and renewing instead of creating territory anew. Geipel (echoing Rogers) emphasized that "the metropolis must be built on the metropolis" (Geipel 2010).

Atelier Castro Denissof Casi: *Capital for Man/Capital for the World*
Of all of the design teams, that of Atelier Castro/Denissof/Casi most directly addressed the "crisis" of the *banlieue*. For Castro, "One of the main questions posed by Grand Paris was raised in the riots of November 2005" (in Cité de l'Architecture et du Patrimoine 2009). In fact, Castro's work on Grand Paris was merely the latest episode in his decades of work on the plight of the *banlieue* and on pathways for transformation of the Greater Paris region (most notable is his involvement in the design project Banlieues 89). Castro and his partners claim that the city's ability to deal with the grave social and economic challenges posed by and in the *banlieues* will determine the future shape of the Paris region.

With poetry as the motif of urbanism and urban life, Castro suggested specific projects to distribute symbolic markers of democratic publicness across the Île-de-France. Beautification and renovation through culture, arts, and urban services were the primary means he proposed to open up the city and restore the promises of the republic to its most disfavored areas. He also proposed new landmarks to celebrate not only the grand historic past but also the complexly woven contemporary urban fabric. Specific critical interventions included a memorial for the nation's "painful memories," a multicultural village with pavilions that would reflect the national makeup of the region, an exhibit of inquiry to reassess French heroes (Molière, De Gaulle, Mandel), and a vista point north of the city from which to view all of Grand Paris in one perspective. These suggestions were paired with more conventional examples of iconic place-making projects: a Sydney-esque opera house in Gennevilliers, a children's playground at Fort de Charenton, a footpath along the national 305 highway, and a waterfront redevelopment along the Canal de l'Ourcq. Taking up the imperatives of social cohesion and vibrant public life, Castro's design sought to remake the capital with the *banlieue* at its core.

MVRDV: *The Great Wager of Grand Paris: Smaller Paris (Capa-City), Intensification*

Like many of the competitors, the Dutch firm MVRDV, headed by Winy Maas, had a history of metropolitan and town planning engagements and is known for focusing not only on isolated buildings but on integral urban systems. MVRDV aimed to use extensive urban data to guide the policy making and planning of Grand Paris and to maximize the efficiency and functionality of the Parisian metropolis.

Indeed, MVRDV was by far the most statistically oriented and media-savvy team of Grand Pari(s). The firm is known for its positivist outlook, exemplified by its famous "Datatown," a design model that purportedly captures and visualizes the essence of a city through "neutral" codes and numbers (Patteeuw 2003). In its Grand Pari(s) submission, MVRDV used similar statistical remodeling and a range of urban indicators through its copyrighted "City Calculator" tool. This calculator evaluated Paris across a series of fields and identified weak and strong qualities that could then be used to optimize the city according to precise algorithms. In essence, the team sought to maximize the "capacity" of the city through a precise datafication of the territory's problems. Maas in his practice imagines urban growth, development, and improvement through the language of statistics. This information, treated as the DNA of the city, then becomes the basis on which "smart" urbanism is based. Quantitative networks of information define the urban form in an atopological and aterritorial manner, and in terms that easily translate into global metrics of competition. With this epistemology, MVRDV approached the future Grand Paris in a spirit of optimism. The atelier's "Paris Plus" (more Paris) stood for progress toward a highly rationalized city designed to meet its maximum potential.

Works of Representation

The history of metropolitan urbanism in Paris displays two contradictory aspects. On the one hand, there is a drive to define clear territorial parameters of the city through fixing walls that delimit an inside from an outside. On the other hand, there is the recognition that urban life exceeds any particular boundary and that suburban, regional, and global relations are necessary for and constitutive of Paris as such. Leading up to Grand Paris in 2007, these two perspectives were in tension. Whereas Paris had features of a large and complex global city region and functionally had expanded well beyond its historical ramparts, it nevertheless lacked adequate representational tools to account for its extensive processes and the meaning of its territory in a global age. A blunt city-suburb framework was the most dominant tool in the representational repertoire.

Today there are deep social, economic, and cultural divisions within Greater Paris. Yet these divisions are not reducible to a binary inside/outside geography. Overcoming the more diffuse configuration of today's walls requires a new understanding of Paris as a polycentric and networked city. Such an understanding must break through the industrial-era representations of the city and reflect the empirical realities of complex urban interdependence. It is a crucial element in convincing regional inhabitants of their interwoven destiny, thus overcoming the social unrest displayed in events such as the 2005 uprisings. A coherent and compelling identity is crucial for political legitimacy, regional collaboration, democratic citizenship, and economic attractiveness. Grand Pari(s) sought to forge this identity and to provide a new way to conceptualize and visualize the constitution of the twenty-first century metropolis.

The architects and urbanists of Grand Pari(s) became privileged actors in shaping the city, with unparalleled capacities to research, reconstruct, and reorganize urban reality (Viganò 2012). Indeed, in the aftermath of the exhibition, Sarkozy (2010) acknowledged the influence of the architects: "A year later, thanks to the work of the architects, our 'mental maps' are no longer the same." In place of a hyperbolic discourse of city and suburb unmoored from any identifiable geography, the architects provided a new language of an integrated and globally connected metropolis. They established a new discourse and new ways to decipher the reality of Paris, its change of scale, and its complex territorial dynamics.

It is important to note that the multidisciplinary teams all focused on the systems, networks, relations, and flows that bring the urban fabric into being, and not on the fixed characteristics of a given territory. Whereas architects once focused on individual buildings or on the construction of unique projects, in Grand Pari(s) the scope of intervention spanned the global urban region. The interventions of networked urbanism today are oriented toward metropolitan assemblages, global connections, and those infrastructures that link people, places, and functions at multiple scales. According to this systems thinking, flows and relations combine with fixed structures and places in a holistic site of architectural intervention (Lerup 2000). In this sense, networked designs set the stage for the large-scale plans of growth-maximizing urbanization that define grand urbanism.

The ten architectural teams created varied and even contradictory visions of what Paris was and what it might be thirty years in the future. The teams used a variety of representational and critical tools to present incomplete and incommensurable understandings of urbanization processes and of urban life. But, taken together, the ten designs became the basis for explaining and illuminating Grand Paris policy decisions to the general public. Not only did they reinforce the idea of a large metropolis, the architectural teams also acknowledged that the metropolis is the relevant scale for the valorization of territory. The processes of renewal and revalorization are predominantly economic, but they also cohere around a new urban imperative that the greater region be dense, compact, green, networked, and innovative; that civility, urbanity, and sustainability prevail. By the end of the consultation, according to Mike Davies, the various levels of government began "to speak similar languages and all agree that strategic priorities are real and cannot be escaped" (Rogers and Davies 2010). These priorities are the unquestionable common sense of twenty-first-century grand urbanism.

The knowledge produced by the architects was multivalent, but the primary task of the Grand Pari(s) consultation as a whole was to transform the vocabularies and images of metropolitan space. The plans were never meant to fix a particular future, in the manner of a master plan. Instead, the designs were orientations for further action. In this way, the consultation was less about the material immediacy of addressing the question of the suburbs or meeting pressing challenges of metropolitan life and more about publicly exhibiting an incipient reality. It established a context and a definition of the metropolitan scenario that also projected and conjured particular futures. How these are taken up and to what ends they are put—that is, *which* metropolis they will ultimately render—is taken up in the subsequent initiatives of Grand Paris.

2 The Shared Dream of Grand Pari(s)

To dream of Grand Paris is to draw plans on a comet named destiny.
—Christophe Barbier, quoted in Leloup and Bertone, 2009

This [Grand Paris] policy will not signal the passage from a dream to a reality of weakened ambition. Because if we all have the same grand desire, and the same grand ambition, we are also fully conscious of the necessary time and rhythms for transforming our dreams into reality.
—Christian Blanc, 2010

A Dream Collectivized

The language of dreams and of the imagination abounds in the literature on metropolitan Paris. Long heralded as a city of opportunity, amusement, and pleasure, Paris is the quintessential landscape of fantasy. A space woven of revolutionary prospects and promises of modernity, of utopian designs, technological innovations, sensual titillations, and dazzling commodities, this network of dreams and desires is cemented in the built environment of the city and intimately tied to the abstract sociality of modern city life. From the bourgeois dreamworld of the nineteenth-century Arcades to the hypermediated twentieth-century mass consumer spectacle, the Parisian urban imaginary has been a crucial arena of social and political contestation. The city is defined as much by its imaginative prospects as by its material constituents, the latter not only reproducing social reality but actively involved in its creation. In casting a trajectory for the twenty-first century, the Grand Paris development plan relies on these time-honored oneiric tropes to articulate what Sarkozy (2009) called a "shared dream" of the utopian future in which, purportedly, all inhabitants can actively partake.

Grand Pari(s) is a state-sponsored and state-managed effort to channel the myriad aspirations for a new city into a particular scenario of reform. According to Sarkozy (2010, 43), the consultation was "essential in crystallizing this diffuse, unconscious feeling into a real awareness in precise images." For the architectural teams, the reflection on metropolitan Paris may be a social project animated by a collective vision, but Grand Pari(s) also works to capture diverse articulations of the future, to rationalize them into consensual technical objectives, and thus to dispossess inhabitants of the city of alternative imaginative worlds. The respective visions of the ten architectural teams participating in Grand Pari(s) thus serve both as the horizon of radical democratic change and as powerful tools in the maintenance of hegemonic power relations in the metropolis. With an emphasis on compromise and popular accord, the consultation effectively created a dominant planning trajectory that elides and suppresses the deliberation of genuine political alternatives. While the ten visions each projected different urban futures, the consultation as a whole was used to justify a particular notion of the good city and to garner civil society support for this ideal.

The aesthetic and theoretical function of the public architectural exhibition, as with many political visions, is to justify and enable the subsequently proposed policies, even when, and in some cases especially when, these may contradict one another. In fact, an essential operation of the public architectural exhibition is one of *communication* and *transmission*.[1] How the dream representations of Paris are articulated, by whom, and for what purposes are crucially important to the establishment of a new regime of urban visuality and new norms of urbanism. What is at stake in the overall redevelopment plan is not merely institutional reform and territorial restructuring to alter the formal functioning and built environment of the city and its surroundings but the very way the city is represented and the implications of this representation for democratic politics.

Broadly, Grand Pari(s) was important insofar as it signaled the imbrication of culture and power in the urban context and demonstrated a potentially new orientation of architectural practice and urban design tied to grand urbanism. The architectural bet suggested the high stakes of refiguring the city, as well as a more general indeterminability of postmodern planning (Dear and Flusty 1998; Jameson 2004). In recognition of the impossibility of omniscient rational design and the limits of totalizing plans and rigid technocratic ventures, the great wager of Grand Pari(s) treated urban planning as an unpredictable and flexible affair. In this sense, Grand Pari(s) was quite unlike previous *grands projets* of the nineteenth and twentieth centuries, despite their shared investments in large-scale territorial reform. The architects contributing to the Grand Pari(s) exhibition could outline the conditions of possibility for a desired world, but ultimately they could not control its execution, and had to surrender design to the unstable flux of urban life and the vagaries of the market. This attitude locates architectural intervention as an essential site of creative transformation, but paradoxically, it also renders architectural practice insufficient in urban redevelopment. Architecture may define the design, the symbols, and the language of grand urbanism, but implementation of planning involves a much wider ensemble of public and private actors and processes.

The architects of Grand Pari(s) defined the urban problematic in Paris and created a new common sense of social life, territorial management, building technology, economic policy, land use, and property at the metropolitan scale. They did not create comprehensive town planning documents but rather a series of broad scenarios about the nature of the twenty-first-century global metropolis—scenarios that could be manipulated and easily inserted into a script of neoliberal urbanism. Despite their variations, the ten projects created a clear common sense around the value of a connected, sustainable, and attractive metropolis. They unanimously described the suburbs as global city sites *in potentia*, sites that could be integrated into the existing metropolis through flexible, green, and networked planning.

While many teams adopted a critical orientation, their works were ultimately put into the service of a state-sponsored strategy of mobilizing regional space for capital gain. Out of the wealth of ideas, only particular notions gained traction, largely those that aligned with the already agreed-upon values and norms of a French neoliberal project. The public nature of the exhibition also worked according to populist reason, based on renderings of a city that "everyone would obviously want." Imagining a generalized city and a generalized subject, this "shared dream" has come to stand in for the stated concerns of inhabitants and their diverse modes of being. The shared dream was thus a depoliticizing move, one that restricted the means of directing the change of the city to all but an elite architectural and planning class. Thus, the consultation provided a convenient screen that allowed the French state simultaneously to disavow master plans for the Île-de-France and local communes and to confirm the planning of the city according to a growth-first market logic of the global city.

In what follows, I revisit the discourses and designs of Grand Pari(s) in order to trace the work the architectural exhibit did in legitimating an overhaul of the urban landscape primarily through inventing a new vocabulary of urban transformation. The chapter considers how the architectural consultation acted as an apology for the neoliberalization of urban policy that is set to refashion twenty-first-century Paris as an elite space that concentrates power, wealth, and influence. I propose that the architectural dream was the necessary foundation for the ambitious transportation project at a regional scale that will see the polycentric metropolis to fruition. Thus the performative work of architecture in urban planning evident in Grand Pari(s) is indicative of the crucial place of architectural practices in the project-led networked paradigm of grand urbanism.

Imagineering the Global City

Architectural vision is particularly suited to the task of endorsing the competitive global city as neoliberalism relies on imaginative speculation as part of its orientation toward a future (Harvey 2005; Jameson 1998; Krivý 2011). Not only is architectural practice materially enmeshed within rapidly growing sectors of real estate and finance, but architecture is also increasingly at the forefront of neoliberal cultural production, providing the aesthetic normativity of rule that legitimates places as recognizable global cities (Ghertner 2011). Today, perhaps even more important than its direct link to construction is the role that architectural discourse plays in the symbolic reframing of urban representations and imaginaries.

With the architectural competition and consultation of Grand Pari(s), Sarkozy participated in—and extended to its logical conclusion—the now almost universal practice of employing architects for national and city promotion and for place marketing (Delanty and Jones 2002; McNeill 2009; McNeill and Tewdwr-Jones 2003; Ren 2008; Sklair 2011). In recent years architectural competitions have been used internationally as a means for local or national governments to build iconic buildings, launch flagship projects, and reinvent cities. Prominent examples include the Guggenheim

Museum in Bilbao, Potsdamer Platz in Berlin, the National Stadium in Beijing (built in advance of the 2008 Olympic Games), and the post-9/11 World Trade Center in New York. Architectural competitions, an aspect of what Fernando Orueta and Susan Fainstein (2008) have referred to as "the new mega-projects," gentrify underproductive sites, and, through major physical overhauls, rebrand urban spaces as inviting to tourists, investors, and elite residents (see also Swyngedouw, Moulaert, and Rodriguez 2002). Design competitions have also been used to disguise the powerlessness of the public in transforming city space (Allen 2006; Crawford 1995) and to generate a populist "postpolitical" consensus around urban reform (BAVO 2007). These design competitions, especially when undertaken at a large scale, are key mechanisms of grand urbanism.

This global phenomenon of publicly financed architectural landmarks is especially salient in France, where avant-garde architecture has significant cultural capital and where architectural works have long been used in the symbolic production of the nation. Paris is a city of monuments, and many of the city's most recent iconic sites, such as the Institut du Monde Arabe and the Parc de la Villette, are the outcome of architectural competitions. The architectural consultation of Grand Pari(s) continued in this legacy, but it was also at the leading edge of a larger national and EU strategy to more thoroughly solidify the role of architecture and culture in metropolitan planning apparatuses (Christine Albanel, in Bertone and Leloup 2009).

Furthermore, the strategic role of architecture in urban planning under Grand Pari(s) was not limited to the creation of discrete symbolic buildings or sites but was directed toward entire infrastructures and systems, thus controlling the narrative of the city as a whole. The angle of view became much wider and the focus less defined than in traditional designs. Architectural intervention becomes systematic and networked rather than discrete and site-specific. The networked aims of grand urbanism address not merely territorial conditions but the flows and connections that define the contemporary metropolis.

Doubtless the Bilbao strategy of employing starchitects to enhance competitiveness through signature works partially explains the emphasis on architecture as a privileged discipline of Grand Paris. Yet this is limited as an explanation when we consider the broader research and design function of the consultation. In the Grand Pari(s) consultation, the architects were tasked by President Sarkozy directly, and while they had free rein with respect to their representations, their work was nevertheless undertaken as part of a pointed political strategy to respond to pressing urban unrest, economic crisis, and political stalemate. Architecture thus had a more instrumental function: legitimizing a massive territorial transformation at the behest of a threatened state through rebranding the city.

Because of the strong centralized state presence, a number of teams at the outset were hesitant to participate and questioned the extent to which they were being employed as political tools to bolster a regime they did not in fact support. Indeed, the known leftist leanings of many of the prominent French teams made them odd collaborators with Sarkozy's conservative Union for a Popular Movement (UMP). While the architectural teams were eager to take up the challenge of refiguring the city and the body politic, they were loath to be pawns of a demagogue (Van der Haak 2009). Balancing the desire for progressive change with the fear of co-optation, the architects were faced with a significant choice as to whether or not to participate.

What force brought together idealistic ex-*soixante-huitards* artists and visionaries with an authoritarian politician? For starters, all parties shared a rejection of purely laissez-faire policies, a belief in state intervention to generate prosperity, and a recognition of the urgency of contemporary metropolitan challenges. Like other of his colleagues, for example, Antoine Grumbach was skeptical at first of the consultation and agreed to participate only after a series of meetings with Sarkozy convinced him of their mutual interests and of the unassailable merit of the project. Swayed by the exigency of the compounded urban crises and the promise that a large-scale design exhibition would give credibility to the architectural profession and publicity to their respective firms, in the end, the participating architects found that the lofty possibilities offered by the consultation outweighed the perils of its misuse.

Not reducible to a guide or prop for urban planning, Grand Pari(s) yielded an extensive and sophisticated archive of research on the contemporary metropolitan form in general and on the dynamics of Paris in particular. The ten projects were remarkable for evoking what the metropolitan region *could be,* and as such, they provided a contrast with what the city *was.* Visions of full employment, affordable and universal housing, accessible and sustainable public space, and local democratic organization challenged existing regional hierarchies and exclusions. The very notion that Paris *could* look very different from the way it did was a critical maneuver that was necessary to spur transformation. In identifying actionable problems and creative solutions, these visions also respectively identified decisive points of politics. While the ten Grand Pari(s) projects stimulated the public imagination and generated hope for a different and improved future, questions of the metropolitan structures, material dispositions, and regimes of centrality on which the visions rest are nevertheless proving determinative. The various actors involved in Grand Pari(s) had differing degrees of power and resources to create, mobilize, and impose representations in order to serve their interests.

As stated in the official objective, "More than a forum of ideas, [Grand Pari(s)] is a matter of a call for projects of research and development whose outcomes will *illuminate decision*" (République Française 2009, emphasis added). The projects, however, did not "illuminate decision" in the sense of forging a particular path for policy makers to subsequently follow. Rather, the architectural exhibits primarily served to elucidate decisions already made, allowing them to be seen in a softer and less controversial light. Indeed, the more critical or esoteric elements of Grand Pari(s) were dismissed as being too intellectual, and many of the most interesting and politically potent aspects of the project were ignored. In the end, only a very limited selection of ideas was taken up in official plans and policies.

In particular, six guiding concepts stand out as definitive of the new urban common sense of Grand Pari(s): the grand city, the governable city, the unified city, the designed city, the flexible city, and the connected city.[2] Each of these six key attributes is multivalent and open to interpretation, but together they can be readily manipulated to reinforce the power of the central state in urban planning over and against local government and inhabitants. In generating a new visual repertoire and a conceptual vocabulary of the greater region, Grand Pari(s) cleaned up the faltering image of Paris, replaced it with a new unified and attractive aesthetic, sold the amenities associated with a global city, and solicited public support for a paradigm of polycentric metropolitan growth. In so doing, it established a symbolic economy conducive to grand urbanism.

Re-presenting the Metropolis

The Grand City

In light of the principal valences of grandeur outlined in the introduction to this book, there were several main ways in which the emphases on a "Grand" Paris and a "grand" vision worked in the architectural exhibition. Primarily, they invoked the nostalgic ideals of majesty and grandeur that have historically defined the city. While the French Revolution was to break the hold of power by *"les grands"* (the elite or wealthy) of the city and implement a new civic universality, the history of Paris remains intimately connected to a legacy of elite culture, power, and wealth. The final exhibition of Grand Pari(s) retold this luminous and grandiose history in a series of background tiles at the visitor's entrance. Ignored in this retelling was any idea of a competing "people's history" of peasant and working-class activity, and the democratic and popular political struggles that have also been so important in shaping the city. The key figures in the official Grand Pari(s) history are limited to those individuals who added to the prestige of Paris and who conspicuously emphasized beauty, luxury, and glory in the city at any cost.[3] While the reign of kings and emperors is prominent, and named state planners got ample consideration in the framing literature, there was little mention of lesser-known historical figures and inhabitants who had influenced the trajectory of urbanization. There was little to no acknowledgment, for example, of the Commune of 1871, May '68, the uprisings of 2005, or other popular urban struggles.

For Sarkozy (2009), one important task of the exhibition was to restore the legacy of imperial planning and to make Paris "not only the most beautiful city which exists, the most beautiful city which has existed, but also the most beautiful city that can exist." Sarkozy was set to direct these hyperbolic reforms through big vision and assertive command. Grand Pari(s) positioned Sarkozy as a heroic savior of the city and bolstered the image of the president as a leader who was willing to take risks and reorient the country in new directions, an image he had been trying to fashion throughout his time in office.[4] He self-indulgently capitalized on the popularity of the Grand Pari(s) plans to firmly implant the idea that he was the sole person capable of bringing the plans to their fruition, the sole person capable of piloting the city into the twenty-first century. Only somewhat in jest did he remark to the architects, "I hope that you will aid me in being reelected because it will take time to do all of this. Five years will not suffice" (*L'Humanité* 2009).

The grandeur of heroic and imperial planning was redoubled in the exhibition's final display, set in the Carlu Gallery temporary exhibit hall of the Cité de l'Architecture et du Patrimoine, located in the Trocadéro, a massive *palais* across from the Eiffel Tower and the site of the 1878 World's Fair. With vaulted ceilings and an impressive interior, the *palais* space is a resplendent reminder of both monarchial sovereignty and the profundity and promise of modern construction. The ten sleek and technologically impressive kiosks, or "modular villages," of the exhibit—filled with data-dense maps, glossy photographs, interactive neon consuls, and videos playing on plasma screens—reproduced this imaginary while updating spectacles of worldliness and progress for contemporary audiences. Innovation, technological expertise, and futurist media were introduced as new additions to the modern symbols of monumentality and civilization.

The discourses of grand development also entrenched the elite nature of architectural practice, which privileges the vision of a single perspective over all others and celebrates the architect-designer over the user-inhabitants. The elite, exclusively European, and mostly male makeup of the solicited visionaries was striking, though unsurprising, and indicated the conservative establishment that has long dominated architectural practices. While the interdisciplinarity of the ten teams was important to reinforce the collaborative nature of project-based reform, this was in marked tension with the architectural "cult of the individual" (McNeill 2009, 59–80) that also drove the consultation. Much effort went into asserting that the design process of Grand Pari(s) was multidimensional, and yet there was still a need (especially in photo opportunities and marketing literature) to attribute authorship of the ten designs to celebrity individual (or occasionally paired) creators. In this way a select cadre of world-class visionaries were acknowledged as having unique capabilities to partake in the high stakes of Paris's redesign.

Not only was a plurality of perspectives explicitly not the point of the Grand Pari(s) "shared vision," but the special status of the starchitects reinforced the undemocratic nature of framing urban imaginaries and producing urban space. Similar to other urban projects undertaken throughout the twentieth century, Grand Pari(s) supported the idea that town planning should be guided by strong leaders and international experts, who presumably sit above the chaos of petty politics and parochial interests (see Phillips 1987). The grand purview of the project and the competitive creativity of the experts in the project served at a basic level to suppress active civic deliberation and reinforce the notion that the future is far too vast and too important to be left in the hands of *franciliens* (residents of the Île-de-France) themselves.

The Governable City

One of the driving forces of the broader Grand Paris initiative is to streamline governance of the more than 1,200 communes, eight departments, and dozens of intercommunal establishments that make up the institutional landscape of the Île-de-France region (see chapters 5 and 6). The official objectives state that "in the competition of globally-ranked cities, Paris occupies a respectable place which suffers nevertheless from a chronic deficit linked to its perimeter and its governance" (République Française 2009). Indeed, political commentators have criticized this "ungovernable" institutional landscape for the social and economic problems that plague the region and have repeatedly suggested that breaking down these institutional obstacles is necessary to bring Paris into the twenty-first century (see Chapon 2011; Gilli 2008a; Subra 2009, 2012).

In their appraisal of contemporary Paris, the ten teams of Grand Pari(s) almost universally agreed that the regional configuration of the French state is confusing, inefficient, counterproductive, asymmetrical, and undemocratic. More than one team referred to the multiple overlapping governing bodies of the region as "vertiginous," while the team Rogers Stirk Harbour + Partners (2009) listed the task "Restructure metropolitan governance in the Île-de-France" as the number one priority in its *10 Principles for Metropolitan Paris*. The architects repeatedly problematized governance, many calling for grassroots control of urban practices and the construction of new cooperative governing structures that would be better suited to the urban regional network. Insofar as it offered a framework for territorial and political management that might stabilize the metropolis, the architectural consultation attempted to address the complexity of problems related to governing and coordinating policy at the scale of the global city region.

Groupe Descartes, for example, argued that Paris is currently overwhelmed by its governance systems, and in lieu of the current arrangements the group proposed the creation of twenty new cities of 50,000 people, to do away with the imbalances in municipal organization and to balance local with metropolitan and global needs. Richard Rogers's team also called for reorganizing governance by creating twenty-three new administrative entities that could counteract the polar power of Paris within the Île-de-France and thus add democratic legitimacy to local politics. They suggested extending the existing structures of local intercommunality through the "progressive disengagement of the State in the management of regional affairs" (Rogers Stirk Harbour + Partners, LSE and ARUP 2009). For these architects, local autonomy was pitted against grand urbanism as a centralized state project.

Despite demands for local and regional thinking within the project, however, the Grand Pari(s) consultation was a top-down venture that structurally supported the central state and legitimized the president's role as spokesman for metropolitan affairs. Many understood Grand Pari(s) as in fact an attempt by the central state to take back the reins of control over metropolitan Paris from the region of Île-de-France and from local communes (many of which are now Socialist or Communist), which gained some power over regional affairs after the decentralization laws of the 1980s (Gilli 2008a; Subra 2012; Wiel 2009b). This power struggle was notably at the forefront of national consciousness in 2009 in the run-up to local elections, in which Sarkozy's UMP party hoped to make major inroads. The consultation gave renewed influence to the central state over the discourses of metropolitan development and institutional reform, and thus served to effectively undercut the actual planning powers of the region through the Master Plan of the Île-de-France Region (SDRIF), as well as the growing importance of the grassroots joint authority Paris Métropole. Indeed, Christine Albanel, the minister of culture who oversaw Grand Pari(s), claimed that the architectural designs would help the existing SDRIF evolve and integrate new ideas (in Leloup and Bertone 2009, 14). The objective, according to Frédéric Mialet, was "to broaden the debate that currently takes place at a regional level by exploring beyond existing urban planning methods and models": in other words, to disable the existing local governing apparatuses (Cité de l'Architecture et du Patrimoine 2009).

Jurisdictional struggles over urban governance and policy are strongly embedded within struggles over the image and form of Paris. Architectural projects are uniquely positioned to intervene in these spatial debates and are among what Gerry Kearns (1993, 93) refers to as "ideologically significant planning instruments." Grand Pari(s) here served an ambiguous function, for though its contributors by and large called for pluralism, negotiation, and collaboration, the consultation on the whole became weaponized in partisan interinstitutional battles. The strategic deployment of architecture in this way is not in itself new. According to Kearns (1993), not only have large-scale architectural projects around Paris been put into the service of place marketing, they can also be linked to particular patrons, and thus serve as important signs of who has the legitimacy to direct urbanization. There is a great similarity between the current debates surrounding Grand Paris, for example, and Kearns's account of François Mitterrand's highly contested *grands projets*, built across the city in celebration of the bicentenary of the French Revolution in 1989. Mitterand's *projets* were a means of asserting both partisan (Socialist) and central presidential power through manipulating memory and nostalgia for particular urban sites, with Paris as the battleground within which these conflicts and battles were waged. Sarkozy's architectural *pari* operated in a similar fashion. However, whereas in the 1980s architects were employed for their site-specific and direct contributions to locational politics and place making, today it is the interconnected and complex region itself that is at issue, with architects playing a more indirect role in reconfiguring the shape of the metropolis and renaming its proper authorities.

The use of cultural events to control the narrative of urban development is further clarified when Grand Pari(s) is compared to a similar exhibition, *Paris, the Metropolis and Its Projects*, curated by the local leaders Bertrand Delanoë (mayor of Paris, 2001–2014) and Anne Hidalgo (elected mayor of Paris in 2014) and by Paris Métropole. Initially created in 2013, *Paris, the Metropolis and Its Projects* is now a permanent exhibit at the Pavillon de l'Arsenal. Unlike the 2009 Grand Pari(s) exhibition, which emphasized big visions, grand plans, and civilizational transformations, the Pavillon de l'Arsenal exhibit stresses many small and mundane projects. It is organized around the innumerable individual projects that have incrementally and in composite created the metropolitan landscape over the past three centuries, with particular attention to changes in the last thirty years. In this framework Paris is not an exceptional model or national bastion built by heroic men but a suburban-urban complex assembled over time by millions of actors in contingent ways. In fact, grand visions, according to this perspective, cannot capture "that which is built each day through projects of elected officials, developed by public and private actors in concert with those who live, who work, who grow and who study. Such an intensity of projects demands a shared knowledge and the essential implication of all" (Anne Hidalgo, in Pavillon de l'Arsenal 2013).

To capture the multitude of projects and people that collectively define the contemporary city, *Paris, the Metropolis and Its Projects* provides a detailed timeline displayed on the walls of the main gallery space. However, the focal point of the exhibit is an interactive "digital maquette" called "Paris 2020" that is projected on a thirty-seven-square-meter screen in the center of the Pavillon de l'Arsenal's main concourse. This impressive projection—synched in real time with Google Earth—is a map of the future Île-de-France landscape, transportation networks, and emblematic architectural constructions ("Paris 2020" is also available online at http://www.parismetropole2020.com).[5] An interactive console allows visitors to zoom in and out, focus on individual development projects, or isolate particular relationships (transportation systems, economic channels, water flows) within the wider metropolitan network, and thus to explore diverse geographies and histories of the region. Overall, this local perspective responds to Grand Pari(s) by offering a more nuanced version of the constitution of the metropolis and urban transformation. It also celebrates heterogeneity, complexity, and a wide array of actors—including, what is most important, citizens themselves—as important producers of space. Interestingly, nowhere in the exhibit is the previous Grand Pari(s) consultation referenced, nor does the name of the new transit network, the Grand Paris Express, appear.[6]

Battles over the design of the future city are still being waged, and regional structures of governance remain an open question. The architectural competition brought this question to the fore, yet it is clear that in the national spectacle of Grand Pari(s), architecture was instrumentalized to legitimize the priorities of the central state and to communicate that the national state was the appropriate scale on which to organize the metropolis and lead the Paris region into the next century.

The Unified City

In the architectural exhibit, the elite nature of redevelopment at the level of the central state was balanced by populist appeals to convince residents of the Île-de-France to see themselves as part of the Grand Paris dream. One of the main functions of the exhibit was to reconfigure what Kevin Lynch (1960) called the "imageability" of the city. Grand Pari(s) gave to the inhabitants of Paris a compass that allowed them to find their location in the ever-growing region and a portrait in which to recognize themselves as Parisian, no matter where they might be. The ability to read the city and imaginatively feel a part of it is necessary for a sense of political belonging and collective public life. These affective aspects of urban life and forms of imaginative citizenship, read through city spaces, are fundamental to any political community but have special relevance to a twenty-first-century postmetropolis in which the formal complexity of the urban defies traditional scalar imaginaries. It is also particularly necessary for a city like Paris, fragmented by often invisible histories of violence, exclusion, and inequality.

Architectural and urban plans are important apparatuses to provide inhabitants with "a coherent and detailed mental image of the city," without which the interaction between self and place would remain fragmented and ephemeral (Sennett 1992, 33). A unified presentation allows the city to become more imaginatively consistent and enables a form of mental mapping by which residents can locate themselves in the larger surroundings and relate to the incomprehensible melee of urban life. In making the city more visually accessible, and thus more legible, to all through regional maps, designs, and perspectives, Grand Pari(s) thus constructed an urban identity to which all inhabitants could hopefully ascribe. For a city without the means to represent itself, the architects succeeded in "giving the city to the people" (Christine Albanel, in LeLoup and Bertone 2009, 14). Grand Pari(s) provided a general depiction of the region, a truly Parisian self-representation for the *banlieue*, and a fantasy of metropolitan conviviality.

Like a mirror, the depictions of the city provided a unified identity to a subject (here Paris and the "Parisian") that had previously been ill defined, and an ideal toward which the city was to strive. Frédéric Mialet, an architectural critic involved with Grand Pari(s), at the time described the need to refocus from the central city to the metropolitan territory in order to "create a veritable identity of the scale of the urban region" (in Le Moniteur Architecture 2009, 11). The studio of Jean Nouvel (Nouvel, Cantal-Dupart, and Duthilleul 2008) took up this task directly, describing Grand Paris as a "shared, happy, attractive identity," while the firm LIN called its contribution a "mental map" and a "spatial model" of the unified region (in Le Moniteur Architecture 2009, 199, 192). Roland Castro, a former analysand of Lacan, even referred to Grand Pari(s) as providing a unified reading of the city-as-subject through the psychoanalytic category of a borromean knot.

In the architectural consultation of Grand Pari(s), the uncoordinated elements of the city and excluded residents were joined not through active political engagement but through architectural artifice that substituted for the unmediated experiences of living and projected an image that simplified and generalized, creating of antagonistic and dissimilar objects a new imposed whole.[7] Existing variations and hierarchies in regional space were effaced in the name of a unified vision at the same time that other differences were actively created and imposed.

Many of the teams agreed that the integration of the city had to be accompanied by the differentiation of its component parts. Giving a unified identity to the territory also had to be accompanied by more local positioning, lest the homogeneity become disorienting. Equally as important as unity to the legibility of the city is the ability to discern local places within the whole. As Finn Geipel described it at the time, "The city dweller perceives neighborhoods through their differences. Certain landmarks such as monuments, traffic nodes, avenues and cultural venues allow him/her to build a mental map and thus *read* the territory" (Geipel, Andi, and Équipe LIN 2009, 48). The text of the city involves an overall spatial connection, but it also requires that sites and signs be distinguished from one another. Together, these give the city what Bernardo Secchi and Paola Viganò (2011) have called "isotropy" and "permeability."

Operationalizing this dual approach, Studio 09 roamed the streets, conducting interviews and trying "to understand what people considered remarkable places, [sites] which had significations in their memory" (in Le Moniteur Architecture 2009, 172). The team then created a map of existing "significant" places, the psychogeography of which demonstrated that the distribution of meaning and attachments within Paris remained extremely uneven and still rested on a unipolar imaginary that concentrated interest in the core. Against this, they thus aimed to monumentalize and localize the suburbs to make them valuable and influential places in their own right. In a similar fashion, Jean Nouvel promoted the creation of new site-specific art, especially outside the historic city core, to add more "destination points" and more splendor to the already richly landmarked city (in Le Moniteur Architecture 2009).

Roland Castro, for whom poetry is the motif of urbanism and urban life, also had specific projects in mind entailing the distribution of symbolic markers across the Île-de-France. Despite his acknowledgment of the poetic and the political nature of collective building and making, Castro's attempts to instill the suburbs with significance underscored how easily this project of resignification could slip into a hegemonic framework of national monumentality and local "place making." "Genuine" places for Castro come into being with imposing landmarks that "incarnate and refound the republican identity" (in Le Moniteur Architecture 2009, 121). While a number of his projects had undeniably critical elements, they were also instruments of city branding. He concluded, without irony, that "in the future Michelin guide of Grand Paris, one will find a multitude of places for a metropolitan voyage. Grand Paris becomes, place after place, an inexhaustible destination." Here Castro nearly echoed the conservative secretary of state for the development of the capital region, Christian Blanc (2010, 146), whose own place based plan of economic and infrastructural investment aimed to "give soul to the metropolis," "create a same language" for the city, eliminate barriers, "restore geographic identity," and promote the emergence of "unifying symbols."

The suburban meaning making exercises of Grand Pari(s) are not necessarily driven by market values, but they are easily embedded within metropolitan boosterism and tourism campaigns. Insofar as they help to create a carefully edited image of the region as a whole that can be promoted and sold to the world, Grand Pari(s) architects are complicit in commodifying metropolitan space. Grand Paris's success relies on the presentation of the suburbs as being venues for exploration, opportunity, and exploitation by global investors, developers, tourists, and residents.[8] With a priority on revalorizing metropolitan territory through select investments in site-specific projects, the language of unification and diversification thus promotes precisely the kind of gentrifying strategies of "equalization" and "differentiation" that drive uneven development (Smith 2008).

The Designed City

The Grand Pari(s) R&D phase and the broader Grand Paris renewal plan each involved extensive open debates, seminars, and consultations with concerned inhabitants and interest groups. More than a blueprint or plan, Grand Pari(s) was a cultural event in the form of a public art project and design exhibition. During its tenure, the exhibition saw an estimated 250,000 visitors, and it also received extensive media coverage in the main daily periodicals (e.g., *Le Monde, Le Figaro, Libération*) and on local and national radio and television news programs. In addition to the official exhibit, each architectural team also produced a supplementary archive of literature, qualitative data, blueprints, and designs that was freely accessible on the official République Française Grand Pari(s) website (http://www.legrandparis.culture.gouv.fr). Christine Albanel at the time described the open, collective, and transparent nature of the exhibition as "above all to permit all Franciliens and beyond to appropriate for themselves their metropolitan future to think it and to discuss it" (in Le Moniteur Architecture 2009, 9). Public relations was a crucial aspect of the architectural work, and each of the ten teams worked to distill its philosophical and empirical contributions into an accessible and understandable display.

The fact that Grand Pari(s) was directed at the public, however, does not necessarily imply that urban denizens were empowered with democratic influence over the production and use of space. When placed in the context of what Rosalyn Deutsche (1998, xii) has called the "dominant paradigm of urban aesthetic interdisciplinarity," the openness, collaboration, and free vision of the Grand Pari(s) public consultation can be seen to be structured by more fundamental exclusions that limit the exhibition's effectiveness as an engaged public sphere. Deutsche notes that from the 1980s on, a rise in the use of large-scale urban developments has coincided with an intensification of official rhetoric about public space and an increase in public art commissions, including architectural competitions. She writes:

> Promoting the participation of art and architecture in urban redevelopment projects, this model neutralizes the political character of both art and the city. It couples an aesthetic ideology positing that art and architecture transcend social relations with an urban ideology that presents the organization of cities as the natural product of biological, social or technological evolutions undergone by a supposedly organic society. These concepts sanction art's role in the urban environment as beneficial while legitimating existing urban conditions as inevitable. (xiii)

Discourses of public space provide urban development with democratic legitimacy, yet these same discourses become authoritarian when they fix single definitions of the "public" and of the "space" in question. If the contours of development have been predetermined, there is no room for deliberation and thus no opportunity for democratic politics. More particularly, the yoking of a public exhibition to a large-scale redevelopment initiative enables some degree of collective participation in the theorization and creation of the city, but this participation is also neutralized in the planning process, reducing it to the consumption of the exhibition alone and foreclosing any real active influence over spatial production. The design emphasis of the networked city leaves transformation open-ended while establishing a public consensus for development. All are encouraged to gaze upon the spectacle, but there is not room for popular oversight.

While Deutsche is mainly concerned with the abuses of urban "public" art as it was expressed in New York's ascendancy in the 1980s and 1990s, this phenomenon is especially pronounced in contemporary Paris, where art and architecture are highly valued as markers of cultural capital and where public intellectuals play important roles as cultural translators. Staging state projects of urban transformation through a public architectural exhibition thus serves to legitimize both the state and architecture. As revered intellectual and aesthetics products, the final designs of Grand Pari(s) had an aura of transcending social relations, partisan politics, and utilitarian rationality, thus enabling them to effectively obscure the political agenda behind them. Moreover, this use of a public exhibition follows the Saint Simonian ideal of the "spatial superiority of art in organizing society" (Phillips 1987).

The limitations on the publicness of the city are further enforced by the aesthetic injunction of urban design to be conventionally beautiful. Indeed, from New York and London to Singapore and Dubai, the global city everywhere consists of glass-and-steel skyscrapers, commodity-filled megamalls, condominium-lined waterfronts, gleaming new office parks, manicured green spaces, and polished "smart" infrastructures. In Paris, this fantasy landscape is set to replace the crumbling housing estates, crowded streets, and formerly industrial brownfields that defined the bleak dystopia of the postwar *banlieue*. Sarkozy's 2005 pledge to "clean up the *banlieue* with a power washer" and rid the periphery of rioting "scum" (promises he made during the uprisings as minister of the interior) was achieved in Grand Pari(s) through what Grant Kester (1993, 35) has described as a hegemonic and "aggressive phenomenology, dedicated to the suppression of all traces of an autonomous working class culture" that defines the imaginary space of postindustrial society. The ten architectural teams rejoiced in the notions of renewal, regeneration, and renovation. They rejected the long-standing depictions of bleak uniform suburbs, instead projecting life, color, and vitality across metropolitan space. Yet their utopian designs nevertheless ignored the possibility that this very redevelopment might bring about its own patterns of displacement and erasure. The idea of the designed city thus suffered from a spatial fallacy that in transforming image, and even in transforming physical space, one solves underlying problems. The aesthetics of the global city ideal and the environmental determinism of many of the proposals masked the exclusions on which they were based.

The Flexible City
Across Grand Pari(s) there was a disavowal of the purely technocratic planning regime of the modernist era and an embrace of a more open and collaborative postmodern form of planning. Grand Pari(s) demonstrated how urban planning and architecture have responded to the conditions of late capitalism and postmodern critiques with a measured reflexivity and have adopted a new series of orientations and guiding principles, replacing strict codes and regulation in the service of future-proofing, with flow, flexibility and openness to change. Unlike Second Empire or post–World War II reforms, the ten teams of Grand Pari(s) also rejected the rational parceling up of space and a homogeneity of form and function, instead focusing their efforts on a series of concerns that included connectivity, mixity, and organicism.

Twentieth-century bourgeois spatial relations that sought a strict separation between public and private realms were refigured through Grand Pari(s) by way of "mixed-use" neighborhoods, where places of work, residence, and leisure would be intertwined. Efforts to "dezone, decode, deregulate," as Roland Castro (in Le Moniteur Architecture 2009, 217) put it, were a welcome response to the regimented order of functionalism. Jean

Nouvel, for example, claimed that livable spaces resist delimitation and cannot be captured by zones or rigid ordinances. Many of the teams also blamed the zoning regimes of the postwar era for ossifying land uses and preventing value from being created in peripheral areas. Imagining a more malleable property and land use regime allowed the architects to turn a simple green space into a multifunctional "central park" or an unused river embankment into a permanent world fair. It also enabled them to champion green garden business towers, to hail mixed retail and transit sites as places of democratic encounter, and to market the wholesale food warehouses in Rungis as places of individual consumption and gastronomic exploration. With flexibility, "Warehouses are transformed into lofts, offices flow into former residential buildings, parking lots are occupied by civic amenities, large estates are not demolished but enhanced, heightened, embellished" (Jean Nouvel, in Cité de l'Architecture et du Patrimoine 2009).

In a slightly different vein, Finn Geipel saw flexibility as an organic element of the aleatory mix of urban encounters. He saw (with perhaps an orientalist eye) "Asian agglomerations" as paragons of multiservice and mixed-use compact developments (in Le Moniteur Architecture 2009, 201). L'AUC also invoked Asian multiservice locales as a model for mixity, citing Japanese train stations as key public, commercial, and infrastructural spaces where, in the words of Roland Barthes, "a train may open unto a sock display" (97).

It is telling that the promise of mixity assumed that proximity would bring about equality and that democratic encounters between luxury shoppers and low-wage laborers might be staged through the spacing of daily movements. While such public encounters are necessary for a progressive politics of propinquity, spatial interventions alone are insufficient without more substantive economic reform. In reality, the flexibility of spaces that Grand Pari(s) purported to underwrite cannot be understood outside the more generalized context of flexible capitalism, which is marked by precarious and unstable labor, weakened unions, a deskilling of industry and service, a breakdown of organizational hierarchies, and a growing divide between the urban elite and urban poor. The "flexicity" (Soja 2002) is the form of the city wrought through the political economy of post-Fordist production.

Moreover, in such an economy, impermanence is expected and desired, and the very fungibility of capital, labor, and spaces gives them value.

Spaces that are mutable and transformable can more easily adapt to marked demands and can be continuously revalued to enable accumulation through property markets. Unlike stable forms of territory, favored by Fordist production, today stability and changeability are seen as interlinked. Today metropolitan spaces are subject to the laws of permanent mutability. According to this logic, "the sustainable city is the transformable city" (Christian de Portzamparc, in Le Moniteur Architecture 2009, 118). A belief in essential flexibility thus underlies the creative destruction of capitalist urbanization and permits the continually shifting patterns of investment and disinvestment in territory that enable widespread gentrification.

As planning shifts from a comprehensive public power over territory to a loose collection of ad hoc and often private collaborative projects, architecture becomes a means of mediating ever more malleable relations between public institutional and market systems. This flexible restructuring is marked by the idea that there is "no long term." The future given is tenuous at best, and therefore the plannability of the city is always tempered by the caprice of the world to come. The lack of control of the future and the inability to fully direct the city absolve the state and inhabitants of responsibility and strengthen the logic of risk and speculation through the paradoxically framed grand urbanism.

The Connected City
All of the architectural teams acknowledged that the metropolis is not a territory with fixed borders but a series of relationships, flows, and interactions. There was unanimous agreement across the ten teams that in order to account for the hierarchical polycentricism of the region and to facilitate flux, connection, and mobility, Paris needed to extend public transit service to the periphery, link disconnected segments of regional territory, and facilitate global movement. Mass mobility was thus the overriding concern of the Grand Pari(s) consultation, a concern that was explicitly taken up in subsequent transport policies. Yves Lion (2010) even claimed that "the main aim of the project of Grand Paris is for those concerned with architecture and urban planning to bring the transport question into the limelight." If the problem of the Parisian metropolis is posed equally as being too diffuse and too global, too segregated and too insular, the connected city discourse of Grand Pari(s) provided the solution of infrastructural networks as a way to coherence and equality.

The architects did differ, however, in their proposals for how to accomplish this networked connectivity. Richard Rogers, for example, called for improving suburban transit offerings through a series of circumferential metro rings extending outward from the core and connecting peripheral hubs to one another and to the existing train and bus network. Jean Nouvel suggested a dense mesh consisting of high- and low-speed networks spread across regional territory. LIN instead favored a bus rapid transit network of "micromobilities," to be integrated into the global transportation system. For Studio 09, transportation at multiple scales was also paramount. The team proposed that the porous city of Grand Paris be defined by "absolute accessibility," where "everyone can travel to any point in the metropolis via a dense network of green routes and public transport services" (Cité de l'Architecture et du Patrimoine 2009). This local lattice would then be integrated into European-wide networks through high-speed rail and international connections through airport connections.

For many of the teams, improving mobility was also explicitly meant as a social policy to combat the segregation and apartheid that currently define the regional landscape. Enabling all people, including those in the underserviced *banlieues*, to move freely and to access the diverse sites of the metropolis is a means of equalizing and democratizing the city, and of liberating its residents. Moreover, teams such as l'AUC even went so far as to link this right to mobility to related socializations of property (through bike sharing, car sharing, and free transit) and the communalization of land use (densification of social housing and autonomous management of services), suggesting, quite radically, that a sustainable city must be premised on a truly equitable distribution of collective goods and collective resources.

Many of the transportation proposals aimed to move people around the city and balance territorial inequities of transit service and spatial capital, but others were more concerned with transit oriented to facilitating global flows of capital and investment. This was especially clear in the designs of Christian de Portzamparc. Like the other architectural teams, de Portzamparc called for new mobility systems and the densification of housing and commerce alongside transit corridors. But for him this involved treating the obsolete *banlieues* as privileged sites of intervention whereby transit infrastructure would explicitly become a lever of gentrifying redevelopment. "The riots [of 2005] brought the metropolitan crisis to even the people of

Paris. ...There are places where the public authorities should step in, *where value should be generated immediately"* (in Sachs 2009, emphasis added). De Portzamparc's vision also involved using transportation to channel investment in already existing economic and technology clusters in the Parisian suburbs. In other words, in order to achieve the private intensification of the city, the network had first to connect elite spaces of economic production and ensure Paris's place in global markets.

It was this economic development model of transportation, not the more social variations, that was taken up by Christian Blanc at the end of the consultation. Indeed, Blanc's "supermetro," the *"Grand Huit"* (Great Eight, for its two interlocking loops), advanced in 2009 at the Grand Pari(s) exhibition, bore little resemblance to a "thick mesh" of service and instead consisted of sparse stations that were not at all integrated with existing networks but were above all designed to connect globally competitive hubs of finance, research, tourism, and international travel.[9] Parodying the political philosophy of Gilles Deleuze (and filtered through the proposal of de Portzamparc), Blanc used the terminology of the rhizome to describe a competitive urban network. Blanc described the differentiated hubs of metropolitan Paris in terms of an economic rhizome that had to be developed for its immanent economic potential. In the metropolitan rhizome, he wrote, "Each element of the territory constructs itself by relation with Paris, but grows by its own energy." The constantly open polycentric assemblage would catalyze regional development as a "potential" for innovation, investment, and growth existed at each node (Blanc 2010, 149–151).

The language of the rhizome, and the relational social ontology that it suggests, provides a way to understand the metropolis as global, and mobility as key to this globality. It also furnishes a model of an urban cluster where nodes can be enhanced for the overall prosperity of the region. If territorial flexibility links Grand Paris to capitalist operations, the plan's market logic is further strengthened by the networked imperatives of connected urbanism. Indeed, the overriding focus on how transportation infrastructure will build urban cohesion replicates an organic conception of the unified republic, while eliding critical understandings of how networks and flows might themselves also be productive of marginality and exclusion.[10]

Moving the Vision Forward

The Grand Pari(s) consultation put questions of urban space at the forefront of national consciousness and prompted a high-profile conversation over the meaning of the metropolis and the politics of architecture. Through their designs and written material, the ten teams created an unprecedented archive of thought on contemporary urbanism and urbanization. Addressing fundamental questions of collective life, social ties, and economic and property relations, Grand Pari(s) reframed what it meant to live in contemporary Paris. Individually and in concert, the designs pointed in many progressive directions for twenty-first-century urbanism and were intensely rich in their layered accounts of what Paris was at the time and could be in the future.

From the outset, it was never clear how the architectural projects of Grand Pari(s) were to be deployed or accounted for by the various institutional networks that collectively govern the metropolitan Paris region. How specifically the projects would "illuminate the path" to the future city was largely left up to political decisions and the discretion of national policy makers and local planners. The uptake of ideas into policy was highly uneven. Elements of the consultation that accorded with Sarkozy's already established agenda were lauded, while those that challenged it were ignored or trivialized. Though the material changes proposed by the ten teams were often fanciful and ambitious, the actual changes instigated by the national government have so far been calculated and unimaginative, limited for the most part to the regional transportation initiative and site-specific megaprojects along its route. Since the exhibition, many of the design teams have banked on their notoriety to win bids to develop projects in greater Paris, but most of the specific Grand Pari(s) proposals will never be implemented.

As many of the plans advocated by Blanc and Sarkozy had been proposed prior to the consultation, what the exhibit did, more than anything, was devise a language and a medium of representation to communicate the projects already conceived. The urbanist and transport expert Marc Wiel (2009b, 175) went so far as to describe Christian Blanc as the "eleventh team" in the competition, "who did not compete because he had already won."

In planning for what is now known as the Grand Paris Express, for example, Blanc and the Société du Grand Paris were accused of ignoring the myriad proposals of the architectural consultation as well as the existing transit proposals of local councils, intercommunal organizations, and Paris Métropole (see chapter 3 for details of this conflict). Indeed, after the exhibition several architects publicly criticized Blanc's treatment of the Grand Pari(s) projects (Jérôme 2009; Le Chatelier 2009; Van der Haak 2009). Nouvel, Lyon, and de Portzamparc all voiced their concerns about the way the technocracy of Grand Paris had responded to the architectural proposals. Even Hollande's more tempered and socially oriented "New Grand Paris" ignored the many radical aspects of the architectural consultation, prompting Michel Cantal-Dupart (2013) to write an open letter to the supposedly more progressive and less dictatorial president condemning his willful ignorance of and disingenuous deployment of the architectural designs.

The fact that the exhibition was based not on competition but on consensus contributed to further eliding any actual disagreements over how the city should be built and the priorities for development.[11] For Blanc (2010, 152), despite "practical and cultural divergences in the manner of vision," the teams, like the wider population they were supposed to represent, were nevertheless "in the same boat and want to arrive at the same port." Thus the architectural consultation, while seeming to be free and open, in effect shut down deliberation and contestation. By leveling the designs to a "shared dream," the architectural visions were instrumentalized as a representational and theoretical basis for new metropolitan policies, in particular those initiated by the central state in the areas of transportation and economic development. The shared dream translates a range of political interests into rational technical objectives.

The architects of Grand Pari(s) all participate to a greater or lesser degree in this practice, acting as intellectual support for what Jean-Pierre Garnier (2010) calls the "contemporary urban counterrevolution." Garnier (2010, 22) accuses the starchitects of the consultation of being *"super-bobos"* (*"bobos"* being slang for "bohemian bourgeoisie") who defend existing social and spatial hierarchies in the name of reformist utopias and highly aestheticized politics.[12] Banishing notions of capitalism, colonialism, exploitation, alienation, class, struggle, antagonism, contradiction, exploitation, and hierarchy from the urban lexicon, the architects of Grand Pari(s) evacuated Grand Pari(s) of its revolutionary and radical goals. Grand Pari(s) established instead a new framework of grand urbanism that rests squarely on a depoliticized imaginary and glossary of urban terms. In particular the renovation and renewal of the metropolis is today directed by idioms of competition (rentability, workability, flexibility), political centrism (civility, solidarity, urbanity, and inclusivity), and prestige (attractiveness, beauty, grandeur).

Through the exhibition, the same public figures who once criticized the urban order—Castro, Nouvel, Grumbach, and de Portzamparc, for example, all of whom emerged from the highly politicized post-1960s French architectural turn—thus crafted a scientific apology for the way things are. Indeed, further to the value added by the consultation as marketing is the value gained by incorporating tempered progressive criticism into the existing planning regimes. What appears as a paradoxical renewal of architecture as a leading urban practice can also be seen as a key moment of the institutionalization of critique. As Łukasz Stanek (2011, 79) has noted, since the 1960s, the French state has founded planning on the knowledge of urban studies, and has used social theory as an operative tool in policy making. With Grand Pari(s), this mode continued, with the knowledges and practices of the ten designs captured by apparatuses of state planning and bound to government projects.

The ambivalence of Grand Pari(s) is even more important as architectural thought and practice have, and are poised to continue to have, a profound influence over Paris's future transformations. In the aftermath of the 2009 exhibition, a permanent nationally appointed public interest group, the International Workshop of Grand Paris (AIGP), was established to continue where Grand Pari(s) left off. For Pierre Mansat, who was elected president of the group in 2014, the AIGP is

> at once a veritable laboratory of reflection/action. ... But also a veritable site of experimentation, of construction. ... Thus, the *atelier*, I believe, has never more aptly carried its name: it is, in effect, a site of boiling, where research, experiments and actions converge, which contribute to interrogate public policies of development and planning and to coproduce innovative practices, a veritable workshop at the metropolitan scale just as much as a place of open, frank and fruitful debate. (In AIGP 2013c, 13)

This workshop, which consists of selected Grand Pari(s) teams as well as new collaborators, is now thoroughly integrated into networks of urban planning and is a significant intellectual and symbolic force in regional affairs, with the capacity to indirectly shape public discourse and policy directions. The AIGP has been influential in moving Grand Paris forward from design to implementation. Indeed, it is precisely the imaginative and intellectual labor of the AIGP architects that enabled a compromise between the state and the region over transportation in 2011 and that set the terms of infrastructural reform in 2013–2014.

Furthermore, the AIGP is also exerting global influence, exporting its vision of the competitive polycentric city around the world through professional seminars and consultations. The tools forged in Grand Pari(s) are defining grand urbanism as a global practice. The visual and intellectual instruments developed by the ten teams in the course of the consultation are not the only ones in global circulation, but they are particularly notable ones for architects and planners practicing at the scale of a large metropolis.

The use of architecture in urban planning under Grand Paris is thus an ambiguous project in that it recognizes the urgency of transforming space, and has elements that are highly critical of the existing spatial distribution of Paris, but also contributes to the reproduction of such a distribution. Urban architecture, situated between competing economic, political, and aesthetic incitements, is at what Winy Maas has referred to as an "impasse" that fundamentally calls into question architecture's revolutionary potential, as well as its ability to direct large-scale social change (Patteeuw 2003). Grumbach articulates a similar indictment of the profession, claiming that architectural reflection over the past twenty years has too often been put into the service of state programs: "In fact, there has been capture of this reflection by bureaucrats, technicians, offices and engineers" (in Leloup and Bertone 2009, 27).

The introduction and incorporation of architecture into state policy is not a simple, linear, or complete process, but insofar as it strengthens the bureaucratic state, its "counterrevolutionary" tendencies would seem to prevail. When Le Corbusier (2008) was presented the choice in 1923 between architecture and revolution, he sided on the practice of architecture as a weapon to stifle revolutionary potential. Housing and roads, rather than canons and guns, would forestall revolt and temper antigovernment sentiments. Sarkozy was more equivocal (and in fact accompanied the Grand Pari(s) project with policies of increased penal rule across France), but it is nonetheless clear that architecture came to be deployed in France as a means of defusing a volatile situation, a deployment Hollande does little to contest. Through Grand Pari(s), the central state is able to secure the perceived coherence of France and of the Paris region and to promote economic growth in peripheral areas to begin to consolidate an internationally recognized global city.

The failure on the part of the Grand Pari(s) architects to achieve a more radical agenda also indicates broader limits to architectural practice in late capitalist society. In his 1998 essay, "The Brick and the Balloon," Fredric Jameson addresses the relationship between urbanism and architecture as fracturing along the lines of the meaning of cultural production under conditions of postmodernism. Given the close connection between architecture and economics, its integration into the commodity market is more pronounced than that of other aesthetic forms. For Jameson, then, the urban question is rooted in the question of "the relationship between the distinctive form land speculation has taken today and those equally distinctive forms we find in postmodern architecture." The alignment of the architectural visions—of a grand, unified, governable, designed, flexible, and connected urban form—with that of an investment plan and economic growth strategy is not accidental. These are the forms given by late capitalism, and each of these exists within a spatiotemporal frame that is bound to the conditions of accumulation.

In general, grand urbanism relies on a future-oriented mode of speculation and vision, and in so doing it posits a parallelism between the artistic utopian representations of the city and the institutionalized governance directing policy and investment. It poses a relationship, as it were, between the aesthetic and the economic through the political. Both the designs and the urban redevelopment project more generally rely on a conception of the future as a structural feature that bears claims of value, both spectral and never given, yet felt in the present forms and lives.

In casting the vision thirty years into the future, the Grand Pari(s) exhibit provided a suitable prediction on which a long-term business plan, for example, could be based. The architectural visions of Grand Pari(s) demonstrated the future added value of the metropolis and thus gave confidence to investors who might wish to invest based on the speculative property markets instituted through the new transit network.[13] The predominant function of Grand Pari(s), therefore, became one of providing an image to a city that had lost its means of representation, and in this way to justify large-scale territorial and economic reformation. The architectural consultation has been primarily used by the state to give a sense of imagined solidarity to the fractured metropolitan populace, to legitimize a massive overhaul of regional space, and to valorize the global city ideal. It thus works as an essential apology to garner civil society support for the subsequently announced material and institutional changes to metropolitan Paris.

II Connecting the Networked City

3 Transit Debates and the Contested Regime of Metromobility

Transportation, again transportation, always transportation!
—Paul Delouvrier, quoted in Merlin, 1967

It is surely transportation which will play the most decisive part [in Grand Paris]. Because the question of mobility is crucial, because the system of regional transportation is out of steam. Because commuting each day to go to work has become a veritable hell for millions of regional inhabitants.
—Nicolas Sarkozy, 2009

The preamble to the 2010 Grand Paris Act introduces the initiative as follows:

Grand Paris is an urban, social and economic project of national interest which unites the great strategic territories of the region of Île-de-France. ... It aims to reduce social, territorial and fiscal imbalances to the benefit of national territory. ... This project is based on the creation of a network of public passenger transit. (République Française 2010)

In line with the architectural consultation, the laws directing Grand Paris orient territorial and economic development toward greater capacities for mobility, and stress the need to improve regional transit above all other concerns. Indeed, Grand Paris is frequently considered a transport plan, and the initiative is fundamentally associated with the ambitious extension of the Métropolitain (or simply metro) urban rail network.

The placement of mobility and flow at the center of grand urbanism attests to the inseparability of the form of the urban and its networks of movement (Bridge and Watson 2011; Dupuy 1991; Offner 1993; Virilio 2006). Urban mobility systems fundamentally shape political economic patterns of production, consumption, and distribution at multiple scales

(Boutros and Straw 2010; Sheller and Urry 2006). Networked infrastructures are intertwined with social services and facilities (housing, schools, parks, clinics) and thus are deeply implicated in everyday urban life. From health to employment, security, education, recreation, and inequality, mass transportation affects virtually every sector of regional policy and planning. Transit also conditions individual and collective movements throughout the city and is an essential element in how inhabitants experience, imagine, and identify with each other and their environment. Not only do changes in transit infrastructure affect who or what is moving (and where, how, and why), but developments associated with any new transit system will change the meaning and function of the urban environment and define the contours of regional growth, quality of life, and governance.

Conflicts over transit projects are thus conflicts over the essence of the metropolis. Moments when transit systems are in question, as they are with the Grand Paris initiative, are key points of opening that reveal diverse interpretations of the city and a range of transformative possibilities. The different architectural renditions of the networked city and the official and unofficial conversations about regional transit must thus be understood as highly contested discourses where new spatial politics are emerging. Jean-Marc Offner (2007) stresses the importance of the mobility debates in Paris, saying that the transport files are analyzers of controversial territorial dynamics that will profoundly change regional political and spatial dynamics (see also Orfeuil 2012; Orfeuil and Wiel 2012). The stakes of this venture are huge and reach to the very essence of urban politics today.

The transit debates of Grand Paris, however, are not merely about urban mobility in the abstract. An overwhelming priority is placed on mass transportation, and more specifically on the metro and Regional Express Network (RER) rail lines over other modalities of urban mobility such as automobile, pedestrian, bicycle, bus, bus rapid transit (BRT), and tram networks. From April 2009 on, when Christian Blanc, then secretary of state for the development of the capital region, first used the Grand Pari(s) consultation as a platform to announce the central state's plan for a new suburban metro network, rapid urban rail projects have dominated discussions of regional mobility.

Metromobility—referring to metro infrastructures of urban rail, the political economic cultures they support, and the ideologies of movement and development that underlie them—is a key force in Grand Paris's reconfiguration of urban space and urban life. Metromobility is also a key aspect of grand urbanism more broadly. Although automobility was the obvious driving force of urbanization and modernization in France in the twentieth century (Orfeuil 2001; Ross 1996), today's return to the metro as a significant vehicle of globalizing cities suggests a renewed role for mass transit in the networked polycentric metropolis. The metro may not be replacing the car as the leading vector of development, but metromobility is one of the key sociotechnical institutions through which the twenty-first-century global city region is being produced.

There are several issues Grand Paris's emphasis on metromobility brings to the fore. This chapter follows two main lines of inquiry. First, what are the main functions of rapid mass transit that make it a privileged vehicle of contemporary urban restructuring? Second, how are mobility megaprojects and the desired twenty-first century city coproduced?

This chapter addresses these questions by analyzing contemporary discourses of transportation and development in Paris, focusing on a series of public debates held from September 2010 through January 2011. While the debates revealed transportation as linked to diverse social, environmental, political, economic, and ethical objectives, this diversity of meaning still affirms an overall planning priority for infrastructure as an economic asset. The most audible voices in the Grand Paris transit debates assumed new urban rail infrastructures would have to be pursued in order to anchor capital in the built environment, catalyze urban rent production, and increase territorial competition and economic growth. The networked city is defined by multiple complex movements, not the least of which is the relentless circulation of capital (Beauregard 2005; Leitner and Sheppard 2002; Sassen 2001).

The Grand Paris regime of metromobility, which prioritizes network connectivity for accumulation, is useful for thinking more generally about the ways in which infrastructures of mobility are linked to processes of urbanization in the contemporary global conjuncture. In looking at how mass rapid transit is theorized, as well as at its real and imagined relationships to other services and sectors, much can be discerned about the multiple material and symbolic *uses* of mobility in urban regional restructuring and the ideological force of transportation in creating a networked twenty-first-century global city.

The Politics of Metromobility

As cities around the world grow in size and complexity, their transport needs also increase and become more complicated. Mobility patterns are transformed when urban functions become suburbanized and decentered. Yet because existing transportation infrastructures—dominated in most cities by highways and automobile networks—represent long-term fixed structures and sunk investments, they tend to have a conservative impact on space. Traffic congestion, long commutes, mobility deserts, and negative environmental impacts are just some of the problems facing large cities today as twentieth-century models of car-oriented urbanization reach their functional limits. It is difficult to retrofit cities with the sort of multimodal networks they desperately need to survive and thrive, and as a result, transportation is one of the most frequent obstacles to metropolitan adaptability. Indeed, improving transportation is one of the primary ways for big cities to organize vast spaces and to enhance economic productivity, quality of life, and regional coordination.

Cities around the world are struggling to transition their mobility systems to meet new metropolitan demands and to manage growth. While the car has by no means ceased to be an influential element in urban policy and planning, it is now but one of a panoply of transport modes that marks the present mobile age (Offner 2013; see also Adey 2010; Cresswell 2006; Urry 2007; Urry and Sheller 2006). Cultural trends and policy shifts indicate that automobility is in decline and that cultures of mass transit are rising to take its place (see especially Geels et al. 2011). In response to the now well-established woes of the automobile-driven urbanisms of the twentieth century, metro-friendly policies and transit-oriented development in particular have become best practices in contemporary planning, promising unfettered movement, speed and progress, environmental improvements, the creation of vibrant mixed-use neighborhoods, easy and universal access to city life, improved territorial balance between home and work, and general prosperity (Dittmar and Ohland 2004). The intensified promotion of and investment in rapid urban rail projects around the world are testament to its relevance to a range of large urban regions.[1]

It is no exaggeration to claim that mass transportation is now becoming an essential element of urban economic and social planning, particularly in metropolitan regions struggling to integrate fragmented territories and to remain competitive in the global marketplace. Robust systems of mass transit, especially rapid urban rail, are also necessary to achieve the essential features of a global, world-class city. As we saw in chapters 1 and 2, transit networks are powerful symbols of twenty-first-century fluidity and of smart, sustainable, vital cities. Metros frequently bear the normative aspirations of urban growth and progress driving development. Urban rail systems are also key features of the political economy of existing and aspiring global city regions. Transit infrastructures link regions internally while establishing external connections to other global nodes. They provide amenities for elite residents, enterprises, and tourists, enable interactions in a polycentric regional economy, and facilitate the growth of clusters of competitive advantage. Here the "network effects" (Dupuy 2008) of metro systems are especially pertinent. The urban rail industry is implicated in the real estate, financial, energy, and communications sectors and is absolutely vital to international engineering and construction consortiums, which profit greatly from a new infrastructure production. Finally, networks of regional transit are sites of complex regulatory articulations and regularizing structures that are transforming contemporary patterns of urban governance in remarkable ways. Transit is crucial to establishing the flexible and systemic mechanisms of interterritorial cooperation and coordination on which the governability of urban regions relies.

Investing in mass transit has become a leading development strategy of globalizing cities. Yet behind the celebratory proclamations of transit advocates and mobility fetishists worldwide lies a set of largely unquestioned material processes and ideological assumptions defining mass transportation's role in social, political, and economic life. Unpacking more precisely how transit infrastructure is involved in the creation of the metropolis brings us closer to understanding the inner workings of grand urbanism.

The concept of metromobility is useful for assessing the multiple linkages between transit networks and contemporary metropolitan processes. Against the narrow scientific discourses of transport planning, metromobility invokes the complex relations between infrastructure, ideology, and contemporary globalizing cities. It thus refers not merely to an engineered structure of steel and concrete but also to a historically situated social world or "mobility system" (Urry 2007) based on networks of urban rail.[2] The meaning of "metro" in metromobility, then, is twofold. On the one hand is a focus on the metropolitan, as in local urban rail (there are various names for these systems around the world—subway, underground, U-bahn—but metro remains the most common). On the other hand, it invokes the metropolis, the large and dynamic urban regional complex that is coming to define life in the twenty-first century.

The analysis presented here is thus not a positivistic report on the transportation planning initiatives connected to Grand Paris. Rather, drawing on the new mobilities paradigm (see, e.g., Cresswell 2006, 2010; Sheller and Urry 2006) it instead focuses on how the emerging transportation system in Paris is mediated through existing social worlds and in turn gives rise to a particular type of society. It pays attention to the economic frameworks shaping regional movement, the political conflicts embedded in transit networks, and the "truths" of mobility created through transit debates. In other words, it narrows in on the shaping forces that make and govern twenty-first-century metropolitan flows, what Steffen Böhm and colleagues (2006) usefully refer to as a mobility regime. An account of contemporary metromobility thus captures the structured relations of power that accrue in and through transportation technologies. These aspects are crucially important when considering how and to what ends cities today are being produced.

The focus on conflictual "regimes" of urban transportation rather than on autopoietic "systems" also dovetails with a related analytical endeavor to study what Colin McFarlane and Jonathan Rutherford (2008) call "political infrastructures." For McFarlane and Rutherford, infrastructures (of mobility or otherwise) are always highly contested material, symbolic, cultural, and political artifacts (see also Young and Keil 2010). According to this perspective, for the political character of networked infrastructures to be appreciated, they need to be understood not merely as organic ecologies or as the neutral results of rational planning but as outcomes of struggle, decision, and power wielding. Infrastructures do not automatically maximize a predetermined collective public good, but they express decisions based on favoring some costs and benefits over others. They are inevitably expressions of "congealed social interests" (Graham and Marvin 2001; see also Amin and Thrift 2002; Gandy 2005; Lorrain 2002). In a fundamental sense, mobility systems or assemblages are complex products of local conflicts, ideological plans, and uneven cementations of capital investment and disinvestment. An analysis of metromobility, then, also invokes a regime of contestation between social classes and political interests over what and who should move in the city, how, and for what purposes (Merlin 1967, 2012).

In Grand Paris, the centrality of new transit infrastructure to metropolitan planning reflects the multivalent dimensions of contemporary metromobility writ large. The intense focus on a new suburban metro system, however, is also rooted in long-standing locally situated conflicts over Paris's transit network. Indeed, the contentious politics of metromobility evident in Grand Paris demonstrate how general global trends of metro-driven growth are articulated in historically and culturally rooted ways. The 2010–2011 transit debates reveal a process of decision making whereby different transit systems—each with purported costs and benefits—are weighed against one another. How diverse stakeholders articulate transit-driven metropolitanization and how these various iterations are eventually compromised on demonstrates some important features of local political dynamics in the greater Paris region. This political process also offers crucial lessons for understanding how large cities are transitioning to a post-automobile world and how such infrastructure planning figures within experiments of grand urbanism.

Moving through Grand Paris

The map of the Paris metro is one of the most frequently produced and most recognizable pieces of cartography ever made. Pierre Mongin, president of the state-owned Parisian Autonomous Transport Operator (RATP), writes,

There is a very intimate link between Paris and its Métro, its design and its Métro map. The birth and development of the Métro transformed an impractical space into a modern connected city, and this is how the system is presented cartographically. There are few metropolises around the world that have such a close connection, so dear a unity between the way a city is 'drawn,' and how it feels to move around it. (In Ovenden 2009, 5)

Metropolitan Paris and its infrastructures of mobility are intimately intertwined in representations of the city, phenomenologies of inhabitation, and in material circulations of people, goods, and capital. The metro in particular is a privileged conduit in the way Paris is represented, conceived, and lived (see also Augé 2002; Dallas 2008; Delaney and Smith 2006).

No other infrastructure defines modern urban space so forcefully as the Paris metro. Throughout its more than hundred-year history, the metro has not merely had the function of moving people through Paris in an efficient manner, it has also played a significant role in defining the city and its limits, organizing and promoting commerce, influencing regional demographics, shaping land use, and connecting landmarks and tourist amenities (Ovenden 2009). The Paris metro has also been emulated the world over both for its unique design features and aesthetics and for its role in civilizing and managing modern city life. The Paris metro is thus an exemplary site in which to understand the workings of metromobility.

Because of its unique power to shape the urban environment and culture, each stage of the Paris metro's development has been marked by conflicts over design, construction, location, costs, financing, and operations management. The values embedded in the metro network at different historical moments thus bespeak the dominant trends of urbanism.

In the last decades of the nineteenth century, for example, when Paris was considering a rapid transit system to rival the London Underground, there were quite fierce debates over whom such a system should serve. More than sixty proposals were scrutinized by officials and planners, but the main cleavage was between the Paris municipal council, which wanted service to be tied to the needs of inhabitants, and the national government, which sought to connect a new metro to existing mainline rail throughout France and to promote international connections with the city of Paris. Whereas local leaders sought to improve access, particularly for the peripheral working classes, Louis Napoleon (and later the leaders of the Third Republic) prioritized the needs of circulation and defense over the lives of citizens. As early as 1878, city administrators had devised a plan for a local metro network for daily movement within Paris and the inner suburbs, but no progress was made because of stalling on the part of the national government and a populist fear that the rail lines would bring the poor and "dangerous classes" from the edges to the center of the city. When the transit plans of the nationally appointed chief engineer Fulgence Bienvenüe were finally adopted in 1896, it was clear that the metro's priority was to showcase the splendor of Paris and its capacity for modern innovation in time for the World's Fair in Paris in 1900. Only secondarily did it meet the actual commuting needs of the time.

In the early twentieth century, metro growth remained largely limited to the historic city center, but both the Prost Plan of 1934 and the Ruhlmann initiative of 1936 envisaged more ambitious extensions to the inner suburbs to promote urbanization and to meet the needs of the working classes, pushed out of the center by high rents. It was not until the 1960 Plan for the Development and General Organization of the Paris Region (PADOG) and the postwar suburbanization plans of the 1960s, however, that suggestions for enlargement of the network and inclusion of the suburbs came to be taken seriously. Indeed, Delouvrier's regional polycentrism was built through RER axes that linked new towns to the city of Paris. Despite these new city-suburban links, in the postwar period local transport officials in Paris and the suburbs were frequently at odds over whether to refurbish the existing system within Paris or to extend a similar level of service to a larger suburban area.

The historical battles between local and national concerns, equality and priority, speed and service, and wealthy and working-class interests continue to define transit in the twenty-first century and are observable today in debates over a transit network for Grand Paris. Perhaps the most prominent line of conflict, today, however, one that cuts across many of the aforementioned antagonisms, is that between Paris and its suburbs. Indeed, one of the most familiar ways of understanding the problem of territorial inequality and the long dominant model of unipolar urbanization in Paris is through the modern mass transportation system, of which the metro is an essential part. The present-day map of the metro, when placed beside one of the rail lines extending into the remainder of the Île-de-France, shows the problem (see figures 3.1 and 3.2).

The metro network, currently operated jointly through the RATP and the Île-de-France Transport Union (STIF), consists of sixteen lines, three hundred stations, and fifty-four transfer points, providing an easily accessible subterranean structure for movement throughout the city proper. It is estimated that the network can be accessed within less than one-half kilometer from anywhere in Paris, and each day some 4.5 million people utilize this resource for daily commutes to and from work, school, or leisure activities. Movement around the city of Paris is well organized, rapid, and convenient, and the infrastructure is imbued with a rich sense of history and place.

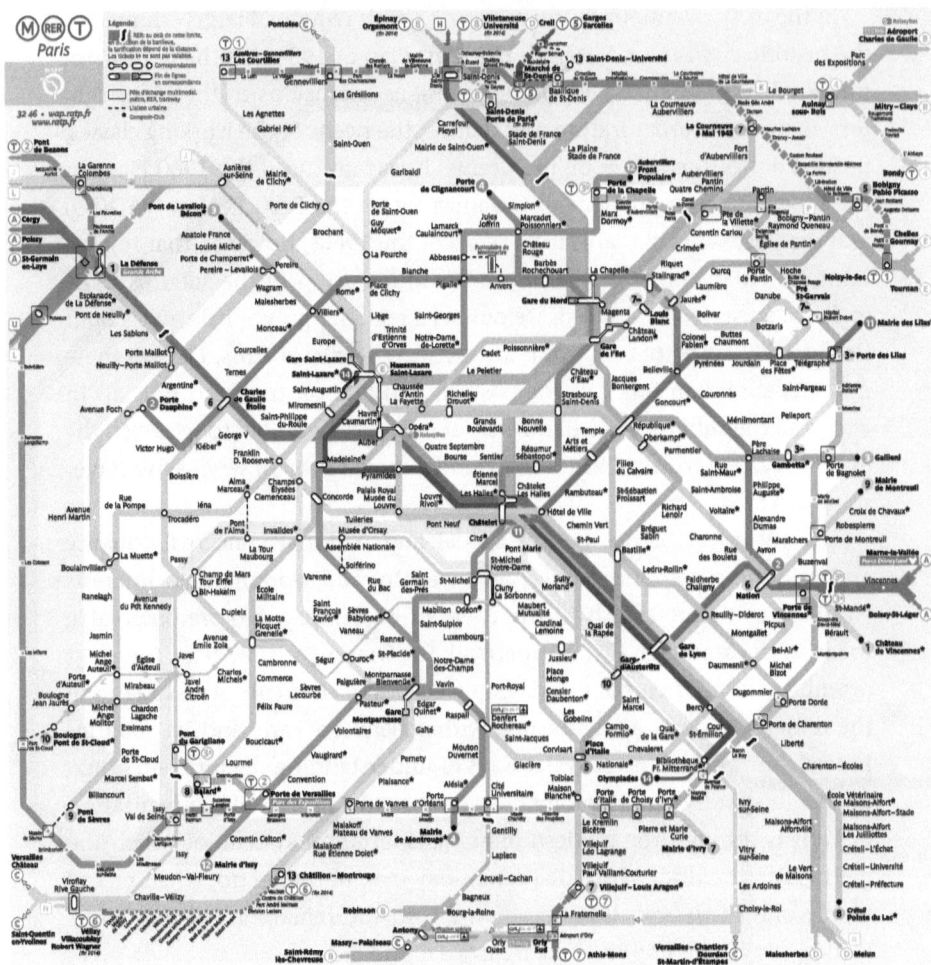

Figure 3.1
Map of the Paris metro.

Transit Debates and the Contested Regime of Metromobility 107

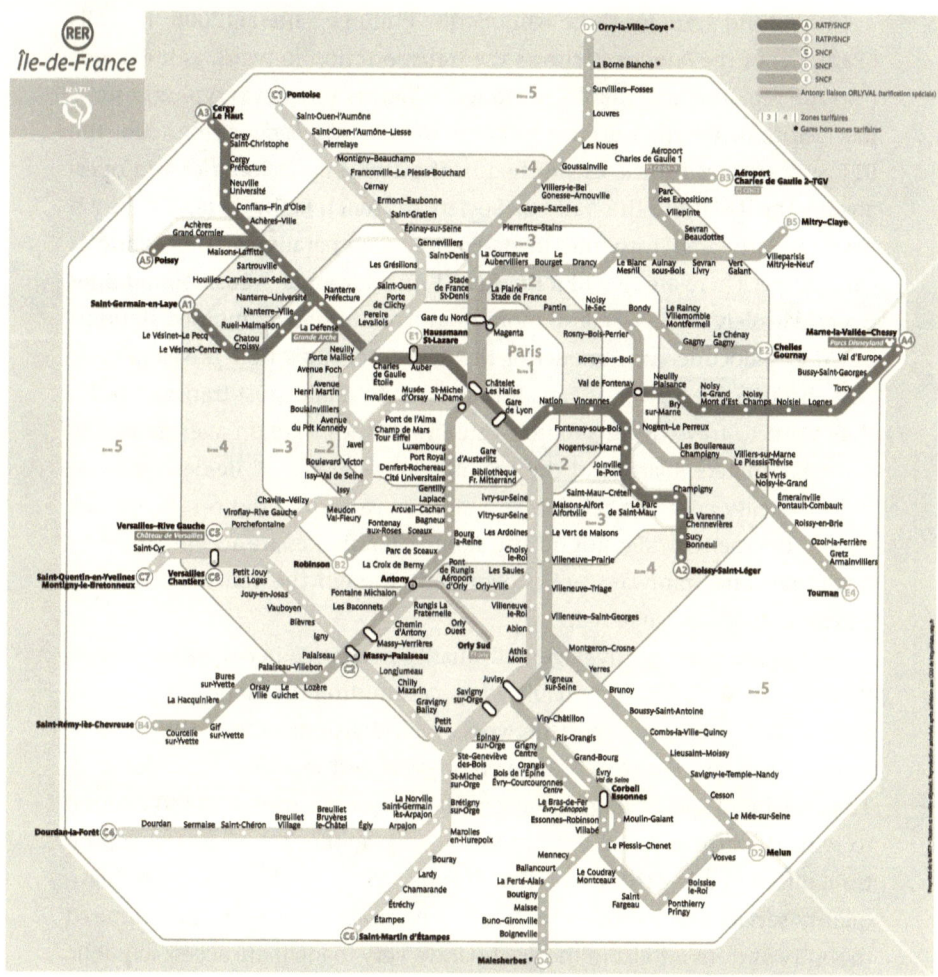

Figure 3.2
Map of the Regional Express Rail (RER) network in the Île-de-France.

The second map, for those whom critic Philippe Panerai (2008, 14) calls "Parisians of the *banlieue*," shows the transportation network as it extends into the remainder of the Île-de-France. Whereas the metro typically stops just before or on the outskirts of the *boulevard périphérique* ring road, the RER suburban rail lines, established in the 1960s by Delouvrier and operated by the RATP and the National Society of French Railways (SNCF), reach beyond Paris well into the Île-de-France. Comparatively, this fabric is threadbare. There are five RER lines (and six additional Transilien rail lines operated solely by SNCF), and more than five hundred combined stations, but the radioconcentric model of the system ensures that travelers must pass through the center of Paris if they want to make most transfers and if they want to travel from suburb to suburb. Stations are on average two to three kilometers apart, and the majority of residents of Île-de-France do not have easy access to reliable and rapid mass transportation. Across the region, the metro underground and suburban rail lines are accompanied by bus routes and tramways not shown here, though the general pattern of service and disservice remains.[3]

The differences in coverage and quality of service between the city of Paris and its suburbs are palpable when commuting throughout the Île-de-France. The public transport networks map divisions within the regional territory and contribute to its uneven physical and socioeconomic patterns. The social and spatial fragmentation that Jacques Donzelot (2009) referred to with the "three-speed city" quite literally applies to urban transportation, differentiating those who live in Paris proper and have access to high-quality service from those who live in periurban areas with more limited mobility options and from those who have very inadequate access to public transit.

While some ten million users partake of the network on a daily basis, making more than three billion trips each year (RATP 2013), the existing transportation infrastructure is ill equipped to meet the needs of the region. The network has failed to keep pace with the demographic and spatial changes that Paris has undergone since the last major transit overhaul brought RER lines to the suburbs. Transport lags behind other restructurings of the global city metropolis. In particular, the westward shift over the past two decades of the center of gravity of employment away from Paris and toward the suburbs presents a problem for static infrastructures and the less mobile residential markets (INSEE 2006). Deep divisions exist between home and work for many inhabitants. These divides are only set to grow, with commutes in the near suburbs predicted to rise by 15 percent by 2020 (APUR 2006).

In addition to the crisis of representation that plagues the region, Grand Paris identifies a generalized "crisis of transit" and claims that an overhaul of regional transportation is needed to improve daily life. Existing offerings are saturated and prone to disruption, suburb-to-suburb links are almost nonexistent (as a result, 80 percent of these commutes are done in cars), commutes are long and arduous (often taking upward of ninety minutes on overcrowded trains), and vast areas of the region remain unconnected to one another in any viable fashion (INSEE 2007, 2010a). Residents of poorly serviced areas also suffer additional burdens, such as exclusion from labor markets and health and social services. A number of recent studies have concluded that Paris has one of the most unequal and centralized urban transit networks in the world, a fact that reflects and embeds more general social and spatial conflicts (APUR 2006; Panerai 2008).[4]

Class- and race-based segregation resulting from existing networks has been apparent for many years, and since the 1970s, mobility has been an important concern of alienated residents of the stigmatized *banlieue*. Popular films such as *La Haine* (2005), in which three suburban youths spend a night wandering around Paris after missing the last train home, and *Paris Je T'aime* (2006), which features a story, "Loin du 16e" (Far from the 16th Arrondissement) about a young immigrant woman who awakes at the break of dawn in a suburban housing block in order to drop her own infant off at daycare so that she may make the extremely long commute into the city, where she serves as a nanny to a wealthy family, dramatically illustrate this divide. The burning of cars and the *rodeos*, in which cars are stolen and driven at high speeds and then destroyed, as well as graffiti on trains and buses, also speak to the symbolic importance of urban mobility in urban conflicts. Whatever the intention of these actions, they reveal the transportation gap between urban and suburban residents as a highly politicized site (see especially Silverstein 2004; Wacquant 2008). Clichy-sous-Bois, for example, where the 2005 *banlieue* uprisings began, is only fifteen kilometers from the city of Paris, but the commute (via bus to an RER line to the metro) takes up to two hours using existing public transportation.

The French urbanist Paul Chemetov (2009) sums up the problem of transit in the city by noting that "the region has followed an inverse path.

While the center is depeopled and a benefactor of a mass transit system, the periphery, where most population lies, is continually underserviced." This is no accident; rather, the sanctioned differentiation of Paris and its *banlieue* is a direct result of twentieth-century planning efforts. In the *banlieue*, the metro and RER are not monuments to equality and progress but instead are reminders of the violent geographic hierarchies that structure the region and the institutional expression of state segregation and population management.

The threadbare network and growing disconnection of the region are also barriers to regional economic efficiency and global competitiveness. Transport is a key quality-of-life indicator for global cities and an essential feature of economic growth. The Paris Chamber of Commerce and Industry (CCIP), which represents business interests in Paris and the *petite couronne*, estimates that without a new transit network, annual GDP in France will be reduced by over €200 billion by 2030 (Property Investor Europe 2013). Because of its lack of effective movement, metropolitan Paris is, according to many, suffering from a dissolution of its fundamental communicative and connective capacities, what Philippe Subra (2012, 36) calls a "nervous system breakdown."

Over the past forty years, there has been a series of failed attempts to renovate the transportation network, but most attempts were set aside because of concerns over cost or abandoned as a result of interinstitutional disputes among the region of Île-de-France—which took primary control of mass transit through the decentralization laws of the 1980s—the central state, and local collectivities.

The 1994 regional *schema directeur*, or master plan, of the Île-de-France (known as the SDRIF) was especially influential in focusing development on suburban regions based on an extensive transportation network outside Paris proper. One of the first projects to propose rapid transit through the *banlieue* post-Delouvrier was the "ORBITALE" (Regional Organization of Congestion-free Transport of the Inner Basin Ring), put forth in the 1990s by the Île-de-France Institute of Planning and Development (IAURIF) and the STIF. This would have consisted of a double *rocade* (ring) of underground rail through the inner suburbs, with additional tramways connecting the region. ORBITALE was written into the SDRIF master plan of 1994 but was ignored in the implementation of the plan of 1994–1998 for cost reasons. "ORBIVAL" (a combination of ORBITALE and the sponsoring department of Val-de-Marne) resuscitated the plan in 2006, proposing a network that would link together the radial lines RER A and RER E to RER B with a suburb-to-suburb arc southeast of Paris, thus decreasing the number of vehicles operating in the department by 40,000 per day (http://www.orbival.fr). Also under consideration in the early and mid-2000s was the Métrophérique rail ring, which was to be located at a greater radial distance than ORBITALE or ORBIVAL, two to five kilometers, from the existing *périphérique* highway. In 2007 the Arc Express then extended the ORBIVAL plan from one to four main arcs in the inner suburbs. It gained support across the region and became the leading transit proposal when inscribed into the 2007–2013 state-region planning contract (CPER) and the 2008 revised SDRIF. While these proposals were being drawn up, the void in the regional system was partially addressed with smaller stopgap projects of construction.[5]

What were originally local plans to increase regional coherence and equality of opportunity through improved daily service in and between *banlieues,* however, were challenged in 2009 by large-scale national initiatives to drastically reconfigure the metropolitan region as a prime space of economic accumulation, thus reestablishing Paris's rank among global cities. The central state repudiated Arc Express and the 2008 master plan that defined it, instead offering the "Great Eight" (also known as the "Double Ring," for its two main loops) metro proposal as part of the Grand Paris initiative. Indeed, with Grand Paris, a state-led *grand projet* replaced the *petit* ones for the Île-de-France.

In the 2010 Grand Paris Act—the law outlining the new transit network and its priority nodes, and establishing the administrative structures to support its execution—Sarkozy also strategically removed power from the regional and municipal levels. The act instead partially reestablished transit and land use planning as capacities of the central state through the creation of the Society of Grand Paris (SGP), an appointed public establishment to oversee the new transportation project. These intergovernmental disputes over transit (a result of decentralization) are also overlaid with partisan battles. During Sarkozy's presidency, the central state was led by the right-wing Union for a Popular Movement (UMP), while the region and the majority of its communes were headed by Socialist Party and other leftist officials. Both lines of conflict, institutional and partisan, are reflected in the divergences in the transit proposals.

Christian Blanc, the first head of the SGP, criticized the SDRIF for its "localism" and lack of economic vision (a perspective shared by the very influential CCIP), and swiftly rejected the popular Arc Express. Instead, Blanc supported the Great Eight as a more business-friendly alternative, one that would create rapid conduits of travel through the main airports of the city and would connect hubs of business and enterprise on the peripheries with the core of Paris.[6] The Arc Express and the Great Eight transit plans came to dominate Grand Paris discussions in 2009 and 2010, with the two options representing seemingly conflicting visions of the future network and the future city.

Debating Regional Futures: From Competition to Compromise

To break the impasse between the two alternatives, in 2009 the National Commission on Public Debate (CNDP), a nonpartisan entity, announced a series of official public debates on the draft documents of Arc Express and the Great Eight, now officially renamed the Public Transport Network of Grand Paris (RTPGP).[7] These two-pronged debates were meant to provide a venue for stakeholders to review the plans and a forum in which to more generally discuss the crisis of regional transportation, as well as potential solutions.

In the weeks and days before the debates, informational flyers were distributed door-to-door and placed in town halls, schools, libraries, community organizations, and private corporations. Posters advertising the debates and the two transit plans adorned university hallways, the walls of metro stations, and the sides of city buses (CNDP 2011b, 36–40). Metropolitan Paris was abuzz with talk over its future infrastructural habitat, and the CNDP asked residents to bring the many conversations taking place on train cars, in classrooms, and at neighborhood cafés into the officially sanctioned public sphere through a range of participation options. In addition to attending public meetings, stakeholders (*intervenants*) could contribute brief written opinions, more argumentative contributions, or comprehensive actor workbooks. Interested parties could also review technical plans and post questions on the respective websites which served as touchstones for the debates.

The debates constituted one of the largest pubic planning review exercises ever implemented by the CNDP. More than 7,100 people attended the twenty-four public meetings on Arc Express, while written submissions consisted of 633 opinions, eighty-nine stakeholder contributions, and seventeen actor workbooks (eighty-eight held jointly with the RTPGP). Some eight hundred questions were posted on the Arc Express website, and 84,000 visitors navigated the site during the debate period (CNDP 2011a). In addition, 15,000 participants attended the fifty-five public meetings on the RTPGP, and participants submitted 518 public opinions, 171 contributions, and 255 actor workbooks. During the five months of the debate, the RTPGP website received 835 questions and almost 200,000 visitors (CNDP 2011b).

There was also extensive media attention to the debates. From September 2010 to January 2011, more than a thousand publications were dedicated to the debates in national, international, and specialist presses, in blogs, and on radio and television programs (CNDP 2011b, 61, 2011c, 17). The press coverage outside the region underlines the fact that the debates were not just a local matter but concerned metropolitan and mobility issues at multiple scales.

The debates were significant insofar as they shed light on some of the most important dynamics of contemporary metromobility, as well as on the main tensions in metro-oriented urban development in Paris. The plans for both Arc Express and RTPGP are rooted in a shared belief that it is in the interest of Paris and of France to strengthen and expand the current transit network, and that public authorities should direct these changes. They also concur that transit, and specifically a new metro, is the best way to *fabriquer la ville,* to make the city. The two plans differ, however, in terms of their goals and features and in terms of the values of urban life that they espouse (see table 3.1).

The aspirations of the two projects are broad and integrative in scope. The stated goals of the Arc Express are to:

1. Service existing large economic and living poles or emerging dense territories in the Île-de-France.
2. Fill today's most important gaps in matters of collective transport.
3. Service zones accommodating new housing and jobs that will enable their effective transformation. (STIF 2010, 1)

Arc Express is a moderate plan designed to bring large parts of the city into the same finely knit transit web and to encourage communication and

Table 3.1
Comparing the Arc Express and RTPGP in the 2010/2011 transit debates

	Arc Express	Grand Huit (Double Boucle)/ RTPGP
Institutional supporters	Regional Council of Île-de-France, led by Jean-Paul Huchon, with the support of STIF and the majority of local departments and communes.	Society of Grand Paris, headed by Christian Blanc, with the support of the national senate and parliament and then president Nicolas Sarkozy.
Goals	• Establish a "fine mesh" of links servicing local inhabitants in daily commutes. • Promote regional balance and equality. • Create short-term solutions to long-standing problems of transit disservice.	• Foster high-speed conduits of travel between sites constitutive of the global city, namely, airports, business and technology centers, and commercial sites. • Increase regional and national attractiveness to global investors. • Ensure long-term economic development.
Features	• Extensive and dense network • Uniform service • Large service area • Many transfer points • Multiple modalities • Priority of the near *banlieue*	• Rapid connections • Reduction in travel times • Large service area • Express trains with few stops • International connections • Prioritized service to strategic development sites
Service	• Underground, automatic vehicles • Single ring around inner suburbs • 60 km in length • 1.5 km between stations • Vehicle speed of 25–40 km/h • Capacity of 1 million passengers/day in peak service	• Underground automatic vehicles • 24-h/day operation • Three lines consisting of two large loops through the outer suburbs and a vertical connection • 130 km in length • Vehicle speed of 65 km/h • Capacity of 2–3 million passengers/day in peak service
Estimated cost	€7.1–€8.3 billion	€21.3–€23.5 billion

interaction between disparate parts of the regional territory. The authors of Arc Express stress that the residents of the near *banlieue* are their top priority, and they promise a "fine service" of interwoven transit options that will *"desenclaver"* (liberate) marginal territories and communities. The network aims at uniform and equalized service to create a more genuine balance in the region. The four arcs that define the ring of the project pass through the near and far suburbs, and though the specific route of the track was still to be decided, the Arc Express explicitly targeted dense residential neighborhoods where existing transport options were few.

The project is thus oriented primarily toward territorial and social development—favoring social equality and cohesion, a reequilibration of services, a reduction in territorial inequalities, and an increase in living standards—but supporters highlight that the improvement of transit services is also a matter of increasing competitiveness and stimulating the economy. In conjunction with its social aims, the Arc Express sought, for example, to "develop a dynamic Île-de-France and maintain its global influence" (STIF 2010, 9). The main justification is one of *solidarité*, but this is firmly couched in the language of global competition.

The RTPGP identified similar official objectives, but focused on different issues to be addressed. The network intended to:

1. Improve the daily functioning of transport in the Capital Region through the creation of new suburb-suburb links that avoid saturated lines in the center of Paris.
2. Dynamize economic development in the Capital Region with the creation of rapid services placed in relation to great economic poles, in particular the two international airports, and to improve people's access to the principal employment poles.
3. Accompany a new politics of development founded on the creation of urban polarities around future metro stations, which favor the densification of populations and employment.
4. Open up territories in difficulty, favoring better access to urban functions in the capital region.
5. Contribute to preserving the environment by encouraging a shift from personal car use, toward mass transport and by limiting urban sprawl. (SGP 2010, 6)

The RTPGP is intended to serve both the center of Paris and the near and far peripheries, with priority placed on connecting Roissy and Orly airports with the business district La Défense and the research-and-development cluster of Saclay (Paris's Silicon Valley). The network also passes through a number of other emerging and prospective scientific, information, and cultural hubs in the national capital region.

The new metro is a catalyst for the Dubai-inspired "clustering" strategy of regional economic development. Depending on the iteration, between six and nine main poles are to be served by the RTPGP. The development of these sites is based on a functional division of labor whereby each territory has a signature industry. La Défense (finance), la Cité Descartes (construction and services for the green economy), Roissy-Villepinte (air travel and international connections), Le Bourget, (aeronautical research), the Saclay Plateau (high technology), and the Seine Valley (biotechnology), along with Paris (tourism and international relations), together form the multipolar metropolis of Grand Paris.

The SGP argued that the RTPGP was necessary in order to create transit amenities to welcome high-value-added industries, restore a lost regional and national attractiveness, and realize the potential values of underutilized peripheral land. Christian Blanc summed up the RTPGP agenda of mobilizing space for advanced production this way: "In this knowledge world, territory is not the framework of the economy, it is its motor" (in SGP 2010, 36). In contrast to the Arc Express, the emphasis here is undoubtedly on economic development, but as with the broad agenda of the Arc Express, economic objectives are seen to be coextensive with the ambitions of territorial balance and social integration.

Materially, the two transit systems were to consist of different structures and would move people in divergent fashions around the city. Arc Express is an underground automatic rail line consisting of a sixty-kilometer ring around the inner suburbs. The stations are located one and a half kilometers apart and connect with thirty-eight existing RER, metro, and tram lines. The vehicles of Arc Express travel twenty-five to forty kilometers per hour, and the network has a capacity of 30,000 passengers in peak hours and one million passengers per day (CNDP 2011a, 4). The estimated cost for the loop, €7.1-€8.3 billion, was to be financed locally by the region and local tax initiatives.

The RTPGP consists of three high-speed underground rail lines completing two large loops (the Great Eight) that cut through Paris and extend toward targeted peripheral hubs at a total length of 130 kilometers. The

Transit Debates and the Contested Regime of Metromobility 117

automated trains run at an average of sixty-five kilometers per hour, significantly reducing travel times between targeted poles. According to estimates, the network would be capable of providing two to three million trips per day (CNDP 2011c, 5). The RTPGP focuses on travel between already established and newly emerging hubs and explicitly prioritizes those areas of the city designated to lead development efforts. The transit project connects advanced service and technology industries around the region and aims to inspire commercial and residential and retail investment in these areas. The gains in attractiveness are said to justify the large state expenses of the RTPGP, estimated at between €21.3 and €23.5 billion, to be financed by stakeholders, new taxes, and debt.

The Arc Express and RTPGP can thus be understood according to two imperatives of urban growth and two conceptions of what a transportation network should do. While Arc Express sees the transportation system as being necessary to facilitate daily commutes, mainly for employees in the *banlieue* to their place of work, RTPGP sees the network as primarily easing travel between nodes of international connection. Urban growth for the former should be carefully managed at a local level, while for the latter, global competition and relevance on an international scale are primary, thus necessitating state involvement. In the words of one debate participant, the plans are "based on different objectives and economic models" (CNDP 2011a, 19). Even where their respective lines overlap and they serve the same poles, they attribute very different roles to those poles. The region and the STIF define the city as a place of habitation and transit as a public good that should be in the service of all, while the SGP defines the city as an economic motor of the national economy and transit in the service of competitive industries.

There are clear differences between them, and yet, as the debates progressed, dozens of actors called for a "fusion," a "rapprochement," or a "convergence" between the two plans (CNDP 2011a 19). The CNDP and the International Workshop of Grand Paris (AIGP), the design and planning organization, responded to these calls and brokered a compromise. In mid-November 2010, halfway through the debate proceedings, Jean-Paul Huchon, the regional president of Île-de-France, announced a merger of the two projects and declared that the remaining scheduled debates should consider not the merits of one or the other plan but the possibility of their consolidation. The CNDP (2011c, 4) followed suit and officially reframed the terms of the debate from comparison, competition, and argumentation to reconciliation, complementarity, and convergence.

This move would prove decisive in the struggles over the future of mass transit in Paris. In what has come to be called an "unprecedented compromise" between the state and the region of Île-de-France, Maurice Leroy, minister of cities charged with Grand Paris, and Huchon announced in January 2011 the blueprint for the combined "Grand Paris Express" (GPE). On May 26, 2011, Huchon and Leroy, along with other key players in regional governance, officially unveiled the GPE network that would finally realize a "Paris for all Parisians." The priorities of the GPE are to renovate RER C and D lines, extend RER E and line 14 of the metro, increase service on the existing tramlines, and above all build a new automatic and twenty-four-hour ring metro. Representing a vast public investment, the GPE network has a projected cost of €32 billion (which is to come from a combination of new taxes, as well as direct investment from the state and local authorities) and is set to be operable by 2025. Although costlier and more ambitious than either of the initial proposals, the GPE "gentleman's agreement" ensured priorities that all could agree on: first, that a new system would be built no matter what, and second, that no personality or institution would lose face (Orfeuil and Wiel 2012, 20). Indeed, there was remarkable approval of the GPE across the political spectrum, and most conservative, Socialist, and Green Party members found it satisfactory merely because it looked to dissolve the political impasse that had stalled transit reform for decades.[8]

Yet the gap between the content of the debate and the final agreement on the GPE was startling. Through this consensus, the focus of Arc Express on short- and medium-term goals and the immediate needs of inhabitants came to be seen as commensurable with the RTPGP's long-term goals of economic development, even though the merger of the plans meant it could take another fifteen years for the system to be functioning. Though concessions were made to include more stations (especially in residential areas) along the transit route, many areas of the metropolis would still be unconnected. Any suggestion that solidarity and economic competition might be at odds with one another was swept under the rug. When details were genuinely contested between the two plans, the state-sponsored interests almost invariably won out.[9]

The GPE plan calls for seventy-two stations along 200 kilometers of new track along four new metro lines (see figure 3.3). The GPE features a 100-kilometer ring route through the inner suburbs (line 15), with branches extending west to Sevran and Clichy-Montfermeil (line 16), north to Charles de Gaulle Airport (line 17), southeast to the Saclay Plateau (through Versailles, line 18), and through the city center (by an elongation of the existing line 14). When finished, the automatic metro is expected to run at an average speed of sixty kilometers per hour, twice as fast as the existing metro network, and will be integrated into the existing system through many interconnecting stations (SGP 2013). Overall, the new lines seek to reduce travel times between international airports and major financial and business centers, to decrease congestion, to promote growth and job creation, to improve territorial balance, and to encourage regional attractiveness.

These goals are pursued through an integrated approach to planning that links national transport policy to regional and local planning tools. In particular, the large-scale design of the network will be achieved through specific Territorial Development Contracts (CDTs). These contracts establish the conditions for growth around new stations and are collaborative agreements to oversee construction and territorial development in strategic sites. They are the main mechanisms to accelerate the construction of the transit network and ensure densification around new stations. This innovation is fundamentally tied to Grand Paris's networked spatial strategy. With CDTs, the dynamic created by the transportation projects is carried through to specific developments.[10] Through targeted developments around the new stations, the GPE is set to dramatically transform the suburbs of Paris.

To a city whose infrastructures have not matched patterns of urban growth, the GPE thus provides new circulatory systems, especially to the periphery. Residents of underserved areas celebrated in the streets when the new stations were announced.[11] The GPE also promises to revitalize the suburbs and to move beyond the core-periphery dualisms structuring the region. Physically and symbolically, the GPE will connect the city and integrate its territories, through supposedly public and green modes of building. The GPE also overcomes institutional and partisan blockages and suggests a new collaborative form of networked urbanism that brings together diverse stakeholders around shared priorities.[12]

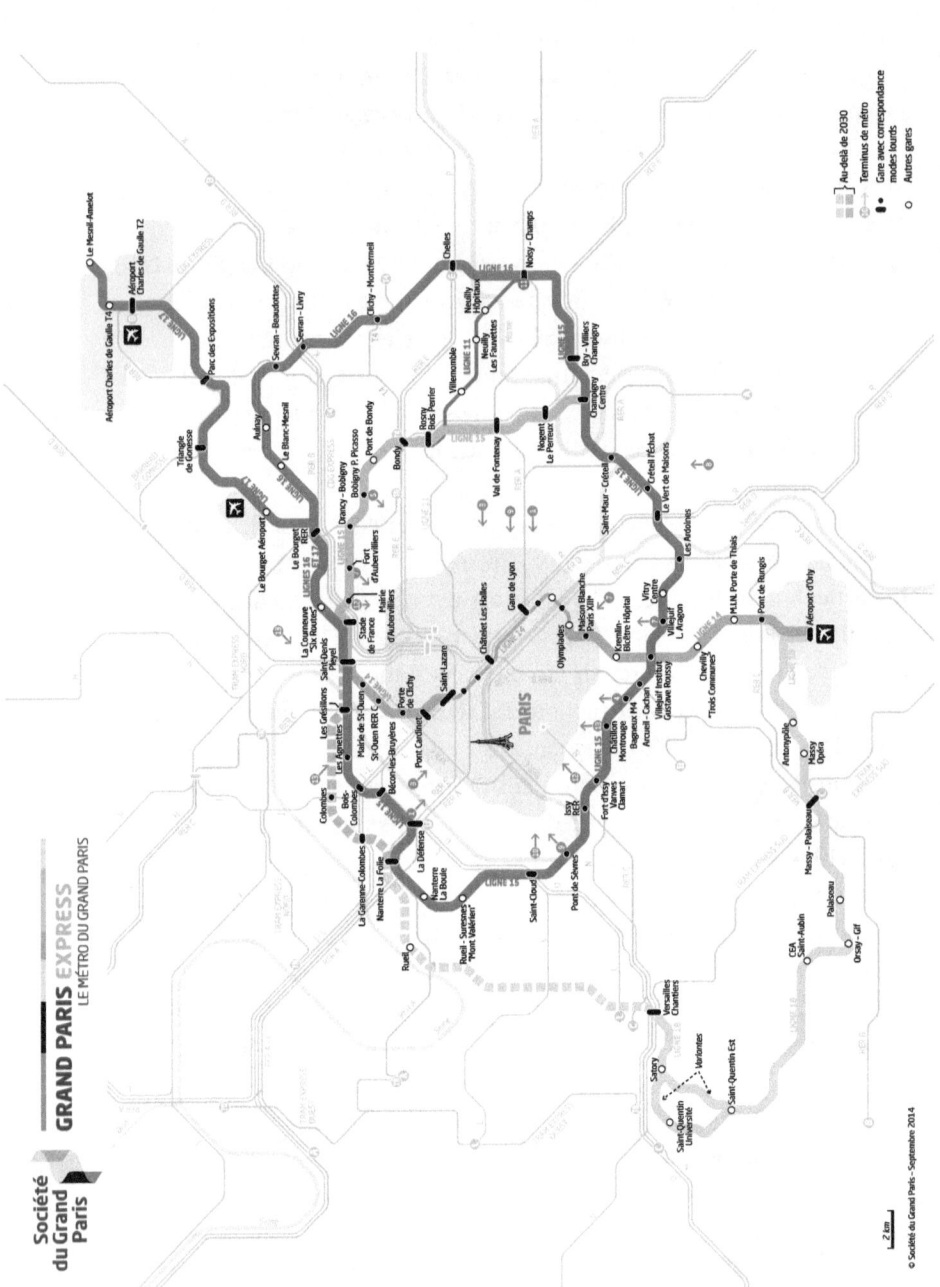

Figure 3.3

A Grand Compromise

The CNDP public debates were described by the organizers as composing "an exceptional mine of information," bringing together suggestions, critiques, analyses, and commentaries from diverse actors (CNDP 2011c, 3). The debates amounted to neither a technical appraisal of two blueprints nor a battle between purely partisan or institutional interests. The discussions passed well beyond "infrastructural technocratics" (Orfeuil and Wiel 2012, 110) and delved into questions of housing and employment, the growing disconnect between employment and residence, and the social and spatial inequalities that cut through the region. Issues of governance, land use, and urban services were frequently voiced, but so too were those concerning the quotidian experiences of commuting. The discussions also spoke to more esoteric issues: the meaning of the metropolitan scale, the collective identities of neighborhoods and communities, the link between urban and economic development, the value of "natural space," and the substance of democracy, the public, equality, and solidarity. Indeed, without celebrating the debates as paragons of deliberative decision making, they undoubtedly represented a rich dialogue on the heterogeneous ways that transit is understood and experienced in the city and the manifold stakes of new infrastructure initiatives.

The debates surrounding mass transit also revealed that metromobility is an ever-changing complex assemblage of human and nonhuman actors, technologies, information, goods, and images. They illuminated how individual experiences of mobility (e.g., of commuting) cannot be considered in isolation but must be situated as part of complex regional, national, and global processes. They also demonstrated quite dramatically that metromobility in Paris remains a highly contested and contestable terrain shaped by economic forces and political conflicts.

The debates produced a remarkable archive of various meanings of urban mobility, the problems of commuting, and perspectives on the nexus of transportation infrastructure and metropolitan development. Yet the limits of the forum were patent. Many mayors complained that no meetings were held in their communes, pointing to the exclusionary nature of public sphere participation. Some went even further, criticizing the debates as being merely consultative and placating. One participant called them a "democratic illusion" as the SGP retained full discretionary power over collective transit planning in the last instance (CNDP 2011b, 24). Perhaps the strongest criticism rested on the fact that many of the most influential participants were not individual citizens but corporate stakeholders, including lobbyist organizations such as business improvement associations, property developers, and construction and utility companies including Vinci, Siemens, and Veolia (CNDP 2011c, 87). For critics the veneer of participation was unable to conceal the debates' depoliticizing effects. From this perspective, the democratic nature of the consultation was thin at best and manipulative at worst. Despite, or perhaps because of, these limits, the debates revealed much about the contested system of metromobility and the struggles over urban meaning in metropolitan Paris. It is particularly notable that the debates *appeared* to remove conflict from the megaproject planning.

The broad discourses of mobility utilized in Grand Paris have narrowed greatly as the initiative unfolded. The myriad meanings of transit and movement in and through the city were progressively reduced to two main possibilities—of enhancing neighborhood connections and sustainable communities and promoting international commutes and competition—which, through careful political maneuvering, were collapsed further into an uneasy unity. Alternative and more politically potent aspects of movement through the city—as a means of generating encounter and political community, as an intimate engagement with the material environment, as a facilitator of communication, as a way to pursue desires and express existential freedoms—become subordinated to the goal of regional rent production. Through the official public debates around transportation, any general conflict over the conditioning factors of movement was rendered null, and indeed incommensurate with urban change. The eventual consensus in support of the GPE established a regime of metromobility in which slippery social, economic, and ecological values of global city development are to be pursued together. With this obfuscation, the possibilities for a critical intervention in the region are further reduced.

The compromise on a single version of metromobility is particularly confounding—not only because of the limiting yet legitimating rituals of democracy performed by debates and consultations but also because "mobility" and "networks" continue to have overly positive connotations. Beyond the ideological and stakeholder differences in the two plans, proponents of both plans agree that transportation networks must be built to ensure development in the region, on the premise that circulation is good for economic and social life. And both agree that the revalorization of territory around the new stations will be good for the region.[13]

In one reading, this agreement on metro-oriented development and gentrification can be understood as the growing centrism of mainstream French political culture and the cross-party use of a shared populist rhetoric. This interpretation is not wrong and is quite powerful insofar as it is an indicator of the pervasive soft neoliberalism underlying contemporary French urbanism. But another interpretation is also needed, one that acknowledges the sheer complexity of transit development in the contemporary conjuncture. Metromobility describes a regime that cuts across diverse sectors of social life, a regime in which a polyvalent ensemble of social forces, paradigms, and actors converge and conflict. Within this regime traditional binaries collapse, but tensions remain. Use and exchange values are not opposed, local and global concerns are almost inextricable, equity solutions do not imply unambiguous transit modality options, and neoliberal and Keynesian economic models are not strictly at odds with one another.

Traditional critiques of bureaucratic and technocratic planning that indict the hubris of the modernist state or the fragmentary knowledges of twentieth-century urbanism are inadequate to assess contemporary mobility planning and the social forms they create. Continued attention to the material and ideological significance of mobility systems is necessary, yet this task is daunting, especially when the broad language of mobility systems is incorporated into policy. The discursive breadth of megaprojects of transportation, like that of "new megaprojects" more generally, makes them difficult to oppose and question (Lehrer and Laidley 2008). Promises of widespread social, cultural, and ecological benefits leave little room for criticism, yet the diverse invocations of mobility and networked urbanism in Paris today do not weave seamlessly into a neoliberal rationality that reveals itself in the idea of the global city.

The compromise on the GPE does not signal the end of conflict or struggle over mobility or over the future of the region but its temporary displacement. Insofar as it brings into focus competing infrastructures, plans, development agendas, forms of regional growth, and modes of urban life, the Grand Paris regime of metromobility is thus an essential site where dominant planning practices are developed and expressed. Indeed, questions still remain over technical plans, details of the route, environmental impact, tariffs, the integration of stations into local neighborhoods, the timeline and priorities for completion, and financing schemes. More profound questions, such as who benefits from a new transit line and what kind of city a transit system should bring about, also remain open.

4   The Mobilizing Myths of the Grand Paris Express

Never has it been more important to choose the most fitting projects and get their economic, social, and environmental impacts right. ... Never has systematic and valid knowledge about megaprojects therefore been more important to inform policy, practice, and public debate in this highly costly area of business and government.
—Bent Flyvbjerg, 2014

Rent operates through a desocialization of the common, privatizing in the hands of the rich the commonwealth produced and consolidated in the metropolis.
—Michael Hardt and Antonio Negri, 2009

After decades of neglect, today mass urban transit is a crucial part of spatial and economic planning in the Île-de-France. The Grand Paris transit debates and the broad discussions they engendered pointed to a popular interest in non-car modalities of movement and highlighted a coherent approach that treats the provision of infrastructures of mass transportation as an integral element in the politics of urbanism. Because mobility and transit are so thoroughly embedded in *francilien* life, they are at the heart of Paris's metropolitan question. Yet the 2010 debates also suggested that any system of mass transit is not merely a technical solution to automobile congestion but a highly contentious urban *problematique*. Indeed, the two transit plans discussed in chapter 3, Arc Express and the Grand Eight/RPGTP, entailed very different metropolitan meanings. Recognizing how seemingly neutral transit proposals are linked to social, political, and economic ideals—that is, recognizing the *politics of metromobility*—is a crucial task for urban researchers in light of the central place of transit infrastructure in grand urbanism.

As the debates over transportation revealed, stakeholders in Paris are seeking investment in mass transit based on divergent objectives. There is considerable disagreement over why and through what means transit can address the growing pains of large urban regions. In Paris as elsewhere, transit and networked infrastructures are not absolute "goods" but are tools wrought by political battles and wielded for conflicting purposes. They can certainly be employed in strategies for social justice, democracy, and freedom, but they can also be apparatuses of segregation, elitism, and authoritarianism. Often they are both simultaneously. The emerging regime of metromobility in Paris is a site of struggle, inequality, and antagonism. Identifying tensions within the regime of metromobility can reveal how mass transit is tied to particular interests and power structures. These tensions were raised in the 2010 public debates but were ultimately glossed over, a move that obscured the contradictory goals toward which transit systems may aim.

This chapter shifts the focus of analysis from the *contests* over transit as exemplified in the public debates of 2010/2011 to the *consensus* on the Grand Paris Express (GPE) that enabled a compromise plan to be created in 2011 and that continues to shape Grand Paris. It thus redirects attention from the political to the postpolitical side of the emerging metromobility regime. Bringing to light moments of friction within the Grand Paris mobility debates is useful for highlighting the conflicts embedded in infrastructure and for drawing out the stakes of transit-oriented metropolitanization. Looking at the shared assumptions that define the GPE compromise is also crucial for illuminating how seemingly unquestionable discourses and practices of mobility function ideologically within grand urbanism and global city pursuits.

Critically assessing the more stable discourses of policy and planning that underlie and suppress its most prominent antagonisms is necessary for a complete picture of the power relations that enable the workings of hegemony (Flyvbjerg 1998). Indeed, the shared common understanding of metromobility as a panacea for metropolitan challenges—typically ignored or taken for granted in research, publications, and public debate—is essential to the prevailing rationality and ideology guiding Grand Paris. This chapter seeks to uncover some of the mystifications of the agreement on the GPE in order to further unpack the dominant norms, assumptions, and knowledges that underlie Grand Paris's transit-led metropolitanization.

The Mobilizing Myths of the Grand Paris Express   127

To claim that the GPE infrastructure is ideological is not to suggest that it is reducible to a single coherent partisan or class position, but it is to maintain that transportation is an important expression of power. As such, metropolitan transport planning is both a terrain of conflict where different projections of urban life are being worked through and a site of compromise where the basic tenets and structures of metromobility, the very terms of political debate, are decided. To understand the GPE as ideological is thus to account for how it condenses and constructs a system of "truths" about mobility and the metropolis. It is also to foreground infrastructure provision as absolutely integral to urban processes of hierarchization and exploitation and therefore to questions of equity and justice.

Such a critical perspective on the GPE thus calls into question the leading knowledges and practices of urban planning on which the Grand Paris plan as a whole is based. A new transit system in Paris has the potential to radically change the metropolitan frontier and to improve the quality of life for all regional inhabitants. Yet it can also easily reproduce the status quo of territorial and social fracture. The latter is more likely when the plans fail to truly interrogate why people are moving and fail to fully articulate how transportation is tied to other material conditions of life, such as housing, poverty, employment, racism, and production. Exposing the operating rationalities of the GPE illustrates how transportation infrastructure furthers the neoliberalization of Parisian space and reveals the problematic nature of transit-oriented development (TOD) as a so-called "best-practice" of contemporary urban planning. In drawing out these ideological features, this chapter exposes what work the GPE transportation network is poised to do beyond being a vehicle of personal movement.

Mobilizing Myths

There is an overriding assumption within the mobility strategy of Grand Paris (as exemplified in the compromise on the GPE) that the myriad objectives of transportation raised in the 2010 debates are complementary and mutually reinforcing. Most notably, the polycentric metropolis of Grand Paris aims to be both "competitive" and "inclusive" (*solidaire*). Yet this assumption or illusion (Orfeuil and Wiel 2012) rests on extremely undialectical understandings of urbanization and mobility as being without conflict and without contest. Perhaps most important, the ideology of mobility embedded in the transit network displays a willed ignorance of patterns of uneven development, and especially of the way in which the production of ground rent (perhaps *the* defining feature of contemporary metropolis) is itself tied to the social inequality, economic disinvestment, and environmental exploitation that mass transportation purports to address.

The lack of attention to the contradictions that stem from transit's role as both a public and private good can be explained through what Henri Lefebvre (2003) calls a "blind field" of urbanism. For Lefebvre, a blind field emerges as a site of occlusion where reality is obscured because of our incomplete or erroneous perception. In particular, blind fields of urbanism are blurred regions in thought, awareness, and knowledge that result from our inability to conceptualize the constantly shifting ground of urban processes. They are commonly found at the disjuncture between industrial ways of knowing and seeing and postindustrial (for Lefebvre, "urban") modes of life. "We focus attentively on the new field, the urban, but we see it with eyes, with concepts that were shaped by the practices and theories of industrialization, with a fragmentary analytical tool that was designed during the industrial period and is therefore reductive of the emerging reality" (29). Blind fields of mobility exist when modernist frameworks of reason, authority, technology, and the state are applied to new forms of life, and when new urban commonsense norms of renewal, flexibility, sustainability, and mixity fail to capture the dialectical relations of contemporary urban life. They exist, in other words, in the gaps between postwar models of urban transport and land use planning and prevailing twenty-first-century realities. Exposing these fields reveals a misalignment between highly complex urban processes and the underlying rationales of planning meant to guide and manage them.

Where blind fields preclude adequate access to spatial dynamics, coherent knowledge is simulated through urban myths. According to Lefebvre (2003, 104–105), a myth "always fills a void" in discourse by recontextualizing dominant tropes and supporting "knowledge that is oriented toward and by practice." Myths of mobility, circulation, and speed abound in the literature on cities and are thus key to urban planning knowledge regimes of the academy, technocracy, and political parties. The transit-led metropolitanization of Paris is facilitated by several prominent "mobilizing myths," a term Marc Wiel (2009b) uses to describe the formative assumptions about transit that are discursively utilized (mobilized) to legitimize political projects. Although he draws not on Lefebvre but on Roland Barthes, Wiel similarly describes myths as discursive practices that conceal and illuminate realities. Myths are not "false" in the sense that they have no bearing on reality; rather, they produce particular truths and realities about mobility that replicate existing power relationships. Enabling and framing our conception of urban affairs, mobilizing myths create policy problems and solutions in line with the epistemologies, organizational frameworks, and institutions of particular political-economic and social systems.

Mobilizing myths are some of the most prevalent ways of thinking through the relationships of collective movement and the urbanization processes of late capitalism. Beyond the partisan differences of the transportation debates lies a common set of ideas and justifications that organizes transportation policy and, by extension, the behaviors and interactions of inhabitants in metropolitan Paris. The dominant myths of transportation effectively demonstrate how global city norms and values are actively and continuously created and enacted through institutions, laws, policies, and languages in ways that confirm the primacy of the market and encourage competition in all aspects of life. These myths are instrumental in reinforcing neoliberalism as the dominant governmentality of Grand Paris.

Mobilizing myths thus provide essential ideological and pseudo-scientific support for an urban governance regime that structures profitable public policy around the values of exchange and efficiency and orients decision making toward optimization logics. Specifically, the five main "myths" mobilized in the GPE transit plan are the following: (1) the assumption that megaprojects of mobility are good for economic and social development, (2) a belief in dense transit-oriented growth clusters as levers of urbanization, (3) the equivocation of different types of mobility (especially the false substitution of daily commuting for residential mobility), (4) the notion that mass transportation is also public, and (5) the presumed incontrovertibility of sustainable TOD. In what follows I examine each of these myths in greater detail. Together they activate a regime of metromobility suited to grand urbanism.

Megaprojects Are Good for Development

The main mobilizing myth of the broad Grand Paris project is that large-scale infrastructure is good for development. This rationale holds that changing the physical distributions of people, places, and functions can improve society and that public investment in large-scale pharaonic projects will resonate across a variety of political, economic, social, and cultural terrains. Unparalleled public sector spending is earmarked for the GPE. The ostentatious state involvement and the enormous cost of the project, especially in a time of crisis and recession, are remarkable, and the purposes of such investments demand judicious consideration.

Vast infrastructural projects have long been the means through which states legitimize power, display technical prowess, monumentalize cultural symbols, civilize populations, and expand control. The modern state territorializes its power and concretizes particular ideals through the built environment. But public investment is never just about the authority or self-aggrandizement of the state alone. Infrastructure is also an important tool of economic development and thus concerns the relation of the state to the historically specific dynamics of the globalized economic order. In many ways, the large-scale territorial management of Grand Paris follows in the footsteps of earlier *grands projets*. Yet megaprojects today differ in a number of important ways from the modernization projects of Haussmannization in the nineteenth century or the postwar reconstructions of the twentieth century.

As in earlier eras, state intervention through infrastructure today aims to reassert fading power and prestige and to counteract economic and social decline. In line with the Second Empire reforms, for example, the GPE works to channel surplus into the built environment, targeting areas of working-class "blight" and unrest. Andy Merrifield (2014, x) calls this tactic of redevelopment based on "upscaling the urban physical environment to alter the social and political environment" a matter of "neo-Haussmannization." While the strategy is showcased in Paris, for Merrifield it is part of a broader phenomenon of gentrification that is "now happening globally ... in all cities, orchestrated by transnational financial and corporate elites everywhere, endorsed by their respective national governments." Whereas Haussmann's reforms bolstered Napoleon Bonaparte and the military power of an imperial hegemon, today's reforms are subtler insofar as they support a more diffuse sovereign matrix of state and corporate power and a more collaborative and cooperative mode of project-led regeneration.

The GPE combines massive transformation of the physical and social territory of the capital region with changes in the share of the region's commonwealth, yet neo-Hausmannization is also not fully comparable to the national redistributive policies of the early and mid-twentieth century. Under Keynesianism, governments invest in infrastructure in hopes of a generalized return through broad social application. State managerialist policies in France aimed to equalize living standards of the population through redistributing wealth, democratizing access to public goods (and public space), and regularizing the attractiveness of territories for investment by ensuring that industry was spread uniformly through space (see Brenner 2004). Current reforms maintain the postwar slogan "all's well if construction's well," but, in contrast to the building strategies of the postwar era, investment in the GPE is directed toward increasing, not leveling, intercity competition and polarity and toward decreasing the distance between the public and private spheres. Under this regime, the state maintains a high level of involvement in leading aggressive territorial reform, but it does so not to correct the failures of the naturally functioning market but to intervene in and commodify those social and political forms that would not otherwise conform to a market logic. Rather than sharing wealth downward to the many, financialized capital and rent production work through processes of upward redistribution whereby collective wealth is privatized in the hands of the few (Hardt and Negri 2009; Harvey 2005).

The contemporary phase of public expenditures in infrastructure and the built environment, which has been described as "roll-out" neoliberalism (Peck and Tickell 2002), primarily works to direct surplus value into the hands of elite investors and developers. Because of its centralized direction, Grand Paris is seen by some as an expression of Jacobin principles and a reversion to the days of the omniscient state, but it is also important to note that the contemporary form of state involvement is far from complete and—what is important—it aims not only toward national glory and social service but also toward private gain (Orfeuil 2010). To see the GPE to fruition, Grand Paris's public policies and urban planning are directed toward measuring "underperforming" areas, identifying sites for redevelopment, and promoting broad-based renewal based on multilevel governance and public-private partnerships. This strategy is coordinated through Territorial Development Contracts (CDTs) around proposed GPE stations. The very meaning of urban politics and urbanism is transformed in this shift, with various government bodies structuring property rights, landownership rules, funding vehicles, land use regulations, and taxes in ways intended to more effectively direct capital into the built environment (Baraud-Serfaty 2012). Central state institutions create or manipulate large-scale infrastructure in order to lead and manage this urban gentrification process.

Moreover, through the GPE, Grand Paris takes the model of the flagship urban megaproject—typically in the form of Olympic villages, airports, waterfront developments, and site-specific architectural masterpieces—and applies it to the scale of the metropolis itself.[1] Indeed, the GPE is a hyperbolic example of a megaproject being used as the preferred delivery model of urban services and the preeminent bearer of urban development (Flyvbjerg 2014; Flyvbjerg, Bruzelius, and Rothengatter 2003).[2]

As the previous chapter showed, the stated benefits of a large-scale suburban metro network are various and profound. Supported through technological, political, economic, and aesthetic "sublimes," the GPE is a seductive project that promises to incontrovertibly change the structure of metropolitan Paris.[3] While the potential gains of contemporary megaprojects are impressive, the drawbacks are equally as staggering. For Flyvbjerg, megaprojects are perilous endeavors beset by inherent risk and frequently marred by weak leadership, conflicting authorities, and rampant misinformation. This leads him to declare the "iron law of megaprojects": they nearly invariably experience cost and time overruns and underachieve benefits (Flyvbjerg 2014). Founded on megaprojects, the ambitious speculative experiments of grand urbanism are a risky and unstable gamble of vital public resources.

The *grand pari* of the Grand Paris megaproject is further exacerbated by postcrisis accountancy organized around debt funding and speculative growth. Paradoxically, megaproject development in grand urbanism is facilitated by an increasing reliance on debt for municipal social service provisions and capital infrastructure. The attractive character of state and municipal debt—its ability to be bought and sold as an asset—amplifies the reliance on large projects, particularly those affecting property markets, to promote metropolitan growth. That is, a reliance on debt actually facilitates and in some cases requires massive ventures and large-scale construction efforts as the primary forms of urban governance (see Hackworth 2006). Massive investment in new networks may seem to be at odds with the post-2008 European atmosphere of recession, but in effect, this stimulus spending actually works to achieve liquidity and reestablish growth.[4] Though

Sarkozy (2009) stated this most explicitly—"a crisis is an opportunity for a *grand projet*"—this perspective is widely held by both the left and the right in France. The austerity-growth dialectic of Grand Paris thus largely replicates a cycle of speculative real estate growth that caused the 2008 crisis in the first place (Enright 2014).

Megaprojects are an attractive means to achieve what austerity is ultimately aiming for: ever new investment, ever new growth, and the ability of the state to borrow more. Through new accommodations between planning and growth, as well as compromises over debt and public financing, the GPE megaproject restructures the economic and political processes of metropolitan space to align with the demands of the twenty-first century. The notion that megaprojects of mobility are good for development is a powerful myth, but one that hides more insidious dimensions of large-scale speculative transformation.

Transit-Oriented Clusters: A Lever for Transformation

The national policy of Grand Paris is an example of a pronounced trend, in Europe and elsewhere, to focus on clusters of economic activity, with the innovative "city region" as the key unit of global competition (Lovering 1999; Moulaert and Sekia 2003). The official means of metropolitanization are thus dictated by the gap between production needs and given spatial distributions. The preamble to the 2009 legislative bill leading up to the 2010 Grand Paris Act describes this transit-development relation as follows:

> The founding principle of the overall project development of Grand Paris rests in the valorization of its potential for the emergence of several economic engines of growth poles. Within these *clusters*, exchanges between disciplines and partners (researchers, designers, enterprises, etc.) will stimulate innovation. The economic, functional and spatial articulation of these major poles, territories of research knowledge and creativity will also have a multiplier effect. The complementarity of their objectives, with economic specialization and forward-looking technology, strengthens the resistance of the economy to cyclical and structural shocks. By connecting these clusters, the primary transportation network, a true central nervous system, provides consistency and efficacy to the entire project of development and management. (Assemblée Nationale, 2009)

The system of mass transit finalized in the GPE is the necessary precondition for the emergence of prospective poles of industry so crucial to the innovation and growth of the region.

Supporters of the transit plan claim that intervention is required to support the information and service industries, presumed to be the only bases for growth in a postindustrial and entrepreneurial economy. Christian Blanc (2010), who as secretary of state for the development of the capital region first presented the bill, argued that the state needed to rapidly intervene in the regional economy to save France from "decline" (*décroissance*, literally "degrowth") and impending "chaos" (see also Blanc 2009). Blanc described the Grand Paris metro as a networked "rhizome" that would increase the intensity of regional interactions and generate new capacities for growth and innovation at each hub.

Clustering in Grand Paris entails identifying functionally differentiated regional poles and actively courting investors to relocate to these designated areas. Economic growth under this industrial policy is premised on

Figure 4.1
The future site of the Arcueil-Cachan GPE station. As expressed in the slogan "Cachan within the metropolis," by hosting a new station, the municipality becomes connected to the economic life of the multipolar urban network. At the same time, the transit network is being used to solidify a "science and health care campus" in the station vicinity.

general productivity gains from transit's influence on agglomeration effects—the positive externalities accrued by concentrating agents, increasing the proximity of labor to employment opportunities and intensifying the exchange of information (Prager and Quinet 2013).[5] Providing public amenities such as transit instigates this process by spurring on other investment in private buildings, homes, and commercial enterprises and (re)activating private enterprises (Karadimitriou, De Magalhães, and Verhage 2013). In particular, the new GPE is meant to enable growth in research and technology sectors.

The commitment to infrastructure and the designation of priority investment zones also, and perhaps just as important, aim to boost property markets. Indeed, clustering rests on the belief that a healthy property market is necessary for a vital and prosperous economy and society (Karadimitriou, De Magalhães, and Verhage 2013). Although in Grand Paris, the cluster is a vaguely defined concept and actual agglomeration prospects are questionable, the identification of hubs may nevertheless still be an effective way to intensify select areas of the city by attracting more dynamic economic activities and private sector growth.[6] In speculating on the development of clusters, various levels of government and private investors coordinate economic activity through urban construction in order to increase the potential for future profits or rent on undervalued land.

One way that speculative development works in Paris is to focus on existing hubs of enterprise and to further specialize already established geographies of industry so as to increase the competitive advantage of the regional network. The thriving hotspots of La Défense in the west and the Saclay Plateau in the southwest have already established symbolic and economic capital, while new reforms will make them even more attractive to high-value investors. A second strategy is to further creative destruction through a dialectic of dystopia and utopia, whereby certain spaces are depicted as deteriorated and useless, ready for redevelopment into a profitable livable space "once again." Decay and obsolescence are thus required to inflate the gap between a space's current use and its potential futures (Baeten 2007). In many ways the *banlieue* as a space of disorder, marked in the popular imaginary by crumbling *grand ensemble* housing projects and rampant delinquency, illustrates the condition that must be overcome through new developments. Together, these two strategies work to create what Hackworth (2006, 69) calls a "regionally differentiated profit landscape" that will eliminate barriers to investment while ensuring a specialization of functions across the territory for maximum value creation.

With the GPE, France has been actively courting foreign investors for sites around the new stations (Invest in France Agency 2014; Leroy 2011; Wallis 2011). Recent reports estimate an additional €40 to €200 billion in private investment in the region while the transit network is being built (Mobilicités 2011; Property Investor Europe 2013). Real estate and financial investors worldwide have taken note and are interested in the project for its ability to catalyze rent production. A 2013 report titled simply *Why Invest in Paris*, by Ernst & Young/Jones Lang Lasalle sums up the valorizing effect of the GPE as follows:

As a prestigious world city, Paris is currently subject to a vast infrastructure project that aims to defend and improve the city's international stature. ... Two [themes] in particular are likely to influence the real estate market in the coming years:

• The development of business districts around Paris which could impact the choice of location for certain companies.
• The creation of a new transport masterplan that will connect important transport hubs with new districts around the city. ... This in turn will help develop local economic activity in these areas.

In a 2013 report titled *All aboard the Grand Paris Express*, J.P. Morgan Chase echoed this positive evaluation of the GPE as a promising investment opportunity: "The key outcome of Grand Paris ... is its impact on property values. ... Property with greater access to transport hubs (mostly proxied by the distance to station) outperforms those with reduced access." A 2011 white paper from CBRE Global Investors stated in even more direct terms,

We believe the Grand Paris Project will stimulate the Île-de-France office property market as a whole. CBRE Investors anticipates that the project will sustain, if not increase, the attractiveness of Île-de-France in the worldwide arena. ... In summary, a successful strategy to capitalise on the Grand Paris Project is to proactively target expanding or upcoming business districts, as well as industrial and logistic areas that are well-suited to setting up European-scale logistics facilities, in anticipation of infrastructure improvements.

In the financialized city, urbanism thus becomes oriented toward projects that create gaps between high- and low-rent uses of space. Thus, through the GPE, the public sector establishes the conditions for value creation, or *rentabilité*, in a twenty-first-century economy. Some of this value is set to be recuperated by the state through value capture taxes and invested back into the network (Carrez 2009; IAU-IDF 2009), but this redistribution does not fundamentally alter the imperative of gentrification.

Speculative development and the revalorization of land and property cannot be fully or directly controlled, but it is a stated priority of the network proposal (Carrez 2009, 32). Through a combination of exceptional rights of preemption, direct oversight of development by the SGP, and the coordinated urbanism of CDTs, the state is involved in delivering clusters and directing territorial revalorization (République Française 2010). Where the state cannot directly intervene in property markets it can change land use patterns through structuring taxes in a manner incentivized toward large businesses and those with high profit rates. The state's mapping capacity—to envision clusters, to carve up regional territory into functionally differentiated segments, and to market these branded hubs to the world through grand designs and growth projections—is its prime function under grand urbanism.

Thus the economic function of metromobility today is not primarily about transporting commodities such as freight, as with nineteenth-century rail systems (Schivelbusch 1986), nor is it about mass consumer consumption or bringing labor to market, as with automobile systems in the twentieth century (see especially Ross 1996). The circulation of capital in the city today demands a different mobility infrastructure and ideology of movement. The global city metropolis does not produce objects and profits but rent, and an effective mobility system today must serve this end. The ability of metro systems to produce rent more quickly and intensely than, for example, bus, highway, bus rapid transit, or tram systems accounts for their crucial role in contemporary urbanization.[7]

Equivocal Mobilities

The movement of people throughout the Île-de-France may not be the primary reason for the massive state investment in GPE, but it is by no means incidental. The dynamics of capital circulation and clustering are closely related to the question of who is moving through the city (e.g., "delinquents" or executives) and for what purposes. People are expected to move in metropolitan Paris in very specific ways, and the transit system is a crucial mechanism for directing and controlling these flows.

The French notion of *déplacement* (or in verb form *déplacer*) invokes multiple aspects of this movement. *Déplacement* refers to the general characteristic of moving from one location to another (displacement), to a commute (typically to and from work), and to the English equivalent "displacement," the forcible removal from a site (particularly in terms of residential relocation). The concept of equivocal mobilities refers to the slippery use of *déplacement* to express movement, commuting, and residential "choice" and to elide their often fraught interrelationships. In particular, exposing this myth reveals that there are inconsistencies in one of the most firmly held ideas about contemporary transit-oriented urbanism: that increasing the speed of the commute will reduce the spatiotemporal divide between home and work.

As the sediment of patterns of a postwar modernization driven by automobiles and the automobile culture, there now exist large distances between residence and employment in the Île-de-France. Commuting today has increasingly become a concern because of what the Grand Pari(s) architect Christian de Portzamparc has called a disconnect between Hestia and Hermes (in Le Moniteur Architecture 2009). Recent data from the National Institute for Statistics and Economic Research (INSEE) show that commutes of all kinds are rising in number across the Île-de-France and that three quarters of employed *franciliens* leave their commune for their place of work, just under one-half also leaving their department (INSEE 2007, 2010a). On average they spend eighty-two minutes per day commuting, and it is not uncommon to spend more than two hours. Many of these commutes are between *banlieues,* as the job market attractiveness of Paris has been partially ceded to the *grand couronne* suburbs, and especially to the western department Hauts-de-Seine (INSEE 2006). In La Défense, for example, there are four times more employment offerings than employed residents, while in the northern municipality of Saint-Denis there are far fewer offerings than residents (INSEE 2006). Today, what Kristen Ross (1996) has called *"l'homme disponible"* (which she translates variously as "available man" and "moveable man") of modern production practices expects to be displaced, and now under a regime of postindustrial flexibility, at ever greater distances from the site he calls home.

Lengthy and time-consuming commutes between work, residence, and leisure destinations can be a problem for the quality of life of urban inhabitants, and also for urbanization more generally. The structures of reproduction are inadequate to meet the needs of contemporary forces of production. Infrastructures must be expanded to broaden the scale of the urban. The GPE promises to create jobs and homes and to reduce the time spent traveling between these sites. However, the model concentrating growth and jobs in hubs attempts to substitute the daily mobility of inhabitants for residential mobility. Leaving aside the important question of unemployment (as high as 35 percent in some communes in the region), the assumption is that reliable public transit is needed to move labor power to the market. While the GPE works to solidify and consecrate poles by moving jobs and people around the city, the project does not do enough to address the mobility of housing alongside the movement of enterprise or daily mobility.

For Wiel (2009b, 177–182), the equivocation of mobilities is misleading because it presumes that a new transit network will increase speed without affecting existing residential and employment access. He suggests instead that the movement of bodies around the city be conceptualized in terms of the deep divide between home and work that underwrites bourgeois urban space, and in terms of the intimate relationship—based on land valorization—between the provision of transit infrastructure and the production of rent. Whereas a polycentric city claims to temporarily overcome the divide between residence and work, between reproduction and production, if the material conditions that generate this divide have not changed, the problems of access and sprawl only become reconfigured as poles multiply.

Indeed, there are several reasons why a high-speed ring metro may not achieve the densification to which TOD aims. First, the specialization of employment zones, especially those in the outer suburbs, encourages recruitment from across the region and thus suggests more and longer commutes (Lacoste 2010). This is especially pertinent as the 2010 Grand Paris debates decided in favor of a scheme that had a lesser impact on job access in marginalized (nonpriority) areas (Gallez and Fol 2014). Second, if ring metros are built in peripheral zones, they may engender further sprawl, as residents could now move farther away from centralized areas and still maintain a reasonable commute (Lacoste 2010; Orfeuil and Wiel 2012). Increases in speed are not necessarily correlated with a more compact living. Indeed, the tax on value-added territory around new stations compounds this perverse effect by pushing development just beyond taxable radius. In both of these scenarios, households and employment move away from one another. Third, agglomeration may in fact mean more people and more industries competing for the same property. As land values increase around new stations and in priority clusters, low-income populations and activities may be priced out of their neighborhoods. Thus even attempts to provide disconnected areas of the city with transit may have the adverse effect of driving inhabitants away from transit. Even with the 70,000 new housing units per year promised under Grand Paris, rising property values pose limits to housing accessibility, already at crisis levels in the Île-de-France.[8] The problems of territorial fragmentation and polarity remain if vulnerable populations are pushed further out to the peripheries, where public transit does not reach.

The linking of housing and employment remains a problem if these are separated into distinct clusters or forced apart through displacement. According to Caroline Gallez and Sylvie Fol (2014), the current calculations of mobility in terms of "time saved" estimates do little to account for actual accessibility and proximity concerns, especially in relation to social inequities. The risk of mismatches between mobility and accessibility is enhanced by competitive land markets and property booms. These concerns about uneven development are especially salient to Grand Paris as its principles of renewal and recycling are explicitly tied to revalorization. Grounded in the ideas of "make with" and building "the city on the city," densification and intensification in Grand Paris target zones "where the land and revitalization potentials justify and inscribe them at the heart of intervention priorities" (AIGP 2013c, 21). The metric of "revitalization potentials" as rent potentials disincentivizes those uses of land, such as social housing (but also other public amenities, such as parks, schools, and green spaces), that do not abide conditions of profitability. Even more insidious, the gentrifying effects of the GPE are also being used as a strategy to actively displace communities in an effort to break up existing class-based and antiracist solidarities.[9]

The view that commuting can stand in for all types of mobility rests on the assumption that transit infrastructure can stand in for the problems that planning has repeatedly failed to solve. The language and concepts of planning on the one hand and traffic engineering on the other treat commute/residence and speed/density relations as isolated from one another. Yet these variables are interdependent and changes to one will invariably influence the others. Residential and individual mobility in particular must be considered to be dialectically related: as Wiel (2009a) asserts, "one cannot substitute for the other." The myth that circulation and efficiency are absolute goods misses the factors that direct movement and the goals to which they are aimed. Without limiting rising property prices, enabling a right of residents to stay put, and providing local jobs opportunities across the metropolis that are appropriate for the skills and needs of particular communities, the acceleration of individual commuting times remains mismatched with the goal of residential densification.

Mass Transit Is Public Transit

The GPE network is being sold as a system that will unite the region. It is also fundamentally described as a "citizen-oriented" "public" space that will enhance urban encounters and urban living. "[A] new public transport offer for everyone ... underground stations that will line the new network's route will be more than mere stops on the metro. They will be open to the city and help shape the metropolis's development towards a more connected, more sustainable, more intense but also more human town" (SGP 2012). The myth that mass transit is public transit implies that the network is pursued with an aim for the common good. The myth is important for what it distorts, that mass transit may be based on an individualized model of private interest and atomized and autonomous mobilities, and that a neutral public mobility stands in for a wide range of experiences of movement throughout the city. The myth of public transit is an instance of the myth of the republican bourgeois public sphere more generally, in which an abstract universal subject (coded white, male, able-bodied, and propertied) is taken to represent the diversity of *citadins* or urban dwellers.

There are many ways to define the "publicness" of a given system of mass transit. The malleability of the word "public" means that it can be invoked to refer to the nature of the system's ownership, the status of its institutional operator, the financing of its construction and functioning, its de jure openness to a universal set of users (an economic public good), its de facto accessibility to a broad population, or its mechanisms of profit distribution. More abstractly, one could also define transit as public insofar as it is a symbolic reference point of quotidian metropolitan life, a terrain on which to deliberate the purpose and constitution of good city, and an essential site of collective aleatory encounter where citizens who would not otherwise have reason to meet are thrown together, if temporarily, in the shared space of a metro *wagon*.

The GPE clearly meets some of these conditions, but with questions remaining about the democratic composition of its creators and beneficiaries and doubts about its universal accessibility, its claims to publicness should also be suspect. The GPE will no doubt be used by large numbers of people, and will affect even more through its ancillary influence, but its broad impact does not translate so directly into the betterment of daily life for the denizens of metropolitan Paris. Indeed, while "mass transit" at first glance implies a service to all in equal measure, so long as speed and movement are based on the conditions of competition and the already exclusive nature of republican belonging, not all people are poised to use or experience transit in the same way. The costs and benefits of any new infrastructure do not accrue equally to all, depending on a variety of social and spatial factors (e.g., class, race, gender, ability, residential location). As Doreen Massey (1994, 148) explains with reference to increased connectivity brought about through new technology more generally, "time-space compression needs differentiating socially." An analysis of the public nature of the GPE must take into account the "power geometry" of the mobilities it entails.[10]

Two aspects in particular draw out these complications. The first is the extent to which the GPE can achieve its social goals of territorial balance, solidarity, and inclusivity. The Grand Paris transport initiative is part of a larger social strategy and in addition to targeting underserviced, often working-class and racialized, residential neighborhoods across the metropolis (a win of the left in the GPE compromise), each station's Territorial Development Contract must account for its local social, environmental, and cultural contributions. Yet the plans for the GPE also explicitly draw attention to the lack of direct investment in social issues. Instead, the Grand Paris initiative relies on the idea that the provision of transportation is linked to the provision of housing, employment, and other social services and that investment in one can satisfy all of the others. Whereas the economic aspects of Grand Paris are clearly articulated and its market goals are instrumentalized in policy provisions, the social equity dimensions are expressed only in vague generalities. This explicit focus on economics over other social welfare concerns (maintained even in François Hollande's New

Grand Paris) indicates a naturalization of the terms of competition, innovation, and economic growth as the baseline metrics of public action. As the housing question has done for centuries, today the "transit question" effectively substitutes for the systemic question of social inequality.

Adding to this, transportation planning remains rooted in technical cultures of economics and engineering that focus on cost-benefit analyses, efficiency, and short-term perspectives. While a reduction in travel times, for example, is a key selling point for GPE boosters, these estimates do not take into account who might be traveling. According to Gallez and Fol (2014, 74), the focus on universal transit mobility instead of differentiated transit accessibility prevents engineers and planners from achieving social goals. "Most transportation projects," they write, "are based on the naïve assumption that they will benefit all users whatever their social position, income or location of residence. The reality is, of course, different." Without breaking down movement into distinct social groups, the real winners and losers of any given scheme cannot be identified. As they stand, the methods used in appraising transport capacity do not distinguish between social groups. Travel time saved, for example, is calculated for a person who can choose where to live, thereby effectively ignoring those who do not have this residential choice. Whereas models of access usually are measured in terms of infrastructural efficiency, the socioeconomic characteristics of amenities are equally as important.

The question of fare structure based on zones (pay for distance) is another way in which affordability prevents access for marginal residents. The pricing for the metro and RER is currently calculated based on a zone structure based on five concentric circles from the center of Paris outward. To travel within zone 1 (roughly the city of Paris proper) on a single ticket costs €1.70, while a ticket from zone 1 to zone 5 (the outer reaches of the network) can cost as much as €8.10. In effect, this means that those who are unable to live in the center of the city are charged far more for daily mobility needs than those already living in the "core." There are efforts to change this pricing, but under the current system, where one travels and one's socioeconomic status have a great influence over transit accessibility. For the French urban expert Jean-Marc Offner (2013, 54), this is indicative of residents' asymmetric "spatial capital," that is, their capacity to use territorial resources to the full ensemble of geographic scales and to mobilize economic, cultural, and cognitive abilities.[11]

In addition to where people move and why, a second aspect of the GPE power geometry affecting transit equity is how the *experience* of transportation is differentiated according to populations. The fact that not all inhabitants experience mass transit the same way has been largely absent from any kind of public debate. In particular, this is a concern for those marked as racial or cultural outsiders.[12] In contrast to the rich affective space of memory and desire that the subway can be for a middle- or upper-class resident of Paris (Augé 2002), for many, especially low-income or racialized youth, the metro and RER are institutions of extreme violence and vehicles of exclusion. For these inhabitants, the metro is both a symbol of exclusion and a very real tool of increased state surveillance and control.

With previous expansions of transit lines to the "dangerous" suburbs, there has been an increase in security and surveillance. In the 1980s, shortly after the completion of regional rail extensions, the SNCF rail authority produced a number of complaints about "losing control" over the lines outside Paris and publicly decried problems of vandalism, graffiti, and muggings, even going so far as to refer to itself as an "unwilling participant in the drug scene" (Silverstein 2004, 111). Depending on where the transit lines go, different rules of treatment for commuter populations are required. Myriad examples in recent years demonstrate the differentiated regimes of governance and the involvement of the transit system in producing and reproducing racialized and criminalized subjects. In the 1989 "security plan" for the metro and RER, surveillance of the transit system was increased, but only on the lines traveling outside Paris, in the so-called "spaces of disorder." In 2005, fear of mobility caused authorities to shut down the major RER stations in Paris to prevent the flames of the suburbs from reaching the center of the city (Murray 2006, 29). In similar fashion, in 2010 heightened security measures were ordered for regional buses, but in effect they applied only to those routes in Seine-Saint-Denis. Ongoing complaints about the nonviability of the Vélib public bicycle-sharing program for the unruly suburbs also echoed this general discourse of the unsuitability of the *banlieue* and *banlieue* residents for modern city amenities.[13]

The racial overtones of transit security are clear. Overall, since the initiation of the Vigipirate security plan (or Vichypirate, as it is colloquially known) of 1978 (heightened after the Métro bombings of 1995 and again after 9/11), police have stopped, in targeted attacks, nearly three million North African– and Arab-looking residents in stations and on transit networks (Silverstein 2004, 111).[14] As Paul Silverstein reminds us, the transportation industry is "an important site in the ambivalent production of the *banlieues* as spaces of order and disorder, tribalism and modernity. ... [It] both delineates racialized compartments and violates them, enables mobility and delimits the possible avenues through such movement can occur" (109). There is nothing in the Grand Paris plans or in the proposals for the GPE that would indicate that the transport industry will not continue to be involved in the invidious linking of race, space, and violence. Indeed, network expansions and the renewed emphasis on cleanliness and security increase the likelihood that transit may serve as a tool of surveillance and control.

To address the unequal way in which the transit network serves and harms populations, then, we must think through transindividual characteristics of mobility. This exercise would recognize the way that mobility is tied to the production of space and the production of subjects through social and economic relationships of, for example, labor, gender, and neighborhood. The organization of travel for the purpose of displacing an abstract body from one location to another without an expenditure of too much time or money hinges on an understanding of society as an ensemble of persons without links to one another. But the conditions of transportation are fundamentally situated within broader social and economic relations such that, to quote Wiel (2009b, 78), "mobility is the result not the choice of one who commutes each morning." A truly communal or public transit network must address the link between transit and housing markets, as well as transit's securitized racial circuitries.

Sustainability as a Watchword

Sustainability (*durabilité*) is absolutely central to Grand Paris and to the legitimation of the GPE. Transportation is a particularly salient sector for sustainable policies because automobile dependence is a major source of greenhouse gas emissions and the environmental benefits of mass transportation are rhetorically powerful, especially in a global city regime that requires a model of green city growth (Suzuki, Cervero, and Iuchi 2013). The consensus over the need for sustainable transit and sustainable metropolitan development, however, hides inconsistencies in the invocations of the post-Kyoto paradigm of Grand Paris.

Heralded as a green and resilient model of urbanism, Grand Paris emphasizes the creation of dense mixed-use neighborhoods, easy and universal access to mass transit, lowered carbon emissions, a reduction in traffic congestion, improved air quality, land conservation, and a rich pedestrian life. Drawing on the possibilities offered by the Grand Pari(s) architectural consultation, Grand Paris promises to integrate the natural world into the fabric of the city, to revitalize brownfield sites, and to pursue environmentally sustainable architecture for new stations and developments (SGP 2014). What the GPE demonstrates quite explicitly, however, is that to the extent that these goals are achievable, they often are available only selectively. This is indicative of the broad challenges of linking ecological and social goals in large urban regions today (Offner 2013, 55).

Grand Paris largely follows the World Bank's (2014) model of sustainability, founded on the three pillars of economic growth, environmental stewardship, and social inclusion. Sustainable development is based on prosperity through coordinated innovation in manufacturing, "green job" creation, improvements in regional economies, and the reduction of negative environmental impacts. Sustainability, as is articulated in the Grand Paris plans, suggests that problems of polarity can be solved and inequitable impacts of growth can be managed. It ties together the goals of social equity and environmental responsibility, with neoliberal growth representing a compromise between communal and environmental well-being and competitive urbanism. This has been described elsewhere as the "new environmental politics of urban development" (Jonas, While, and Gibbs 2010).

It would be an overstatement to claim that the sustainability promises of Grand Paris are nothing more than a means of "boosterism" for world city status. Indeed, the GPE has mobilized environmental activists and has given rise to coalitions between socialist and green party interests around the construction of lasting ecological and social urban improvements Moreover, for Cècile Duflot (of Europe Écologie, or EE—i.e., the Green Party), made head of the SGP by François Hollande, the goals of environmental durability are tied in to refusing a speculative model of hypergrowth. "We will not become Dubai on the Seine," she quipped in 2012 (in de Ravinel 2012).[15] Yet sustainability under Hollande's New Grand Paris scheme nevertheless remains tied to pro-growth megaprojects. While the GPE compromise and Hollande's New Grand Paris pay much more attention, and in meaningful ways, to green ends, they have not resolved the underlying tensions that see competiveness and accumulation (and dispossession and exploitation) at odds with more radical green alternatives.

Even the most obvious assumption that the GPE consists of primary new underground tracks (influenced by heavy lobbying on behalf of the construction firm Vinci) calls its environmental virtuousness into question. The ecological ramifications of such a massive undertaking are huge, and many have criticized the plan for its wanton restructurings and for ignoring the less disruptive multimodal networks of light transit suggested by the majority of Grand Pari(s) architects. Frédéric Léonhardt (2011, 2012), for example, has criticized the underground project as being impractical for the kind of commuting necessary in the suburbs and singles out Paris as the one of the few modern metropolises that continue to push for underground service outside a historically dense core. Pierre Merlin, an expert on Parisian transport history, has also claimed that because of urban rail's capacity to overhaul land-use patterns, a peripheral ring subway under current property and growth conditions will engender further urban sprawl, not dense infill. "It is imperative to determine on this occasion, if the choice of transport (ring rail) is coherent with the choice of urbanism (compact city)" (Merlin 2012, 199). A heavy transport system organized around priority development clusters is a far cry from the "porous city" suggested, for example, by Studio 09 in 2008. It also ignores the warning given by l'AUC that the contradictions of sustainability, mobility, and growth cannot be overcome as long as the city suffers from a disconnect of use and property.[16]

Despite the reorientation toward more substantive environmental regulation with the leftward shift of the project, concerns over its ecological impacts remain. The nongovernmental organization Environment Île-de-France (IDFE), a regional union of associations for the protection of the Paris environment, suggested in a 2014 public consultation brief that the GPE would be expected to cause flood risks, waste management problems, excessive vibrations on vulnerable soils, forest encroachment, and the destruction of vital agricultural lands (IDFE 2014). Recent studies across France have also raised doubt about the assumption that a polycentric metropolitan model will encourage compact growth, reduce automobile travel, and be better for the environment (see especially Aguilera and Mignot 2004; Bouf and Hensher 2007). In this sense, it is important to demystify the spatialist fallacy that posits a direct link between sustainability and urban form.

Moreover, the post-Kyoto paradigm of the GPE is directly tied to the speculative futures on which the broader Grand Paris venture is premised. Christian de Portzamparc sums this up concisely: "It's a matter of appreciating and creating urban textures and neighborhoods with a plasticity, a flexibility. Neighborhoods and buildings can change their properties, functions and be replaced. This capacity of appropriation by future generations is the secret of successful cities. It is also that of the sustainable city. *The sustainable is the transformable*" (in Le Moniteur 2009, 118; emphasis added). Sustainability as development that meets the needs of the present without compromising the future contradicts the kind of risk-oriented speculation that is meant to drive development in the GPE. Yet these contradictory discourses are held in tandem throughout Grand Paris in the curious motto, "The sustainable is the transformable." The myth of flexible sustainability is insidious insofar as it accelerates the creative destruction that drives uneven development. New potentials for redevelopment must be ceaselessly created, and new projects to transform the region must be pursued interminably. When sustainability is tied to grand urbanism's terms of competitiveness and profitability, what is being maintained for future generations is the status quo of inequality. What is made resilient is the global city itself.

Development in Saclay and La Gonesse

A closer look at two prospective clusters, Saclay Plateau and the Gonnesse Triangle, and their CDTs (Paris-Saclay Territoire Sud and Val-de-France/Gonesse/Bonneuil-en-France), illustrates how the GPE mobilizing myths gain traction in practice at local scales. Even though CDTs must define local development according to a range of urban planning priorities, including "housing, transport, travel, and the fight against urban sprawl, commercial facilities, economic development, sports and cultural development, protection of natural, agricultural and forest landscapes and natural resources," the nature of these goals is amorphous (République Française 2010). Overall, as illustrated in the following examples, existing contracts demonstrate the priority given to exchange value and productive industries (e.g., high technology, finance, real estate, management, tourism, sport, leisure) and regeneration in pursuit of maximal profits.

Investing in Saclay

The Plateau de Saclay, also called Silicon Valley Européenne, is an area approximately twenty kilometers southwest of Paris between the departments of Essonne and Yvelines. The territory has a long agricultural tradition but more recently has also become host to world-class universities, research centers, and private scientific and technology corporations. The Saclay campus, "a hub of global research" (EPPS 2014), was recently ranked by the MIT *Technological Review* one of the world's top eight innovation clusters (cited in Invest in France Agency 2014).

Saclay is the pivotal project of Grand Paris and the only location to be explicitly targeted by the Grand Paris Act.[17] The initiative aims to make use of the growth potential of the area and to transform the existing research facilities into an even more world-class scientific cluster, taking advantage of synergies between education and enterprise. The transformation of Saclay is one of Europe's largest urban planning projects and is the decisive element in the overall Grand Paris mission (République Française 2010). Modeled after the development of Silicon Valley, Saclay is to lead the way in enhancing research and development, promoting educational and private sector partnerships, and rendering the region attractive to business and highly skilled workers from around the world (see especially Blanc 2010). In a 2013 speech given at the future site of the Université Paris-Saclay, Prime Minister Jean-Marc Ayrault (2013) confirmed the continuation of the state's exceptional support for the cluster, describing the development of Saclay as an "exemplary illustration" and "source of inspiration" for the new French model of territorial development.

Both the CDT and the broader *schema de développement territorial* (SDT, which defines the strategy and orientation for projects within a given pole) plans for regeneration prioritize the linking of knowledge and industrial economies. The CDT includes, for example, the creation of the Université Paris-Saclay campus (featuring some twenty-two research organizations linked to private initiatives), a scientific excellence pole at Moulon, intensification of the area surrounding the École Polytechnique in Palaiseau, an incubator for hotel enterprises, as well as improvements of local infrastructure and the creation of parks and green space. The CDT estimates the creation of approximately five thousand new residential accommodations each year (including student, family, and individual models and social housing), as well as 25,000 new jobs by 2030 (Prefecture de la Région d'Île-de-France 2013).[18] The plans also place a priority on startups and cultural facilities. Specific development priorities include the Mov'éo business cluster, the construction of a velodrome in Saint-Quentin-en-Yvelines, and renovation of the National Golf Course in Guyancourt in anticipation of the Ryder Cup in 2018 (EPPS 2012).

Clustering activity in Saclay rests on the ability of firms to connect with one another and with the other functionally differentiated hubs around the Paris region. Thus transportation improvements are crucial. To ensure accessibility and reduce transport congestion, there are planned renovations of the RER B, local bus lines, and highways. In addition, line 18 of the GPE is set to be the "backbone feeding and connecting Paris-Saclay" (EPPS 2014). The GPE has eleven future stations planned for the Saclay Plateau, with three occurring in the CDT-defined territory (at Saclay-CEA, Orsay Gif, and Palaiseau). Mobility here is formative of and necessary for the proposed territory and its capacities for growth (Prefecture de la Région d'Île de France 2013).

Certainly the CDT promotes mixed-use development around the GPE and integration of the territory into global circuits and facilitates the movement of people, ideas, and goods into and out of the region. But this cohering activity of the transit network scarcely ensures a socially and ecologically grounded urbanization strategy. For one thing, the production of new networked spaces is predicated on the destruction of Saclay's existing agricultural and rural ecosystems. Critics have pointed out that even though the metro line through the territory will be raised and not underground so as to minimally affect the agricultural territory, the environmental consequences of the intense growth are dire (COSTIF 2014).

In addition, while the CDT promotes growth for a privileged class of technological and knowledge workers, it largely ignores surrounding communities. Although there are provisions for new housing around stations, this is largely to accommodate an affluent population of executives, researchers, and students. Despite the optimistic job projections, employment is extremely polarized and concentrated in high-end sectors. The

International Workshop of Grand Paris (AIGP 2013a), while not outright critical of the plan, nevertheless also identifies the need to focus on particular areas of improvement ("points of vigilance"), including improved integration with the surrounding territories and adjusted goals for affordable and mixed-use housing.

Silicon Valley is one of the world's leading centers of innovation, driving global knowledge and high-tech economies. But it is also a lifeless, abstract space of sprawling suburbs, environmental degradation, economic inequality, and intense racial and class segregation. These latter aspects are ignored when cities look to it as a model. The grand urbanism of transit-based territorial reform of Saclay prioritizes international influence over local balance and promotes a polarized and polarizing growth. Saclay is not Palo Alto, but the networked growth it aims for based on the concentration of high-tech industries creates contradictions that suggest that similar problems to those of its American counterpart may be on the horizon.

Urbanizing Val-de-France/Gonesse/Bonneuil-en-France

In contrast to the upgrading of the existing cluster of Saclay, the Val-de-France/Gonesse/Bonneuil pole is premised on repurposing an underachieving urban space that is yet to be developed to its limits, and therefore is ripe for change.[19] The Gonesse Triangle refers to a piece of "underdeveloped" agricultural and post-industrial territory northeast of Paris in the department of Val d'Oise. Line 17 of the GPE is meant to solidify the objective of transforming Gonesse into an economic engine and to enable the entry of Val d'Oise into Grand Paris (Prefecture de la Région d'Île-de-France 2014). Through inclusion in the public transit network, the Gonesse Triangle is slated to become a center of business, leisure, and commerce and a key site within the Bourget and Charles de Gaulle airport complexes.

The CDT for Val-de-France/Gonesse/Bonneuil-en-France was signed on February 27, 2014. It develops one part of the larger Grand Roissy cluster centered on growth in infrastructure and the transportation field.[20] The CDT spans six municipalities in the Val d'Oise department, Gonesse, Garles-lès-Gonesse, Sarcelles, Arnouville and Villier-le-Bel, and Bonneuil-en-France, an area home to close to 166,000 inhabitants. While not as strongly branded as the research hub of Saclay, the CDT outlines four major sectors that will meet the corporate needs of the two nearby international airports and lead local urban regeneration efforts: leisure, airport and aerospace, health care, and culture (Prefecture de la Région d'Île-de-France 2014).

In particular, urban regeneration is centered on three main strategic sites: the Gonesse Triangle, featuring Europa City (including commercial, entertainment, and cultural venues); a hub around the Garges-Sarcelles transit station featuring the Dôme Arena (a Formula One racetrack and multifunctional stadium); and a mixed-function development of the Avenue de Parisis (mainly retail and housing improvements). The clustering strategy aims to produce 30,000 new jobs by 2025, to build 14,000 residential units over the next twenty years, and to increase the population of the area by 5,000 new residents, all while upgrading the area and preserving natural spaces (Prefecture de la Région d'Île de France 2014).

Development of the Europa City site is the most important facet of the growth pole, ensuring that the area in question meets its full economic potential. Europa City is a proposed megamall and entertainment villa designed as a signature "gateway to Paris." The French retailer Auchan has outlined plans for a vast €1.7 billion retail, cultural, and entertainment complex, aimed primarily at tourists, to be built on an eighty-hectare site. The complex is set to include five hundred shops, a dozen hotels, numerous high-end restaurants, a lavish exhibition hall, and a convention center, as well as an indoor ski slope, a waterpark, an amusement park, and a circus. An estimated 30 million visitors a year (twice as many as visit Euro Disney) are expected to partake of this "multidimensional experience" of leisure and consumption (Auchan 2014). Situated around the future site of a line 17 GPE station, and thus accessible by regional and international travelers, Europa City calls itself a *"Glo/cal* boasting an optimal situation directly accessible by transports."[21] Sarkozy (2010) celebrated the urbanism at Europa City as "commercial urbanism with a human face" that would define the contours of the new Grand Paris.

Privileging investors, tourists, and consumers over inhabitants of the area, the initiative demonstrates how the transit system is a vector of spectacular territorial commodification and general regional gentrification. Indeed, based on the provisional plans for Europa City, surrounding property throughout Gonesse is already subject to development pressures. Property markets are taking off, with buyers and sellers both flooding the area, hoping to make a profit from speculative revalorization processes.

Figure 4.2
The future site of Europa City. With a megaproject on the horizon, much of the surrounding area in La Gonesse is for sale.

Europa City has come to symbolize outlandish luxury and has brought to light the immense divides between the existing community and the imagined elite spaces of Grand Paris. Unlike other local plans, many of which have managed to pass their pro-growth agendas without controversy, the hyperbolic nature of this development has prompted a growing and militant resistance from groups in the vicinity. The Collective for the Gonesse Triangle (CPTG) was formed in March 2011 following the announcement of Europa City. Today it consists of eighteen associations in Val d'Oise and Seine-Saint-Denis (including IDFE, as well as Val d'Oise Friends of the Earth and Environment 93). The CPTG (2013) claims that the current plan "has nothing that can qualify as 'territorial development' ... opportunities relevant for the attractiveness of Île-de-France, but certainly not the development of territory for the benefit of inhabitants of Val-de-France and Gonesse." The AIGP (2013b) reiterates this concern and claims that for development of the area to be effective, the residents of Roissy themselves must be the ones to profit from new activity. If there is to be growth (as local municipalities themselves desire), it should be accompanied by qualitative improvements to quality of life and a thorough redistribution of surplus to inhabitants. Many far left local officials, for example, want the CDTs to be used to address inequalities first and to redirect benefits of transit-induced growth into ambitious social programs, particularly housing.

Development driven by the Europa City project may benefit Auchan and the multinational developers, retail giants, hotel chains, and entertainment corporations investing in the La Gonesse site, but it is unlikely to meet the needs of local residents. While inhabitants are desperate for jobs, mobility options, and improved living standards, the growth plan is out of step with the skills, patterns of movement, and residential preferences of those in the area. This has led the CPTG to frame its opposition explicitly around collective consumption concerns, rejecting the logic of *"projets inutiles et imposés"* (useless and imposed projects). The CPTG (2012a 2012b) also opposes the uselessness of the Europa City project because it will contribute to urban sprawl, destroy vital agricultural territories, provide little noncommodified cultural value, and, based on misleading estimates of visitors and jobs, may result in expensive local bailouts.

The Val-de-France cluster is perhaps the most egregious example of gentrification founded on undemocratic planning and symbolizes the high social cost of becoming incorporated into the Grand Paris global city network. The GPE network here enables exchange, production, and profit distribution, but to the benefit of capital, not the social reproduction needs of users and inhabitants. The physical connections of the GPE network are poised to link the Val-de-France territory to elite global city spaces worldwide through the Charles de Gaulle Airport, and speculative growth in the vicinity of new stations will trigger flows of investment and an increase in exchange value, but these glocal transformations offer little use value to the community.

Metropolis Derailed

In October 2013 the architect Michel Cantal-Dupart, who took part in the Grand Pari(s) consultation, issued an open letter to President François Hollande. In it he repudiated the limited and deleterious (even violent) way

The Mobilizing Myths of the Grand Paris Express

Grand Paris was being implemented. He criticized the reduction of the vision for the Grand Paris plan to the GPE at the expense of concerns about solidarity and integration, and he described the economic focus of local developments as "an assault on residents." Not only had Grand Paris ignored inhabitants' concerns, he claimed, but the cluster-led local CDT developments also ignored the guiding principles of just urban planning (Cantal-Dupart 2013). The local scale of the development plans, he wrote, had not achieved more "human" outcomes"; rather, the "small projects have killed the grand intentions" of the metropolis.

Cantal-Dupart's criticisms amplify other concerns about TOD clustering and the social costs of the networked metropolis to which they contribute. In the Saclay Plateau and the Gonesse Triangle, the privatized densification and diversification on which GPE is based creates a contradiction: it risks further peripheralizing marginal populations, thus reducing access to the city and mobility, and it precludes if not outright defies the goals of territorial balance and regional equity (equalization of territory merely amounts to the suburban land markets being equally unblocked). There is a fundamental incompatibility in the plans for the GPE between the economic goals of land valorization around new stations (resulting in gentrification and growth) and the social goals of accessibility (including affordable housing and service provision for low-income populations) that is ignored in commonsense narratives of both local and national perspectives. Thus, weaving new territories into the metro network replicates the conditions of the urban (and suburban) crises it purports to address.

Indeed, the two cases display a host of negative consequences of mobility networks geared toward competition based on land rent valorization: the use of spectacular projects that do not meet the needs of residents, the destruction of scarce resources, the segregation of space caused by polar growth strategies, land speculation, the gentrification of the *banlieue*, and the denial of the powers of local authorities to genuinely pursue alternatives (COSTIF 2014). These are repeated across other Grand Paris sites, and more progressive localities have not completely avoided these traps. While the development of innovation poles has been variable thus far, and there is evidence of their potential for progressive local government reforms (Gallez 2014), it is still doubtful whether this interstitial resistance can subvert the dominant mission to realize the global city vision of metromobility.

The mobilizing myths of the GPE are absolutely central to the new metropolis of Grand Paris. They yoke regional mobility concerns inextricably to market values and real estate speculation. With an emphasis on strategic sites for renewal, territorial polarity is no longer an externality or unforeseen consequence of planning strategies but is the very pillar of urbanization and urban transformation. Intensification of these zones promises compact development, but greater density comes at the cost of privatization and sprawl. Even though there is a real priority placed on mass transportation, it is not clear that resources are being effectively marshaled for the benefit of Parisians.[22]

As a result of these tendencies, the proposed network may also fracture or "splinter" (Graham and Marvin 2001) urban space, further segregating territories into those with a GPE station and those without, and populations into those who can capitalize on mobile resources and those who cannot. Insofar as the GPE acts as an anchor for increasingly mobile global investment, it is a prime example of the "gleaming new glocal infrastructural fixes of contemporary capitalism" (Graham and Marvin 2001, 418). The polycentric clustering strategy of urban development provides an immediate solution to political and economic problems, but it shifts costs to other times and places. It also supports a fundamental practice of transferring public funding to the private sector and to high-productivity economic activities through the built environment based on socialization of costs and privatization of benefits.

The GPE is both a reaction to and a vehicle of uneven development. While it purports to create territorial balance and equality by reconstituting vectors of mobility and access and reconfiguring where value lies in the Île-de-France region, it has elements that cannot but cement and entrench the given unequal spatial order. The GPE will create a new map of the Paris metropolis, and while *banlieues* as they currently are imagined may be supplanted by silicon landscapes of business zones and research hubs, the winners and losers of global city development will remain.

III Governing the Competitive City

5   A Thousand Layers of Governance

The Metropolis, which is already a reality in the daily world, should now be a part of the law and legal framework.
—Mairie de Paris, 2012

Modern city government is increasingly like an empty shell whose territory marks out the once-meaningful boundaries of the political.
—Engin Isin, 1998

The 2009 Grand Pari(s) architectural exhibition and the 2011 agreement on the Grand Paris Express (GPE) established the imaginary and physical conditions for metropolitan social and spatial arrangements. In symbolic and material ways Paris is functionally integrated with its *banlieue,* and there is now widespread recognition of the existence of a novel urban agglomeration. Yet neither the construction of a polycentric urban identity nor the creation of a transit-connected region has pointed toward a single scenario for how the metropolis should be managed and governed. The political space of the metropolis lags behind its speculative and technical correlates such that the experiential reality of Paris is "out of step with its political and administrative reality" (Sarkozy 2010, 43). To complete the transformation from a monocentric city to a multipolar urban region, Paris requires the construction of new governance arrangements and related transformations in urban authority, legitimacy, management, decision making, citizenship, and democratic life.

In Paris as in other large cities around the world, the unsettled borders of the globally networked metropolis call into question the territorial foundation of administration. In such a situation it is a challenge for local, regional, and national actors to construct political communities and institutions adequate to the complex geographies of contemporary urban life and responsive to the practical challenges that they pose. The program of a conference run jointly by the City of Paris and Paris Métropole describes some of the difficulties of governing today:

> Whether states or cities, the territorial base is constitutive of contemporary governments. This power structure is deeply upset by the arrival of powerful logics of mobility and by increasing entanglements at different scales (and legitimacies) in the resolution of localized problems. This is especially the case for the world's major cities. Their perimeters are increasingly undecided, their contents and residents are moving, they are part of territorial and actor systems with highly variable temporalities and scales. Institutions and systems involved in recent decades have questioned their ability to project themselves into the new system: should we invent new ways of coordinating institutions or must we invent new institutions? (Mairie de Paris 2011)

The contemporary upheavals of Paris's governance system rest on two interlinked processes: (1) the globalization of the regional economy and the associated integration of local governments with private markets and actors, and (2) the decentralization of the French state, resulting in a proliferation of institutional authorities. The networked metropolitan polity, however, is not achieved through a straightforward reorientation in state administration from welfare concerns to market entrepreneurialism or through a linear shift from centralized dirigisme to local autonomy. Rather, the metropolis is being fabricated through complex institutional reworkings. Conflicts among a wide range of individuals, associations, and coalitions (each with its own organizations, interests, and ideologies) form the generative tensions that are shaping new political structures. Grand Paris is neither a functional submission to global neoliberal imperatives nor a purely domestic power struggle; rather, the Parisian metropolis is being forged through localized actions situated within a rapidly changing global urban environment.

Metropolitanization is thus not an organic and inevitable calibration to globalization but is an ongoing political dynamic that takes a particular form in the twenty-first century.[1] The making of the Parisian urban region entails the creation of an imagined community, a set of social relations and regulations, an economic market, a bundle of public policies, and an institutional framework that operates in and through a particular scalar arrangement.[2] This is forged through often deep-seated struggles between classes, territorial factions, political coalitions, and governmental agencies. To

A Thousand Layers of Governance

address the overall question of the meaning of twenty-first-century Paris and how it is being built, it is essential to recognize these lines of conflict. Together they shape the emergence of the political metropolis as an object of analysis and deliberation and the instruments, rules, norms, organizations, and procedures through which it is being governed.[3]

Building on the analyses of previous chapters, this chapter turns more directly to the making of Grand Paris as a properly *political* project and to the juridical and administrative supports on which it is being founded. Starting from a nascent metropolitan fact, it traces a genealogy of metropolitan governance to more fully understand the constellations of power and authority that define the region today. It provides a critical analysis of how grand urbanism works "on the ground" by tracing the shifts in institutional landscapes and authority relationships in the greater Paris region leading up to the construction of the new metropolitan government, the Métropole du Grand Paris, in 2014. With a focus on enduring historical rationalities of the state and new techniques of metropolitanization, it seeks to answer the question, through what mechanisms and processes are the political institutions of Grand Paris being built?

The Challenges of Metropolitan Governance

It is clear today that globalization has radically changed the territorial and political composition of large cities. Globalization and the rise of supranational institutions, especially the EU, have undermined the presumed sovereignty of the nation-state form and have reduced the scope of centralized power. The denationalization of the economy has also undercut state management of industry. This has engendered a reorganization of global authority into select cities and has exposed cities to the shocks of international capital and to heightened territorial competition. Over the past forty years cities around the world have been subjects of profound restructuring. In many important ways, the metropolitanization of Paris is not unique but is emblematic of changes that have been occurring in large cities everywhere in this context.

The pressures from a deregulated global system, the expansion of urban areas, and the intensification of cross-border interdependencies have led to large globally networked urban ensembles. In these urban regions there is increasingly a divide between administrative and jurisdictional borders and other kinds of functional organizations. That is, the political boundaries of urban regions rarely align with "urbanized" settlements, and even less so with economic relationships, labor and commodity markets, residential units, collective identities, infrastructure networks, private and public service catchments, or natural ecosystems. Moreover, with increased mobility in all areas of life and with residents and stakeholders increasingly defined by their multiple and overlapping relationships to places, what constitutes a political community as such is in a constant state of flux. The territorial base of contemporary local governments has thus been overturned; authority itself is multiple, complex, and difficult to pin down; and local officials are unable to autonomously control the spaces over which they preside.

As a result of intensified connectivity in different realms, interdependencies and externalities (both negative and positive) between administrative units pose problems for public service delivery and spatial and economic planning. For Michael Storper (2014), the permanent divide between functional and administrative territories results in a "principal-actor mismatch" whereby responsible institutions are misaligned with the problems they must solve. As a result, in large metropolises there is a continual cycle in which new agencies are created, only to quickly become ill adapted to the changing realities they must address. The case of transit here is particularly revealing. "A larger urban area will, for example, generate a natural need for a more extensive transport system. But the preexisting boundaries for transit operators and financing more services tend to trap the principals behind the agents whose boundaries are no longer the right ones to serve new needs as they arise" (Storper 2014, 120). The conflicts over the GPE (and the battles between the state and region and between the RATP, STIF, and SGP over its operation) are exemplary of this dilemma. Moreover, insofar as different policy sectors and planning endeavors will inevitably have their own particular geographic terms, it is nearly impossible to coordinate all of the service delivery, infrastructure, and policy making on the metropolitan scale within a single fixed territorial unit.

Widespread processes of decentralization have exacerbated these problems in many countries, leading to a fragmentation of power, policy failures, and inveterate intergovernmental disputes. The political, economic, and social causes of decentralization are variable, but over the past few decades states across Europe have almost invariably reduced the direct national management of urban issues and devolved or downloaded responsibility for welfare and economic development functions to local levels of government. Local collectivities (be they communes, districts, municipios, or any other of the many designations for local government around the world) are on the front lines of welfare state restructuring, but in many cases the emerging roles for these governments (and the urban agglomerations they comprise) are at odds with the constitutional and legal spaces in which they are expected to operate. With increased responsibilities but diminished capacities and resources, large cities frequently lack the key political instruments to control their foundations. As Jon Pierre (2011, 23) has written, "One of the main challenges to urban governance rests in the circumstances that the levers controlled by cities are far inferior to the forces that threaten social cohesion and the long-term prosperity of the city."

Decentralization and devolution not only multiply the formal institutions operating at the metropolitan level, they also necessitate the inclusion of nonstate actors in the management of urban and regional affairs (see Stone 1989, 2005). The shift from municipal government to metropolitan governance traces the widening realm of influential actors and the extension of political authorities "beyond the state." To meet the needs of growing urban populations, accomplish basic operations, and pursue more active economic development, multiple levels of government have normalized the practices of seeking resources (e.g., funding, expertise) from the private marketplace. In large cities where these dynamics are most pronounced, the blending of resources with corporate and civil society actors in order to undertake urban capital projects and to provide quotidian urban services is now the status quo.[4] Indeed, the metropolis or the "urban region" is the presumed natural scale for these new growth regimes (Brenner 2003; Krätke 1999).

A further consequence of decentralization and its thickening web of subnational institutions is increasing confusion as to the roles of various actors in urban affairs. While the devolution of power means that the viability of cities is now dependent on new forms of inter-administrative cooperation and public-private partnerships, the fragmentation of authority also causes conflict. Vertically, this has resulted in problems of multilevel governance over jurisdictional authority, administrative competency, fiscal responsibility, and political legitimacy. Horizontally, it has led to cross-border competition between localities for power and resources and between public and private coalitions over accountability, risk bearing, and the distribution of surplus. The global city region and its unwieldy tangle of flexible institutions have thus generated many new issues of governability (Jouve and Lefèvre 2002; Kantor et al. 2012; Le Galès and Vitale 2013).

The micropolitical aspects of managing this bewildering array of actors and institutions should not be overshadowed by more functional analyses of the emergence of new social and economic configurations. The metropolitan scale may indeed be a spatial fix to the economic transformations of the global economy, but it is by no means guaranteed that this political scale can be taken for granted (Lefèvre 2010). Without attention to the political dynamics ordering urban life in the twenty-first century and the transformed conditions of the boundaries and functions of state assemblages, we are left with a truncated version of how global city regions arise and the consequences of this political ordering. Of particular interest to unpacking the workings of grand urbanism today is identifying the mediating role of governments and political institutions in not merely coping with change but actively instituting change within these "struggling giants" of global city regions (Kantor et al. 2012).

The making of Grand Paris concerns the creation of the metropolis, that is, the way in which contemporary processes of globalization take place and become embedded in territorial and spatial arrangements. A grounded critical analysis of this process demonstrates, however, that this formation is not merely the top-down response to transformations in firm networks and financial flows (i.e., the formation of Sassen's global city) but is equally about local projects of reform. Considering the creation of the Parisian metropolis thus calls attention not only to the importance of the urban regional scale worldwide but also to the idiosyncratic rescaling of the state, understood as an ongoing localized engagement with general globalizing trends.

The matrix of political relations that constitutes the Paris metropolitan region is notoriously complex, and the administrative landscape of the Île-de-France is infamous for its multitudinous, competing, and overlapping governmental and nongovernmental structures that collectively organize and manage the region.[5] Described colloquially as a *"mille-feuille,"* a pastry consisting of a "thousand layers" of dough, governance in the capital region of France is complicated, impenetrable, unstable, and fragile. This configuration has been criticized for impeding policy formation and implementation and making the functions of regional governance—the organization of production, the provision of social services, the regulation of activity—inefficient, ineffective, and undemocratic, not to mention difficult to analyze.

According to local officials, "the urban area of Paris is faced with all the challenges of a twenty-first-century metropolis, but like the majority of worldwide metropolises, still has to cope with the tools of the twentieth-century government and with the administrative limits of the nineteenth century" (Mairie de Paris 2013).[6] The region suffers from what Mancur Olson (1982) described as "institutional sclerosis," a situation in which the institutions of governing have not kept pace with the organizational patterns of contemporary metropolitan life. Indeed, political commentators on all sides of the political spectrum have criticized the extant arrangements for deepening the social and economic problems that plague the region and have suggested that breaking down these institutional obstacles is necessary to bring Paris fully into the twenty-first century.[7]

In line with the diagnosis of the Grand Pari(s) architects that the regional configuration of the French state is vertiginous, confusing, inefficient, counterproductive, asymmetrical, and undemocratic, one of the driving forces of Grand Paris as a state-sponsored plan is to agglomerate the city politically and to streamline governance of the more than twelve hundred communes, as well as the seven departments and dozens of intercommunal establishments that make up the institutional landscape of the Île-de-France region. This national vision is matched by local initiatives of reform founded on the idea that pressing policy issues—especially unemployment, lack of housing, social marginalization, congestion, and environmental sustainability—require integrated and collaborative metropolitan-wide administrative solutions.

Paris is an exception among large French cities that otherwise have metropolitan authorities, and is also unique among its competitor global cities in Europe that have metropolitan structures. London, for example, has had almost continuously since 1963 an areawide Greater London authority with power over select regional issues and functions. The political metropolis, as an entity with strong legitimacy, autonomy from other levels of government, wide-ranging jurisdiction, and appropriate territorial borders (Lefèvre 1998), is not yet present in Paris. In his cross-national study of metropolitan governance, Christian Lefèvre (2004) suggests in particular that strategic political action and public accession are necessary to combat this lack of institutional capacity and recommends a more concerted "metropolitan plan" to intentionally address the fragmentation of urban governance and the ossified context of policy making.

The consolidated power structures of Paris are difficult to change, and collective-action problems have plagued institution reform, but in the last fifteen years there has been a series of movements to restructure the boundaries of administrative territories, to streamline services such as police across the region, to implement interlocal regulatory policies (especially with respect to the environment), and to promote formal and informal collaborations, with the goal of metropolitanization.

Although a farsighted institution at the metropolitan scale is a widely shared desire of diverse actors within the Île-de-France—indeed, "the metropolis" has taken on new life as a metanarrative of urbanization in Paris today—there remain significant conflicts over what form that institution should take, who should make up its ranks, and what the scope of its mandate should be. The state, the region, and intercommunal authorities such as Paris Métropole each have quite distinct interests in metropolitanization. Officials from Paris, the *grand couronne*, and the provinces each have a unique stake in transformation, as do *franciliens* with different political affiliations. As with the previous debates over envisioning and transport, the deliberations around governance reveal divergent urban meanings and are an important terrain where the future of Grand Paris is being decided.

The Multidimensionality of Metropolitanization

The debates over the Parisian metropolis are telling expressions of how France is adapting to globalization. The rise of the Grand Paris metropolis is an essential feature of broader changes in the meaning and function of the state form in the twenty-first century. The framework of "state rescaling" effectively describes the deconcentration of national capacities and responsibilities and the changing territoriality of the post-Fordist French state (see especially Brenner 2003, 2004). Brenner's (2004) claim, for

A Thousand Layers of Governance

example, that the construction of a regional governance arrangement with competitive and pro-growth policies is a key strategy undertaken by national and local elites in response to global capitalist crises is extremely helpful for situating the making of Grand Paris. Beyond the dichotomy of decentralization and centralization, the notion of rescaling also emphasizes the multiform and often incoherent ways in which the state divides and spatializes its functions in a nonbinary manner. Furthermore, it escapes an economistic reading of globalization by maintaining a focus on the nation-state as a powerful actor within the formation of a new regionalism.[8]

However, the struggles over the existing Parisian metropolis defy the linearity of this process and refute the claim that authority will necessarily devolve to the municipal scale as cities gain more importance in global economic circuits. Some even argue that local political struggles in France have been effective counterweights to these political-economic imperatives (Pinson and Le Galès 2005). Drawing on the notion of rescaling, but with a greater emphasis on situated conflicts over greater Paris, this section traces key lines of force defining metropolitan governance. There are four main axes along which the transformations are currently taking place: central and territorial authorities, Paris and the provinces, Paris and its *banlieue*, and left-right ideologies. Each of these represents a key terrain of conflict, cooperation, and negotiation over the shape of the metropolis and its techniques of authority. These are the main axes giving form to the global city polity.

Central and Territorial Authorities

The first dimension of metropolitan transformation concerns the political tension within French republicanism between a unitary and universal authority and more disparate and diverse territorial arrangements. Debates between Jacobinism (a system founded on a highly ordered and powerful central command) and Girondism (in which power is decentralized into diffuse factions) have existed since the time of the Revolution. France is known for prioritizing the former, but is equally defined by the latter. The nineteenth-century work of statecraft—creating a new unified public space around the ideals of Frenchness and strengthening the sovereign power of military and civilian infrastructures—centralized power in the national government, but did so incompletely (Keating 2003; Tilly

1975). This legacy has been inherited by successive regimes. Under the Fifth Republic the central government has retained a prominent role in organizing national affairs, coordinating everything from universal educational curricula, to nativist cultural policy, to territorial and industrial production. There have, however, also been significant devolutions of authority to subnational levels of government that have threatened the centralization of national power.

The general conflict between central and territorial authorities in France takes on a special character in Paris, where the state has always sought to maintain exceptional mastery. Paris is the seat of centralized authority, but it is also a site where this authority is most contested. Indeed, Paris's independent power and revolutionary zeal have long destabilized the centralizing power of the state. Not only do territorial elites concentrate in Paris, but at the level of civil society, from 1779 to 1968 to 2005, Paris has been a hotbed of popular revolt against centralized power.

Since the late 1970s, decentralization across France has created numerous levels of governmental authorities that divide functions and share responsibilities, such that the central state can no longer exert unilateral influence over policy. While this situation requires new forms of cooperation between governmental authorities, it also engenders redundancy, institutional disagreement, and complexification (Nicholls 2005). The current state-regional debate over Grand Paris's mass transit system is but one example of the difficulties of policy provision in this climate of competing priorities. In fact, in many sectors, from health care and education to welfare, policing, and basic infrastructural services (e.g., water, sewage), there are ongoing vertical and horizontal conflicts over who is responsible for issues, how power should be shared, and how the costs and benefits of policies should be distributed. Territorial alliances and political coalitions at the subnational level compete with each other and with the central state for authority.

On the one hand, the French republic rests on a statist regime, which continues to forestall the deepening of any uniquely urban power (Pinson 2010). On the other hand, the opening up of state space to new territorial actors suggests a potentially new form of political ordering. "When looking at the French local and regional system," write Pinson and Le Galès (2005, 9), "one should never underestimate the weight of local politicians vis-à-vis the central State and the importance of political competition within

A Thousand Layers of Governance

dynamics of institutional change."[9] Depending on its structure, the creation of a powerful global metropolis can strengthen the central authority of the state or it can counter state authority with localized municipal autonomy.

Establishing who has the right to organize metropolitan space is one of the most fundamental questions in French politics today. The conflicting agendas, for example, of Delanoë, Huchon, and Blanc are not merely the result of divergent opinions among technical urban experts but reflect the opposed interests of different parts of the state apparatus. The recomposition of the internal architecture of the state is thus a matter of "local geopolitics" (Subra 2012) in which rival powers oppose one another for the control of territory and the ability to define the borders of the global city metropolis. This geopolitical character is a highly pertinent aspect of the metropolitan debates.

Paris and the Provinces

Decentralization and the conflicts between central and territorial authorities are compounded by the second axis of governance reform, the asymmetries between Paris and the French provinces as a result of the preeminence of the capital region. What is known locally as the national "macrocephaly" refers to Paris's exceptional weight with respect to population, economic productivity, infrastructure, and political control in relation to the rest of the country. This swollen-headed condition results in two main contradictory depictions: Paris as national flagship and Paris as a drain on national resources.

The former, exemplified in the idea of Paris as the face of France (Blanc 2010; Burgel 1999; Leroy 2010), is the belief that the Paris is the bellwether of national success (or failure) and that the city should be prioritized in any national growth agenda. Based on the idea that the concentration of wealth and population makes the nation dependent on the success of its capital city, those who value macrocephaly claim that the central state has a special interest in the territories of the Île-de-France and in its social and economic functions. As a result, Paris is and should be subject to more state involvement and more targeted measures than other parts of the country. While typically a national narrative, this is also the mantra of local elites, for whom the grandeur of Paris is justification for exceptional resource and investment demands.

The latter depiction is best expressed through Jean-François Gravier's (1947) famous thesis of "Paris and the French desert." Gravier denounces the extreme concentration of political and economic activity within the Paris region and condemns the capital's monopoly of national resources as pathological. Rather than invigorating the provinces, Paris's magnitude causes it to behave like a tentacled monster that devours national patrimony (Gravier 1947, 111). According to this perspective, which largely guided Keynesian distributive policies, the growth of Paris needs to be limited and territorial investment widespread to ensure a balanced national planning. This theme is particularly relevant for other large cities in France (e.g., Marseilles, Lyon, Toulouse) that are also struggling to adapt to global conditions.

In many ways it is clear that decentralization has not upset France's priority on the Île-de-France (until 1977, for example, there was no elected mayor of Paris but a nationally appointed prefect who administered municipal affairs). Against the constitutional principle of nonhierarchization among local collectivities, Paris clearly has more clout and receives more national attention in terms of investment than other communes and departments on the same formal footing. External elites still resent the special treatment of the capital, but it is unclear whether or not Gravier's paradigm applies today (Gilli 2014). Local representatives of all political stripes claim the opposite, that the state has not adequately prioritized the Île-de-France and that in order for the metropolitan region to flourish, more targeted investments are needed.

Urban-Suburban Divides
The third axis of institutional reform concerns the overdetermined relationship between Paris and its suburbs. Metropolitanization is above all about the "suburbanization of urban politics" and the establishment of a regionalist view of municipal operations (Keil 2000, 777; see also Ekers, Hamel, and Keil 2012). Through the GPE, Grand Paris is poised to capitalize on the territory around Paris and radically alter its built environment, but it has yet to consolidate the greater urban region politically.

Because of the history of regional centralization, it is difficult today to achieve a shared agenda between the city of Paris and the surrounding suburbs. Mistrust and ignorance on both sides are legacies of the asymmetrical history, and conflicts persist over where to locate developments, who should pay for the externalities of growth, and who should decide on regional priorities. Officials in the city of Paris are hesitant to relinquish their long-held power in metropolitan power structures, while suburban representatives are skeptical of regional relations repeating historical patterns of annexation and exploitation.

One of the central developments driving the political processes of metropolitanization is a shift in the balance of power toward the periphery. Over the past decade there has been a "revenge of the suburbs" (Gilli and Gonguet 2015), bolstered by changes in the demographic and economic influence of the *banlieue*. This revenge is not so much an active attack on the center by suburban forces as the suburbs' refusal to submit to the will of Paris and the assertion of a uniquely suburban power bloc. While obstacles to metropolitan government remain, and interterritorial disputes between Paris and its suburbs or between the suburbs themselves (especially the *petit* and *grand couronne*) are not likely to be resolved in the near future, metropolitanization has seen a more concerted effort by local officials to organize and cooperate across boundaries and to transcend parochial concerns in pursuit of common goals and projects.

Partisan Ideologies

The final dimension in the ongoing process of building metropolitan Paris is that of political and ideological cleavages. Cutting across all of the aforementioned dynamics is the conflict between right and left forces, exemplified today in partisan divides between the leading political parties in France, especially the Union for a Popular Movement (UMP, renamed Les Républicains in May 2015) and the Socialist Party. If the *trente glorieuses* functioned on a consensual opposition between Gaullists and communists to realize a national mutation that was both economic and urbane, today a similar compromise is at work in the creation of a competitive and sustainable global city.

Local elites at the municipal, departmental, and regional levels are divided by left-right affiliations. The city of Paris has traditionally been a stronghold of the right surrounded by the red belt of the *petit couronne*, but the 2001 mayoral victory of Delanoë marked a watershed leftward shift in the city at both the local and national levels. The regional council also reflected this change, with a (weak) left alliance in power since 1998.[10] The path to Grand Paris and the making of the metropolis have occurred in this highly politicized atmosphere. The political divides between the left and right have hindered metropolitan reform and restructuring. Among local officials, divergent visions of the goals of metropolitan life and growth have prevented, for example, a clear agreement on entrepreneurial spatial policies, on the one hand, and fiscal redistribution to address social, environmental, and economic disparities on the other. This partisan impasse was amplified under Sarkozy when conservative state-led urban policies conflicted with the center-left plans of Huchon and the Regional Council.

While ideological cleavages are an impediment to institutional reform, there is new momentum for compromise. Factions of the left and right seem to favor the construction of a metropolitan government and metropolitan policies, though each faction has its own reservations. The conservative government under Fillon and Sarkozy, for example, desired a Greater Paris authority that would fulfill its national ambitions but was simultaneously hostile to the emergence of rival institutions at the grassroots level that might rival state power or organize metropolitan development around progressive or working-class interests.[11] Obversely, the originally left-leaning Paris Métropole was absolutely vital in instigating metropolitan reforms yet balked at the uptake of metropolitan discourses by Sarkozy in 2008. The metropolis currently rests on an uneasy coalition between these conservative and socialist aspirations. At the same time, however, the collapse of the far left nationally and the rise of other parties, such as the National Front and the Green Party, complicate these partisan relations and have the potential to recast the traditional ideological groundwork for or against the construction of metropolitan institutions.

The Metropolitics of Grand Paris

The *mille-feuille* of governance that defines metropolitan Paris today is a product of all four of these constitutive tensions. Together these dynamics combine in a process of "unregulated competitive decentralization" (Kantor et al. 2012, 171) the outcome of which is a fragmented political landscape where neither the state nor local actors have sufficient capacity or legitimacy to govern unitarily. A brief sketch of recent changes in this fragmented landscape will clarify the conditions of possibility for the

Table 5.1
Major Forces of Metropolitan Transformation

	General Metropolitan Aspirations	Examples of Changing Relational Dynamics in the Process of Metropolitanization
Central and territorial authorities	• The central state desires the metropolis as a national asset, primarily for economic development. • Local authorities seek pragmatic solutions to ongoing policy challenges at the metropolitan scale.	• Modern dirigisme declines with global pressures from the 1970s on. • Acts I (1982) and II (early 2000s) of decentralization devolve power and responsibility to territories. • Decentralization is partially countered by "steering from a distance." • Intergovernmental partnerships and intermunicipal associations proliferate in the 1990s. • The Île-de-France takes control over regional planning in 2005. • The 2010 Grand Paris Act reasserts central power over affairs in greater Paris and puts in place new top-down institutions to guide metropolitan restructuring (e.g., the SGP, Ministry of Development for the Capital Region).
Paris and the provinces	• Greater Paris seeks special metropolitan status to strengthen its development capacities and to attract priority investments. • The provinces prefer a national landscape of metropolises to enable more balanced growth.	• Of the twenty or so priority urban developments designated as Operations of National Interest (OINs), almost half are located in the Île-de-France. • The Balladur Report (2009) calls for eleven metropolitan regions across France. • The Grand Paris Act (2010) names the Parisian metropolis as the flagship territory of national development.
Paris and its *banlieue*	• Recognizing the growing power of the suburbs, Paris seeks metropolitan cooperation to prevent its irrelevance. • A polycentric metropolitan arrangement is attractive for collectivities in Greater Paris because of its potential to enhance the power of the suburbs with respect to the central city.	• Led by Bertrand Delanoë, Paris begins a process of reparation and collaboration with suburban municipalities. • Paris Métropole forms in 2009 as a voluntary joint authority to address inter-territorial concerns in greater Paris.
Left and right ideologies	• Leftist politicians and residents desire a metropolitan structure that can address social inequalities and territorial disparities at a grand scale. • Right-wing factions seek a viable metropolitan platform to organize economic development activities and to enhance global competitiveness.	• Battles over the 1994 SDRIF pit regional environmental concerns against economic imperatives for development. • In 2000, Plaine Commune emerges as a left-wing power bloc within greater Paris. • From 2009 to 2013, Paris Métropole shifts from a left-leaning organization favoring democratic municipalism to a more pragmatic cross-partisan alliance.

metropolitan plan of Grand Paris and the emergence of the official Métropole du Grand Paris (MGP).

The Municipal Turn

The high era of modern state dirigisme began to decline in the 1970s as a result of internal and external pressures. As industry in France struggled to maintain a competitive position in the face of global markets, there was a shift in territorial planning from nationally oriented efforts at equalization and distribution to urban-based locational policies (Brenner 2004). The state was incentivized to orient production toward the urban scale even if this required ceding some power in order to do so. In France the move toward more local political arrangements, however, was not just a result of the drive to secure capital investments but it was also imbued with intense ideological stakes. Decentralization and the institutional strengthening of localities were a particular priority of the Socialist Party, which built up strength in localities and had constructed an agenda around democratic ideals of *"autogestion"* and self-management. Indeed, decentralization was presented by the Socialist Party in 1980 as "one of the most powerful levers of the rupture with capitalism, which will permit citizens to take the most direct path on the immense enterprise of social transformation which will be undertaken when the state has been conquered by the left" (in Keating 1983). Strengthening local municipalities was about direct and popular control against centralized statecraft.

The Defferre Laws of 1982 (known as Act I of decentralization) began the far-reaching transformations of intergovernmental relations and the movement of substantial decision-making power and policy responsibilities to subnational levels of government. Touted by some as the Socialist Party's François Mitterrand's "greatest domestic policy accomplishment" (Bernier 1991), the laws dramatically shifted power relationships within the French state system. Most important, the laws established the three official tiers of subnational government and their competencies that continue to define the French state.[12] They also established new norms for how these institutions would interact. The three levels of government are arranged horizontally based on the principles of shared functions and nonsubsidiarity. Many important policy issues (e.g., economic development, spatial planning) are under the control of several levels at once, and while each level may have the lead responsibility over particular issues, there is no domination exercised by one level over those under it. The first law of decentralization stated, for example, that regions, departments, and communes could respectively "take measures necessary for the protection of the social and economic interests of the population" as long as the measures did not contravene the master plans for development (in Keating 1983). Both nonsubsidiarity and shared functions continue to be underlying tenets of French governance.

This did lead to a new significance for subnational bodies, but by spreading out its powers the state did not fundamentally change the geopolitics of urban planning and policy making. For many, decentralization paradoxically amounted to a new form of central power whereby the state could shed unwanted functions while maintaining the capacity of "steering at a distance" (Cole 2006, 2008). In a time of global economic downturn and national fiscal austerity, the Deferre laws enabled the state to "decentralize the recession" by divesting itself of costly expenditures and inflationary functions (Cole 2006; Keating 1983). Thus, according to Henri Lefebvre (in Lefebvre, Brenner, and Elden 2009, 128–129), these reforms merely continued a pattern wherein "political elites have attempted a simulacrum of decentralization ... of transferring the problems, but not the privileges of the central power to grassroots organizations and associations." The opening of barriers to international markets and the deregulation of finance accompanying France's "Little Big Bang" in the early 1980s similarly had the effect of strengthening centrality by spurring on national capital markets and expanding the role of the competitive state in financial management (Cerny 1989).

Early decentralization processes, however, did have effects on the mechanisms of policy delivery at the local level, on the scope of reform, and on the form of subnational institutional coordination. With new responsibilities and fewer state transfers, departments and communes began to rely increasingly on private capital markets for development projects as well as for quotidian operations (Bernier 1991; Cerny 1989). Local governments also began to alter their spatial policies, implementing new infrastructure and amenities and pursuing place-based rebranding campaigns to attract economic investment (Nevers and Hoffmann-Martinot 1989). Thus, from the 1980s on, at the same time that the state itself became oriented to regional and municipal scales (Brenner 2004; Jessop 2010; Keating 1983), spending became increasingly channeled into investments such as real estate that would drive up financial assets and improve territorial attractiveness and rentability.

With new responsibilities at the local level but inadequate capacity, new contractual arrangements, collaboration, and public-private arrangements proliferated. In the wake of dirigisme emerged new regulatory arrangements of "negotiation, partnership, voluntary participation and flexibility" (Lefèvre 1998, 18). Local councils in the Paris region had significant responsibilities but were too small and had insufficient resources to address the devastating urban impacts of deindustrialization such as unemployment, lack of affordable housing, and growing sociospatial marginality. At the same time, the region of Île-de-France was better situated to deal with these broader urban policy geographies, but its powers were weak and its competencies minimal. Cross-border coalitions became necessary for the operation of community power.

Collaborative Coordination

The French practice of intercommunality (or intermunicipality) refers to any of several types of cooperation between local governments.[13] Initially intercommunal bodies were created for service provision, such as water distribution and waste collection, but these institutions, especially in the form of public authorities for intercommunal cooperation (EPCIs) (with fiscal capacities), have been clamoring to direct larger initiatives, such as regional economic development, social welfare, and physical infrastructure, including public transportation. Interinstitutional cooperation has thus been able to partially counter the fragmenting effects of decentralization. In adding extra layers to urban governance, however, these institutions often compound the problems of fragmentation they were meant to address. Emmanuel Négrier (2003, 176) has called this an "overcrowding solution for solving overcrowded patterns of government," while for Subra (2009, 25), intercommunal structures are both "the problem and solution" of agglomeration. Intercommunal structures can therefore widen the gap between functional and political territories as much as they can suture territories together for shared purposes.

The French political culture of partnership and collaboration between local collectivities is also visible in contractual relations between the state and other levels of government, and between the state and nonstate actors. State-Region Planning Agreements (CPERs) between the state and the

Regional Council are important tools, for example, to contract financing and action for particular projects over a five-year period. Cooperative (and competitive) contracts are also paralleled in practices of corporatism, which remained common after decentralization, especially with respect to urban policy.[14] In both these cases, however, contracts with the central state tended to be directed by and favorable to the state. Relative to American development regimes or British locational policies, the multiscalar urban governance in Paris during the early waves of neoliberalism was able to prioritize social concerns, but in general, these collaborative forms of governance still remained, even under socialist governments, more conducive to nationally steered collective growth strategies. Wealth distribution and sociospatial marginality remained sticking points in the Île-de-France that could not be adequately addressed through voluntary collaboration.

Debates about solidarity, territorial inequalities, and the power balance between the central state and local collectivities came to the fore in 1994 over the regional plan for the Île-de-France. In many ways the 1994 SDRIF elaborated by the socialist government of Michel Rocard followed that of Delouvrier, but was adapted to an era of heightened competition and new environmental realities. The plan aimed to strengthen competitiveness by opening up new areas to polycentric urban growth concentrated around priority developments. It also outlined an ambitious environmental policy for the protection of the regional greenbelt and improved public transportation. This caused significant disagreement between the state, the regional council, and certain departmental general councils. Whereas environmentalists wanted to protect natural territories and maintain planned regulated growth, others called for opening up vast territories to urbanization. Most local officials rejected the plan that had not taken into account regional concerns and represented an unsatisfactory centrist compromise. In the end the plan was forced onto municipalities by the state.

When the Île-de-France took control of regional planning in 2005, the Regional Council under Huchon opened up the 1994 plan to revision. This marked a significant turning point in terms of strengthening regional powers vis-à-vis the central state. Ideologically, struggles over the SDRIF concerned to what extent economic development would be integrated into urbanism. Structurally, they concerned the role of the region in making this decision. In the early 2000s greater regional influence over planning (the SDRIF still required state approval) was accompanied by increased power over transportation (the STIF replaced the Paris-based authority in 2000 and came under the control of the Regional Council in 2006) and development (the Regional Development Agency, ARD, was created in 2001).[15] As an exception, despite the creation of a region-wide land development agency (AFTPR) in 2006, control over land was not fully transferred to the region and remains in fragmented agencies. These reforms were bolstered by a series of reforms by conservative Prime Minister Jean-Pierre Raffarin to enhance regional powers and strengthen the departmental role in social policy (together these reforms compose Act II of decentralization).

The period from 1999 to 2007, during which regional authorities gathered strength, was also marked by a general intensification of debates over the political basis of the metropolis and in particular over the development of new forms of local coordination.[16] In 2000 the most powerful of the *communautés d'agglomeration*, Plaine Commune, was formed with five municipalities of the northern Parisian suburbs (Aubervilliers, Épinay-sur-Seine, Pierrefitte, Saint-Denis, Villetaneuse). Arising out of a long history of working-class organizing and shared socialist and communist leadership, Plaine Commune has become a coherent stage for territorial planning. Through partnerships with public authorities, local chambers of commerce, and unions, it has also established significant influence over urban planning, transportation, economic development, urban policy, and facilities. Under the leadership of Patrick Braouezec (formerly of the French Communist Party, now a member of Front de Gauche), it has become a significant counterforce for progressive regional policies and an effective coalition for growth organizing to attract coveted investment to the northeastern suburbs. *Communautés d'agglomeration* such as Plaine Commune thus have a significant geopolitical function: to weigh in on debates on governance in the face of the state, the region, the departments, and the city of Paris and to push for a more confederate style of coordination at the scale of the metropolis (Subra 2012).

The emergence of intermunicipal partnerships between Paris and its cross-border suburbs was another key development in local affairs. In particular, after his election as mayor of Paris in March 2001, Bertrand Delanoë began playing a key role in metropolitanization. His election was a watershed moment: it saw the right-wing stronghold of Paris swing left, and it also changed the character of relations between Paris and the *banlieue*. Delanoë and his mayoral adjunct, Pierre Mansat, became involved in a "process of atonement ... which has gradually turned into true cooperation between Paris and its neighbors" (Mansat 2012, 12). Through this leadership, Paris showed its commitment to establishing the metropolis by entering into cooperation agreements, engaging in common projects with neighboring municipalities, and encouraging metropolis-wide policies.[17] Delanoë and Mansat were also instrumental in the creation of the joint authority (*syndicat mixte d'études*) Paris Métropole, which aimed to "put a definitive end to the traditional relationship between Paris and the suburbs" (Mansat 2012, 13).

Established in April 2009, Paris Métropole has brought to the fore the question of metropolitan governance and has highlighted the need to act collectively on regional redistributive concerns, in particular housing and transportation. With an emphasis on multiplicity and flexibility, Paris Métropole suggests that innovative forms of political organization are needed to meet the deterritorialized dynamics of the contemporary city. Crucially, the form of metropolitan governance supported by Paris Métropole rejects a single overarching structure of national centrality and instead defines regional coordination as an overlapping series of multilateral partnerships rooted in the complex realities of the polycentric urban fabric.[18] Paris Métropole is founded on the principles of voluntary participation and equal representation. Each territory can elect membership and is represented through a "one local authority = one vote" policy. As of December 2014 it had grown to encompass 214 partners (one region, eight departments, forty-four intercommunal organizations and 161 communes), more than 9.3 million inhabitants, and more than 2,546 square kilometers (Paris Métropole 2014).

While Paris Métropole originally consisted mainly of left-leaning collectivities wishing to revive a democratic municipalism (and *autogestion*), its constitution has become less partisan over time and its activities and rhetoric more centrist as the organization has grown in membership and (mainly symbolic and intellectual) power. Despite being opposed to Sarkozy's Grand Paris on a number of fronts, it is nevertheless a collaborator on many state-led projects. Paris Métropole was consulted, for example, and served as an interlocutor in the creation of the GPE, is a member of the International Studio of Grand Paris (AIGP), and is involved in recommendations for Territorial Development Contracts (CDTs).[19] Today its actions are guided by the "conviction that the two dimensions of attractiveness and solidarity of the metropolis capital are closely linked ... the best way to serve their territory is to work together in the general interest, in order to devise solutions to deal adequately with current issues" (Paris Métropole 2013). While Paris Métropole has strong legitimacy, significant influence, and a high public profile, it has no formal competence to put in place new metropolitan policies. Rather, it acts primarily as a forum for deliberation, a model for collaboration, and an agency for agenda setting.

In a departure from the decades-long taboo among regional representatives of collaborating with Paris, today a new consensus is emerging on the need for some metropolitan institutions. Calls for a metropolitanization have come from the central state (with Sarkozy and the Balladur Report) and from the grassroots (with Paris Métropole). These calls are supported by Paris and the *banlieue,* and by diverse coalitions of right and left actors. According to Pierre Mansat, although it has taken a long time to establish positive and effective intercommunal relations, the region has entered a period of consolidation of metropolitan governance (in Chapon 2011).

The Return of the State
If the central state was ambiguously involved in subnational and especially metropolitan affairs in the 1990s and early 2000s, it has recently returned as a palpable presence. In 2007 the state confirmed the importance of several key National Interest Operations (OINs) in the region and gave new support to powerful pro-growth development institutions to guide their creation (the public operators EPADESA in La Défense and Paris-Saclay being the most notable).[20] In the case of the development of La Défense, in fact, the central state unilaterally approved a proposed development extension that had previously been rejected by the region. Most notably, however, the state's return in urban affairs is marked by its denial of the revised 2008 SDRIF and the counteracting launch of the Grand Paris initiative.

The Grand Paris Act of 2010 furthered this agenda by harnessing the energy of metropolitan reform toward statist ends (République Française 2010). This act established the Society for Grand Paris and endowed it with unprecedented powers in terms of land use and transportation—two essential areas of policy that were unsettled at the regional and local levels. To build the new transit network of Grand Paris (eventually the GPE), the

SGP was given exceptional rights of preemption, the capacity to establish subsidiary groups or companies, and the legal ability to create new tax instruments and structures to ensure revenue flows. The SGP model of arbitration and exceptional decision is at odds with the regional culture of negotiation and partnership (although it fits well within the competitive aspects of decentralization).

In the early days of Grand Paris (2010–2012), the state's presence was also assured by the new Ministry of Development for the Capital Region (originally headed by Blanc) and by the Ministry of Cities (headed by Maurice Leroy). In this capacity, for example, Leroy (2010) announced the appointment of Pierre Charon (UMP) to be a "facilitator" in the development of Grand Paris at the urban level and to ensure that national priorities were met by local policies. The state used these new institutions and appointments as steering mechanisms for the overall priorities of Grand Paris, a move recalling the centralized administration of prefect rule. Although new trust between the central state and local governments emerged in the wake of the François Hollande's New Grand Paris, the tools enabling state control over key infrastructure have remained.[21]

Perhaps the most relevant aspect of the state's return through Grand Paris, however, is its proposal for a new metropolitan structure. When Sarkozy suggested the creation of an urban community in greater Paris in June 2007, he was immediately met with opposition from both local officials and the media, who denounced the plan as a political maneuver to take over positions of power. Huchon initially described such a plan as "the death of the Île-de-France in its cohesion and its solidarity" (in Subra 2009, 95). For Huchon, a structure of government of agglomeration would completely invert the powers of the region, which have been slowly growing since the 1980s, and reassign the management of the territory, economic development, and transportation to the national state, leaving the region as a figurehead with a toothless SDRIF master plan. Sarkozy's initial proclamation was also interpreted as an electoral ploy and was understood to be a partisan attempt to seduce the region and the three most powerful institutions—the City of Paris, the Île-de-France, and the General Council of the Hauts-de-Seine—from the left in the run-up to local elections.

Despite the resounding opposition from local representatives to metropolitan reform, Sarkozy commissioned former prime minister Édouard Balladur to lead a commission on national democratic governance and institutional arrangements. Published in March 2009, the Balladur Report, as it is commonly known, outlined plans to change the national political map by shaking up regional and local government and breaking up the *mille-feuille* of Paris. Among other amendments to the constitution regarding, for example, the strength of the executive and parliament, the Balladur Report advocated for the creation of eleven "metropolitan regions" across France with special rights and responsibilities, similar to those of departments. In particular, the report proposed the creation of a new Grand Paris administrative unit comprising the City of Paris and the three departments of the *petite couronne*, with competencies over planning, housing, and transportation. Like Sarkozy's initial speech, however, the Balladur Report was met with virulent criticism, from the left in the Île-de-France (which had just recently solidified its hold on power) and from local officials across the political spectrum, who were wary of losing autonomy and being structured out of existence.

The Métropole du Grand Paris

The impasse following the Balladur Report was broken in 2012 by Paris Métropole when it released a green paper on metropolitan governance with the twofold aim of leading the debate and making specific proposals for reform.[22] The green paper was an open ("*(ou)vert*") tool to establish a pathway for discussions and action. It aimed to stimulate conversation and action and to set the agenda for regional change on the key issue areas of housing, mobility, revenues, and attractiveness.

On the specific question of a new institutional authority, Paris Métropole proposed three main figures of metropolitan governance. The first aimed to unify governance and to simplify the institutional map through an "integrated metropolis." This family of propositions emphasized the need for streamlined institutions, a reduction in collectivities, clear decision-making procedures, and unitary strong leadership. The second, a "concerted metropolis," suggested an evolved institutional system arranged through existing structures. This metropolitan scenario was founded on the constitutional principle of the free administration of collectivities and valued the capacity of communes to create their own development. It aimed not at dismantling existing arrangements but at the development of a sharing culture of negotiated metropolitanization through exchange, interconnection, and dynamic collaboration. The third scenario, that of a "confederated metropolis," sought the creation of a metropolitan institution through the coordination of existing collectivities. This middle-ground set of proposals maintained the polycentrism of the concerted version but within a unified and integrated government capable of more binding decision (Paris Métropole 2012). These options thus represented different means of balancing institutional flexibility and local autonomy with coordinating capability.

The green paper set in motion a national legislative bill (*Law on the Modernization of Territorial Public Action and the Affirmation of Metropolitan Areas*, or MAPTAM) by Prime Minister Ayrault on the creation of new metropolitan government structures, with special provisions for the Metropolis of Grand Paris.[23] Through the opposition it identifies between the integrated and concerted metropolitan figures (the confederated version largely collapsed into the latter in subsequent discussions), the green paper also set the terms of the legislative debate and public discourse around the MGP. In the time leading up to the law, the battles over the institutional form of the metropolis were oriented around these two main competing visions, each corresponding to different principles and modalities of authority.

On one side, proponents called for the dismantling of existing administrative organizations and the obligatory regrouping of all territorial arrangements into a united metropolitan institution with significant powers that would be located at a scale between departmental and regional governments. This streamlined and simplified version of the metropolis would, they said, be better situated to manage the "big" problems of housing, territorial inequality, unemployment, and environmental policy that have thus far eluded decision-makers. A coherent single-tier institutional arrangement would also be effective in bringing economic stakeholders (development agencies, transportation authorities, and city boosters) into metropolitan development initiatives. Here supporters, including national and local Socialist Party representatives, claimed that ad hoc collaborations that had thus far defined metropolitan governance were insufficient and that more permanent and fixed authorities had to be put in place. They argued that a high degree of centralization and obligatory integration was necessary for ambitious policy and lasting decision and political legitimacy,

Table 5.2
Two Proposals for the Métropole du Grand Paris

	Integrated Metropolis	Concerted (Federated) Metropolis
Operational features	• Streamlined institutions • A reduction of collectivities • Clear decision making procedures • Strong leadership • Obligatory participation	• Negotiated arrangements between existing collectivities • Strong mechanisms of coordination and collaboration • Shared capacities • Voluntarism
Goals and priorities	• Enable ambitious policies, lasting decision, and strong political legitimacy • Build institutional capacity to manage large-scale problems such as housing, environment, and territorial inequality • Develop official and longstanding partnerships with private stakeholders	• Maintain local policy and decision-making powers within existing municipal structures • Strengthen cooperative arrangements at the metropolitan scale • Build intermunicipal capacity to articulate diverse and flexible metropolitan strategies and projects in context
Constitutional rationale	• Institutions should be structured to uphold the integrity of the unitary state. • Integration must check parochialism.	• Institutions should honor the principles of nonsubsidiarity and autonomy of collectivities • Localism must check central despotism.
Proponents	• National and local Socialist Party officials	• Plaine Commune • Many Front de Gauche representatives • Local UMP officials • Paris Métropole

and that parochialism had to be checked by formal interdependencies. This model represented a significant rupture from previous strategies of intermunicipality, including the initial premise of Paris Métropole (Lacoste 2013). Many Front de Gauche representatives opposed such a strong metropolis on ideological grounds for its dismissal of local autonomy (and hence direct democracy). At the same time, many municipal UMP officials who gained in the previous election and would risk losing power back to the left if a metropolitan authority were created also opposed the integrated institution on strategic grounds.

On the other side, supporters of the federated version emphasized the importance of existing intercommunal structures and the culture of grassroots partnership. The federated metropolis, a "Metropolitan G20," would respect the powers of local collectivities (especially the fiscal powers of *communautés d'agglomeration*), they said, while organizing them into a larger administration with certain capacities for planning at the metropolitan scale. The federated and multitiered arrangement sought to maintain local policy making and deliberation within existing municipal structures while enabling cooperation and administrative functions at the metropolitan scale. Plaine Commune in particular mobilized a plural organization in combination with other local agglomerations in support of a radically federated institution that would maintain local power, claiming that intermunicipality was the pertinent scale at which to articulate metropolitan strategies and urban projects. As head of Plaine Commune, Patrick Braouezec (2011) explained his support for intermunicipality on the grounds that a centralized metropolitan strategy would worsen territorial inequalities and insufficiently enable a polycentric or multipolar emergence. He was joined in support by other conservative representatives, who maintained that communal autonomy and identity were at risk of being sacrificed in the face of a top-down mandate.

Through a process of negotiation and extensive consultation, a middle-ground version of the law gained enough support in the parliament and senate. After prolonged debates, MAPTAM was finally adopted and ratified on January 27, 2015 (known as Act III of decentralization). The final version of the act was a compromise in terms of both the structures it proposed for the new authority and the ends of metropolitanization to which it aimed. The MGP came into existence in January 2016.

The new MGP covers an administrative area that includes Paris, the three departments (124 municipalities) of the *petit couronne,* and five additional municipalities of the *grand couronne.*[24] The law thus establishes for the first time an institution capable of governing the roughly seven million inhabitants who make up the urban core of the Île-de-France. The MGP takes over a number of functions "in the metropolitan interest" from member municipalities, particularly in metropolitan development, housing, urban and environmental policy, crime prevention, and economic and social development. The MGP is responsible, for example, for the development of a Metropolitan Master Plan, a metropolitan housing policy, economic development, participation in mega-event applications and planning, and devising a climate and energy plan. As an EPCI, the MGP will also have tax-raising capacities to fulfill these activities, and MAPTAM permits quite extensive tax harmonization and revenue sharing.

The MAPTAM law is also significant for what it excludes. In terms of urban planning, the new metropolis must elaborate a Metropolitan Plan for Sustainable Development (PADD) that is compatible with the SDRIF and local PLUs (*plans local d'urbanisme*); however, it does not alter the functioning of the public development agencies (EPAs), which constitute the most powerful levers of urbanization within the region. In addition, the national legislature was clear that even though the new MGP has responsibilities for spatial planning and economic development, it will not have power over transportation (calling into question the extent to which transport and development will be integrated at the metropolitan scale). In fact, the law leaves network operators such as STIF (and those of water, electricity, and waste) in an ambiguous position, directed by the state, organized at a subnational scale, and formally in the hands of large private companies. In light of the importance of infrastructure, and particularly public transportation, to the making of the new metropolis, this surviving gap between the connected global city and its governing institution is very significant (this argument is considered more extensively in chapter 6).

The MGP thus outlines significant new functions for metropolitan management, but also raises new lines of criticism. For Lacoste (2013), in privileging the urban but not the wider suburban and exurban region (the *grand couronne*), the MGP excludes vital parts of the territory and prevents truly metropolitan coordination. The MGP risks widening the gap between the most urbanized areas of the Île-de-France, where jobs and enterprises are concentrated, and the periphery, and thus extending existing spatial segregation (IAU-IDF 2014b). This is especially troubling as the political space of the MGP does not sit neatly atop the much broader polycentric economic area envisioned by the GPE and elaborated through CDTs. Many questions about urban regional governance also remain. These questions include how competencies should be transferred from local to metropolitan levels, how to ensure a balance between the new responsibilities of the MGP and the resources at its disposal, how to ensure cooperation and equity between the demarcated territory of the MGP and the rest of the Île-de-France, and how to arbitrate divergent interests and territorial relations.

Despite these uncertainties, in terms of its stated goals, the MGP repeats the now familiar promise to bring about the trifecta of grand urbanism—a competitive, inclusive, and sustainable global city.

While the world's major cities such as London, New York and Tokyo have entered the 21st century, Paris fears being surpassed in economic attractiveness, in tourism and in quality of live. To avoid losing the race, Paris must develop is potential and be more visible internationally to maintain its rank as world capital. ... Such a metropolitan project must also for greater equity, be able to develop better territorial solidarity, reduce regional inequalities and propose a rebalancing in terms of access to housing, employment, training, services and facilities. It is in this overall dynamic that the attractive, inclusive and sustainable twenty-first century metropolis will be constructed. (Métropole du Grand Paris Mission de Préfiguration 2015)

This political compromise on the Metropolis of Grand Paris thus echoes that of the Grand Pari(s) architects and the GPE transportation planners.

Conclusion

Historically, Paris has been essential to French statecraft, and the city's institutions, academies, and seats of power have consolidated the democratic republic. Today Paris suggests a new order, that of the global city metropolis, as a significant form of political organization. In a globalized world the nature of the city and the nature of the nation are changing in concert, and the making of the Metropolis of Grand Paris provides a unique window onto this incipient reality. The contemporary questions surrounding the governance of the Paris metropolis are about Paris's relationship to

France and to the world at large (Veltz 2012). They are also questions about the kind of polities that will organize collective life in the twenty-first century.

The rescaling and reterritorialization of political action in metropolitan Paris have thus overturned traditional institutions of urban governance, and the emerging political arrangements of Grand Paris present an opportunity to reflect on the meaning and limits of local government in a global age. The stakes of these conflicts certainly concern the uniquely French processes of contractualization, negotiation, and partnership building that are increasingly coming to define decision making at the metropolitan scale. They also concern the nature of territorial autonomy, the prospects of local democracy, the legitimacy of the state, and the pragmatic ability to address the big issues that threaten the future of the region, and even the future of the planet.

The metropolitan consensus brings together a range of interests. The need for a metropolis is expressed by coalitions of local officials, who want to coordinate social policy, and by local growth regimes with entrepreneurial goals that aim to mobilize resources at the regional scale. It is supported by the authoritarian national government, which benefits from an attractive global city, and by local enterprise and corporations, which potentially benefit from an improved atmosphere of competition and investment. Even those against the metropolis—local autonomists (in radical democratic or conservative guise) and mid-range regional bureaucracies—are warming to the reality in one form or another.

In the construction of metropolitan Paris, there is no easy correlation between Jacobin and Girondist models of authority, urban and suburban priorities, capital and provincial logics, or left and right ideologies, on the one hand, and the kind of metropolitan plan that has come into existence on the other. Rather, a more complex set of overlapping divisions, tensions, and compromises defines the shape of reform. While the same divides between hard and soft versions of neoliberalism that define the architectural and transit debates are palpable in the conflicts of metropolitanization, these partisan differences cut more diagonally across the issues of governance. The desire to build a metropolitan space does not directly further the ends of a liberal market economy based on possessive individualism, nor does it clearly engender alternatives of social justice and environmental sustainability. Grand Paris is thus not a common target but a zone of contestation between competing versions of metropolitanization. On all sides there are more open or closed processes, more equitable or hierarchical policies, and more democratic or authoritarian institutions. The making of the metropolis may be merely a geopolitical struggle for power, or it may reveal innovative territorial organizations and planning instruments that gesture toward an alter-globalization. Thus, in addition to how the metropolis is being made and by whom, what rationalities guide its transformation will define its political horizons. The next chapter considers this latter question in more detail.

6 Metropolitan Governance and Global City Productivism

We should welcome gentrification but it needs to be designed and managed well.
—Richard Rogers, in ARUP, 2014

No one believes that you can make a plan for a megalopolis. So we have to work out a system of projects that are more strategic plans than traditional planning … we have to find a sort of Urban Acupuncture.
—Antoine Grumbach, in Grumbach, Ramo, and Upmeyer, 2013

Systematic transformations in the political economy of global capital and local geopolitical battles within the French administrative system have brought about dramatic changes in the spatial governance of the Paris metropolis. In the imbroglio over the construction of Grand Paris, there has been a multiplication in the units of government involved in the production of urban space, an extension of the nature of these actors beyond the statutory state, and a shift in the manner in which these actors come together to pursue particular initiatives and policies. The thickening web of institutional relations is marked by an intensification of competition and cooperation between territories and between public and private actors, and by more transverse and networked forms of authority that organize around specific project-based reforms. Couched in an initial and necessary grand vision, the metropolitanization of Paris is nevertheless achieved by targeted spatial interventions, interinstitutional contracts, and temporary partnerships between various state bodies and corporate and civil society actors.

The creation of the Metropolis of Grand Paris (MGP) signals a restructuring of metropolitan governance that establishes new competencies for subnational administrative institutions, at the same time that it has strengthened the state's role in organizing and facilitating urban economic development. Internally, arrangements such as the MGP define a new dynamic of citizenship and a new scale of social life, while externally they reposition Paris in a competitive global marketplace. The construction of new administrative institutions, however, is only a small part of the metropolitan governance regime. The MGP is connected to a range of other formal and informal partnerships and regulatory norms that define how the metropolis is being organized politically.

To understand the changes to governance accompanying the making of the metropolis, it is necessary to look beyond the traditional dualisms of centralization and decentralization, the capital and the provinces, Paris and its suburbs, and left and right partisan positions. The project of metropolitanization involves polymorphic and multilayered conflicts that are collectively reshaping the means of producing urban space. Further, in assessing the causes and implications of Grand Paris, it is inadequate to assume the metropolitan scale as an inevitable outcome of macrolevel capitalist restructuring. Local political dynamics are driven by a variety of interests and objectives that defy and exceed a crude economistic script.

The claim that the making of metropolitan Paris is grounded, complex, and contradictory, however, does not imply that this process is not driven by strategies and tactics—if incomplete and internally fraught—to create new conditions for economic growth. Though Paris is not following an abstract and universal neoliberal process of regulation, and though salient differences exist between the different proposals for metropolitan arrangements, there is nevertheless a clear pursuit of institutions at the urban regional scale and a common context of reform fundamentally related to accumulation. Kantor and coauthors (2012, 8) may be correct in claiming that "how much politics matters in containing pro-growth policy bias in GCRs [global city regions] remains a question," but across ongoing conflicts and very real struggles, there is an emerging consensus among variously situated elites that the global city as an economic entity requires similarly scaled political institutions.

The first objective of this chapter is to elaborate the relation of state rescaling in Paris to new forms of global capitalism. While Paris's rise as a key global city of finance accounts for part of the story, a purely global city narrative does not capture the role of the state in initiating and encouraging particular spatial economies, nor does it explain the role of planning and policy making in generating urban and suburban value. The chapter aims to draw out how the making of Grand Paris is shaped by contextually embedded transformations in the tools of capitalist urban regulation. The second objective of the chapter is to understand the significance of the regulatory transformations that accompany the targeted, contractual, and collaborative urban initiatives. Though there has been considerable debate over the shifting scenarios of governance and the organizational difficulties of Grand Paris, there has been little normative critique of the common paradigm of grand urbanism that defines them. As a result, questions of governance have largely been divorced from the kinds of values that they embody. Against a narrow consideration of governance in instrumental or functional terms (i.e., "good governance"), I argue that it is also necessary to consider the "governmentality" (Foucault 2000, 2009) of Grand Paris and the way in which new tools, technologies, and practices of planning produce and reproduce particular ideals and behaviors.[1]

To address the state's involvement in Grand Paris and the politics to which grand urbanism is aimed, the discussion first situates the changing forms of governance (including the creation of the MGP) within a financialized regime of global capital relations. Though the nation-state's capacity to organize territory on a large scale and to coordinate mobilities remains especially salient in these reforms, the management and administration of urban populations and functions are being pluralized as sovereignty is ceded to supra- and subnational scales and to nonstate actors. Drawing out the political economic particularities of state rescaling, I argue that the new metropolitan form, while not the inevitable outcome of neoliberalization, nevertheless facilitates new modes of state-economic relations geared toward advanced production. After tracing the global city form of productivity, the discussion specifies more particularly some of the main institutional techniques and mechanisms of governing the global city. It explains that through tools such as contrats de développement territorial (CDTs, Territorial Development Contracts), public-private partnerships, and real estate investment trusts, metropolitan governance is made polymorphic, consensual, participatory, contractual, and spatial policies are increasingly oriented toward private concerns. The chapter ends with an analysis of how changes in metropolitan governance affect the prospects for substantive democracy and justice. I argue that global city productivism privatizes decision making and that grand urbanism marks a significant shift in public policy from welfare to market goals and in planning from comprehensive regional schemes to speculative "wagers" (*paris*) on the future.

The Productivist State in an Urban Age

Over the past thirty years, the French state has relinquished its dirigiste spatial planning and economic management and in its place established more diffuse forms of economic governance (though these forms are still heavily influenced by the ideals of republicanism and by strong state traditions). These new styles of political-economic intervention are notably expressed in the creation of new metropolitan state spaces (Brenner 2004) and in investments in the global city of Paris as a "national champion" (Crouch and Le Galès 2012). With the consolidation of competition ideals, the rise of global finance, and the extensive growth of the suburbs, Paris today is more than simply a place to manage consumption following the movement of industry; rather, it is implicated in production itself. Instead of exercising direct control over this development, the state's main influence is now felt through its indirect oversight of territorial relations and infrastructural flows.

Neil Brenner's (2004) articulation of a "rescaled competition state regime" provides a useful description of how recent efforts to create productive spaces in France's urban areas contrast with earlier national managerialist models. He writes that this arrangement is

rescaled, because it rests upon scale-sensitive political strategies intended to position key subnational spaces ... within supranational ... circuits of capital accumulation; a *competition state*, because it privileges the goal of economic competitiveness over traditional welfarist priorities such as equity and redistribution; and a *regime*, because it represents an unstable, evolving institutional-geographical mosaic rather than a fully consolidated framework of statehood. (260)

The state-facilitated construction of the globally attractive Grand Paris metropolis gives credence to the continued relevance of this thesis.

Yet perhaps even more relevant to the present case is the conceptual framework from which Brenner largely derives his analysis, that is, Henri Lefebvre's (1976a, 1976b, 1977, 1978) concept of the "state mode of production" (SMP). The concept of the SMP and the related ideology of "state productivism" highlight the fundamental connections between and among space, territory, and capitalist production. Lefebvre's understanding of a state that manipulates national territory for accumulation can be usefully extended in the present day to illuminate the dynamics of grand urbanism, to elaborate recent transformations of metropolitan governance, and to highlight the essential aspects of pro-growth development driving this reform.

For Lefebvre, the SMP refers to a transformation of the state form linked to the urbanization of capital. What Lefebvre (1977) refers to as the SMP is therefore the institutional and territorial means for directing and controlling accumulation, one that invokes all the diverse strategies of the state (e.g., new forms of knowledge, material shifts in production, institutional innovations) to order the spatial and social relations of modern capitalism. This state productivism sees the state take charge of economic growth in an active and interventionist manner, most notably through establishing conceptual and technical resources of urbanism and through channeling investment into the built environment for production, consumption, circulation, transportation, and social ends. Lefebvre (in Lefebvre, Brenner, and Elden 2009, 238) argues that "only the state" can take on this task of managing space "on a grand scale." The productivist state represents neither an ideological support superstructure for a more fundamental economic base nor a regulationist addition that facilitates market functions but is an agent that is actively involved in planning the economy, especially through creating and using space.[2] The SMP establishes rule through the rationalized technocracy of urbanism.

Lefebvre's antiproductivism was founded in an acknowledgment of the antidemocratic consequences of the centralized control of spatial production (Brenner and Elden 2009). The notion of the SMP has also been used to attack the class compromise on which the French postwar social democracy was founded, whereby the left's accession to the growth imperative undercut anticapitalist alternatives. Of importance for Lefebvre, not only does the mobilization of space for production commodify everyday life and create a differentiated landscape where certain territories and populations benefit over others, but the SMP stands in opposition to citizen control of the production of space and direct democracy through autonomous organizing, or *autogestion* (Lefebvre 2009, 134–136).[3]

In the twenty-first century—an era of a consolidated service economy, generalized gentrification, growth in the real estate sector, and the financialization of space—Lefebvre's specific conclusions do not apply, but his perspective on state productivism remains crucial. Though Lefebvre's theory of the state is tied to the grammar of late Fordism, in describing the various strategies through which states mobilize space as a productive force, he may be especially useful in accounting for the intense uneven development of metropolitanization today, the hybrid assemblages of neoliberal governance, denationalized forms of statehood, and concerted pursuits of the global city region (Brenner and Elden 2009; Merrifield 2006). Brenner (2001, 799) in particular notes the sustained relevance of the SMP, calling the contemporary form of the state "hyperproductivist" and suggesting that we may currently be witnessing the emergence of a historically new form of the SMP, in which "the state's function as an agent for the commodification of its territory—at once on national, regional, and urban scales—has acquired an unprecedented supremacy over other regulatory operations within the state's institutional architecture." In this light, metropolitan governance can be understood as the attempt to secure accumulation in the form of networked flows of financial capital through the built form and to stabilize the political tensions that would otherwise hinder this historically specific mode of accumulation.

Insofar as Grand Paris reveals the desire of the French state to endlessly create commodifiable spaces as well as infrastructures of reproduction and collective consumption, it is emblematic of an emergent global city state mode of production. This historically new form of the SMP today rests on two main pillars: First, it rests on the national promotion of global cities as a means to international competition and the use of networked infrastructure as a lever for economic growth, particularly in financial and real estate markets. Second, it relies on negotiated metropolitan institutions that will ensure these economic ends while simultaneously purporting to address the demands of social reproduction and to solve the administrative crisis that prevents the state from effecting the welfare policies for which it claims responsibility. The internal conflicts of the *mille feuille*, while important for the shape of metropolitanization, all operate within this framework.

Thus, approaching Grand Paris and grand urbanism through the perspective of global city state productivism reveals that the problems with contemporary metropolitanization in Paris pertain not merely to the internal contradictions of capitalism but to a deep political crisis of democracy, governance, and the state form. The global city SMP undermines democracy through its rule of urban experts and through rendering the assumption of growth uncontestable. The contradictions of this SMP are particularly visible when financial capital becomes become global, and governing becomes unmoored from its traditional territorial groundings.

The Governance of Capitalist (Sub)urbanization

There are four main dimensions to Grand Paris's global city productivism. First, successive central governments since at least 2005 have affirmed stimulating development in Paris as a national growth priority. Second, a series of legislative reforms has established intergovernmental partnerships as a key tool of metropolitanization that has replaced modernist master planning with contractualized project-based reforms. Third, the central state has organized these projects within a framework of infrastructure provision that links the creation of the connected metropolis with networked collaborative governance. Fourth, action by local and national elites has facilitated the financialization of the built environment and urban planning rationales, particularly at the metropolitan scale.

From Dirigisme to Collaborative Governance

Since the crisis of Fordist Keynesianism, political elites across the world have been searching for an "institutional fix" compatible with the transformations in capitalist social and spatial relations (Peck and Tickell 1994). Variously located stakeholders are struggling to build administrative capacity within the large global city. As a result, there has been an intensification of institutional building at the urban regional scale, with "new institutional spaces" of urban regions poised as key sites in which neoliberal states orchestrate governance, planning, and policy provision (Harrison and Hoyler 2014; Jonas 2013; Jones 2007; MacLeod and Jones 2007). Moreover, as these large and powerful units grow and become key economic engines, countries across the world are adopting policies that promote urban regions as national assets (Crouch and Le Galès 2012). Adopting the strategies of what Oleg Golubchicov (2010) calls "world-city entrepreneurialism," nation-states today no longer seek to increase their economic weight by expanding territory and hence broadening their resource base and scale of industry; rather, they orient activities toward select global cities that concentrate the productive forces of the new economy.

In his reflections on Paris's role in the twenty-first-century world, Pierre Veltz (2012), director of the Paris-Saclay Public Authority (EPPS), takes the logic of "national champions" to its extreme, claiming that the future of the French state relies on the expansion and intensification of the Parisian metropolis. The creation of what he terms "a metropolis called France" goes beyond the program of Grand Paris and invokes the weaving together of a single national metropolitan fabric. Overcoming once and for all the division between Paris and the French desert, for Veltz (2012, 16), Grand Paris gestures toward a horizon where national territory and space are reoriented toward a "sort of distributed metropolis." While Veltz's hyperbolic vision of networked urbanism may seem far-fetched (and certainly there are local obstacles in the way of this achievement), the macrocephaly of Paris under grand urbanism is intensifying.

From the perspective of the French state, the need for a metropolitan region, in terms of both an organized economy and a consolidated administrative structure, stems from a climate of international competition. Once a stronghold of Europe and a key player in global affairs, France today risks losing this position. Threatened both by traditional foes such as Germany and the UK and by the rising BRIC countries, France's global influence is decreasing materially and symbolically.[4] The construction of and support for an attractive global city is a way of revalorizing national space. This has consistently been the primary justification for Grand Paris.

> The Grand Paris (Greater Paris project) plan was launched in response to a critical question for our country: how to ensure that France keeps its prominent position as a sustainable place in the international economic competition? The world has been advancing at dazzling speed for the past several decades and countries that just yesterday appeared to be lagging behind are now growing at full speed. In this context, large emerging countries ... are arming themselves with new tools: global cities. (Ministère du Logement, de l'Égalité des Territoires et de la Ruralité, 2014)

Participating in the worldwide battle to ground mobile capital in their territory, French leaders are subsidizing the Paris region as an attractive site for leading-edge manufacturing and service sectors (including information and communications technology, biological sciences, aeronautical engineering, creative and cultural industries, and financial services). According to the Ministry of Housing, Territorial Equality and Rurality, Grand Paris aims to "leverage the capital region" by building physical and institutional infrastructure that will channel growth by stimulating property markets and opening up the city to investment (Ministère du Logement, de l'Égalité des Territoires et de la Ruralité 2014). The promotion of competitive clusters through fiscal incentives, deregulated labor laws, and more open immigration policies is also a means of dynamizing what the *Economist* (2012) has called a "deeply anti-business culture."

Simultaneous with national reforms, local actors are also pursuing the global city metropolis in order to overcome the city limits of globalization. The coordination of Paris and its suburbs is tactically advantageous in competitive development. According to Christian Lefèvre (1998, 22):

> If central cities agree to play the game, it is because they are now aware that they need the peripheries in order to develop, or quite simply, to keep their place, in the ranks of world cities. The urban hierarchy of today is international. ... In this respect, the metropolitan territory has become the scale on which the central cities reason. To do so, they must free themselves and go beyond their own administrative limits. The metropolitan government is to them, both a necessary instrument and an advantage in attaining their objective.

Through both intermunicipal cooperation and metropolitan institutions, local officials by and large agree on the pursuit of some sort of collective action at the urban regional level to respond to the pressures of global city competition. In these cases, the creation of new governance arrangements is crucial to the urbanization of capital. The creation of the MGP is thus equivalent to "an institutional 'big bang'" (IAU-IDF 2014b) to reposition Grand Paris in a global marketplace. As discussed in chapter 5, in Paris the local demands for the global city are voiced simultaneously with calls for redistribution. These are not insincere, but they have become embedded in the productivist imperative. It should be noted that under grand urbanism, global city formation at the grass roots is justified through discourses of growth and of the necessity for coordinating reproduction and collective consumption (see Jonas 2013; Jonas, While, and Gibbs 2010).

Across all levels of the state and across political parties, one of the main perceived advantages of metropolitan governance concerns its ability to increase the attractiveness of the territory for growth. This has not eclipsed social welfare concerns, but it is their precondition. In this context the central state has reworked tools designed for the national equalization of territories into mechanisms to service priority global cities. In 2006, for example, the Interministerial Delegation for Territorial Planning and Regional Attractiveness (DATAR), created in 1963 under Charles de Gaulle, was renamed the Interministerial Delegation for Development and Territorial Competitiveness (DIACT). The explicit change in wording from "regional attractiveness" to "territorial competitiveness" reflects a policy shift away from equalization of growth and toward targeted place marketing, and away from national plans for territorial management and toward strategic city forecasting. Although Cécile Duflot would later reclaim the original name and fold this institution into the General Office on Equal Territories, the mandate of the institution has been successfully reoriented toward building pro-growth coalitions around large city-regional projects. Similarly, the Voynet law of 1999 also marked a change in policy from territorial interventions to address imbalances and help disadvantaged regions, to the promotion of already successful areas. According to the 1999 law, "the politics of territorial development must favor the emergence and the concretization of projects founded on the valorization of resources, more than the compensation for handicaps and the reparation of damages" (Pinson 2009, 87).

Furthermore, unlike their dirigiste predecessors, state territorial interventions today are less likely to be centrally controlled and more likely to be founded on partnerships. In these arrangements the central state still provides the broad framework for reform, but multiple stakeholders subsequently carry through particular interventions. Exemplary here is the designation of the National Interest Operations (OINs) and the collaborative development agencies (EPAs) to build them. These too represent postwar inheritances retooled for the new priorities of grand urbanism. In the past, EPAs were used for large-scale plans directed by central authorities, such as the building of the *villes nouvelles* or the construction of La Défense. Today, however, while the EPAs remain under the supervision of the Ministry of Housing, Territorial Equality and Rurality, they are not centrally managed and controlled, but they are guided establishments geared toward bringing multiple stakeholders into growth coalitions. Even the progressive agendas of the EPAs are tied to ambitious growth. The EPAs have welfare and service mandates but limited resources to deliver these, and thus seek private partners to build their capacities. In attracting new Grand Paris Express (GPE) stations, densifying and anchoring iconic buildings, these development agencies can, for example, raise the value of land and property taxes in the hope of meeting both economic and social ends (Baraud-Serfaty 2012).

There is limited space for development outside the competitive urban framework.

It is thus only in relation to mutations in the productive spheres that the variety of metropolitan agendas make sense. Under this framework all levels of the state are incentivized to valorize comparative advantages through signature urban territories and to reconfigure space for economic advancement and, to a lesser extent, social welfare (Karadimitriou, De Magalhães, and Verhage 2013). The relationship of nation-state to global city is thus not one of progression or replacement but one of overlap, interpenetration, collusion and contradiction. The territorialization of state action through Grand Paris thus achieves a rescaled competition regime at the scale of the metropolis. In the creation and promotion of the global city, key decision-making powers remain with the central state, but operational functions are also distributed among developers, financial institutions, government bodies, technical experts, architects, and—often only marginally—users. In retooling itself to the production of the global city, the role of the state becomes less direct, managerial, and "hands-on" and more focused on facilitating and enabling.

Between Master Planning and Urban Projects

Europe-wide state retrenchment, neoliberal management, and skepticism of modernism have led to a retreat from comprehensive spatial planning (Albrechts 2006). Ironically, despite its panoramic perspective, grand urbanism is generally implemented and operated through more limited "project-based" urban policy and area-based agendas to organize private and public stakeholders around shared goals. As the Grand Pari(s) architect Antoine Grumbach notes in the epigraph to this chapter, a plan for a megalopolis is unrealistic. The large-scale vision of the Grand Paris megaproject must be focused and achieved through discrete—if networked—subprojects.

Grand Paris is the apogee of the French variation of this megaproject-driven development agenda (Fainstein 2008). Like other advanced industrialized economies in Europe, France has adopted site-specific projects as the privileged form of public and private investment in the twenty-first century. Pinson (2009, 2010) identifies project-oriented planning, or "governing the city by project," as a new instrument of policy being used to organize local political systems and bring together plural forces of government with private actors. These devices incentivize association, recruitment, and mobilization and enable coherent collective action in a context of organizational fragmentation and dispersion of resources. French project-based growth is articulated in part out of the histories of decentralization, contractualized policies such as *politique de la ville*, and the pluralization of corporatist governance. In the Île-de-France, projects are thus also compelling antidotes to the institutional pathologies caused by the administrative failures of the existing *mille-feuille*.

Grand urbanism extends this model operationally, by enlarging the scope and size of project-based reform, and geographically, by moving the project targets from the central city to the suburbs. In Grand Paris, megaprojects of mobility such as the GPE organize collective action at the metropolis level by bringing together multiple levels of government and nongovernmental actors around a series of shared initiatives "facilitated by the revision of regulations that too often block bold projects" (Ministère du Logement, de l'Égalité des Territoires et de la Ruralité 2014). The regionwide GPE is exemplary here for combining ambitious territorial mapping on behalf of the central state with contractualized transit-oriented development projects in identified growth clusters.

Indeed, the primary role of the central state in grand urbanism is not to exercise coercion but to mobilize cognitive capacities and to forge connections among political, social, and economic stakeholders:

> The Project uses an approach based on responsibility and partnerships between institutional social and economic stakeholders in the Capital Region. Built on a common ambitious vision that goes beyond geographic, administrative and social borders, driven by a dialogue and coordinated by new institutional players bringing a metropolitan perspective to issues of general interest, a common project was developed through identifying the potential contributions of each stakeholder and acquiring the means to implement them. (Ministère du Logement, de l'Égalité des Territoires et de la Ruralité 2014)

The state plays an essential role in shaping an urban vision and in orienting the contractually organized projects. These projects, however, are not managed directly by the state but are overseen jointly by the region, municipalities, private investors, planners, and community organizations.

Projects are necessary, as the costs and risks today for any actor—including the central state—to attempt a large-scale urban development project through noncooperative means are insurmountable. According to Sarkozy (2010, 53),

> We must be clear. In the twenty-first century the State cannot create a new city, nor can it create centers of growth, nor can it decree where people are going to live. This is just as true for other authorities as it is for the State. On the other hand, public authorities must give support to movements and encourage dynamics that are largely spontaneous. They must also solve problems and avoid any form of impasse, whether economic, social, cultural, or ecological. Between interventionism and "laissez-faire," we must carry out regulatory and corrective action, with flexible and adaptable planning, rather than through large rigid plans.

The success of Grand Paris depends not solely on the central state but also on a complex assemblage of overlapping authorities:

> The State plays an essential role, particularly regarding transportation issues and the overall coherence of development. But this large-scale common project will be developed and implemented with the signing of contracts, mutual commitment and mobilization on all levels from the region and its districts to town, from international investors to small innovative businesses, from researchers to urban planners, and from large companies to neighborhood associations. (Ministère du Logement, de l'Égalité des Territoires et de la Ruralité 2014)

There is no doubt that there has been a shift with Grand Paris from comprehensive planning to project management. Sarkozy had considerable influence over the narrative of Grand Paris and firmly set the agenda with his call for a prosperous networked global city driven forward by ambitious transit plans. Yet this general grand vision is shared by Hollande, and by local officials too. Based on a tenuous agreement, it can be implemented only through a "negotiated urbanism" of agreements, compromises, and experiments (Belkind 2013).[5] Whereas the state has reasserted its authority in instituting large-scale reform, it has retreated from its prerogatives for implementation.

The project-driven urbanism of Grand Paris is thus articulated on the ground through what Haughton, Allmendinger, and Oosterlynck (2013) refer to as "soft spaces" of governance, those in between, often temporary sites outside or alongside the "hard" statutory spaces of territorial boundaries and administrative structures. With this planning model there are thus more fluid and complex frontiers between institutions and between public and private development (Gilli 2014).[6]

The CDT is one of the main mechanisms through which the soft governance of Grand Paris is assembled. These contracts define the conditions for development, but in line with a predetermined agreement on the competitive, inclusive, and sustainable metropolis. CDTs are comparable to other global development arrangements whereby formalized decentralized tools are used a means of urban policy creation and implementation (see Douay 2010; Geddes and Bennington 2001; Pierre 2000; Rhodes 1997). These collaborative governance structures articulate macrolevel policy priorities and goals at more diffuse horizontal scales and enable a variety of competing interests and participants, including politicians, technical experts, planners, stakeholders, users, or residents, to negotiate based on deliberative, communicative models of decision making with a shared vision as the desired outcome.

Since their emergence, twenty-one CDTs have been negotiated as part of Grand Paris and nine have been signed to date. The agreements cover some 157 municipalities and 4.4 million inhabitants (representing 38 percent of the regional population) (IAU-IDF 2014a). The constitution of existing and proposed CDTs is quite varied, with some comprising isolated municipalities and others large areas spanning multiple departments and intermunicipal organizations. Their content too is heterogeneous. Most CDTs are organized around one or two multifunctional megaprojects (e.g., a mall, sports stadium, university, residential community, cultural facility, or employment zone), and their function within the larger system of urban labor is defined by these elements. Indeed, many of the Grand Paris CDTs have a particular brand, such as "health," "culture and creativity," or "sustainability," associated with them and written explicitly into the contract. These labels serve to reinforce the federated nature of Grand Paris at the same time that they work as local territorial marketing.

While the initial backlash over the "exceptional" logic of control set out in the 2010 Grand Paris Act has largely waned, the combination of increased state involvement in regional affairs and the inclusion of plural local actors in planning efforts has brought a number of governance problems to the surface. The CDTs must mediate often very different conceptions of development, solidarity, and public interest, and in situations of competition over plans and ideas it is not always entirely clear who has authority (Gallez 2014). The details of the contracts are also fuzzy on some issues (taxation being one), leading to significant gaps in coordination. Thus, in many ways what precisely is meant by contractualization is still being worked out (IAU-IDF 2014a). This has led the Institute for Urban Development in the Île-de-France (IAU-IDF) (2014a) to describe the CDT not as a financial or legal contract but as a "moral contract." As such, the CDT's main contribution is in the establishment and solidification of norms and principles, not necessarily their concrete implementation.

Through the GPE and the CDTs the French state is able to retain extraordinary powers to control global flows, at the same time that it ensures local coordination for productive sites such as housing estates, megamalls, research campuses, ports, and office complexes. A core feature of grand urbanism is this creation of vast infrastructure networks in order to release land into the hands of developers. The state directs this process while also setting the ideological parameters for spatial transformation. The state simultaneously channels vast territory into global economic networks, at the same time that it secures consent for development among stakeholders and generates agreement over physical design and architectural aesthetics (on the role of the state in consensus creation, see also Béhar 2013; Lovering 2010; and Pinson 2009).[7] The neoliberal state favors the creation of a rule regime to facilitate urban projects as bearers of metropolitanization. Instead of directly involving itself in the particularities of design and implementation, however, here the state acts primarily to facilitate private sector activity and to organize urban regional territory.

Locating the State in Networked Urbanism

Paris's urban-suburban conurbation in the twentieth century relied on and was regulated through nationalized industries and infrastructures. Today, however, the networked metropolis of Grand Paris is enmeshed within global political and economic structures that stretch well beyond France. The architectural consultation of Grand Pari(s) represented an explicit attempt to grapple with the empirical realities and theoretical implications of this new phenomenon. Christian de Portzamparc (2010) provides one of the most compelling descriptions of the twenty-first-century global metropolis:

> It is parallel to the internet and cyberspace. It's parallel to a credit economy and fast returns on investments. It's parallel to a moment when the elected representatives are having difficulty making projects for infrastructure during their term in office. ... This metropolitan fact forces us to see that it's no longer a classic city, it's no longer

the city with a hierarchy in proximity to which everything is organized according to the key word: "space." Here it's about connections. ... It's the possibility of connections that defines the space or the use and needs in terms of connections, thus creating a kind of constellation.

If the metropolis is understood in terms of flow and connection, as an amorphous mix of dynamic overlapping movements, and as a series of possibilities, then it is clear that traditional territorial administrations are radically inadequate to produce and direct this reality. These inadequacies are patent in the persistent blockages to metropolitan policy and planning at the metropolitan scale.

Whether out of local necessity to meet the quotidian needs of urban populations or out of a desire to more effectively harness the metropolis's relational potentials, the debates over Grand Paris show actors trying to come to terms with planning in terms of these flows. To govern the mobile urban region means to take into account the porosity of frontiers and borders and to accept "a more fluid, less patrimonial, conception of population and territory" (Estèbe 2013, 25). It also entails more networked forms of urbanism that are based not on building within fixed zones and boundaries but on developing particular types of connections.

What Gabriel Dupuy (1991, 2008) has called "network thinking" is today more than ever an essential aspect of planning. Network thinking is attuned to the fundamental interdependence of component parts and the flux of urban life, and it sees mobility, land use, and everyday life as being necessarily related. It acknowledges connections between the morphological structure of places and their dynamics of development at multiple scales and is imperative for addressing challenges of organizing collective life in an interdependent world (Dupuy and Offner 2005). Integrated physical networks and infrastructures (of, e.g., water, electricity, waste, or transportation) have thus become key sites of urban development in the twenty-first century (Graham and Marvin 2001).

Infrastructure, through the seemingly *apolitical* practices of engineering or design, thus takes on significant functions of governance. According to Keller Easterling (2014, 15),

Some of the most radical changes to the globalizing world are being written not in the language of law and diplomacy, but in these spatial, infrastructural technologies. ... As a site of multiple, overlapping or nested forms of sovereignty, where domestic and transnational jurisdictions collide, infrastructure space becomes a medium of what might be called extrastatecraft—a portmanteau describing the often undisclosed activities outside of, in addition to, and sometimes even in partnership with statecraft.

Despite their seemingly technical nature, infrastructural design and urbanism are essential to the ordering of space and populations, and are thus key, often concealed, features of contemporary politics. The coordination of metropolitan networks relies on the multiple knowledge authorities and urban experts who create the epistemological conditions for making the metropolis and its essential forms of connection.

Grand Paris aims at developing innovative institutions and tools for planning based on this networked reality, in particular through its transit-connected metropolitanization agenda. The infrastructural space of the GPE, for example, is being constructed through a mix of traditional statecraft and softer governance arrangements. The state has retained control over metropolitan transportation, yet infrastructure is planned, built, and operated through a range of public and private collaborations. Here "networked thinking" refers both to the primacy of infrastructure in metropolitan development and to the "networked" cooperative, dynamic, and transverse forms of governance developed to address dynamic and multivariate urban problems.

The complex dynamics of governing regional transportation illustrate many of the challenges of arranging infrastructure across jurisdictional borders and bureaucratic silos (of land use, transit planning, environmental sustainability, job creation, housing, etc.). For example, in executing the broad plans for the new transit network, the Society of Grand Paris (SGP; itself composed of a diverse array of experts) must collaborate with the central government (the Ministry in Charge of Grand Paris, the Transport Ministry, the Ministry of the Economy, the Budget Ministry, the Paris Prefecture, the Police Prefecture, regional governmental delegations), local authorities (municipalities, intercommunal bodies, departments, and the Île-de-France), transport partners (STIF, RATP, SNCF, RFF), associations of elected officials (the Île-de-France Mayoral Association, Paris Métropole), socioprofessional organizations (AIGP, public land and development authorities for the Paris region, consular chambers of commerce, the Regional Development Agency for Paris Île-de-France), and citizens (SGP 2012).

The construction of a single GPE station thus may involve the SNCF, RFF, RATP, and STIF, which are simultaneously forced to collaborate with one another and with private construction teams, engineering firms, developers, and architects. Each of the seventy-two GPE stations is also linked to local urban development in its vicinity (through CDTs or through the sole direction of the SGP). Thus a whole range of additional actors is also involved in the integration of the station with other plans and priorities.[8]

Looking at CDTs as innovative instruments of network urbanism that facilitate transportation and land use coordination and mediate the grand vision of Grand Paris at the local scale is instructive in demonstrating the mechanisms of contemporary governance rescaling and their embedded norms. The harmonized governance facilitated by CDTs attempts to overcome the often segregated, fragmented, hierarchical, and territorial (zone-based) model of transit planning and development in favor of a more relational approach that focuses on the coevolution of multiple urban functions and the dynamic interplay of local nodes within wider metropolitan and even global systems. CDTs enable multiple actors—often with highly divergent interests—to agree on development priorities around new stations and thus are meant to be flexible spatial planning tools that can circumvent the rigid, fragmented, and exceedingly complex structures of existing territorial regulations. In addition, CDTs have the potential to integrate a variety of transit-oriented development nodes within a broader system and to vitalize local agency in directing large-scale reforms. They thus highlight the tactical pragmatic approach of contemporary grand urbanism.

The use of CDTs, however, raises crucial questions about the function of networked infrastructures in urban and regional reform. Even though the GPE is linked to myriad social, environmental, political, economic, and ethical objectives—objectives to be instrumentalized through CDTs—as the case studies of Saclay and La Gonesse demonstrate (see chapter 4), there is nevertheless an overall planning emphasis on transit as an economic asset. Based on collaboration, the CDTs reduce outlier opinions, limit the scope of reform, and thus reproduce the status quo. The political implications of Grand Paris concern not only a changing "balance" of territorial institutions but the harmonization of urban vision across metropolitan actors. Indeed, when coalitions of state and private actors devise policies in pursuit of growth, they encourage very particular types of development.

The equitable redistribution of surplus, for example, is not achievable as a primary objective through collaboration because elite partners will simply not agree to a vision that reduces their political, social, and economic capital. Thus local Grand Paris projects tend to aim not at class or welfare concerns but at populist urban ideals of culture, creativity, innovation, tourism, and leisure. At both large and small scales the contractual nature of Grand Paris projects leads to cross-class coalitions and compromises on postmaterialist concerns, in lieu of broad progressive ambitions (Cantal-Dupart 2013). Thus, while projects of grand urbanism are often framed in terms of social policy, the techniques and rationalities of governing the metropolis prevent their success. As a result, welfare benefits are nearly invariably couched within the hegemonic economistic framework of competition, attractiveness, and growth, and the pretensions of equality, redistribution, and welfare become dependent outcomes of property development.

As it stands, the urban network of Grand Paris prioritizes the goal of increasing accumulation by invigorating local production capacities and by placing metropolitan Paris in global circuits of capitalist exchange. Even if one takes into account the considerable variation in how these objectives may be pursued, according to local dynamics of collaboration, CDT structures seem to coordinate reform according to market imperatives first and social concerns only tangentially. Based on contractualized and consensual objectives, CDTs tend to place limits on the scope of public policy and foreclose the horizons of decision making.

As metropolitanization aims to orient institutions to the challenges of global flows, the issue of transportation is particularly salient in terms of defining the overall shape of the urban region and in terms of coordinating local project-based reforms. Large projects of mobility such as the GPE are thus essential aspects of grand urbanism and are crucial vehicles of global city production. In the networked urbanism of Grand Paris, mobility defines the excessive and relational character of the metropolis even as its infrastructures territorialize flows in embedded contexts.

Governing the "City Seized by Finance"

If state rescaling and urban development in Paris are today oriented toward project-driven networked forms, the flows of finance capital have underwritten this transformation in multiple ways. Stimulating and managing the financial and real estate sectors are at the heart of the global city SMP.

The financialization of urban space preceded Grand Paris, but is nevertheless accelerated by its various initiatives.[9]

Certainly the imbrication of finance and urban renewal is not unique to the contemporary era. As David Harvey (2003) shows in his now famous study on the nineteenth-century modernization of Paris, Haussmann's transformations required the creation of an elaborate credit system and new tools of financing and debt. Indeed, for Harvey (1985), financial instruments are always crucial to the "urbanization of capital." In Paris, flows of debt and credit facilitated not only the Second Empire reforms but also the postwar processes of suburbanization. Financial tools in particular have simplified "capital switching" between industrial sectors of the economy and the secondary circuit of real estate (see also Lefebvre 2003). Debt in the form of national bonds or personal mortgages has enabled surplus capital to be channeled into the built environment in times of overaccumulation, thus forestalling and geographically dispersing endemic economic crises. These "fixes" have been essential to the growth and transformation of the *banlieue*.

Harvey's general thesis on urbanization continues to apply, but a contextually specific rationality and ensemble of actors characterize the "financialization of urban production" (Halbert and Le Goix 2012, 39) in the Grand Paris metropolis. The relationship between the financialization of real estate and processes of urban planning and policy making are not well explored in the French context, though several authors have begun to make these connections (Baraud-Serfaty 2011; Lorrain 2002; Nappi-Choulet, 2011, 2013; Nappi-Choulet and Loubière 2012; Renard 2008). Indeed, these authors have identified in various ways a new type of privatization in the city, heightened in recent years, that is linked to the postreconstruction emphasis on real estate and urban infrastructure, and the increasing financialization of capital. According to Vincent Renard (2008), Paris today is a "city seized by finance."

The Grand Paris spatial reforms must be understood in this context, that is, linked to place-specific regulatory structural and political-economic transformations that have enabled the growth of the financial sector in France and facilitated its more thorough integration with real estate markets. Various regulatory moves at the national and local levels have restructured capital flows through real estate markets. On the one hand, these provide a legitimate framework for capital switching in a time of crisis. Here professional actors such as property developers (often through contracts with state bodies) invest in new office, commercial, or residential spaces in order to get a return from the appreciation in value of the built form over time. On the other hand, an institutional framework has also been developed to enable the securitization of the built environment. New tools and institutions permit the debt on which the construction of space depends to be bought and sold, and investment funds, insurance agencies, business banks, sovereign funds, and pension funds have acquired buildings and securities in real estate portfolios. Investors are interested in real estate not only as a real asset but also as a securitized asset whereby real estate portfolios can garner profits through the asset's appreciation on the stock market. Grand urbanism depends on both.

State-local development projects are a powerful anchor for available global credit. Over the past fifteen years, there has been considerable increase in foreign investors seeking speculative short-term property investments across Paris and a growth in high-risk, high-return opportunity funds, which has led to the financialization of the property sector and an increase in urban rents across the region (Nappi-Choulet 2012). The capacity for projects to attract investment is especially pronounced in the suburban peripheries, where rent gaps can be more effectively exploited than in the highly urbanized city of Paris. Large multifunctional clusters where risks can be diversified and sustainable building projects are especially attractive for investors (Nappi-Choulet and Décamps 2011; Nappi-Choulet and Loubière 2012). The acquisition of large swaths of suburban land by domestic and international developers for dense luxury development has corporatized land and territory across the Paris region.

This transformation in land ownership was enabled by a series of policy shifts at the municipal and national levels. In the early 2000s, actors at multiple scales tried to intervene in these patterns and to rationalize the way in which global capital flowed to Paris's metropolitan property markets. In addition to broad changes such the privatization of state development companies and the opening of markets to foreign property firms and contractors, specific strategies include the legalization and promotion of public-private partnerships (PPPs) and the creation of American-style real estate investment trusts REITs (Baraud-Serfaty 2011).

Since the first stages of state devolution in the 1980s, local municipalities around Paris have dealt with fiscal constraints by increasing taxes, borrowing from global capital markets, reducing services, and selling off assets to the private sector.[10] Local actors in Paris also turned in the 2000s to PPPs carried by large operators and directed by financial organizations (Baraud-Serfaty 2011). Though the use of PPPs has historically been limited in France, the national Ordinance 2004–559 of June 17, 2004, sets up a legal framework for their development and lends support for their widespread adoption. This created a new form of contract that reworked the partnership models of *politique de la ville*. Since their inception, different models of PPPs have been employed. Stadium projects associated with the Euro 2016 UEFA championships, for example (also nominally under Grand Paris), illustrate the range of funding options, from a strict PPP, to a public concession of land, to private legal projects financed by local communes. In the case of the future stadium of Racing-Métro Arena 92, the construction of which will be directed by Grand Pari(s) architect Christian de Portzamparc (associated with the developer Vinci), financing will come though entirely private funds, but the land is given in a lease by the mayor of Nanterre for a period of ninety-nine years. Whatever the form of partnership, PPPs have been very popular, generating €3.5 billion between 2004 and 2010 and predicted to generate €60 billion between 2010 and 2020 (Baraud-Serfaty 2011). With a vision based on development projects, a map for investment, and a legal regime that enables more private involvement in development, Grand Paris further facilitates the growth of PPP use.

The financialization of urban development in Grand Paris is also related to the development of U.S.-style real estate investment trusts, *"foncières cotées,"* or *"sociétés d'investissement immobilier cotées"* (SIIC), which own and manage income-producing real estate on behalf of shareholders. In France, REITs were initiated in 2001 and approved in 2002 by the Federation of Real Estate and Financial Societies (FSIF), as well as by the national government, to improve the competitiveness of property companies listed on the Paris Bourse. The trusts are supported by the state for their ability to "provide the Paris financial sector with a vehicle to facilitate the financing of nonresidential real estate, allow France to catch up with other countries," and generate a solid tax base for national and local authorities (FSIF 2014). The introduction of REITs was a strategy to address the globalization of financial markets and the growth in speculative property funds and to dynamize depressed financial markets. In addition to market stabilization and rescue, these REITs are also purported to contribute to environmental sustainability and social goals, in particular through integrating local developments into the wider urban fabric. They are now key stakeholders in urban development and urban policy making.

This legal innovation is an important factor in the evolution of the market insofar as it reinvigorated the property sector and led to an overall increase in rentability of the Paris region. In the 1990s, the financialization of the real estate sector in Pairs represented less than 1 percent of market capitalization, but by the end of the 2000s it was close to 3.6 percent (Nappi-Choulet 2013). Real estate trusts also enabled some key large-scale projects during this time. For example, Unibail, currently the largest commercial real estate company in Europe, in conjunction with Goldman Sachs and Whitehall investment funds, managed the development of the Coeur Défense office building in the business district of La Défense (Nappi-Choulet 2011, 2013). They are set to play an even more integral role in Grand Paris megaprojects.

Icade, the leading commercial real estate company for offices and business parks in the Île-de-France and a private subsidiary of the Caisse des Dépôts et Consignations, is the first French REIT to develop a strategy and appoint management to deal specifically with Grand Paris.[11] Icade has millions of square meters of holdings and investments in areas that will benefit from Grand Paris (in the vicinity of emergent development poles), and is a signatory to five CDTs, in Roissy-Villepinte, Saint-Denis–Pleyel, La Défense–Nanterre, Val-de-France–Gonesse, and Orly–Val-de-Bièvre. The company is poised to play an essential role in leveraging territory and providing the resources for development.

> In Paris and in the region, our objective is to create value for territories through identifying economic development potential in territories as well as dynamics that shape it. …With communities as with private players, the prospect of Greater Paris opens for us great opportunities of projects around future stations and in particular clusters under development. These clusters, for example, cannot establish themselves but through the mobilization, very early, of an economic and thematic community organized around a strong political will. … Being the partner of choice of those who make the city is the role of Icade. This means becoming from today on, an accelerator, a facilitator, an illuminator for the Grand Paris of tomorrow. (Icade 2014)

Their involvement in the planning and implementation of Grand Paris reconstruction and growth demonstrates the extent to which the private sector is embedded in land-use arrangements and in the public infrastructures of governance. Increasingly, decisions about who builds, what, where, and how are vested in private hands but supported by public expenditures.

The participation of real estate and financial actors such as Icade and Unibail in Grand Paris has profound implications for the deepening of a financial logic in urban planning. Planned and governed as urban projects, more and more spaces become subject to financial calculations—promising positive returns for developers, investors, and shareholders. Renard (2008) claims that that it is precisely the "financial aspect" that defines twenty-first-century urban space. "The novelty is to give autonomy to the financial aspect of a building ... the building becomes a "financial product" represented by securities, shares, listed on the stock exchange." New developments are defined less by their use value than by the property values that they inflate. The financial success of global cities depends on this ability to create and manipulate dynamic disparities in real estate values, and to transform real assets into highly liquid financial products. Thus, through the GPE and its related projects, that is, through controlling infrastructure and financial flows, the public sector establishes the conditions for value creation in a twenty-first-century economy.

One consequence of grand urbanism driven by financialized real estate production is that the future becomes less predictable and less secure. Debt-financed project-based developments require redevelopers to garner their funding up front, based on the future promise of increased land values. Public and private investments are literally great wagers on imagined urban futures. The state thus borrows to invest money in projects, claiming the rent increase will provide fiscal revenues in years to come. In this paradigm, public benefits are deferred to a future date, while private gains and public costs are realized in the present. Moreover, the guiding rationale for public investment is now the ability to financialize, to produce speculative rents in the long term and to maximize future revenue streams. In such a system, dirigisme loses its macroeconomic functions. In providing the legal framework for finance and in coordinating the metropolitanization of capital through a grand plan, the state retains, however, a "tactical dirigisme" (Cerny 1989, 190). In Grand Paris, metropolitan state rescaling is achieved through a series of networked projects intractably tied to the financial sector. Through this the state is able to produce the innovation clusters, housing estates, megamalls, research campuses, entertainment complexes, and waterfront parks that define the global city.

Prospects for Metropolitan Democracy

In 2014 a public survey found that 76 percent of residents of the Île-de-France thought of Grand Paris primarily as a transportation scheme, and almost half felt that the plans would not improve their daily quality of life (Delahaye 2014). While there may be an administrative fix at the metropolitan scale, this has yet to be accompanied by democratic legitimacy or by meaningful forms of citizen participation and influence. Residents of the metropolis are increasingly removed from where decisions happen, and Grand Paris is distanced from ordinary citizens in all but the most ritualized ways. As a youth journalist with the *Bondy Blog* put it, "For now, Grand Paris says nothing to no one. It concerns only a certain elite, architects, urbanists, journalists. ... But that doesn't speak to people, it remains vague and far removed from reality" (in Merlino and Bidou 2013, 14). New metropolitan institutions are poised to intervene in key aspects of growth, but the political class has yet to generate a genuine forum by which citizens and their needs can be brought back into the conversation.

The broad implications of metropolitan organization for life in the Île-de-France and for the fabric of the *banlieue* are hardly part of the civic discussions of Grand Paris. Instead, public consultations and engagements tend to focus on the technical minutiae of transit construction or the bureaucratic details of institutional design. Citizens are encouraged to participate in planning consultations, debates, and oversight exercises, but by and large, the terms of urbanism have already been decided on. Everyday citizens have very little control over grand urbanism, despite their populist inclusion in the dreams of the global city.

More inclusive planning techniques and practices carry the hope of a democratization of the production of space. Similarly, diffuse and cooperative policy making would suggest a less centralized production of space. Yet as states and local administrations become less able to control global flows of people, goods, and information, new players, especially private enterprise, obtain important capacities of spatial governance. With the proliferation of project-based development, spatial production today is increasingly influenced by those who do not claim to speak for a common good. A technocracy of planners and architects who are not bound to the electorate or the populace increasingly formulate knowledge of the metropolis, while contracts are negotiated at a level abstracted from democratically elected councils. Combined with the fact that local electoral representatives are losing their legitimacy in the eyes of the electorate, governance is moving farther away from accountability and from the majority of those who live in the city, instead becoming concentrated in the hands of a "plural" but elite class. This implies a different conception of public action than forty years ago—a public-private "coproduction" of the urban. Such an SMP indicates profound changes in the structuring of the city, in patterns of governance, and in the role of democratic institutions.

The temporary, experimental, and ad hoc forms of construction and management in Paris may enable progressive policies, but, tied to a competitive productivist logic of the global city SMP, they seem to be trending in the opposite direction. Thus it is not enough to proclaim the virtues of stakeholder cooperation: a just and democratic metropolitan governance is not grounded in "coalition" alone. Political fragmentation and disagreement under collaborative forms of networked governance are overcome with a common logic and aim, a form of rule that can be as or more insidious than explicit authoritarian rule. The very idea of collaboration is premised on high levels of trust and the tacit assumption that the oppositional agendas can be compromised on. Such collaborative planning and policy making may dissuade hard-line neoliberal reforms (such as those proposed and discredited by Christian Blanc), but they also erase truly progressive possibilities.

Collaborative governance—rooted in liberal notions of harmonizing institutions—rests on a center that denies agonism and that thus cannot fundamentally address the exploitative and dominating relations of capitalism. Collaboration requires pluralism and the multiplication of interests while at the same time "preventing their translation into universalizing demands that cannot be accommodated for in the current social order" (Haughton, Allmendinger, and Oosterlynck 2013, 222). Balancing profit and public investment is the challenge of cities under the global mode of production, but one that is fraught from the start.

Indeed, consensus in Grand Paris projects tends toward centrist positions and excludes the ability to contest the rules of the game themselves.

The very notion of urban governance deemphasizes adversarial forms of politics, dismisses questions of domination and exploitation, and emphasizes coalition building and regime formation, thus supporting postideological and postpolitical thinking (Mouffe 2005; Swyngedouw 2009). The soft governance arrangements, for example, allow stakeholders to be heard and concerns to be voiced, but not in a way that can subvert the existing sociopolitical order or question the market-led development based on a global, inclusive, and sustainable city. Moreover, "territorial regulation," described by Gallez (2014) as the "process whereby the conflicting views of public actors at different levels on the best course of action within a specific territory coalesce into a set of common rules that make collective action possible," risks reproducing consensual forms of decision making. Once the terms and ideals of a program have been set, there is relatively little room for maneuvering. Contractual and project-based planning thus tends to fit uneasily within broad agendas for things like social justice, territorial equality, and the right to the city.[12] Suburban residents remain effectively disenfranchised, while social and economic polarization goes unaddressed.[13]

When the state itself is so thoroughly implicated in the planning of space for capitalist accumulation, partisan divides nationally and locally narrow considerably. Both the left and the right are complicit in grand urbanism, and are incentivized to reinvent Paris as a twenty-first-century global city through courting high finance and enterprise. This aligns with the movement away from mass politics of the twentieth century and toward what Eleanora Pasotti (2010) has called "brand politics." Urban representatives are no longer relying on established parties for their resources, ideology, or organizational support or patronage, which is often, in neoliberal times, no longer available. This has led to a new form of politics that rests instead on a "brand" or vision of the city to be enacted through redevelopment. The necessary breadth of these brands undermines the formerly divisive discourses over how the city should be organized and the values it should embrace, and thus the scope of debate and contention narrows significantly. The branding of urban politics also turns citizens into consumers of space and consumers of services, and not active participants in deliberative processes. The logics driving politics and markets have converged as "both spheres increasingly pursue their goals of consensus and profit maximization by manipulating preferences and striving to shape new values and identities" (13). Both the left and the right in France today largely support the program of Grand Paris and agree on the consensus of the need for growth and the promotion of accumulation through metropolitanization. Though their modes of accomplishing this differ, the productivism of the state remains.

Moreover with grand urbanism's focus on revalorization and incessant territorial redevelopment, local politics is no longer primarily concerned with fostering a particular population base but with growing a particular revenue base. Projects to raise property values are pursued interminably, often in lieu of, for example, projects to secure high levels of prosperous employment for constituents. In fact, under the financialized model of local governance, regions that remain populated by taxpayers (residential and low income) are merely underutilized rent.

For Lefebvre, the SMP revealed the extent to which a critique of capitalism must also be leveled at the state. Because of its centralization of control over the creation of the city, the state mode of production was antithetical to democracy, that is, antithetical to collective control by individuals and communities over the conditions of their own lives. In the global city, centralized control has given way to diffuse mechanisms of public and market coercion and state facilitation, but the lines of influence remain concentrated in the hands of a few and thus the SMP is similarly demobilizing.

Conclusion

The rise of networked metropolises around the world poses fundamental questions about how to govern bigness, complexity, and flux. The importance of city regions as leading sectors of the economy also suggests that these are sites for innovation in political institutions and belonging. Thus, argue Harrison and Hoyler (2014, 2250), city regional governance is "more important today than ever before." Public and private authorities concerned with large metropolises are faced with the question, what forms of authority are poised to guide urban change in unsure environments organized according to proliferating and interdependent institutions?

The making of Grand Paris does not represent a shift from an interventionist to a noninterventionist state or vice versa, and neither does it represent a pure decentralization or recentralization of state power. Rather, in the transformations that mark Grand Paris's progress, both the central state and local actors increasingly turn their attention to urban regional concerns. In this reorientation, the political rationalities, institutional forms, planning apparatuses, and legal tools that define city politics are beginning to align with what has been identified as a global city mode of state productivism. These strategies have the effect of facilitating accumulation and promoting exchange values at the same time that they affirm state authority.

Under today's SMP, metropolitanization itself is the preferred instrument of economic production and expression of political power. This productivism is not limited to governance in "the political sphere" as an isolated realm of official state institutions. Rather, the global city productivism relates to the many diverse interventions for creating, ordering, inhabiting, and exchanging urban space. Indeed, in each of the sites examined in this book—architectural representation, transportation, and governmental restructuring—there is an emergence of a new consensus of grand urbanism, one that centers on necessary growth, global competition, and financial speculation, as well as on reworked republican notions of solidarity, state providence, and development. Under this regime, real estate and property markets are paramount; governance is polymorphic, consensual, participatory, and contractual; and spatial policies are increasingly oriented toward the private concerns of business, finance, and economic growth. Urban infrastructure plays an especially important role in securing and driving this regime.

In these transformations there is a coalition of the state, elite local interests, and civil society and private sector actors, each adjusting to and reifying the metropolitan fact. The French state plays a crucial if restructured role in these processes. It is involved both at the planning and strategic level and at the operational level through semipublic development and financial institutions, and it retains key territorial and economic functions, namely, the ability to organize and sign contracts, the capacity to create large plans and territorial borders, the maintenance of infrastructure, and the reregulation of finance. These are the mechanisms through which the state intervention produces developable private space and financializable rent gaps.

The metropolitanization of Paris draws a new political map and the productivism of Grand Paris represents a significant shift in public policy. What we see in Grand Paris is a regime of accumulation contiguous with neoliberal entrepreneurial governance but subsumed within a grand state vision. While there are competing and coexisting regional governance approaches, both formal and informal, that render coherent and straightforward policy implementation impossible, increasingly these competing forces are dovetailing around similar strategies of competitive metropolitanization whereby governance at all levels is oriented toward production within global financial markets. With this, there is a reconcentration if not recentralization of power over the right to affect the future of the city, yet a simultaneous diffusion of the rights and duties of the state into the hands of private developers and investors. In an era of revived, or perhaps refigured, state capitalism, further attention to the implications of this mode of economic growth, political organization, and spatial organization is needed.

Conclusion: Grand Urbanism in Perspective

Paris is not Paris anymore.
—Manuel Castells, 1983

What a strange idea to make plans for Grand Paris! Grand Paris already exists, it is here in front of our eyes.
—Eric Hazan, 2011

Grand Urbanism beyond Grand Paris

Grand Paris builds on earlier modes of urban governance and spatial production in France. For centuries there has been collusion between the state and the elite economic classes to organize and regulate social and economic life in order to maintain capitalist relations. From Haussmannization through to the present, the state has pursued massive investments in territory to channel the productive capacities of space. The national state has retained a primary position in spatial patterning and urban planning and through a variety of means has leveraged national (and sometimes extranational colonial) sites through the hierarchical differentiation of spaces and populations. Over the past two centuries specific plans have vacillated between statist megaproject reforms to gentrify the periphery and socialist attempts to provide local services to working-class areas and to enhance regional democracy. In the process of tearing down and rebuilding city walls and drawing and redrawing centers and peripheries, the creative capacities of producing urban space have been granted to some and denied to others.

Today's Grand Paris inherits the historical trajectory of earlier regional planning schemes; however, it also is situated in a new political, technological, environmental, and economic context. With its dominant focus on marketing the city, creating transit-connected hubs of economic activity, and installing project-based governance, Grand Paris is ushering a long-standing modernization project into an era of neoliberal reforms and global city development.

In today's mode of global city production, it is the mechanisms of dezoning, decoding, and deregulating that entrench the power of the state and of capital. Spatial planning aims to create polycentric, networked, and rhizomatic cities where designated clusters and hubs of excellence produce value in the global knowledge economy. Mass transit is a privileged means to urban growth as it promises to link these priority territories to one another while also promoting resiliency and environmental sustainability. Public expenditures are undertaken for private growth through debt-financed public works. Leading the metropolitan process, flagship territories and site-specific megaprojects are created and supported through an emphasis on polarity itself as a model of growth. In this regime, real estate and property markets are paramount; governance is polymorphic, consensual, participatory, and contractual; and spatial policies are increasingly oriented toward private concerns.

In many ways the making of Grand Paris is undeniably French. This single case study has illuminated the particularities of one city's emergence into the twenty-first century based on particular cultural, spatial, and political inheritances. Yet insofar as it reveals the working of grand urbanism in a global context, it also provides useful analytics that are applicable elsewhere. Indeed, Grand Paris is not as unique as it might first appear, and one need not paper over the place-specific traits of metropolitanization and reformation to recognize broader patterns of global urbanism and urban politics. The challenges that Paris faces in the twenty-first century—economic instability, political strife, social inequality, territorial apartheid, inadequate housing, infrastructural gaps, municipal austerity, outdated and fragmented administrations, environmental degradation, a decline in the quality of life, loss of hope for the future—are ones that large cities everywhere are facing. Certainly the local articulation and combination of these issues is context-specific, but there is also much shared structural commonality across cases as cities adapt to a postindustrial metropolitan resurgence (Scott 2008). Cities around the world are adopting large-scale growth plans with similar designs, land use plans, and governmental arrangements.

The idea of grand urbanism helps conceptualize the local response to Paris's idiosyncratic metropolitan challenges and a globalized and globalizing paradigm of regional planning in the twenty-first century. That is, grand urbanism captures the growth paradigm specific to Grand Paris, but it also reflects an increasingly generic practice combining the intensification of speculative urbanization, investments in major infrastructural networks at the regional scale, and experiments in metropolitan institutional arrangements. The Grand Paris initiative is one highly spectacularized version of this more common model of spatial production and management that aims to coordinate design, growth, and governance across urban and suburban territory as a whole.

The preponderance of state-led investments in metropolitan megaprojects suggests that the Grand Paris mode of planning is becoming increasingly widespread today. Indeed, what I have described as grand urbanism resonates with what Guy Baeten (2012) calls "Keynesianism for the rich." Global reforms, from courting business in postsocialist St. Petersburg (Golubchikov 2010), to large-scale urban development projects across China (Broudehoux 2007; Olds 1995; Ren 2011), to mega-events such as the 2012 London Olympics (Raco 2012, 2014), all involve the prominent leadership of the state in delivering flagship projects, ordering territory, and ensuring the regulatory framework for competition based on the concept of an extended and improved city space connected by world-class modern infrastructure. Grand Paris also bears uncanny resemblance to other major urban regional visioning and development projects such as PlaNYC, Plan Abu Dhabi 2030, Greater Helsinki Vision 2050, and Tokyo Vision 2020.

The reiteration of similar planning strategies and land use patterns around the world is evidence that grand urbanism hardly "originates" in Grand Paris. Indeed, the representations, plans, and policies of Grand Paris are infused with many befores and elsewheres—global Silicon Valleys, Docklands, Central Parks, opera houses, eco-cities, and Guggenheims mark the imagined landscape. Grand Paris architects and planners also explicitly sought lessons from other regions, most commonly London (the Olympic and Crossrail developments and the Greater London Council are frequent models) but also Tokyo (the multi-use transit station), Dubai (functionally differentiated regional clustering), Hong Kong (transit and land use development and financing), Bologna (polycentric metropolitan governance), and Bogotá (regional transit integration), to name a few. Grand Paris is exemplary of grand urbanism, but it is by no means the natural representative or arbiter of this endeavor. It is, however, one important node of translation and conversion where the ideas and practices of grand urbanism that are circulating globally are taking shape.

Grand Paris is poised to set the agenda for grand urbanism moving forward as it is rapidly becoming a key reference point for other cities through various practices of policy and knowledge mobilization and mobility (McCann 2011; McCann and Ward 2012). Paris may have lost its principal position of global influence, but it still has a special (if romanticized) cachet in urban design, planning, and policy-making markets. Elites in Paris are eager to spread their unique knowledge and skills abroad, and they find a willing audience in globalizing cities seeking solutions for metropolitan revitalization.

The knowledge created in Grand Paris, for example, comes from architects who have a global presence. The teams of Grand Pari(s) and participants in the International Workshop of Grand Paris (AIGP) are taking the knowledge created in Paris and using it in other works and initiatives around the world. Similarly, as a result of thick networks of information sharing between metropolitan governments, key Grand Paris policies are on their way to becoming global best practices. This is especially true for regional transport planning, where members of the Scientific Committee of the Society of Grand Paris (SGP) have traveled to meet with colleagues in London, Milan, and Toronto, to name just a few. More generally, since 2007, Grand Paris officials have advised Sydney, Hong Kong, Moscow, Tokyo, São Paulo, Buenos Aires, Caracas, Berlin, and Brussels on the merits of the proposed projects and on what can be learned from Paris. As Laurence Cassegrain, project director for public politics relating to Grand Paris, has commented, "Cities around the world have sought to understand, develop and apply similar processes. The list is growing quickly, as the cities of the world realize that they have to find a new way to address their issues" (in Williams 2011). What is being forged in Grand Paris could soon find its way into other urban planning initiatives in diverse contexts.

Grand Paris in this sense is not a single prescription or unified planning package that is being transferred whole cloth to other places. As a bundle of technical and normative images, designs, policies, laws, dreams, and calculations, it is, however, a highly mobile discourse. Across each of these political technologies, processes of citation, aspiration, comparison, and competition link Grand Paris to grand urbanism in other cities around the world. Grand Paris is thus a key facilitator of what Ananya Roy and Aihwa Ong (2011, 10) call "spatial practices in the dual sense of gathering and dispersing, of circulating ideas, forms and techniques ... constitutive of emerging globalized spaces." Paris's global influence may be waning in the twenty-first century as the city has been forced to cede ground to financial boomtowns and emerging megacities, but it nonetheless continues to have profound currency in urban planning. As Grand Paris in particular and grand urbanism in general become more influential, it is necessary to understand what acts of political and cultural translation must accompany the reception and mimicry of the plan abroad, and the political implications of the adoption of the "grand" paradigm in aspiring global cities.

Grand Moscow

A focus on one particular translation of grand urbanism—from Grand Paris to Grand Moscow—illuminates some provisional dynamics of how the grand paradigm is shaping global urban space. The agglomeration and development initiative of Grand Moscow was announced in 2011 based explicitly on the French example. The transmission vectors between the two plans are many and range from visiting dignitaries traveling from one city to another, joint conferences for Russian and French business associations, international contracts for construction and real estate development, and shared expertise through urban planning and architectural design consultations. In material and symbolic ways, Grand Paris's urbanism is translated across these urban contexts. The Grand Paris model, however, is not merely delivered to Moscow in its entirety. Rather, the plan is stylized and circulated through local political cultures, spatial histories, policy-making contexts, and regulatory institutions, and is influenced by the organizational dynamics of cultural producers and private firms and developers. In this case, international architects are the key intellectual and cultural producers in the policy dissemination of grand urbanism.

In the first decade of the twenty-first century, Moscow was facing many of the same challenges as Paris. Rapid population and territorial growth in suburban areas had not been accompanied by appropriate infrastructural, institutional, or social development. As a result, problems of traffic congestion, housing shortages, high living costs, overcrowding, economic volatility, and power struggles among a fragmented political class plagued the region and were reducing the urban quality of life. When then president Dimitri Medvedev decided in 2011 to address these concerns through a Grand Moscow (Bolshaya Moskva) project that would double the surface of the city and transform it into a modern polycentric metropolis, he looked to international, notably French, expertise for assistance. According to Alexandre Missoffe, director of the presidential cabinet of the SGP, "The Russians asked for our advice for general planning, for transport growth.... They are searching for a model for methods of development" (in Quénelle 2013). The supporters of Grand Paris were eager to offer lessons.

As in Paris, problems of urban expansion in Moscow originated in the specific pathways of urban development established in the twentieth century. Growth in Moscow has long been characterized by concentric spatial patterns. Centralized Soviet urban planning in the early years of the twentieth century saw monumental projects such as the metro system and Stalinist skyscrapers take root in central areas of the city. Mid-century, these infrastructural developments gave rise to the concrete suburban microdistricts of Khrushchev. Since the 1960s, however, urban developments have been sparse and fragmented, and although Moscow's population has nearly doubled, administrative facilities and public services and infrastructure have not kept apace. This has led to patterns of segregation between the core and periphery (almost two-thirds of jobs are located in the center, while most housing estates lie in the periphery), as well as socioeconomic disparities between urban and suburban populations (Kolossov, Vendina, and O'Laughlin 2002). With an uneven distribution of employment throughout the Russian Federation's capital, millions of residents are forced to commute each day from distant peripheries to the overpopulated historic city center, thus causing serious transportation, ecological, and social problems.

Despite these problems, because of the city's enormous potential for redevelopment and growth, Russian and foreign investors have expressed a growing interest in Moscow since the turn of the twenty-first century. At least until the sanctions imposed on Russia following the annexation of Crimea, global capital poured into Moscow, and speculators keenly watched its property markets, but there is no overall plan for where or how to build, which risks accentuating existing concerns. In a 2013 interview with the French newspaper *Les Echos*, vice mayor of Moscow Andrei Sharanov

Conclusion 227

claimed that Moscow has a "paradoxical reputation" for being a great place to do business, but also for having a difficult bureaucracy and a low standard of living (in Quénelle 2013). These negative features are obstacles to advancing the attraction of large-scale investors and cosmopolitan residents. The goal of Grand Moscow is to better balance these elements in order to increase quality-of-life standards and improve its international reputation. In August 2011 the city announced that the entire region would be brought up to "international living standards" so that the territory as a whole could become more available for investment, development, and financial growth (Argenbright 2011). Grand Moscow is the key element in this rebranding and restructuring strategy to secure global city status and organize the city's economic resurgence.

The main thrust of the Grand Moscow plan is to expand the space of Moscow and relocate federal agencies to the periphery as a way of deconcentrating and decentralizing the city. Grand Paris and Grand Moscow both demonstrate that the typically monocentric focus of the metropolitan region has become increasingly large and polycentric or multinodal. Indeed, as of July 1, 2012, Moscow had grown by 148,000 hectares, expanding 2.5 times its existing limits through the incorporation of twenty-one new municipalities (in the southwest between Varshavskoye and Kievskoye Shosse) and increasing its population by 300,000 inhabitants. In addition, more than 40,000 government officials (the state is still one of the largest employers in the city) will be relocated into the new territories, in particular to "New Moscow" or the "New Federal District."[1] The expansion plan for New Moscow was approved by the Moscow City Duma and Federation Council in July 2011.

Medvedev also instructed Moscow's Mayor Sergey Sobyanin and governor of Moscow Oblast (the Moscow region) Boris Gromov to come up with a combined plan for the Grand Region as a whole that would include a new financial center designated for the Rublevo-Arkhangelskoye area and a future "Silicon Valley" in Skolkovo (Argenbright 2011). The overall project aims to divert attention outward from the center of the city and to encourage the city's growth in peripheries (*troitsk*) through poles of excellence in advanced producer services. The annexed areas will be developed into differentiated hubs of research, leisure, tourism, medicine, and business and finance. As with Grand Paris, the Grand Moscow project also aims to reduce traffic between these hubs by increasing the offerings of public transportation (including the construction of an ambitious new metro along the southwest growth axis by 2020) to the new employment and residential poles, moving away from "ring" developments toward polycentric connections and building multimodal mobility links. To make Grand Moscow, the state plans to invest a prodigious sum of €185 billion over three decades (Jégo 2012). Like Grand Paris, the project rests on a multi-pronged approach featuring architectural designs for a new city identity, expanded infrastructure networks, and innovative governance arrangements. Each of these key policy areas was influenced by French practices.

Perhaps the most significant and direct way in which Grand Moscow was modeled after Grand Paris was through its architectural competition. The project to expand Moscow's borders to the southwest, joining cities and towns to the border of the Kaluga Region, was propelled forward by a competition for the best urban development project for the newly annexed territories. What became known as the Moscow City Agglomeration Competition was launched on January 13, 2012, by the president of the Russian Federation, the Moscow City and Region, the Union of Architects of Russia, and the Academy of Architecture and Civil Engineering. It solicited plans for

- the creation of conditions for Moscow to develop as a global city and international center for finance, education, innovation, and tourism;
- the construction of new centers for the agglomeration, with the different attributes of a capital city and those of a global city;
- the dynamic deployment of transport infrastructure, in particular a regional rail network for passenger transport to ensure the development of the Moscow Agglomeration's polycentric structure and the interconnection of that development with neighboring areas. (EPADESA 2012)

With this competition, Moscow aimed to develop a new identity and scale for the city that would be driven by the imaginative work of architectural teams, and to rebrand the region as a truly distinctive yet global city. "In the context of strong international competition, to distance itself from Chinese, American and European cities, Moscow wants to position itself and to find a good urban and economic strategy," explained Parisian Bertrand Lemoine, general director of the AIGP and a member of the Russian selection committee (Veran 2012).

In 2012 the Architectural Department of Moscow City Government (MosComArhitectura) announced a short list of teams, each composed of foreign and Russian architects as well as interdisciplinary urban experts.[2] Included on the short list were several architectural studios who had worked directly on Grand Paris, including Antoine Grumbach et Associés, l'AUC, and the Italian design firm Studio Associato Secchi-Viganò. In addition, the SGP, the Public Development Authority for La Défense Seine Arche (EPADESA), the Public Authority for Paris-Saclay (EPPS), and the Russian-French Centre for Energy Efficiency also consulted to one of the teams on the development of a financial pole, the transport development plan, and the development of a science and technology cluster, and evaluated the plans in terms of technical, financial, and legal feasibility.[3]

Unlike the pure "consultative" work of Grand Pari(s), the Moscow City Agglomeration competition explicitly aimed to select a combination of winners to work on different phases of the project, with the goal of actually implementing their designs. Because of this pragmatic focus, the object of the Moscow consultation was much less free than the Grand Paris consultation. At each stage of the competition the teams responded to one of three questions, respectively how to transform the saturated city, how to work on the extension of 150,000 hectares in the southwest, and how to move state services from the city to the periphery (Laugier 2013). Unlike in Grand Pari(s), where Sarkozy asked architects and urbanists to "dream big" and make proposals without any constraints, the Moscow City Agglomeration design consultation was organized according to a more specific program of extending the city.

While round one of the competition was won by the Rotterdam-based OMA (Office for Metropolitan Architecture) and round two by the Russian urbanist Andrey Chernikhov, in the third round of the competition the French team, headed by Antoine Grumbach and his partner, Michel Wilmotte, was awarded the victory. Their designs to develop Greater Moscow along the banks of the river Moskva mirrored closely their Grand Pari(s) design based on the Seine Métropole and similarly featured dense networks of multimodal rail, tram, and metro lines to enhance flows throughout the city and boost regional environmental sustainability. The growth plan along the Moskva river aimed to do away with the Soviet-style urbanism that marks the region and to infuse new life, including new green spaces, into the city. The "nature-city" vision also stressed the coextensive goals of more public transit and ecological preservation, with the creation of new towns, including Federal City, as anchors for regional economic growth.

Beyond the architects, official delegations at multiple levels of government (traveling from Moscow to Paris and vice versa) and technical conferences of financial and business experts also served to develop extensive collaborations between actors in Paris and Moscow. It should be noted that the considerable French involvement in the architectural competition and other aspects of the development initiative is not altruistic. Public and private sector actors from Paris have significant interests in supporting the Grand Moscow project. For politicians the positive affirmation of the Grand Paris model adds legitimacy to the grand paradigm. For corporate bodies, greater Moscow represents a new market for products and services. Indeed, the Russian government is looking for partners for public-private partnerships (PPPs) as well as foreign investors to see the plan to fruition, and French construction, real estate, and commercial firms are positioned to benefit greatly from Grand Moscow. Hoping to win lucrative government contracts or to speculate in property markets, French business associations have a large stake in the Grand Moscow plans (as they do in Grand Paris). In promoting the Île-de-France and its enterprises abroad, the French state has been able to sell Grand Paris in more ways than one.

To facilitate exchange between French and Russian professionals and politicians, the Franco-Russian Chamber of Commerce (CCIFR) also held two large conferences in 2012, one in June, titled "Greater Moscow-Greater Paris: Modern Agglomeration and Public Private Partnerships," and the other in November, titled "From Russia to France: Presentation of Russian Projects in the Field of Transportation to European Investors." These conferences brought together a wide range of stakeholders to discuss the experiences of development and investment programs of the Grand Paris project and the prospects of Grand Moscow. "The Grand Paris and Grand Moscow projects constitute important steps in the history of the development of the two agglomerations, designated to become megapoles of world importance," noted the president of the CCIFR, Emmanuel Quidet (CCIFR 2012). The conferences also dealt with the important question of how to establish PPPs between investors and governments in both projects and how to finance the planned urban and infrastructural extensions through incorporation of the private sector.

In additional to more general musings on how to manage large metropolises today, official state delegations discussed the administrative aspects of PPPs and governance of the two plans over the course of 2011–2013.

Maurice Leroy, former French minister of urban planning, advised Russian and Moscow delegates on several trips to Moscow, while in March 2012 Moscow mayor Sergei Sobyanin traveled to Paris to meet with Jean-Paul Huchon, president of the Regional Council of Île-de-France, Paris mayor Bertrand Delanoë, and representatives of the SGP. According to the Moscow City Government External Economic and International Relations Department, the main subject of this meeting was how to strengthen economic ties of the global cities and the "common investment goals" that united the two projects (DEEIR 2012).

As a result, French business interests have affirmed their commitment to invest in projects in Moscow and the mayor of Moscow has already awarded substantial contracts to French firms. Alstom Transport has a contract to build new tramways in the Moscow region, and Vinci Construction is in charge of building 35,000 parking spots in peripheral sites. The Russian Skolkovo Foundation and the French Fondation Mov'eoTec have also signed on to a long-term partnership for the development of mobility innovations in the respective "Silicon Valleys" of Paris and Moscow.

Despite the broad similarities of the two plans and the extensive transversal links between them, the Russian authorities and practitioners made it clear that their intention was never a blanket application of Grand Paris but a transformed and translated version to meet the particular needs and conditions of the local context. The translation of Grand Paris is not straightforward because although the traditional ideologies of Soviet urban planning no longer suit Greater Moscow, neither can Moscow's urban dynamics be captured in the discourses of Western urbanism (Menu 2013). Chief Moscow architect Sergei Kozlov also reports that the French project is not a template but rather a general concept. "Given the importance of this project only the most successful elements from various concepts will be used in developing new project plans for Moscow" (Kopteva 2013). The precise means of global city development solutions cannot be identical in Eastern Europe as in the West.

The use of Grand Paris furthers the postsocialist neoliberalization of Moscow (Argenbright 2013; Golubchikov 2004; Golubchikov and Phelps 2011; Kolossov and O'Loughlin 2004), but in incomplete ways. As Jamie Peck (2011, 789) writes, "the project of neoliberalization did not simply 'arrive' in eastern Europe, but neither was it unilaterally imposed by western powers. In fact, it was constructed through several decades of (asymmetrical) dialog and (mis)-communication." A similar sort of ongoing dialogue between many transnational actors is currently shaping grand urbanism in Grand Moscow. Whereas the language of the global city, and the terms of sustainability, growth, and competition were consistent across these exchanges, they were inflected with a Russian accent. Similarly, Grand Moscow is led by a global city SMP involving massive investments in territory and infrastructure for the purpose of private growth and increased competition, but these reforms are being negotiated through idiosyncratic institutional structures and political cultures.

There are two main lessons about grand urbanism that the Grand Paris–Moscow nexus provides. First, the diffusion of urban practices from Paris to Moscow speaks to the hybrid nature of urbanism today. In both Grand Paris and Grand Moscow, the central state was a key instigator of territorial transformation and was required to mobilize regional space and map new growth plans and infrastructure projects. Yet the grand plan of Paris was not merely transferred at the level of official diplomacy. Instead, the mobility of policies involved overlapping actors who negotiated, adopted, adapted, emulated, and contested grand urbanism through multiple channels and at multiple scales. Along each of these pathways policy is not merely "technical, rational, neutral and apolitical" but rather is shaped by relational asymmetries, contingent forces, and place-based conflicts (McCann and Ward 2013). Transnational policy making certainly involves state delegations and the formal sharing of best practices, but a great deal of the diffusion of the Grand Paris paradigm is also occurring through nonofficial circuits. Networks of international architectural and urban design professionals are particularly important in influencing how grand urbanism is taking shape through these globalizing spatial activities.

Second, the complex planning assemblages of grand urbanism that cut across local places call into question a simple narrative of global "urban competition." Although the competitive race of global cities for investment and prestige is the milieu out of which grand urbanism emerges, networked cities are not universally at odds with one another, interacting purely out of isolated and calculated self-interest. The social, political, and economic connections among global city regions mean that Moscow and Paris are closely linked through a variety of interpenetrating flows. Each globalizing city may struggle to individually maintain its comparative rank, but there is also a shared project to grand urbanism at a global scale whereby the

Conclusion

transnational capitalist class (Sklair 2005) of elite architects, developers, politicians, and planners reproduces its own conditions for survival through cooperation, negotiation, and compromise in and against the interests of isolated cities or their nation-states. In this sense, grand urbanism is an ideological practice that operates not only within select metropolises but also increasingly within a networked global field. Global city competition frequently entails cooperation, partnership, and the maintenance of common oligarchical rules amongst otherwise adversarial urban sites.

Taking Account of Grand Paris

Grand Paris is a far-reaching social, political, and economic enterprise that is redefining the future of the city in dramatic ways. This book has shown how assorted understandings of space, politics, and the "good" of urban life have been created, deployed, and operationalized through various policy sites and how an amalgam of urban techniques has come into being to create a new metropolitan reality. The argument of the book is anchored in the contention that Grand Paris is restructuring the French capital and its urban-suburban relations in response to political-economic pressures at multiple scales. The analysis has deciphered these transformations by investigating tensions in the processes of producing, realizing, and distributing urban space and urban value. I interpret the contemporary redevelopments in greater Paris as an expression of grand urbanism, a paradigm of urban development that reaches its apex in Paris but that indicates an increasingly prevalent form of planning and policy making being articulated by large metropolises around the world.

In particular, I have considered the making of Grand Paris in three main dimensions: the imaginary, the economic, and the juridico-political. Across each of these essential policy terrains I have shown how twentieth-century planning models based on an urban-suburban agglomeration are being adapted to the prevailing realities of the twenty-first-century global city metropolis, and the challenges associated with such a process. I began by identifying the aesthetic and intellectual conditions of Grand Paris. Projecting the face of the metropolitan Paris region thirty years into the future, the Grand Pari(s) architectural exhibit created an ersatz city to be brought about through subsequent policies. It also solidified an unquestionable language of global urbanism rooted in the trifecta of competitiveness, inclusiveness, and sustainability. Giving a unified representation to a fragmented region, the exhibit popularized a collective dream of a connected polycentric metropolis that broke with Paris's long-standing monocentric history. This "shared dream" was then concretized in large part through the Grand Paris Express mass transit initiative. The nationally sponsored GPE megaproject has enabled the state to mobilize the suburban territories of Paris for capitalist production by linking future transit stations with strategic enterprise zones to be developed as productive hubs in a global informational economy. Mass transit's function as a mode of everyday travel for urban dwellers is here rendered subordinate to its capacity to catalyze speculative real estate development around new stations, closing the rent gap in underdeveloped peripheral areas. This regime of speculative (sub)urbanization is supported by the creation of a shifting and inchoate regional institutional structure that provides the regulatory framework to make the dream of Grand Paris a reality. The Metropolis of Grand Paris and new mechanisms of collaboration and partnership are the foundations of the regulatory arrangements of state productivism.

In the empirical and theoretical analysis of Grand Paris, three main arguments emerged. First, with respect to the theme of neoliberalism, the analysis underscored the pervasiveness of the logic of market optimization in French urban planning and governance. The case of Grand Paris demonstrates that the rationalities and practices of neoliberal urbanism have become dominant both through pro-growth market-based competitive locational policies and through social democratic domains that define themselves as progressive alternatives. Indeed, in Grand Paris there is a paradoxical interdependence of explicit plans to capitalize metropolitan space and leverage the city into global markets and those that seek regional cohesion, solidarity, and sustainability. This is particularly evident in the collusion of state productivism and the development of sustainable infrastructure. The shared language of right and left in relation to urban transportation and development marks, on the one hand, a pragmatic need for compromise in order to operationalize policy, and on the other an increasingly pronounced consensus around maximizing the value of urban territory across an increasing number of domains of urbanism and urban policy. Generalized gentrification (or sometimes the less controversial *embourgeoisement*) is understood nearly universally by Grand Paris actors to be a natural and progressive process of urban change that should be accelerated through public action.

Those on the right, for example, say that to reach its economic goals, the government should intervene to make city building more flexible, efficient, and cost-effective. Those on the left call for redistribution after and through the same building practices. The right lauds free exchange, the left hails the return of "state providence," but both support the state-led marketization of metropolitan territory. The GPE transport system is exemplary here in achieving this compromise. While creating proximate developments around new stations and servicing collective consumption needs, it still submits everything and everyone to the general law of circulation. The differences between different metropolitan plans no doubt matter on the ground and in the streets, but they both rest fundamentally on pillars of project-led productivism.

When compared with the stark privatization models of urban restructuring in the United States or the UK, the bleak urban austerity across much of southern Europe, or the violent accumulation by dispossession that is driving urbanization across the global south, France may appear to have exceptionally resilient policies of social democracy. The very real particularities of France's political culture of republicanism, based as it is on the articulation of an unbreakable social bond tied to a providential state, should not, however, cloud the reality of its own neoliberal engagements. In France until recently, the creep of the private sector in urban planning has been matched by a fighting welfare state. With Grand Paris, however, there has been a decisive shift in favor of market-led strategies of growth and reform. The practice of neoliberalism *à la française* (in both hard and soft versions) involves the pursuit of solidarity and sustainability alongside the entrenchment of profit-driven models of administration in general and competitive place-based urban policies in particular. As a result, through the socially conscious veneer of grand urbanism, capitalism remains "'the impassable horizon of our times,' to say nothing of those to come" (Garnier 2010, 127).[4]

Second, in considering the territoriality of France, the book has demonstrated how Grand Paris has accelerated and transformed processes of state rescaling. In Grand Paris's privileging the creation of Paris as a global city, the nation-state is reconfigured as both ineluctably interdependent and emphatically urban. Tracing the precise mechanisms of this process, the book fleshed out empirically attempts to make the new economic spaces of global capital commensurate with the political spaces of metropolitan regions.

Against theories of urban entrepreneurialism and municipally led growth machines, the analysis of grand urbanism demonstrates the emergence of a new common sense of collaborative yet state-led metropolitan coordination. In France there is recognition by multiple administrations and actors of the necessity of a functional metropolis to secure local competitive advantage and to address the urgency of social disintegration accompanying global city reforms. Through multiple parallel processes of metropolitanization, the global city region is created as a common identity, scale of collective action, and horizon of social, economic, and political success.

In addition, the concept of grand urbanism invokes networked planning as an absolutely essential component of contemporary state rescaling, and it argues that the French state has strategically retained functions of infrastructural (especially transport) and financial management as a means to control large territories. The tactical dirigisme of managing infrastructure combines anticipatory visioning and large-scale territorial distribution with soft forms of collaborative local governance and project-based reform to alter the built environment. Capital-dense projects of rapid urban rail are particularly salient political infrastructures for grand urbanism as they require extensive administrative coordination across territories. They also have the capacity to dramatically restructure physical landscapes, patterns of mobility, and the orienting ideals of land use planning, thus transforming the regulatory and regularizing structures of urban governmentality.

In general, global city state productivism positions the metropolis as the engine of national growth, at the same time that it encourages within the metropolis an ever deeper web of transnational economic, and especially financial, connections. Thus the book troubles traditional narratives of how the nation-state capitalizes territory by rearranging domestic space and promoting its interests overseas. In so doing, it connects contemporary forms of hybrid sovereign rule to the facilitation and direction of multiscalar flows.

Third, on the issue of uneven development, grand urbanism suggests a new metropolitan mediation for the equalization and differentiation of territory. Capitalist urbanization has always been beset by problems of growth misaligning with development and social conflict rising alongside putative economic prosperity. With grand urbanism, these patterns operate at large urban and regional scales. While the contemporary gentrification of the city of Paris, for example, has been noted in popular and scholarly literature (see especially Clerval 2012), the present study has illuminated similar dynamics extending to the suburbs as well. The annexation and revalorization of greater Paris are based on channeling investment to priority regional hubs. Such suburban polarizing reforms raise land values and alter land uses in ways that threaten to push low-income residents even further afield and into the multiplied interstices of the global city network.

The notion of grand urbanism was mobilized to understand the intensification of this type of urban planning scheme unabashedly aimed at raising the value of land in underperforming regional territories through targeted megaproject developments. Uneven development of suburban territory through the accelerated but selective upgrading and revitalization of the metropolitan fabric is no longer an externality or unforeseen consequence of planning strategies but the very pillar of urbanization and urban transformation. Grand urbanism orients urban processes toward the production of exchange value in the form of rent. In this climate, grand urbanism quite literally amounts to betting on city futures.

Conclusion

Nine years into the project, Grand Paris still appears largely aspirational. The physical landscape imagined by the initiative has only just begun to take shape. It is too soon to accurately predict what the future contours of Grand Paris will look like and feel like, for the development of the built environment is only beginning to materialize. Yet in this short time the intellectual and geopolitical landscape of Grand Paris has been dramatically transformed. Increasingly there is little discursive space to think about urbanization outside the overriding grand urbanism agenda. Although the city walls of Grand Paris are still being built, the writing on them is already clear.

In each of the Grand Paris policy sites studied in this book, there are very real conflicts between the constitutive goals of democratizing and redistributing, or concentrating and privatizing, the common wealth of the city that play out in planning deliberations. These conflicts—inherent in capitalist social organization—are, however, subtended by a more thoroughgoing consensus among lawmakers, urban planners, architects, developers, public officials, and even "participating" citizens around the goals of networked regionalism, global competition, and economic growth. In response to the overarching question, *What makes a city grand?*, the answer is a resounding chorus of the attractive global city. As a process of policy making and ordering urban life, Grand Paris actively distributes the populations, spaces, and functions that make up the twenty-first-century city in alignment with the demands of global finance capital.

The consequences of this could be dire. From its populist spectacles of urban design, to its orchestrated dynamic of regional gentrification, to its privatization of public concerns, the Grand Paris reforms are diminishing democracy and equality. Paris is being symbolically and physically transformed by an elite cadre of state officials, technical experts, aesthetic and intellectual leaders, and financial institutions in order to improve its reputation as a high-ranking world metropolis and thus to become more attractive to choice residents and investors. Owing to the logic of commodification on which Grand Paris development is based, benefits will not accrue to all places or to all *citadins* (city dwellers) in the same way. Everyday inhabitants are denied the ability to collectively produce spaces according to their desires and needs, decision-making capacity is concentrated in a small class of state functionaries and business leaders, and opposition is made incomprehensible according to the accepted terms of urban deliberation. Moreover, the logic of optimizing economic growth, which is the lodestone of grand urbanism, is poised to exacerbate existing social, economic, and political problems while contributing to the peripheralization of unwanted populations and the suppression of critical ideas and praxis. In other words, Grand Paris will deny an equal and generalized right to the city (Harvey 2008; Lefebvre 1996; Schmid 2012). If the analysis presented here reveals the specter of the future Île-de-France, it is increasingly a neoliberal landscape of social fragmentation, inequality, and political complacency.

While Grand Paris is hardly a unitary plan, its debates and discourses tend to rest on this overall common sense that never questions the logic of metropolitanization that fragments as it unifies, peripheralizes as it centralizes, impoverishes as it makes prosperous. Endemic to grand urbanism is a ground rent incompatibility between the achievement of a livable, self-sustaining, democratic, and just community and the maintenance of relations of accumulation. Whereas grand urbanism seeks consensus and compromise, to truly question the manner in which urban space is productive of inequality, urban planning cannot merely be a matter of balancing the forces of growth and sustainability or competition and equality while maintaining the competitive global city as the a priori condition of decision making.

Although I claim that Grand Paris is delusional, the aim of this book is not to reject the project outright. Rather, the book has sought to draw out the main features of this emerging planning paradigm in order to clarify its internal dynamics and its specific promises and limits. As elaborated throughout, the production of the new space of Grand Paris opens both progressive and regressive possibilities. Clearly, the project offers a wealth of insight into the particular history of Paris and the contemporary metropolitan form more generally. It also serves as a prescient reminder of the revolutionary potential of spatial transformation. There were many indications in Grand Pari(s) of critical practices that would see the building of Paris reshape the city in a form other than in the image of capital given by the powers of developers backed by finance, corporate capital, and an interventionist state. Similarly, the battles won by the left to expand Grand Paris transit and bring urban services to underprivileged parts of the city are important reminders of the possibility of contesting centralized elite plans and the importance of networked infrastructures as fundamental to urban equity. The gains made in policies for new social housing, sustainability, and fiscal redistribution through the Métropole du Grand Paris are also meaningful if incomplete indicators of how to organize space in more collective, ecologically sound ways. Indeed, all of these insights should be drawn out and explored for their political purchase. Together they point to urban futures not shackled by the contradictions of the present.

The fact that Grand Paris is a living project that has not yet fully left the ground means that its trajectory can be altered. Paris, like global cities elsewhere, can yet be made otherwise. But this is possible only if we understand the limits to the current path and expose its complex internal contradictions. In an era of widespread urban upheaval and exploitation the exigencies of theorizing the urban in this manner are pressing. In a public and spectacular fashion, Grand Paris demands a rethinking of how and to what end the city is made. The debates surrounding the Grand Paris project in particular and grand urbanism in general involve deep examination of the political, perhaps the essentially political, questions: What is the City? How are cities made? And who benefits from transformations?

This book is a practical, critical, and historical endeavor that addresses these questions in order to disclose more just and democratic ways of building communities and environments. The analysis presented here is part of an ongoing intellectual project to provide a fuller account of the limits to existing urban discourses, and in so doing to imagine how urban planning and architecture—as quintessential techniques of spatial transformation—might work in ways that are not co-opted into the state productive machinery. This work is crucial if we are to make cities that are decidedly not grand.

Notes

Introduction

1. All translations are mine unless otherwise noted.

2. The terms used to speak of these territorial objects are quite slippery. In general, "Paris" designates the City of Paris, the proper name of the administrative municipality (Paris has the unique distinction of being both a "commune" and "department," the two most local subnational levels of government in France). Paris, in other words, is the internationally known city composed of twenty *arrondissements intra muros* (between the walls) of the *boulevard périphérique*. Grand Paris and metropolitan Paris, on the other hand, both refer to a more amorphous urbanized fabric that extends *hors les murs* (beyond the walls) of the municipality. The Île-de-France is the administrative "region" (sometimes simply "the Region") containing Paris and seven other departments. Other terms, such as *zone dense* (dense zone), *center d'agglomeration* (agglomeration center), *zone central dense* (central dense zone), or *aire urbaine* (urban area), are also variously employed to describe particular territorial formations.

3. This is a significant departure from the existing writing on Grand Paris in France. A number of recent French-language publications have examined different aspects of the Grand Paris plan with a focus on questions of governance. Philippe Subra's *Le Grand Paris* (2009), Frédéric Gilli and Jean-Mark Offner's *Paris métropole hors les murs* (2008), and Marc Wiel's *Le Grand Paris: Premier conflit né de la décentralization* (2009), for example all consider how different agglomeration scenarios effect institutional dynamics and policy provision. Philippe Panerai's *Paris métropole: Formes et échelles du Grand-Paris* (2008) does not address the question of governance as such, but instead explores the malleable form of the new Parisian metropolis in terms of both its varied representation and its legal and regulatory limits. None of these works deals comprehensively with the political economic structures that are shaping the geography of Grand Paris. While the rest of the world has been closely watching Grand Paris, there are to date no comprehensive foreign language publications on the initiative, and few English-language publications have emerged on Grand Paris,

save brief news pieces and special interest (architectural and transit) reports. This book in large part introduces the debates of Grand Paris to an English-language audience.

4. Michel Foucault's (1982, 49) account of discourse as practices "that systematically form the objects of which they speak" is also particularly illuminating as a guide for this sort of analysis (on this mode of poststructuralist policy analysis, see also Bacchi 2000; Danziger 1995; Fischer 1995; Flyvbjerg 1998; Foucault 1980; Shapiro 1992).

5. After Hollande's election, his government rebranded the initiative "New Grand Paris" to signify a break from the tutelage of Sarkozy and to claim the initiative as a Socialist intervention. While the rhetoric associated with Grand Paris shifted, the main features of the initiative and its overall orientation have remained remarkably unchanged.

6. Like Grand Paris, the concept of the *banlieue* defies easy translation. It is a highly relative "composite discursive nebula" (Wacquant 2007, 9). The *ban-lieue* in medieval times originally referred to the area one league (*lieue*) from the center of the city, which was still subject to the sovereign power or *ban* of the ruling urban authority. Though the urban landscape has changed dramatically since this use, the uneven politics defining center and periphery remain. The term *banlieue* now translates most directly as "suburb," but the suburb of reference is quite different from the postwar single-family housing developments that are conjured up in the North American imagination. Though there are wealthy *banlieues* in France (e.g., the hometown of Sarkozy, Neuilly-sur-Seine), the term is most often used to refer to low-income neighborhoods on the outskirts of major cities. In this sense the *banlieue* is often associated with North American–style inner-city "ghettos" (although there is good reason to be skeptical of this comparison). Typically in French the singular, *banlieue,* is used to refer to the general condition of the suburb. However, the plural, *banlieues,* will also be used throughout the book to highlight the heterogeneity of the neighborhoods and territories that compose the regional landscape.

7. The direct rivalry between Paris and London is an especially prominent undercurrent to Grand Paris. The soaring growth of London's financial sector and the spectacular redevelopment of the Docklands have been inspirations for Paris. But London's success over the past two decades has also instilled profound fear in the French capital. With London beating out Paris in the bid for the 2012 Olympic Games and surpassing Paris in tourist visits each year, Paris risks losing the race of European global prestige to its long-standing competitor. This threat lends urgency and importance to the overall project.

8. The Paris urban region is often taken as a metonym for France. While the Île-de-France represents just a fraction of the physical area of France, it is home to almost one-fifth of its population and accounts for one-third of its GDP.

Notes to Introduction and Chapter 1   243

9. The Grand Paris architectural firm MVRDV identifies the economic stakes of the juncture, saying, "The consultation exactly coincides with the profound moment of reconsideration of the global financial crisis. If in the immediate future, it reduces the number of investments, in one way or another, it will redefine the direction of the world economy, from which will follow immense spatial consequences. What society will we have after a crisis? What collective responsibilities must be assumed?" (in Le Moniteur Architecture 2009).

10. Blanc also expresses this perspective more thoroughly in his 2006 book apocalyptically titled *La Croissance ou le chaos* (Growth or Chaos).

11. Bruno Jobert and Bruno Théret (1994) describe a unique variant of neoliberalism in France that paradoxically relies on the republican ideals of a paternal social state, masking reforms to privatize, deregulate, and discipline labor as large-scale initiatives to improve the health and well-being of the citizenry.

12. While the initial announcement of Grand Paris in 2007 occurred before the onset of the financial crisis, the crisis became the backdrop for the initial phase of the architectural project and was very much present in the language of the project throughout 2008–2014. With the transition in leadership from Sarkozy to Hollande in May 2012, there were severe doubts as to whether the crisis-growth scheme of Grand Paris would be implemented. However, despite concerns over the project's financing (Auzannet 2012) Hollande continues to support Grand Paris even in a climate of austerity (Enright 2014).

13. I use the word "grand" instead of "greater" to signify more closely the French connection of this paradigm and to highlight the aspects of grandiosity, progress, and largess that fundamentally underlie this perspective.

Chapter 1: Paris and/Is Its Suburb

1. Here we may consider, for example, the image of Paris one confronts on exiting a plane at Charles de Gaulle Airport (which is not located in Paris proper) or on viewing a typical tourist map. This image presents the old city of Paris walled at its perimeter, floating in a sea of unidentified hinterland.

2. The Commune was a political trial between the working classes and bourgeoisie over social space, over who has the power to occupy the city and which community can rightfully declare itself "Paris." Violent reaction to the Commune on behalf of the French army and the execution of thousands of communards provided a temporary answer, yet the question of who has the legitimacy to build and manage social space remains to this day (see especially Ross 1988).

3. With the development of new modes of transportation, above all the automobile, the centrality of Paris also came into question in this period. With generalized

commuting, the suburbs developed rapidly, and the sedentary city was replaced by the mobile city (Donzelot 2009).

4. While a full account of the complexity of planning efforts in this time is beyond the scope of this book, it should be noted that the urbanism and architecture of the postwar era were never directed by a complete or closed ideology enforced by a unitary and omniscient dirigiste state. Rather, these were evolving practices enacted by an assemblage of forces and actors. Cupers's *The Social Project: Housing Postwar France* (2014) is useful for untangling the vicissitudes of postwar planning and design apparatuses and their ambivalent politics.

5. In the 1980s a number of former *soixante-huitards* pushed forward a progressive agenda of architecture and urbanism in Paris. They demanded action to reduce inequality, marginality, and extreme alienation, and also alluded to more postmaterialist values, such as the promotion of urban playfulness, harmony, beauty, and pleasure. The Banlieues 89 program undertaken by Roland Castro and Michel Cantal-Dupart is emblematic of these attempts of urban design and policy to address the "problem of the *banlieue*" and to change the image associated with suburban territories. Through a series of projects, exhibitions and conferences, and strategic plans, but mainly through its role as a think tank, Banlieues 89 set the stage for thinking about Paris as a polycentric city of interconnections where the suburbs were as important as if not more important than the city proper (Banlieues 89 1990). They even had a project in 1990 titled "Le Grand Paris: 6 Paris des Cinq Paris," which aimed at territorial and social solidarity and prefigured the designs of Grand Pari(s). For the most part, however, these initiatives substituted symbolic projects based on environmental determinism for systematic initiatives of social redistribution.

6. In 2001 the municipality of Paris instigated a new dialogue to challenge the domination of Paris and develop a plan for more fluid and robust forms of interterritorial collaboration. These engagements, which led to the 2006 metropolitan conference (out of which Paris Métropole was formed), insisted that Paris was but one of a range of municipalities that make up the metropolis. Building on existing and proposed partnership accords between the city of Paris and local collectivities in the Île-de-France, these engagements sought to recast the relations between the city and the *banlieue*. The officials who came together to reform municipal relations were convinced that the construction of a metropolitan identity and scale was necessary to effectively and legitimately govern in the twenty-first century (Mairie de Paris 2013; Mansat 2012).

7. The two should not be easily conflated, however. As I argue in the next chapter, Grand Paris provides a new language for urbanism and a dream of an inclusive metropolis, but largely fails to address the conditions producing urban fragmentation and inequality.

8. In the context of contemporary French urbanism, "mixity" is used to denote mixed-use spaces, but moreover, "social mixity" of multiclass and multicultural integration.

9. The language of an architectural *concours* is used throughout the Grand Pari(s) literature, but Grand Pari(s) was not, it should be noted, a traditional architectural competition. Although the ten teams were initially selected from a larger pool, in the consultation there was no panel of judges and no mechanism in place to select a single winner at the end whose blueprint designs would be implemented. Indeed, most of the visions will never be executed. Yet insofar as the exhibition performed the other tasks of an architectural competition—creating public awareness and support for changed landscapes; generating design innovation, reflection, and debate; and boosting the profile of individual architectural firms—the appellation applies.

10. The post-Kyoto framework refers to the international regime that resulted from the 1997 Kyoto Protocol under the auspices of the United Nations Framework Convention on Climate Change. The Kyoto convention was a watershed in environmental regulation and saw a renewed international effort to reduce greenhouse gases through institutional means, including the market model of emissions trading.

11. From the Latin *ad* (toward) and *glom* (a ball or mass), agglomeration is a process whereby separate parts are moved together to form a cluster or heap. Described by Edward Soja (2002, 12–15) as a unique logic of urbanization, agglomeration has a more specific meaning in contemporary critical urban theory.

Chapter 2: The Shared Dream of Grand Pari(s)

1. This timeline was never linear, however, and in many ways the policies existed in nascent stages prior to their implementation, with Grand Pari(s) merely translating them for a wider public (Wiel 2009b).

2. In his work on the ideologies of modern planning, for example, Robert Beauregard (2005) has identified an interplay between representation and reality through the notion of such "adjectival cities." Each adjective chosen to describe a city distills the priorities of the speaker, and "because each adjective represents a different city, a different type of intervention is implied" (25). For Beauregard, adjectival urbanism is dangerous because adjectives also work to reduce complexity and conflict and make one aspect of the city stand in unitarily for all others.

3. In his book written to justify Grand Paris, *Le Grand Paris du XXIe siècle* (2010), Christian Blanc traces a narrative of Paris back seven thousand years, throughout which the site of Paris has invariably played an important role in local and regional economies. From a strategic trading axis in Bronze Age Europe to the residence of

the Roman emperor Julian to the seat of the eighteenth-century Enlightenment, Paris, it would seem, has long been important, a natural and immutable pole of power, wealth, decision making, culture and art, science and technology.

4. Sarkozy saw declining poll ratings and weakened ambition over his term as president. Without popular support for measures such as large-scale pension reform, Sarkozy attempted to raise his standing with desperate populist measures rooted in xenophobia, such as the war on Paris's Roma population in the summer of 2010 and the banning of the Islamic headscarf. The Grand Paris project was in many ways another attempt to rescue his faltering image (see especially Badiou 2009; *Economist* 2010; Hewlett 2011; Marlière and Szarka 2009).

5. This was made possible through corporate sponsorship by Google and by JCDecaux, among others. The use of Google Earth (a centralized planetary database) in this alternative depiction of Paris suggests perhaps that with "smart" technologies the grand and mundane urbanisms are actually rather synchronous.

6. Finn Geipel and Giulia Andi of LIN architects worked on both projects.

7. What Haussmann initiated and the subsequent zoning regulations reinforced was an idiosyncratic "Parisian style," such that topography was regular and buildings were immediately understandable as uniquely belonging to Paris. The legacy of these zoning practices in the city of Paris—continuous building façades, vertical limits, uniform ornamentation, and so forth—contrasts sharply with the unregulated growth outside the municipal limits. In many ways, the deregulation of Paris and redesign of the suburbs represent an attempt to provide a more recognizable fabric to the metropolitan region through giving to the *banlieues* markers of Parisian identity and through breaking down the stylistic uniformity of the historic city core while adding new unity to the margins.

8. In the wake of Grand Pari(s), several tourist campaigns have focused on enticing tourists away from the core and into the suburbs. In the summer of 2011, for example, the magazine of Greater Paris, *Megalopolis,* published a vacation guide, "Cet Été, Partez En Banlieue!" (This summer go to the suburbs!) to encourage exploration of "100 fun sites on the other side of the *periph.*"

9. Blanc's initial plan was met with vehement opposition from transportation and land use planners from across the region. They criticized the hasty and haughty plan for ignoring planning recommendations, for not accounting for actual travel patterns, and most generally for failing to address the pressing needs of commuters.

10. Indeed, in "no longer speaking of the *banlieue,*" grand urbanism loses its ability to identify the contradictions of capitalist metroplitanization and to describe the mechanisms of exclusion inherent to global city building. As a result, the urban ideology that emerges out of Grand Pari(s) is largely without a critical edge.

11. The end result of the concourse is not "winner take all" but that "all are winners" in the shared dream of Grand Paris.

12. "Multimillionaires in euros or dollars thanks to huge projects that they have authored, at the head of agencies with large workforces, enjoying privileges of the status as internationally recognized designers, it is unclear what could link these members to the old 'bohemia', except for some shallow anti-capitalism, repudiated and forgotten, that they professed in architecture school when they were students" (Garnier 2010, 21–22).

13. Jameson (1998) sees this condition as fundamental, the "colonization of the future as a fundamental tendency in capitalism itself, and the perpetual source of the perpetual recrudescence of finance capital land speculation."

Chapter 3: Transit Debates and the Contested Regime of Metromobility

1. Currently there are at least thirty-two metros under construction worldwide, and of the more than 190 systems in fifty-four countries, 132 have been extended, often quite dramatically, in the last decade alone. Around the world, massive amounts of public funds are being channeled into urban transportation projects (a good archive of these constructions can be found at www.urbanrail.net).

2. Urry (2007, 51) writes, "Historically, most societies have been characterized by one major mobility system that is in an evolving adaptive relationship with that society's economy, through the production and consumption of goods and services and the attraction and circulation of the labor force and consumers."

3. The RATP is responsible for most of this additional transport in the region, although the Professional Transport Organization of Île-de-France (OPTILE) also regulates select suburban bus routes under the authority of STIF.

4. While the use of public transportation has risen across the region in the past ten years, use in Paris is much higher than in surrounding departments, and its rate of transit use has risen faster than either the inner or outer suburbs (Ministère de l'Écologie, de l'Énergie, du Développement durable et de la Mer 2010). As of 2008, only 12 percent of commutes in Paris were undertaken using the automobile, while this number rose to 47 percent in the inner suburbs and to 71 percent in the outer suburbs. In addition to the better offerings, the difference partly owes to the extraordinary efforts to discourage automobile use in the city of Paris. Since his election as mayor of Paris in 2001, Bertrand Delanoë, has made reducing car use and increasing public transportation and cycling top priorities (he introduced, for example, the famous Vélib bicycle-sharing program and hefty parking fees within Paris, and has turned urban expressways into city "beaches"). However successful these efforts were, they also benefited Paris over the *banlieue,* and some cases had the unwanted

effect of villainizing car-dependent suburban communities and forcing low-income suburban residents to pay more for their access to the city.

5. Since 2006, for example, seven tramways have been completed in the region. Trams are preferred in these ad hoc plans as they are far cheaper to build than subways and can work well in less dense suburban neighborhoods where there is no peak demand.

6. Blanc even published his plan for the Grand Huit network in the UMP-supported conservative daily newspaper *Le Figaro* on March, 29, 2009, a month before it was officially announced by President Sarkozy.

7. The CNDP is an independent authority established by the 1995 Barnier law on environmental protection. The authority is responsible for ensuring public participation in development and infrastructure projects in the interest of the state that have high socioeconomic stakes or that have potentially significant impacts on the environment or on territorial planning. Ensuring that "all have a say in *grands projets*," the CNDP can organize debates and consultations on a wide range of projects, from highways, railway lines, waterways, nuclear installations, airports, gas lines, and hydroelectric dams to industrial, sports, cultural, and tourist facilities.

8. Subra (2009, 117) notes how leftist mayors in the region were faced with a particularly difficult political and ethical choice in demonstrating support for either transportation initiative. Strapped for cash, and in urgent need of transit options, many supported plans that were essentially opposed to their political agendas. When Blanc announced his transit plan, many communists in fact announced their immediate support on the sole basis that the plan included their particular municipality. For Subra, the dilemma facing leftist officials in Grand Paris consisted in that in being against either plan, "they risk[ed] losing control over the sociological evolution of the cities they manage," and in supporting the plans, "they pass[ed] to the side of opportunities of financing and development they cannot refuse." A concerted front was elusive as municipal officials were pitted against each other for new developments that might alleviate the grave social conditions in their respective communes. With officials forced to compete for scarce resources, local and particular demands took precedence over broader class-based demands of class or a more amorphous *banlieue* solidarity.

9. The compromise over service to Saclay, the "Silicon Valley" of Île-de-France, is the most blatant demonstration of how consensus became capitulation to state authorities. Fierce battles occurred between environmental activists, who understood the Saclay Plateau as a green space in need of conservation, and firms that wanted to open high-tech plants and headquarters in the booming territory. The local collectives were nuanced in their debate opinions but generally did not want to interfere with the development operation or risk being denied the future revenue from new enterprises in the area. Whereas the Arc Express was not set to pass

through this vulnerable territory, service to Saclay was absolutely crucial to the RTPGP. Local business interests threatened that if the line to Saclay were dropped, the state would fail to facilitate the destiny of the region in the global economy (CNDP 2011c, 106). The CCIP and the Chamber of Commerce and Industry for Essonne stated this speculative relationship in even stronger terms, claiming that because of the future growth of the technological industry, "the service to the Saclay Plateau is inseparable from Grand Paris." The initial GPE compromise featured eleven stations on an aboveground light rail system instead of a more disruptive underground network. Yet this did little to address the demands of conservationists and supported the idea that the transportation network is imperative for the success of the scientific and technological cluster. Notably, while debates over the Saclay site have been waged before on a local level, in widening the scope of the conflict and reframing the issue at the metropolitan and national levels, environmental groups lost out to economic development interests who were more powerfully situated at these scales.

10. CDTs enable shared and contractualized territorial projects. They establish operational partnerships between municipalities, the state, and the SGP (with intermunicipal organizations and institutional actors such as Paris Métropole and the AIGP as optional signatories). CDTs permit discussion among multiple stakeholders and encourage the sharing of information and pooling of financial resources in support of often ambitious economic and social development projects. They also produce diagnostics and action agendas in convergence with existing planning documents, such as the regional SDRIF, intermunicipal *schémas de cohérence territoriale* (SCOTs), and municipal *plans locaux d'urbanisme* (PLUs). In principle, a CDT must outline broad goals of territorial development and specify details such as housing unit projections, any beneficiaries of rights to preemption, a calendar for realization, and cost estimates. Each contract lasts for a length of fifteen years, corresponding to the time until the completion of the GPE.

11. The neighborhood of Arcueil-Cachan, for example, held a celebratory inauguration ceremony for the GPE in 2011 featuring artistic performances and a symbolic "laying of tracks." Thousands of residents came out to acclaim the arrival of the long-promised suburban metro.

12. Despite near consensus among local and national officials on the merits of the GPE, however, the plan has been met with criticism from a number of prominent transport experts who were dissatisfied with the territorial compromise and skeptical of both the vision and the optimistic projections introduced to justify it. Gérard Lacoste (2010), for example, claims that the clustering and network effects are overestimated and that the job creation estimates are ill matched with projections of the working population. He further claims that the GPE presents only a "caricatured vision of polarization" that inadequately accounts for or plans for the complex realities of metropolitan functions. Jean-Pierre Orfeuil and Marc Wiel (2012) and Pierre

Merlin (2012) concur in their suspicion over the numbers and statistics used by the SGP. More fundamentally, they also argue that the plans do not adequately take into account the relationship between the metro extension and land and real estate markets. They also independently question the ability of a ring design to promote equitable and polycentric urban development. These criticisms have largely gone unheeded.

13. Unquestioned support for mass transit is rooted most deeply in the notion of the *maillage*, which at once invokes the fine mesh of service and the corporate-speak of "networking" and connecting. In this networked society (Castells 1996) framework, all areas and peoples are supposedly bound to each other through various nonhierarchical means. The networked, connected metropolis is a powerful symbol that promises universal access, freedom and prosperity, and benefits. Yet it should be noted that in practice these are not undifferentiated, nor are they guaranteed. Disaggregating the progressive from regressive aspects of infrastructural networks, especially those of mass transit, is exceedingly difficult.

Chapter 4: The Mobilizing Myths of the Grand Paris Express

1. The prevalence of large-scale urban development projects (UDPs) across Western Europe illustrates how the shifts in state intervention in the economy dovetail with recentralized modes of governance. In their study of thirteen large-scale UDPs in Europe, Swyngedouw, Moulaert, and Rodriguez (2002) found that they are increasingly being used as a "new scalar gestalt of governing" marked by the creation of urban coalitions, a shift from social to economic policies, enhanced city marketing, strengthened targeted locational policy, and the production of urban rent.

2. Flyvbjerg (2014) defines megaprojects as "large-scale, complex ventures that typically cost US$1 billion or more, take many years to develop and build, involve multiple public and private stakeholders, are transformational, and impact millions of people."

3. Flyvbjerg (2014) identifies these four sublimes as drivers of megaproject development. From awe at scientific innovation, to the rapture of popular attention, to the delight in profits, and the pleasure of beautiful design, megaprojects involve intense affective (not merely financial) investments.

4. The legislation leading to the 2010 Grand Paris Act uses the 2008 crisis to justify exceptional spending and powers: "The current crisis, of unprecedented scale, reinforces the urgency of a strong action by public authorities to increase the capacity of adaptation.... The current challenges justify the urgent and exceptional measures of this bill which allow the extension and the strengthening of the measures of consultation and contractualization, with the will asserted by decompartmentalization and by efficiency, just as the British did for the realization of the Olympics of London" (Assemblée Nationale 2009). Having lost out to London in the competition for the

Olympics, growth-seeking actors in Paris turned to Grand Paris as an alternative lever for urban regeneration.

5. The clustering strategy of Grand Paris is an element of other national initiatives to bring investment and talent to France in general and to the Île-de-France in particular. As of 2014 there were seventy-one innovation clusters in France, with those in Grand Paris representing the largest and most profitable hubs of private companies, educational institutions, and research in key technology sectors. The attractiveness of France is being pursued simultaneously, for example, by the National Pact for Growth, Competitiveness and Employment, unveiled in November 2012, which in part aims to make it easier for exceptional foreign talent to stay in the country; the National Investment Program, launched on July 9, 2013, which promises €12 billion to be spent on research priorities such as energy, aerospace, the digital sector, health care, technological excellence, and training; and Pact for Competitiveness of French Industry, published in November 2012, which seeks a "competitiveness shock" to reduce labor and business costs, encourage small business growth, and stimulate innovation (Gallois 2012; Invest in France Agency 2014).

6. Lacoste (2010) questions the very definition of "cluster," pointing out the extreme variability in how the term is used. The growth poles targeted by the GPE, for example, are anywhere from 30 to 250 square kilometers in size, home to populations ranging from 180,000 to 1.2 million inhabitants, and host anywhere from 50,000 to 500, 000 jobs.

7. Indeed, rail and metro lines in France have long served the function of opening territories and making neighboring land around stations more profitable (Merlin 1967, 2013).

8. Jean-Pierre Garnier (2010) estimates that nationally there are 5.7 million people living in precarious housing (those without homes, in overpopulated conditions, or living with friends or family) because of financial or professional conditions—almost 12 percent of the French population.

9. Garnier (2010, 13), for example, makes the case that urban regeneration and renewal are targeted state strategies to disperse the poor and render them less visible. With the specter of the *banlieue* revolts still threatening capital flight, breaking up the *grands ensembles* is a key yet understated aspect of the Grand Paris plan.

10. One way the GPE has been effective at differentiating mobility socially is on the axis of physical ability. Indeed, "accessibility" was at the forefront of many public meetings over the GPE, yet overwhelmingly this term meant the physical accessibility of stations and trains for those with physical disabilities. The SGP guarantees that the GPE will be a "fully accessible" system, open to all travelers regardless of how they move. Responding to the 2005 Equal Rights and Opportunities Law, the GPE will meet international standards for accessibility and is designed to ensure a simple

and intuitive movement to the blind, those hard of hearing, or those with reduced mobility (see, e.g., SGP 2014). These efforts are by no means insignificant, yet they still conceive of access as an isolated individual characteristic.

11. Offner (2013, 68) suggests that in order to account for the unevenness of mobility in the Île-de-France, we should abandon speed as a main criterion of the efficacy of transport modes and instead shift our attention "from the right to transportation to a right to access." In this way a transit system is considered not only as a means to get from one place to another but as a tool to access services and the common wealth created by the city.

12. While questions of gender are not the focus of this study, it is clear that spatial capital is also divided along gender lines (INSEE 2010a). Women's access to and use of transit is an important aspect of broader equity struggles.

13. This enemy-at-the-gates mentality that fears opening up the suburbs for what might then come back into Paris is exemplified in popular press treatments of the *banlieues* as ghettos in the 1980s and 1990s, including a cover story in the weekly magazine *L'Express* titled "Thugs: Drift of the Ghetto" (see Wacquant 2008 and Dikeç 2007a for an account of these representational tactics).

14. Silverstein's data are from 2004, and it can be assumed that the numbers have increased since then. With the most recent anti-Islamic backlash following the November 2015 terrorist attacks on Paris, transit surveillance is again expected to increase.

15. No small part of the references to Dubai or "the Gulf States" stems from a tacit racism. If Parisians see London as the "good" model of financialization and urban revitalization, the Arab Gulf invariably represents its perverse extremes.

16. Indeed, a number of the 2007 visions supported this idea and proposed decommodifying transit through collectively owned taxis, bicycles, and car-pool systems.

17. The French government has identified Saclay for an Operation of National Interest (OIN) and has committed to investing €5 billion in the area to support projects for teaching, research and innovation, learning, technology and science, and, of course, transport. In addition to this public investment an estimated €15 billion of private funds will to be invested over the next decade in housing, accommodation, private research centers, and business institutions.

18. Existing and planned industries include automotive (Renault, PSA, Daimler Chrysler), information technology (Thalès, Alcatel Lucent, Dassault System, Bouygues Telecom), energy (Air Liquide, Alstom, EDF, Inéo), engineering (CG Veritas, Altran); construction (Bouygues, Vinci, Egis), aerospace (Thalès, EADS, Safran), and food (Danone, Kraft Foods) (EPPS 2012).

19. In the GPE project, many depressed localities are excited to bring investment to the area and celebrate the creation of new development and revitalization to

accompany proposed stations. Both domestic French and international investors are courted with the promise of the opportunity to take part in the creation of a new magnificent Paris (Wallis 2011). The proposed stations in the northeastern working-class department of Seine-Saint-Denis—highly targeted by the network—conform to this logic, as do many of the proposed stations in the eastern department of Val-de-Marne (Observatoire Régional du Foncier en Île-de-France 2011).

20. Since 2011 the Grand Roissy organization, under the prefect of the region, has been involved in directing development efforts in the northern territory. There are four CDTs for Grand Roissy. Each CDT is supported by most local politicians and government officials (including the Plaine de France Public Development Authority, SNCF, Regional Prefecture, and the General Council of Val d'Oise).

21. Next to Europa City there are plans for 200,000 square meters of office space. The usefulness of this should also be subject to scrutiny given the fact that almost five million square meters of office space are vacant in the Île-de-France (Cazenave 2013).

22. Moreover, as Léonhardt (2011) notes, "this urban strategy writes the metropolis into a situation of complete dependence to the realization of the network" such that contestation becomes futile or suicidal.

Chapter 5: A Thousand Layers of Governance

1. French metropolitanization (*métropolisation*) is the dominant narrative of post-Fordist urbanization, referring both to the general creation of what in the Anglo-American literature would be the "urban region" and to the governing institutions that manage their growth. The *métropole* (metropole) of Paris, of course, has a longer lineage in France's imperial history as the organizational center of colonial relations.

2. Peter Miller and Nikolas Rose's (1990) work on governing the national economy is particularly helpful for elucidating the dialectical movement of scalar arrangements and the institutions to oversee them.

3. While attentive to individual actors and institutions, this chapter aims not to expose "who rules" in Grand Paris but to question how metropolitan power structures are coming into being. Chapter 6 continues this analysis looking more particularly at the planning and policy rationalities at work across a variety of governing bodies.

4. Governance describes the new system of actors involved in managing communities that lack a single sovereign authority. While the term is used to describe the international realm (states in an anarchic system) it is also applicable to cities under globalization where a complex of competing authorities establish norms, rules, laws and behaviors. For Le Galès (2002, 17), governance "relates to all the institutions,

networks, directives, regulations, norms, political and social wagers, public and private actors that contribute to the stability of a society."

5. Questions of metropolitan governance in Paris have been particularly salient since the 1990s, when a literature on governance emerged within France to explain the changing national systems of authority and power, especially at the local level (see Jouve 2003; Jouve and Lefèvre 2002; Le Galès 1995 2002).

6. Pierre Veltz (2012, 14) echoes this from a more national perspective: "Our territorial organization has serious faults and produces entropy and waste, notably, as a result of a totally outdated but unfortunately hyperstable institutional structure."

7. See especially the debates from 2008 to 2014 in the online magazine *Métropolitiques* (http://www.metropolitiques.eu).

8. The state here, it should be noted is not a unitary or fixed actor. By the French state most generally, I refer to a multiscalar assemblage of institutions and regulations that collectively govern national space. This assemblage is replete with tensions and contradictions. The "central state," or frequently just "the state," is also shorthand for the national level of government in France (i.e., the executive and legislative bodies, including the presidency and parliament). Because of the institutional structure of the French national government, even within the central state, there can be virulent disagreement and contradiction, exemplified in periods of cohabitation. Nevertheless the central government invariably is structured around particular national priorities.

9. The *cumul des mandats*, which allows elected and appointed officials to maintain positions at several different government levels simultaneously also shapes this relationship.

10. The departments within the Île-de-France typically are split between the wealthy Hauts-de-Seine and Yvelines as a base for the right and Essonne, Seine-Saint-Denis, Seine-et-Marne, Val-de-Marne, and Val-d'Oise on the left. While historically variable, Paris too has been shifting leftward.

11. Here Sarkozy no doubt recalled the experiences of the Greater London Council, dismantled by Margaret Thatcher for partisan reasons.

12. Municipalities or communes gained considerably from decentralization and are responsible for many local policy sectors, including public transportation, housing, local planning, and development. Departments too became stronger with decentralization, taking on area responsibilities for education, social affairs, and roads and highways, and also some aspects of economic development, training, and culture. The twenty-two new regions were established primarily to organize economic development, and whereas they have gained responsibilities since the early 1980s, especially in terms of regional master planning, public transportation, and professional training, they remain relatively weak institutions. Though the 1981–1983 laws saw a

series of radical decentralizations that supported the financial and political autonomy of the communes in particular, these early forms of *autogestion* were for the most part subsequently revoked.

13. These have taken a variety of forms over time: *syndicats intercommunaux à vocation unique, à vocation multiple, districts; communautés de communes, communautés de ville, syndicats mixtes, chartes intercommunales*, and so on. There are two basic forms of intercommunality, those with fiscal power and those without. The intercommunal structures without fiscal power are traditionally referred to as syndicates of communes; they are voluntary organizations that form to deal with one or more matters. While such a practice dates to 1890 and allows single-purpose entities, it has seen increasing use since the 1980s, especially after the Chevènement law of 1999.

14. The *politique de la ville* urban policies of the 1980s onward, for example, were based on partnerships between and among the central state, local governments, civil society actors, and local nongovernmental organizations. Urban politics largely relied on a series *"contrats de ville,"* "urban contracts," between the state and local governments. Targeted urban intervention (in areas such as poverty relief and job creation) was simultaneously local, contractual, and statist. Like decentralization more generally, the corporatist *politique de la ville*, however, did not achieve more autonomous democracy or welfare. According to Walter Nicholls (2006), for example, the policy is guilty of "associationalism from above," whereby the state fosters partnerships with third-party organizations to generate benefits for the state while bureaucratizing civil society.

15. Although there are clear exceptions to this, private and civil society actors as well began to organize on a more regional scale.

16. The 1999 Chevènement law, for example, recodified and rationalized the system of intermunicipal organizations with the aim of reining in these proliferating structures. It established three main categories to replace the existing web of arrangements: *communautés de communes* (for rural areas), *communautés d'agglomeration*, and *communautés urbaines* (for urban areas). In so doing, it also endowed these intermunicipal organizations with new powers and legitimacy that rivaled regional and state powers, and balanced the hegemony of Paris.

17. In February 2011, Paris and Seine-et-Marne signed a cooperation protocol on water management, conservation, and biodiversity. In March 2012, Delanoë and Huchon jointly wrote a statement, published in *Le Monde*, confirming their commitment to a metropolitan housing authority.

18. The logo for Paris Métropole captures this effectively. Outlines of the myriad political borders of the region are superimposed atop one another, giving the effect of a layered, overlapping, and multipolar assemblage. This nonhierarchical and nonpolarized image represents the many constituents (communes, departments, EPCIs, etc.) that make up the authority.

19. In 2010 Paris Métropole, in conjunction with the AIGP, for example, launched a program of 110 initiatives across the territory to revitalize the region, promote citizen engagement, and aid in metropolitanization.

20. This state-driven development is not the only use of EPAs. For example, The EPA of Plaine de France, presided over at one point by Jean-Paul Huchon, is more autonomous and operates a variety of economic and social programs.

21. After 2012 in the Ayrault cabinet, Grand Paris was shuffled between several ministries before eventually settling in the portfolio of the Ministry of Territorial Equality and Housing, led by Cécile Duflot (of the Europe Écologie party, the Greens) until she stepped down in March 2014. This move was symbolically significant insofar as it delineated a shift in the overall goals of Grand Paris at the national level (from the development of the capital to territorial equality). While Duflot seemed less interested in holding the reins of the project (and, when she did, steered it in a markedly different direction), the national presence in Grand Paris still carries considerable weight.

22. In June 2014 the AIGP launched the "12 Keys to Inventing the Metropolitan Project of Grand Paris" as the foundation for the next stage of its work, dealing with governance and administration.

23. While the act also applies to metropolitan structures in Lyon and Marseille, Articles 12 and 14 of the law are specifically devoted to Paris.

24. The forty-six communes bordering the inner suburbs have the option of joining the MGP if they wish.

Chapter 6: Metropolitan Governance and Global City Productivism

1. Urban governmentality, then, not only concerns how services are delivered and the efficiency of institutions in achieving their objectives, it also considers how mechanisms of authority produce spaces and subjects that pursue particular standards of value. The distributions of power and transformations of state spaces accompanying Grand Paris cannot be separated from the conditions and objectives of the urban society—increasingly a competitive and marketized urban society—that they enact.

2. In this sense, Lefebvre differs from other Marxist thinkers of the time, such as Louis Althusser or those of the French regulation school.

3. For Lefebvre, the critique of growth and state productivism applied equally to the social democracies of Western Europe and the planned economies of Eastern Europe and the USSR. Today the global city SMP applies, albeit through variegated rationalities and practices, to liberal, social democratic, authoritarian and developmentalist state regimes.

Notes to Chapter 6

4. BRICs refers to the growing economies of Brazil, Russia, India, and China.

5. Whereas state-managed master plans that precisely defined the future were possible in an era of stable and plentiful resources when authority was arranged hierarchically, targeted projects of collaboration are more suited to the contemporary moment of limited and contingent resources and horizontal and plural governance. As a consequence of the multiplication of authority structures domestically and the greater volatility of an interdependent global political economy, the prospective aspects of master planning have disappeared. All stakeholders act rather in a world of financial, social, and environmental uncertainty (Callon, Barthe, and Lascoumes 2001). The production of space through grand urbanism is no longer a matter of predicting the future but of preparing for it; projects are anticipatory rather than obligatory (Pinson 2009).

6. The private sector has been particularly instrumental in carrying out the mandate of Grand Paris. Although the Chamber of Commerce and Industry of Paris (CCIP) covers only Paris and the *petit couronne*, it nevertheless plays a particularly notable role in regional governing through consultations, working groups, and committees. The CCIP is also active internationally through workshops and trade missions, where it sells the amenities of Paris as well as the services of French firms. And additional private stakeholders have emerged to organize at the metropolitan scale. Le Club des Entreprises du Grand Paris (the Business Club of Grand Paris) was launched in 2012 to secure a more formal role for the private sector in the radical transformation of the regional territory. The club represents forty representatives of enterprises, belong to various sectors (including infrastructure, energy, services, construction and public works, transport, engineering, services for residents, real estate, hospitality, and distribution), who coordinate on various projects and on lobbying public decision makers. The Grand Paris Investment Agency also works to accelerate the economic development and growth of Grand Paris.

7. Pinson (2009, 163) argues that "in a context of limited rationality and of the multiplication of participants in urban politics, it is now a matter of constructing action orientations, shared visions which will have become the object of consensus in the interactive and iterative process of consensus, of mutual adjustments between the relevant actors. … Its effectiveness is cognitive and political more so than juridical."

8. The GPE station is also a particularly notable example of how new technologies of power are created through the interaction of aesthetic and technological norms. Insofar as the GPE stations are set to be central showpieces at the Universal Exposition in 2025—promising avant-garde design, cutting-edge green architecture, and smart digital technologies—they are key emblems of grand urbanism and the modernizing metropolis.

9. The degree of financialization of a city is marked for Rachel Weber (2010) by "the increase in municipal debt, the privatization and securitization of public assets, the size and scope of the financial services available to city governments, and the investor-orientation of critical collective consumption decisions." Across all of these terrains, the Grand Paris metropolis is becoming more financialized.

10. In Paris, for example, the iconic market turned shopping mall of Les Halles was transferred from the City of Paris to Unibail in November 2010.

11. The Caisse des Dépôts et Consignations (or Caisse des Dépôts) is a public group to ensure long-term investments, first established to restore financial confidence after the Napoleonic wars. The group invests in development projects that the market is unable to meet alone. While nominally public, the group consists of many subsidiary private companies. Caisse des Dépôts announced in 2014 that it will mobilize €4 billion in loans for Greater Paris.

12. Challenges to this model are made difficult because the construction of formal institutions at the metropolitan level has not yet been accompanied by the scaling up of civil society. While some institutions such as COSTIF have been mobilizing at the urban regional scale, thus far opposition has mainly taken the form of site-specific neighborhood organizations resisting gentrification of middle-class or agricultural neighborhoods. For example, the group Ecology Europe and the Neighbors of Saclay oppose the extension of the metro through the agricultural plateau. Similarly, the Community for the Gonesse Triangle denounces the gigantism of the project and the financing of the contract-based development plan. Local groups have also opposed developments in Nanterre, in Sevran, and in Clichy-sous-Bois. Yet on the level of the metropolis, these individual expressions of dissent do little to challenge the general logic upon which Grand Paris is based. Without a single locus of exploitation, domination is spread across the territory and resistance becomes disoriented.

13. Without a clear strategy to deal with the contradictions inherent in the creation of new economic territories and the capacity to manage polarities within them, Grand Paris may thus be merely a temporary solution to quell unrest. Comparing Grand Paris to spatial struggles in Taksim Square of public space and gentrification and in São Paolo and Rio de Janeiro over transit and infrastructure, Carine Merlino and Dominique Bidou (2013, 1) write, "In the Paris region the risks of an uprising are less large, but certain banlieues could enflame again, anytime, and this time on the fact of unjust territorial inequalities."

Conclusion

1. Grand Moscow builds on existing plans for the agglomeration of the city and region of Moscow into one institutional and functional unit.

2. The ten teams are led by Ostozhenka Architects (in partnership with the French architects Ateliers Lion Associés and the French organizations SGP, Paris-Saclay, and EPADESA); the Andrey Chernikhov Architectural Studio; the Moscow Architectural Institute; Central Research and Project Institute of Urbanism/Russian Academy of Architecture and Building Science; Antoine Grumbach et Associés and Wilmotte & Associés; l'AUC (in partnership with the French firms Sestra and Franc Boutte Consultant); OMA; Ricardo Bofill Leví; Studio Associato Secchi-Viganò; and Urban Design Associates.

3. Each short-listed team was paid €250,000 to further develop its concepts over the course of six months.

4. Indeed, officials are planning several mega-events, including bids for the 2024 Olympic Games and the 2025 World Expo, to ensure that grand urbanism remains the dominant paradigm of metropolitan planning into the near future.

References

AIGP (L'Atelier International du Grand Paris). 2013a. *Avis de l'Atelier International du Grand Paris sur le CDT Paris-Saclay Territoire Sud.* Paris: AIGP. http://www.ateliergrandparis.fr/aigp/conseil/avis.php.

AIGP (L'Atelier International du Grand Paris). 2013b. *Avis de L'Atelier International du Grand Paris sur le CDT Val de France/Gonesse/Bonneuil-en-France.* Paris: AIGP. http://www.ateliergrandparis.fr/aigp/conseil/avis.php.

AIGP (L'Atelier International du Grand Paris). 2013c. *Habiter le Grand Paris.* Paris: Archibooks.

Adey, Peter. 2010. *Mobility.* London: Routledge.

Aguilera, Anne, and Dominique Mignot. 2004. "Urban Sprawl, Polycentrism and Commuting: A Comparison of Seven French Urban Areas." *Urban Public Economics Review* 1:93–113.

Albrechts, Louis. 2006. "Bridge the Gap: From Spatial Planning to Strategic Projects." *European Planning Studies* 14 (10): 1487–1500.

Allen, John. 2006. "Ambient Power: Berlin's Potsdamer Platz and the Seductive Logic of Public Spaces." *Urban Studies (Edinburgh, Scotland)* 43 (2): 441–455.

Amin, Ash. 1995. *Post-Fordism: A Reader.* Malden, MA: Wiley-Blackwell.

Amin, Ash, and Nigel Thrift. 2002. *Cities: Reimagining the Urban.* London: Polity Press.

APUR (Atelier Parisien d'Urbanisme). 2006. *La mobilité dans le centre de l'agglomération parisienne.* A contribution to the Metropolitan Conference, November 9. http://www.apur.org/etude/une-contribution-apur-conference-metropolitaine-9-novembre-2006.

Argenbright, Robert. 2011. "New Moscow: An Exploratory Assessment." *Eurasian Geography and Economics* 52:857–875.

Argenbright, Robert. 2013. "Moscow on the Rise: From Primate City to Megaregion." *Geographical Review* 103 (1): 20–36.

Assemblée Nationale. 2009. *No. 1961 Projet de loi relatif au Grand Paris*. http://www.assemblee-nationale.fr/13/pdf/projets/pl1961.pdf.

ARUP. 2014. "Guardian Live Event: Designing Livable Cities." Twitter post. December 9, 12:42 p.m. https://twitter.com/ArupGroup.

A.T. Kearney. 2014. *Global Cities, Present and Future: 2014 Global Cities Index and Emerging Cities Outlook*. http://www.atkearney.com/research-studies/global-cities-index/full-report.

Atelier Christian de Portzamparc. 2008. *La métropole internationale de l'après Kyoto*. Executive Summary for Le Grand Pari(s) de l'Aggglomeration Parisienne. Paris: Atelier Christian de Portzamparc. http://www.legrandparis.culture.gouv.fr/sites/default/files/equipes/synthese_portzamparc_chantier_1.pdf.

Auchan. 2014. *EuropaCity*. http://www.europacity.com/.

Augé, Marc. 2002. *In the Metro*. Minneapolis: University of Minnesota Press.

Auzannet, Pascal. 2012. *Rapport de la mission sur le calendrier pluriannuel de réalisation et de financement du projet de Grand Paris Express*. Paris: Ministère de l'Égalité des Territoires et du Logement. http://www.territoires.gouv.fr/IMG/pdf/Rapport_Auzannet_Grand_Paris_Express.pdf.

Ayrault, Jean-Marc. 2013. *Discours de Premier ministre sur Paris-Saclay*. Paris, October 10. http://www.ile-de-france.gouv.fr/gdparis/Slider/Discours-de-Jean-Marc-Ayrault-au-pole-scientifique-et-technologique-du-plateau-de-Saclay-le-10-octobre-2013.

Bacchi, Carol. 2000. "Policy As Discourse: What Does It Mean? Where Does It Get Us?" *Discourse* 21 (1): 45–57.

Badiou, Alain. 2009. *The Meaning of Sarkozy*. London: Verso.

Baeten, Guy. 2007. "The Uses of Deprivation in the Neo-liberal City." In *Urban Politics Now: Re-imagining Democracy in the Neo-liberal City*, ed. BAVO, 44–57. Amsterdam: NAI Publishers.

Baeten, Guy. 2012. "Resilient Neoliberal Practices: Continuation, Restoration, Appropriation." Paper presented at the Association of American Geographers Annual Meeting, New York, February 26.

Balibar, Étienne. 2007. "Uprisings in the Banlieues." *Constellations* 14:47–71.

Banlieues 89. 1990. *Le grand Paris: 6 Paris des cinq Paris*. Paris: Banlieues 89.

Baraud-Serfaty, Isabel. 2011. La Nouvelle privatisation des villes. *Esprit* 3:149–168.

Baraud-Serfaty, Isabel. 2012. "La fabrique des projets d'aménagement métropolitain sous contrainte financière." Presentation at "Governing the Metropolis: Powers and Territories" international conference, Paris, November 25. http://www.ibicity.fr/blog/public/Article_governing_metropolis_novembre_2012.pdf.

Barré, François et al. 2005. "Un appel pour le grand paris." *Le Nouvel Observateur*, March 10.

Baudelaire, Charles. 2010. *The Painter of Modern Life*. London: Penguin.

BAVO, ed. 2007. *Urban Politics Now: Re-imagining Democracy in the Neoliberal City*. Rotterdam: NAI Publishers.

Beauregard, Robert. 2005. "Planning and the Network City: Discursive Correspondences." In *The Network Society: A New Context for Planning*, ed. Louis Albrechts and Seymour Mandelbaum, 24–33. New York: Routledge.

Beaverstock, Jonathan V., Richard G. Smith, and Peter J. Taylor. 1999. "A Roster of World Cities." *Cities* 16 (6): 445–458.

Beck, Ulrich. 1992. *Risk Society: Towards a New Modernity*. New York: Sage Publications.

Begag, Azouz. 2007. *Ethnicity & Equality: France in the Balance*. Lincoln: University of Nebraska Press.

Béhar, Daniel. 2013. "Les paradoxes du rôle de l'État dans la gouvernance du Grand Paris." *Métropolitiques*, January 28. http://www.metropolitiques.eu/Les-paradoxes-du-role-de-l-Etat.html.

Belkind, Lara. 2013. "The Negotiated Urbanism of Grand Paris Express." *Metropolitics*, June 12. http://www.metropolitiques.eu/The-Negotiated-Urbanism-of-Grand.html.

Benjamin, Walter. 2002. *The Arcades Project*. Cambridge, MA: Belknap Press of Harvard University Press.

Bernier, Lynne Louise. 1991. "Decentralizing the French State: Implications For Policy." *Journal of Urban Affairs* 13 (1): 21–32.

Blanc, Christian. 2006. *La Croissance ou le chaos*. Paris: Odile Jacob.

Blanc, Christian. 2009. "L'ambition nationale du Grand Paris." *Le Monde*, November 13.

Blanc, Christian. 2010. *Le Grand Paris du XXIe siècle*. Paris: Le Cherche Midi.

Böhm, Steffen, Campbell Jones, Chris Land, and Matthew Paterson. 2006. "Impossibilities of Automobility." In *Against Automobility*, ed. Steffen Böhm, Campbell Jones, Chris Land and Matthew Paterson, 3–16. Malden, MA: Wiley-Blackwell.

Bouf, Dominique, and David A. Hensher. 2007. "The Dark Side of Making Transit Irresistible: The Example of France." *Transport Policy* 14 (6): 523–532.

Boutros, Alexandra, and Will Straw. 2010. *Circulation and the City: Essays on Urban Culture*. Montreal: McGill-Queen's University Press.

Boyer, Robert. 1990. *The Regulation School: A Critical Introduction*. New York: Columbia University Press.

Braouezec, Patrick. 2011. "De la gouvernance du Grand Paris." *Métropolitiques*, February 11. http://www.metropolitiques.eu/De-la-gouvernance-du-Grand-Paris.html.

Brenner, Neil. 2001. "State Theory in the Political Conjuncture: Henri Lefebvre's "Comments on a New State Form." *Antipode* 33 (5): 783–808.

Brenner, Neil. 2003. "Metropolitan Institutional Reform and the Rescaling of State Space in Contemporary Western Europe." *European Urban and Regional Studies* 10 (4): 297–324.

Brenner, Neil. 2004. *New State Spaces: Urban Governance and the Rescaling of Statehood*. New York: Oxford University Press.

Brenner, Neil, and Stuart Elden. 2009. "Introduction: State, Space, World: Lefebvre and the Survival of Capitalism." In *State, Space, World*, ed. Neil Brenner and Stuart Elden, 1–51. Minneapolis: University of Minnesota Press.

Brenner, Neil, and Roger Keil. 2006. *The Global Cities Reader*. New York: Routledge.

Brenner, Neil, and Christian Schmid. 2014. "The 'Urban Age' in Question." *International Journal of Urban and Regional Research* 38 (3): 731–755.

Brenner, Neil, and Nik Theodore. 2002a. "Cities and the Geographies of 'Actually Existing Neoliberalism.'" *Antipode* 34 (3): 349–379.

Brenner, Neil, and Nik Theodore, eds. 2002b. *Spaces of Neoliberalism: Urban Restructuring in North America and Western Europe*. Malden, MA: Wiley-Blackwell.

Bridge, Gary, and Sophie Watson. 2011. "Reflections on Mobilities." In *The New Blackwell Companion to the City*, ed. Gary Bridge and Sophie Watson, 155–168. Malden, MA: Wiley-Blackwell.

Broudehoux, Anne. 2007. "Spectacular Beijing: The Conspicuous Construction of an Olympic Metropolis." *Journal of Urban Affairs* 29 (4): 383–399.

Brown, Wendy. 2003. "Neo-liberalism and the End of Liberal Democracy." *Theory & Event* 7 (1).

Buck-Morss, Susan. 1991. *The Dialectics of Seeing: Walter Benjamin and the Arcades Project*. Cambridge, MA: MIT Press.

Burgel, Guy. 1999. *Paris, avenir de la France*. Paris: Editions de l'Aube.

Callon, Michel, Yannick Barthe, and Pierre Lascoumes. 2001. *Agir dans un monde incertain: Essai sur la démocratie technique*. Paris: Seuil.

Cantal-Dupart, Michel. 2013. *Vivre un Grand Paris: Note ouvert au President de la Republique sur le Grand Paris*. Paris: Michel Cantal-Dupart. http://cantal-dupart.com/vivre-un-grand-paris.

Carrez, Gilles. 2009. *Grand Paris: Financement du projet de transports*. Paris: La Documentation française. September 30. http://lesrapports.ladocumentationfrancaise.fr/BRP/094000480/0000.pdf.

Castells, Manuel. 1983. *The City and the Grassroots: A Cross-cultural Theory of Urban Social Movements*. Berkeley: University of California Press.

Castells, Manuel. 1996. *The Rise of the Network Society: The Information Age: Economy, Society, and Culture*. Malden, MA: Wiley-Blackwell.

Cazenave, Frédéric. 2013. "Des bureaux qui restent vides sur fond de crise du logement." *Le Monde*, January 29. http://www.lemonde.fr/immobilier/article/2013/01/29/des-bureaux-qui-restent-vides-sur-fond-de-crise-du-logement_1823806_1306281.html.

CBRE Global Investors. 2011. *The Grand Paris Project: Real Estate Opportunities and Risks*. Global Investment Research Report, March. CBRE Global Investors.

CCIFR. (Chambre de Commerce et d'Industrie Franco-Russe). 2012. *Grand Moscou: S'inspirer du Grand Paris?* http://www.ccifr.ru/index.php?pid=7&id=330&page=93.

Cerny, Philip G. 1989. "The 'Little Big Bang' in Paris: Financial Market Deregulation in a Dirigiste System." *European Journal of Political Research* 17:169–192.

Chapon, Jean-Paul. 2011. "'Le temps des collectivités est un temps long' ou le Grand-Paris à petits pas de Pierre Mansat." *Paris est sa banlieue* (blog), July 3. http://parisbanlieue.blog.lemonde.fr/2011/07/03/le-temps-des-collectivites-est-un-temps-long-ou-le-grand-paris-a-petite-vitesse-de-pierre-mansat.

Chemetov, Paul. 2009. "Pour que Paris soit grand." *L'Humanité*, December 18.

Chemetov, Paul, Francis Godard, Philippe Laurent, Pierre Mansat, Bertrand Ousset, Jean-Baptiste Vaquin, Antoine Loubière and Annie Zimmerman. 2003. "Le Grand Paris en debat." *Urbanisme* 333:40–49.

Cité de l'Architecture et du Patrimoine. 2009. *Le Grand Pari(s): Exhibition of the Results of the International Consultation on the Future of the Paris Metropolis*. Press package. Paris: Cité de l'Architecture et du Patrimoine. http://www.citechaillot.fr/data/expositions_bc521/fiche/22844/dpgrandparisangbd_1123c.pdf.

Clark, Terry Nicholls. 2000. "Old and New Paradigms for Urban Research Globalization and the Fiscal Austerity and Urban Innovation Project." *Urban Affairs Review* 36 (1): 3–45.

Clark, Timothy J. 1984. *The Painting of Modern Life*. Princeton, NJ: Princeton University Press.

Clerval, Anne. 2013. *Paris sans le peuple: La gentrification de la capitale*. Paris: La Découverte.

CNDP (Commission Nationale du Débat Public). 2011 a. *Compte-rendu du débat public Arc Express*. http://cpdp.debatpublic.fr/cpdp-arcexpress/docs/bilan/compte-rendu-du-debat-public-arc-express2-31-03-2011.pdf.

CNDP (Commission Nationale du Débat Public). 2011 b. *Réseau de transport public du Grand Paris: Compte rendu du débat public*. http://cpdp.debatpublic.fr/cpdp-grandparis/site/DEBATPUBLIC_GRANDPARIS_ORG/DEBAT/COMPTE_RENDU_ET_BILAN_DU_DEBAT.HTM.

CNDP (Commission Nationale du Débat Public). 2011 c. *Bilan du débat public sur le réseau de transport public du Grand Paris*. http://cpdp.debatpublic.fr/cpdp-grandparis/site/DEBATPUBLIC_GRANDPARIS_ORG/DEBAT/COMPTE_RENDU_ET_BILAN_DU_DEBAT.HTM.

CNNMoney. 2010. "Global 500: France." *CNNMoney*. http://money.cnn.com/magazines/fortune/global500/2010/countries/France.html.

Cole, Alistair. 2006. "Decentralization in France: Central Steering, Capacity Building and Identity Construction." *French Politics* 4 (1): 31–57.

Cole, Alistair. 2008. *Governing and Governance in France*. Cambridge: Cambridge University Press.

COSTIF (Coordination pour la solidarité des territoires d'Île-de-France et contre le Grand Paris). 2014. "Plateau de Saclay." COSTIF. http://costif.parla.fr/plateau-de-saclay.

Cox, Kevin R. 1993. "The Local and the Global in the New Urban Politics: A Critical View." *Environment and Planning D* 11 (4): 433–440.

CPTG (Collectif pour le Triangle de Gonesse). 2012a. *Lettre ouverte aux candidat(e)s à l'élection présidentielle*. http://voe95.fr/cptg/?page_id=62.

CPTG (Collectif pour le Triangle de Gonesse). 2012b. *Note sur la gare du projet Grand Paris Express sur le Triangle de Gonesse*. http://voe95.fr/cptg/?page_id=507.

CPTG (Collectif pour le Triangle de Gonesse). 2013. *Avis du Collectif pour le Triangle de Gonesse: Enquête publique sur le CDT Val de France-Gonesse-Bonneuil-en-France*. http://voe95.fr/cptg/wp-content/pdf/aviscdtvaldefrance.pdf.

Crawford, Margaret. 1995. "Contesting the Public Realm: Struggles over Public Space in Los Angeles." *Journal of Architectural Education* 49 (1): 4–9.

References

Cresswell, Timothy. 2006. *On the Move: Mobility in the Modern Western World.* New York: Taylor and Francis.

Cresswell, Timothy. 2010. "Towards a Politics of Mobility." *Environment and Planning D* 28 (1): 17–31.

Crouch, Colin, and Patrick Le Galès. 2012. "Cities as National Champions?" *Journal of European Public Policy* 19 (3): 405–419.

Cupers, Kenny. 2014. *The Social Project: Housing Postwar France.* Minneapolis: University of Minnesota Press.

Dallas, Gregor. 2008. *Métro Stop Paris: An Underground History of the City of Light.* New York: Bloomsbury Publishing.

Danziger, Marie. 1995. "Policy Analysis Postmodernized." *Policy Studies Journal: The Journal of the Policy Studies Organization* 23 (3): 435–450.

Davis, Mike, and Daniel Bertrand Monk, eds. 2008. *Evil Paradises: Dreamworlds of Neoliberalism.* New York: New Press.

de Portzamparc, Christian. 2010. Grand Paris 04 Atelier Christian de Portzamparc, Institut d'Urbanisme de Paris. YouTube video, posted by citearchitecture, January 19. https://www.youtube.com/watch?v=ivgGFdwUkZE.

de Ravinel, Sophie. 2012. "Duflot : 'Le Grand Paris ne sera pas Dubaï-sur-Seine.'" *Le Figaro*, June 26. http://www.lefigaro.fr/actualite-france/2012/06/26/01016-20120626ARTFIG00738-duflot-le-grand-paris-ne-sera-pas-dubai-sur-seine.php.

Dear, Michael, and Steven Flusty. 1998. "Postmodern Urbanism." *Annals of the Association of American Geographers* 88 (1): 50–72.

DEEIR (Department of External Economic and International Relations). 2012. *Common Goals Unite Grand Paris and Greater Moscow.* http://investinmoscow.cnews.ru/en/news/byid/common_goals_unite_grand_paris_and_greater_moscow.

Delahaye, Olivier. 2014. "Le Grand Paris? Un réseau de transport pour 76% des Franciliens." *Grand Paris Métropole*, October 15. http://gpmetropole.fr/blog/le-grand-paris-un-reseau-de-transport-pour-76-des-franciliens.

Delaney, Arnold, and Geoffrey Smith. 2006. *Paris by Metro: An Underground History.* Northampton, MA: Interlink Books.

Delanty, Gerard, and Paul R. Jones. 2002. "European Identity and Architecture." *European Journal of Social Theory* 5 (4): 453–466.

Deleuze, Gilles, and Félix Guattari. 1987. *A Thousand Plateaus: Capitalism and Schizophrenia.* Minneapolis: University of Minnesota Press.

Derudder, Ben, and Frank Witlox. 2008. "What Is a 'World Class' City? Comparing Conceptual Specifications of Cities in the Context of a Global Urban Network." In *World Cities and Urban Form: Fragmented, Polycentric, Sustainable?*, ed. Mike Jenks, Daniel Kozak, and Pattaranan Takkanon, 11–24. New York: Routledge.

Deutsche, Rosalyn. 1998. *Evictions: Art and Spatial Politics*. Cambridge, MA: MIT Press.

Dikeç, Mustafa. 2006. "Two Decades of French Urban Policy: From Social Development of Neighbourhoods to the Republican Penal State." *Antipode* 38 (1): 59–81.

Dikeç, Mustafa. 2007a. *Badlands of the Republic: Space, Politics and Urban Policy*. Malden, MA: Wiley-Blackwell.

Dikeç, Mustafa. 2007b. "Revolting Geographies: Urban Unrest in France." *Geography Compass* 1 (5): 1190–1206.

Dittmar, Hank, and Gloria Ohland. 2004. *The New Transit Town: Best Practices in Transit-Oriented Development*. Washington, DC: Island Press.

Donzelot, Jacques. 2009. *La ville à trois vitesses*. Paris: Editions de la Villette.

Douay, Nicolas. 2010. "Collaborative Planning and the Challenge of Urbanization: Issues, Actors and Strategies in Marseilles and Montreal Metropolitan Areas." *Canadian Journal of Urban Research* 19 (1): 50–70.

Dunham-Jones, Ellen, and June Williamson. 2009. *Retrofitting Suburbia: Urban Design Solutions for Redesigning Suburbs*. Hoboken, NJ: John Wiley & Sons.

Dupuy, Gabriel. 1991. *L'urbanisme des réseaux: Théories et methods*. Paris: Armand Colin.

Dupuy, Gabriel. 2008. *Urban Networks—Network Urbanism*. Amsterdam: Techne Press.

Dupuy, Gabriel, and Jean-Marc Offner. 2005. "Réseau: Bilans et perspectives." *Flux* 4: 38–46.

Easterling, Keller. 2014. *Extrastatecraft*. New York: Verso.

Economist. 2010. "Nicolas Sarkozy: The Incredible Shrinking President." *Economist*, September 9.

Economist. 2012. "The Time-Bomb at the Heart of Europe." *Economist*. November 17.

Ekers, Michael, Pierre Hamel, and Roger Keil. 2012. "Governing Suburbia: Modalities and Mechanisms of Suburban Governance." *Regional Studies* 46 (3): 405–422.

Enright, Theresa. 2014. "The Great Wager: Crisis and Mega-project Reform in 21st-Century Paris." *Cambridge Journal of Regions, Economy and Society* 7 (1): 155–170.

EPADESA (L'Établissement public d'aménagement de La Défense Seine Arche). 2012. *L'Epadesa au côté des architectes français pour la consultation internationale sur le Grand Moscou.* http://www.epadesa.fr/actualites/actualites/article/lepadesa-au-cote-des-architectes-francais-pour-la-consultation-internationale-sur-le-grand-mosco.html.

EPPS (L'Établissement public Paris-Saclay). 2012. *Paris-Saclay: Schéma de développement territorial* http://www.media-paris-saclay.fr/wp-content/uploads/2012/01/Saclay-SDT.pdf.

EPPS (L'Établissement Public Paris-Saclay). 2014. *Paris-Saclay: A Connected Territory.* http://www.epps.fr/en/a-global-cluster/a-connected-territory.

Ernst & Young/Jones Lang Lasalle. 2013. *Why Invest in Paris.* Paris: Ernst & Young/Jones Lang Lasalle. http://www.ey.com/Publication/vwLUAssets/Why_Invest_in_Paris_2013/$FILE/Why%20invest%20in%20Paris%20(2013)_vEN.pdf.

Estèbe, Pierre. 2013. "Gouverner la ville mobile." *Cahiers de la Métropole* 3 (Automne): 22–26.

Fainstein, Susan S. 2008. "Mega-projects in New York, London and Amsterdam." *International Journal of Urban and Regional Research* 32 (4): 768–785.

Ferry, Jules. 1868. *Comptes fantastiques d'Haussmann.* Paris: Le Chevalier.

Fillon, François. 2009. "Grand Paris: Quel sera le visage de la future métropole francilienne?" Paris: Office of the Prime Minister, December 18. http://archives.gouvernement.fr/fillon_version2/gouvernement/grand-paris-quel-sera-le-visage-de-la-future-metropole-francilienne.html.

Fischer, Frank. 1995. *Evaluating Public Policy.* New York: Nelson-Hall.

Flyvbjerg, Bent. 1998. *Rationality & Power: Democracy in Practice.* Chicago: University of Chicago Press.

Flyvbjerg, Bent. 2014. "What You Should Know about Megaprojects and Why: An Overview." *Project Management Journal* 45 (2): 6–19.

Flyvbjerg, Bent, Nils Bruzelius, and Werner Rothengatter. 2003. *Mega-projects and Risk: An Anatomy of Ambition.* New York: Cambridge University Press.

Foucault, Michel. 1980. *Power/Knowledge: Selected Interviews and Other Writings, 1972–1977.* New York: Vintage.

Foucault, Michel. 1982. *The Archaeology of Knowledge.* New York: Vintage.

Foucault, Michel. 2000. *Essential Works of Foucault (1954–1984)*, Vol. 3, Power, ed. James D. Faubion and Robert Hurley. New York: New Press.

Foucault, Michel. 2009. *Security, Territory, Population: Lectures at the Collège de France 1977–1978.* New York: Picador.

Fourcaut, Annie, Emmanuel Bellanger, and Mathieu Flonneau, eds. 2007. *Paris/Banlieues: Conflits et solidarities*. Paris: Editions Créaphis.

French, Shaun, Andrew Leyshon, and Thomas Wainright. 2011. "Financializing Space, Spacing Financialization." *Progress in Human Geography* 35 (6): 798–819.

Friedmann, John, and Goetz Wolff. 1982. "World City Formation: An Agenda for Research and Action." *International Journal of Urban and Regional Research* 6 (3): 309–344.

FSIF (Fédération des sociétés immobilières et foncières). 2014. *French Listed Real Estate Investment Companies: A Success Story*. Paris: Editions Abécédaire. http://www.fsif.fr/Default.aspx?lid=1&rid=123&rvid=215.

Gallez, Caroline. 2014. "Territorial Development Contracts in the 'Grand Paris' Project: Towards a Negotiated Networked Development." *Town Planning Review* 85 (2): 273–286.

Gallez, Caroline, and Sylvie Fol. 2014. "Social Inequalities in Urban Access: Better ways of Assessing Transport Improvements." In *Urban Access for the 21st Century: Finance and Governance Models for Transport Infrastructure*, ed. Elliot D. Sclar, Måns Lönnroth and Christian Wolmar, 46–87. New York: Routledge.

Gallois, Louis. 2012. *Pacte pour la compétitivité de l'industrie française*. Paris: La Documentation française. http://www.ladocumentationfrancaise.fr/rapports-publics/124000591/index.shtml.

Gandy, Mathew. 2005. "Cyborg Urbanization: Complexity and Monstrosity in the Contemporary City." *International Journal of Urban and Regional Research* 29 (1): 26–49.

Garnier, Jean-Pierre. 2010. *Une violence éminemment contemporaine: Essais sur la ville, la petite bourgeoisie intellectuelle et l'effacement des classes populaires*. Paris: Agone.

Garreau, Joel. 1991. *Edge City: Life on the New Frontier*. New York: Doubleday.

Geddes, Mike, and John Benington, eds. 2001. *Local Partnerships and Social Exclusion in the European Union*. London: Routledge.

Geels, Frank et al. 2011. *Automobility in Transition?: A Socio-Technical Analysis of Sustainable Transport*. New York: Routledge.

Geipel, Finn. 2010. Grand Paris 08 Lin, Finn Geipel + Giulia Andi. YouTube video, posted by citearchitecture, January 19. https://www.youtube.com/watch?v=UHu4eHaDN9A.

Geipel, Finn, Giulia Andi, and Équipe LIN. 2009. Grand Paris métropole douce: Hypothèses sur le paysage post-Kyoto/propositions for the post-Kyoto metropolis. Paris: Nouvelles Éditions Beauchesne.

References

Ghertner, D. Asher. 2011. "Rule by Aesthetics: World-class City Making in Delhi." In *Worlding Cities*, ed. Ananya Roy and Aihwa Ong. Malden: Wiley-Blackwell.

Giacone, Alessandro, ed. 2010. *Les Grands Paris de Paul Delouvrier*. Paris: Descartes & Cie.

Gilli, Frédéric. 2005. "Les statistiques astigmates et la recomposition de la géographie francilienne." *Cybergeo: European Journal of Geography*. https://cybergeo.revues.org/3045.

Gilli, Frédéric. 2008a. "Du local et du métropolitain: Paris, métropole multi-échelles." *La Vie des idées*, November 12. http://www.laviedesidees.fr/Du-local-et-du-metropolitain-Paris.html.

Gilli, Frédéric. 2008b. "Les nouveaux contours de la métropole parisienne." *La Vie des idées*, November 5. http://www.laviedesidees.fr/Les-nouveaux-contours-de-la.html.

Gilli, Frédéric. 2014. *Grand Paris: L'émergence d'une métropole*. Paris: Presses de Sciences Po.

Gilli, Frédéric and Jean-Pierre Gonguet. 2015. "Le Grand Paris, une métropole de techniciens sans vision politique." *La Tribune*, January 16.

Gilli, Frédéric, and Jean-Marc Offner. 2008. *Paris Métropole hors les murs*. Paris: Presses de Sciences Po.

Gilroy, Paul. 2005. *Postcolonial Melancholia*. New York: Columbia University Press.

Golubchikov, Oleg. 2004. "Urban Planning in Russia: Towards the Market." *European Planning Studies* 12:229–247.

Golubchikov, Oleg. 2010. "World-City-Entrepreneurialism: Globalist Imaginaries, Neoliberal Geographies, and the Production of New St Petersburg." *Environment & Planning A* 42 (3): 626–643.

Golubchikov, Oleg, and Nicholas A. Phelps. 2011. "The Political Economy of Place at the Post-socialist Urban Periphery: Governing Growth on the Edge of Moscow." *Transactions of the Institute of British Geographers* 36:425–440.

Graham, Stephen, and Simon Marvin. 2001. *Splintering Urbanism: Networked Infrastructures, Technological Mobilities and the Urban Condition*. New York: Routledge.

Gravier, Jean-François. 1947. *Paris et le desert Français*. Paris: Editions Flammarion.

Grumbach, Antoine et Associés. 2009. *Seine métropole: Paris, Rouen, le Havre: Le diagnostic prospectif de l'agglomération parisienne*. Paris: Archibooks.

Grumbach, Antoine, Beatriz Ramo, and Bernd Upmeyer. 2013. "Unlimited Greatness: Interview with Antoine Grumbach." *MONU* 19: 4–11.

Hackworth, Jason. 2006. *The Neoliberal City: Governance, Ideology, and Development in American Urbanism*. Ithaca, NY: Cornell University Press.

Haila, Anne. 1988. "Land as a Financial Asset: The Theory of Urban Rent As a Mirror of Economic Transformation." *Antipode* 20 (2): 79–101.

Halbert, Ludovic, and Renaud Le Goix. 2012. "Capital financier et production urbaine." *Urbanisme* 384: 40–41.

Hardt, Michael, and Antonio Negri. 2001. *Empire*. Cambridge, MA: Harvard University Press.

Hardt, Michael, and Antonio Negri. 2009. *Commonwealth*. Cambridge, MA: Belknap Press of Harvard University Press.

Harrison, John, and Michael Hoyler. 2014. "Governing the New Metropolis." *Urban Studies* 51 (11): 2249–2266.

Harvey, David. 1985. *The Urbanization of Capital: Studies in the History and Theory of Capitalist Urbanization*. Baltimore, MD: Johns Hopkins University Press.

Harvey, David. 1989. "From Managerialism to Entrepreneurialism: The Transformation in Urban Governance in Late Capitalism." *Geografiska Annaler* 71 (1): 3–17.

Harvey, David. 2003. *Paris, Capital of Modernity*. London: Psychology Press.

Harvey, David. 2005. *A Brief History of Neoliberalism*. New York: Oxford University Press.

Harvey, David. 2008. "The Right to the City." *New Left Review* 53:23–40.

Haughton, Graham, Phil Allmendinger, and Stijn Oosterlynck. 2013. "Spaces of Neoliberal Experimentation: Soft Spaces, Postpolitics, and Neoliberal Governmentality." *Environment & Planning A* 45 (1): 217–234.

Hazan, Eric. 2010. *The Invention of Paris: A History Told in Footsteps*. London: Verso.

Hazan, Eric. 2011. *Paris sous tension*. Paris: La fabrique.

Hewlett, Nick. 2007. "Nicolas Sarkozy and the Legacy of Bonapartism: The French Presidential and Parliamentary Elections of 2007." *Modern & Contemporary France* 15 (4): 405–422.

Hewlett, Nick. 2011. *The Sarkozy Phenomenon*. Charlottesville, VA: Societas.

Higonnet, Patrice. 2009. *Paris: Capital of the World*. Cambridge, MA: Harvard University Press.

Hussey, Andrew. 2007. "Battle for the Soul of the City." *The Guardian*, October 27. http://www.guardian.co.uk/travel/2007/oct/28/paris.features1.

IAU-IDF (Institut d'Aménagement et d'Urbanisme de la Région d'Île-de-France). 2009. "Valorisation foncière et financement des infrastructures de transport." *Note rapide* 477. http://www.iau-idf.fr/savoir-faire/nos-travaux/edition/valorisation-fonciere-et-financement-des-infrastructures-de-transport.html.

IAU-IDF (Institut d'Aménagement et d'Urbanisme de la Région d'Île-de-France). 2014a. "Les CDT à l'heure du Grand Paris: Une dynamique en marche." *Note rapide* 650. http://www.iau-idf.fr/savoir-faire/nos-travaux/edition/les-cdt-a-lheure-du-grand-paris-une-dynamique-en-marche.html.

IAU-IDF (Institut d'Aménagement et d'Urbanisme de la Région d'Île-de-France). 2014b. "Métropole du Grand Paris et mobilité: Quels impacts? Quels enjeux?" *Note rapide* 664. http://www.iau-idf.fr/savoir-faire/nos-travaux/edition/metropole-du-grand-paris-et-mobilite-quels-impacts-quels-enjeux.html.

IDFE (Île-de-France Environnement). 2014. *Enquête publique sur les lignes 14, 16 et 17 Réseau Grand Paris Express*. November 23. http://idfe.eu/images/doc/grand_paris/Avis_IDFE_lignes_14-16-17_141123.pdf.

Icade. 2014. *Le Grand Paris Mérite un Grade Icade*. Paris: Icade.

INSEE (Institut National de la Statistique et des Études Économiques). 2006. *Déplacements domicile-travail: un desserrment de l'emploi parisien vers la grand couronne*. No. 265. Paris: INSEE.

INSEE (Institut National de la Statistique et des Études Économiques). 2007. *Les déplacements domicile-travail amplifiés par périurbanisation*. No. 1129. Paris: INSEE.

INSEE (Institut National de la Statistique et des Études Économiques). 2010a. *Les Franciliens consacrent 1 h 20 par jour á leur déplacements*. No. 331. Paris: INSEE.

INSEE (Institut National de la Statistique et des Études Économiques). 2010b. *Produit intérieur brut regional (PIB)*. Paris: INSEE.

Invest in France Agency. 2014. *France Welcomes Talent and Investment*. Paris: Invest in France Agency. http://www.invest-in-france.org/Medias/Publications/1897/France-welcomes-talent-and-investment-2014.pdf.

Isin, Engin F. 1998. "Governing Toronto Without Government: Liberalism and Neoliberalism." *Studies in Political Economy* 56:169–192.

Jameson, Fredric. 1998. "The Brick and the Balloon: Architecture, Idealism and Land Speculation." *New Left Review* 228:25–46.

Jameson, Fredric. 2004. "The Politics of Utopia." *New Left Review* 25:35–54.

Jégo, Marie. 2012. "Le 'Grand Moscou' en marche." *Le Monde*, December 21. http://www.lemonde.fr/international/article/2012/12/21/le-grand-moscou-en-marche_1809524_3210.html.

Jérôme, Béatrice. 2009. "Grand Paris : Faut-il croire au pari de Christian Blanc?" *Le Monde*, November 23.

Jessop, Bob. 1990. "Regulation Theories in Retrospect and Prospect." *International Journal of Human Resource Management* 19 (2): 153–216.

Jessop, Bob. 2002. "Liberalism, Neoliberalism, and Urban Governance: A State-Theoretical Perspective." *Antipode* 34 (3): 452–472.

Jessop, Bob. 2010. "Towards a Schumpeterian Workfare State? Preliminary Remarks on Post-Fordist Political Economy." *Studies in Political Economy* 40:7–39.

Jobert, Bruno, and Bruno Théret. 1994. "France: La consécration républicaine du néo-libéralisme." In *Le tournant néo-libéral en Europe*, ed. Bruno Jobert, 21–86. Paris: L'Harmattan.

Jonas, Andrew E.G. 2013. "City-regionalism as a Contingent 'Geopolitics of Capitalism.'" *Geopolitics* 18 (2): 284–298.

Jonas, Andrew E.G., Aidan H. While, and David C. Gibbs. 2010. "Managing Infrastructural and Service Demands in New Economic Spaces: The New Territorial Politics of Collective Provision." *Regional Studies* 44 (2): 183–200.

Jones, Martin R. 2007. "Spatial Selectivity of the State? The Regulationist Enigma and Local Struggles over Economic Governance." *Environment & Planning A* 29 (5): 831–864.

Jones, Gareth A., and Maria Moreno-Carranco. 2007. "Megaprojects: Beneath the Pavement, Excess." *City* 11 (2): 144–164.

Jouve, Bernard. 2003. "Les formes de gouvernement urbain en Europe." *disP—The Planning Review* 39 (152): 37-42.

Jouve, Bernard, and Christian Lefèvre. 2002. *Métropoles ingouvernables*. Montréal: Édition Elsévier.

J.P. Morgan Chase. 2013. *All aboard the Grand Paris Express*. Europe Equity Research, February 11. New York: J.P. Morgan Chase & Co.

Kantor, Paul, Christian Lefèvre, Asato Saito, and H. V. Savitch. 2012. *Struggling Giants: City-Region Governance in London, New York, Paris, and Tokyo*. Minneapolis: University of Minnesota Press.

Karadimitriou, Nikos, Claudio De Magalhães, and Roelof Verhage. 2013. *Planning, Risk, and Property Development: Urban Regeneration in the England, France, and the Netherlands*. London: Routledge.

Kassovitz, Mathieu., dir. 2007. *La Haine*. DVD. Criterion Collection.

Kearns, Gerry. 1993. "The City as Spectacle: Paris and the Bicentenary of the French Revolution." In *Selling Places*, ed. Gerry Kearns and Chris Philo, 49–102. Oxford: Pergamon Press.

Keating, Michael. 1983. "Decentralization in Mitterrand's France." *Public Administration* 61:237–252.

Keating, Michael. 2003. "The Invention of Regions: Political Restructuring and Territorial Government in Western Europe." In *State/Space: A Reader*, ed. Neil Brenner and Nik Theodore, 256–277. New York: John Wiley and Sons.

Keil, Roger. 2000. "Governance Restructuring in Los Angeles and Toronto: Amalgamation or Secession?" *International Journal of Urban and Regional Research* 24 (4): 758–781.

Kester, Grant H. 1993. "Out of Sight Is Out of Mind: The Imaginary Space of Postindustrial Culture." *Social Text* 11 (2): 72–92.

Kolossov, Vladimir, and John O'Loughlin. 2004. "How Moscow Is Becoming a Capitalist Mega-city." *International Social Science Journal* 56:413–427.

Kolossov, Vladimir, Olga Vendina, and John O'Loughlin. 2002. "Moscow as an Emergent World City: International Links, Business Developments, and the Entrepreneurial City." *Eurasian Geography and Economy* 43:170–196.

Kopteva, Maria. 2013. "Translated from the French." *World Economic Journal*, May. http://world-economic.com/articles_wej-254.html.

Krätke, Stefan. 1999. "A Regulationist Approach to Regional Studies." *Environment & Planning A* 31 (4): 683–704.

Krivỳ, Maros. 2011. "Speculative Redevelopment and Conservation: The Signifying Role of Architecture." *City* 15 (1): 42–62.

Lacoste, Gérard. 2010. "Le Réseau de transport du Grand Paris: Principles, Postulats et Questions à débattre." Presentation prepared for IAU-IDF, December 17.

Lacoste, Gérard. 2013. "La Métropole du Grand Paris: Intégration ou confédération?" *Métropolitiques*, September 9. http://www.metropolitiques.eu/La-Metropole-du-Grand-Paris.html.

Laugier, Alexandra. 2013. "Interview. Le Grand Moscou d'Antoine Grumbach et Jean-Michel Wilmotte." *CôtéMaison*, March 22. http://www.cotemaison.fr/chaine-d/creation/interview-le-grand-moscou-d-antoine-grumbach-et-jean-michel-wilmotte_17891.html.

Le Chatelier, Luc. 2009. "Jean Nouvel accuse Christian Blanc d'enterrer le Grand Paris." *Télérama*, October 23. http://www.telerama.fr/scenes/jean-nouvel-accuse-christian-blanc-d-enterrer-le-grand-paris,48680.php.

Le Corbusier. 2008. *Toward an Architecture*. London: Frances Lincoln Ltd.

Le Galès, Patrick. 1995. "Du gouvernement des villes à la gouvernance urbaine." *Revue Française de Science Politique* 45 157–95.

Le Galès, Patrick. 2002. *European Cities: Social Conflicts and Governance*. Oxford: Oxford University Press.

Le Galès, Patrick, and Tommaso Vitale. 2013. "Governing the Large Metropolis. A Research Agenda." Working papers of the Cities Are Back in Town program. Paris: Presses de Sciences Po.

Lefebvre, Henri. 1976a. *De l'État. Tome I: L'État dans le monde modern*. Paris: Union Générale d'Éditions.

Lefebvre, Henri. 1976b. *De l'État. Tome II: De Hegel à Mao par Staline*. Paris: Union Générale d'Éditions.

Lefebvre, Henri. 1977. *De l'État. Tome III: Le mode de production étatique (M.P.E.)*. Paris: Union Générale d'Éditions.

Lefebvre, Henri. 1978. *De L'État. Tome IV: Les Contradictions de l'État Moderne La Dialectique et/de l'État*. Paris: Union Générale d'Éditions.

Lefebvre, Henri. 1991. *The Production of Space*. Malden, MA: Wiley-Blackwell.

Lefebvre, Henri. 1996. *Writings on Cities*. Ed. and trans. Eleonore Kofman and Elizabeth Lebas. Malden, MA: Wiley-Blackwell.

Lefebvre, Henri. 2003. *The Urban Revolution*. Trans. R. Bononno. Minneapolis: University of Minnesota Press.

Lefebvre, Henri, Neil Brenner, and Stuart Elden, eds. 2009. *State, Space, World: Selected Essays*. Trans. G. Moore, N. Brenner, and S. Elden. Minneapolis: University of Minnesota Press.

Lefèvre, Christian. 1998. "Metropolitan Government and Governance in Western Countries: A Critical Review." *International Journal of Urban and Regional Research* 22 (1): 9–25.

Lefèvre, Christian. 2004. *Délégation générale à la coopération territoriale. Paris et les grandes agglomérations occidentales: Comparaison des modèles de gouvernance: Barcelone, Berlin, Lisbonne, Londres, Madrid, Manchester, Milan*. Paris: Mairie de Paris.

Lefèvre, Christian. 2010. "The Improbable Metropolis: Decentralization, Local Democracy and Metropolitan Areas in the Western World." *Análise Social* 45 (197): 623–637.

Lehrer, Ute, and Jennifer Laidley. 2008. "Old Mega-projects Newly Packaged? Waterfront Redevelopment in Toronto." *International Journal of Urban and Regional Research* 32 (4): 786–803.

Leitner, Helga, and Eric Sheppard. 2002. "'The City Is Dead, Long Live the Net': Harnessing European Interurban Networks for a Neoliberal Agenda." *Antipode* 34 (3): 495–518.

Leloup, Michèle, and Marion Bertone. 2009. *Le Grand Paris: Les coulisses de la consultation*. Paris: Archibooks + Sautereau.

Le Moniteur Architecture. 2009. *Le Grand Pari(s): Consultation internationale sur l'avenir de la métropole Parisienne*. Paris: AMC Groupe Moniteur.

Léonhardt, Frédéric. 2011. "The Fantastical Accounts of Grand Paris." *Metropolitics*, September 28. http://www.metropolitiques.eu/The-Fantastical-Accounts-of-Grand.html.

Léonhardt, Frédéric. 2012. "Des solutions nouvelles à la crise des transports franciliens." *Métropolitiques*, January 13. http://www.metropolitiques.eu/Des-solutions-nouvelles-a-la-crise.html.

Leroy, Maurice. 2010. *Le Grand Paris, C'est le visage de la France de demain*. Paris, December 13. http://archives.gouvernement.fr/fillon_version2/gouvernement/maurice-leroy-le-grand-paris-c-est-le-visage-de-la-france-de-demain.html.

Leroy, Maurice. 2011. "The Greater Paris Project: Financial and Investment Opportunities." Seminar given in London, July 12.

Lerup, Lars. 2000. *After the City*. Cambridge, MA: MIT Press.

L'Humanité. 2009. "Ils ont osé le dire." *L'Humanité*, March 17.

Libération. 2002. "Les Français on-ils peur de tout?" *Libération*, April 8.

Lion, Yves. 2010. Grand Paris 02 Groupe Descartes. YouTube video, posted by cite-architecture, January 19. https://www.youtube.com/watch?v=Uh8t0nMFuZk.

Lipietz, Alain. 1987. "Rebel Sons: The Regulation School." *French Politics and Society* 5 (4): 17–26.

Lorrain, Doninique. 2002. "Capitalismes urbains: la montée des firmes d'infrastructures." *Entreprises et Histoire* 3 (30): 7–31.

Lovering, John. 1999. "Theory Led by Policy: The Inadequacies of the 'New Regionalism' (illustrated from the case of Wales)." *International Journal of Urban and Regional Studies* 23 (2): 379–395.

Lovering, John. 2010. "Will the Recession Prove to Be a Turning Point in Planning and Urban Development Thinking?" *International Planning Studies* 15 (3): 227–243.

Lynch, Kevin. 1960. *The Image of the City*. Cambridge, MA: MIT Press.

Macleod, Gordon, and Martin Jones. 2007. "Territorial, Scalar, Networked, Connected: In What Sense a 'Regional World'?" *Regional Studies* 41 (9): 1177–1191.

Macleod, Gordon, and Martin Jones. 2011. "Renewing Urban Politics." *Urban Studies* 48 (12): 2443–2472.

Mairie de Paris. 2011. "Le Défi de la Gouvernance. Séminaire international." Paris, December 1–2. Conference program.

Mairie de Paris. 2012. "Introduction." Mairie de Paris, *Les Cahiers de la Métropole* 2:51–53.

Mairie de Paris. 2013. "Innovations and the Making of Metropolitan Identity International Conference." Paris, November 26–27. Conference program.

Mansat, Pierre. 2012. "Opening Speech of the Seminar." Mairie de Paris, *Les Cahiers de la Métropole* 2:12–13.

Marcuse, Peter, and Ronald van Kempen, eds. 2000. *Globalizing Cities: A New Spatial Order?* Malden, MA: Wiley-Blackwell.

Marliere, Philippe, and Joseph Szarka. 2009. "The Sarkozy Presidency: From Rupture to Crisis? Introduction." *Modern & Contemporary France* 17 (4): 371–373.

Maspero, François. 1994. *Roissy Express: A Journey through the Paris Suburbs*. London: Verso.

Massey, Doreen. 1994. *Space, Place, and Gender*. Minneapolis: University of Minnesota Press.

Massey, Doreen. 2007. *World City*. London: John Wiley and Sons.

MasterCard. 2008. Worldwide Centers of Commerce Index http://www.mastercard.com/us/company/en/insights/pdfs/2008/MCWW_WCoC-Report_2008.pdf

McCann, Eugene. 2011. "Urban Policy Mobilities and Global Circuits of Knowledge: Toward a Research Agenda." *Annals of the Association of American Geographers* 101 (1): 107–130.

McCann, Eugene, and Kevin Ward, eds. 2011. *Mobile Urbanism: Cities and Policymaking in the Global Age*. Minneapolis: University of Minnesota Press.

McCann, Eugene, and Kevin Ward. 2013. "A Multi-disciplinary Approach to Policy Transfer Research: Geographies, Assemblages, Mobilities and Mutations." *Policy Studies* 34 (1): 2–18.

McFarlane, Colin, and Jonathan Rutherford. 2008. "Political Infrastructures: Governing and Experiencing the Fabric of the City." *International Journal of Urban and Regional Research* 32 (2): 363–374.

References

McNeill, Daniel. 2009. *The Global Architect: Firms, Fame and Urban Form.* New York: Taylor & Francis.

McNeill, Daniel, and Mark Tewdwr-Jones. 2003. "Architecture, Banal Nationalism and Re-Territorialization." *International Journal of Urban and Regional Research* 27 (3): 738–743.

Menu, Flavien. 2013. "From the Kremlin to Dachas." *MONU* 9:121–126.

Merlin, Pierre. 1967. *Les Transports parisiens.* Paris: Masson.

Merlin, Pierre. 1991. *Les villes nouvelles en France.* Paris: Presses Universitaires de France.

Merlin, Pierre. 2003. *L'Île-de-France: Hier, aujourd'hui, demain.* Paris: Documentation Française.

Merlin, Pierre. 2012. *Transports et urbanisme en Île-de-France.* Paris: Documentation Française.

Merlino, Carine, and Dominique Bidou. 2013. *Le Grand Paris: Terre d'échanges.* Paris: Éditions Autrement.

Merrifield, Andy. 2006. *Henri Lefebvre: A Critical Introduction.* New York: Routledge.

Merrifield, Andy. 2014. *The New Urban Question.* New York: Pluto Press.

Métropole du Grand Paris Mission de Préfiguration. 2015. *Métropole du Grand Paris.* http://www.prefig-metropolegrandparis.fr.

Miller, Peter, and Nikolas Rose. 1990. "Governing Economic Life." *Economy and Society* 19 (1): 1–31.

Ministère de l'Écologie, de l'Énergie, du Développement durable et de la Mer. 2010. *La mobilité des Français, panorama issu de l'enquête nationale transports et déplacements 2008.* La Défense: Commissariat Général au Développement durable. http://www.developpement-durable.gouv.fr/IMG/pdf/Rev3.pdf.

Ministère du Logement, de l'Égalité des Territoires et de la Ruralité. 2014. *Grand Paris.* http://www.territoires.gouv.fr/Grand-Paris.

Mobilicités. 2011. "Will the Grand Paris Infrastructure Project Attract Foreign Investors?" *Mobilicités.* http://www.mobilicites.com/en_news_will-the-grand-paris-infrastructure-project-attract-foreign-investors--_0_77_1049.html.

Mouffe, Chantal. 2005. *On the Political.* London: Psychology Press.

Moulaert, Frank. 2000. *Globalization and Integrated Area Development in European Cities.* Oxford: Oxford University Press.

Moulaert, Frank, and Farid Sekia. 2003. "Territorial Innovation Models: A Critical Survey." *Regional Studies* 37 (3): 289–302.

Murray, Graham. 2006. "France: The Riots and the Republic." *Race & Class* 47 (4): 26–45.

Nappi-Choulet, Ingrid. 2011. "La financiarisation des quartiers d'affaires: l'exemple de 'Cœur Défense.'" *Esprit* 11:30–43.

Nappi-Choulet, Ingrid. 2013. "La financiarisation du marché immobilier français: De la crise des années 1990 à la crise des subprimes de 2008." *Revue d'Économie Financière* 2:189–206.

Nappi-Choulet, Ingrid, and Aurélien Décamps. 2011. "Is Sustainability Attractive for Corporate Real Estate Decisions?" ESSEC Working Paper 1106. ESSEC Business School, Cergy-Pontoise Cedex.

Nappi-Choulet, Ingrid, and Antoine Loubière. 2012. "Esquisse d'une histoire de la financiarisation immobilière et urbaine: Entretien avec Ingrid Nappi-Choulet (ESSEC)." *Urbanisme* 384:42-45.

Négrier, Emmanuel. 2003. "A French Urban Powershift? The Political Construction of Metropolization." *French Politics* 1 (2): 175–198.

Nevers, Jean-Yves, and Vincent Hoffmann-Martinot. 1989. "French Local Policy Change in a Period of Austerity: A Silent Revolution." In *Urban Innovation and Autonomy: Political Implications of Policy Change*, ed. Susan Clarke, 182–212. New York: Sage.

Nicholls, Walter J. 2005. "Power and Governance: Metropolitan Governance in France." *Urban Studies* 42 (4): 783–800.

Nicholls, Walter J. 2006. "Associationalism from Above: Explaining Failure through France's Politique de la Ville." *Urban Studies* 43 (10): 1779–1802.

Nouvel, Jean, Michel Cantal-Dupart, and Jean Duthilleul. 2008. *Le Grand pari de l'agglomeration parisienne*. Paris: Conseil Scientifique de Grand Pari(s). http://www.legrandparis.culture.gouv.fr/documents/NOUVEL-AREP-MCD_Livret_chantier_1.pdf.

Observatoire Régional du Foncier en Île-de-France. 2011. *Les enjeux de la valorisation foncière autour des pôles de transport*. Paris: Observatoire Régional du Foncier en Île-de-France. http://www.orf.asso.fr/uploads/attachements/rapport_transport_siteorf.pdf.

Offner, Jean-Marc. 1993. "Les 'effets structurants' du transport: Mythe politique, mystification scientifique." *L'Espace Geographique* 22:233–242.

Offner, Jean-Marc. 2007. "Le Grand Paris." *Problèmes politiques et sociaux* 942. Paris: La Documentation Française.

Offner, Jean-Marc. 2013. "Les mobilités." In *Repenser l'urbanisme*, ed. Thierry Paquot, 53–73. Paris: Infolio.

Offner, Jean-Marc, and Frédéric Gilli. 2010. *Paris métropole: Hors les murs*. Paris: Presses de Sciences Po.

Olds, Kris. 1995. "Globalization and the Production of New Urban Spaces: Pacific Rim Megaprojects in the Late 20th Century." *Environment & Planning A* 27 (11): 1713–1743.

Olson, Mancur. 1982. *The Rise and Decline of Nations: Economic Growth, Stagflation, and Social Rigidities*. New Haven, CT: Yale University Press.

Orfeuil, Jean-Pierre. 2001. "L'automobile en France: Comportements, perceptions, problèmes, perspectives." Paper presented at a conference, "Colloque International de l'Institut pour la Ville en Mouvement," Marne La Vallée. http://ville-en-mouvement.pagesperso-orange.fr/interventions/Jean_Pierre_Orfeuil.pdf.

Orfeuil, Jean-Pierre. 2010. "Grand Huit, grand pari, gros problem." *Métropolitiques*, December 6. http://www.metropolitiques.eu/Grand-Huit-grand-pari-gros.html.

Orfeuil, Jean-Pierre. 2012. "Le Grand Paris, ambitions et intendance." *Urbanisme* 385:4–5.

Orfeuil, Jean-Pierre, and Marc Wiel. 2012. *Grand Paris, sortir des illusions, approfondir les ambitions*. Paris: Scrineo.

Orueta, Fernando Diaz, and Susan S. Fainstein. 2008. "The New Mega-Projects: Genesis and Impacts." *International Journal of Urban and Regional Research* 32 (4): 759–767.

Ovenden, Mark. 2009. *Paris Underground: The Maps, Stations, and Design of the Métro*. New York: Penguin Books.

Panerai, Philippe. 2008. *Paris métropole: Formes et échelles du Grand-Paris*. Paris: Éditions de la Villette.

Paris Métropole. 2012. *Livre Vert: Pour une métropole durable: Quelle gouvernance?* Paris: Paris Métropole. http://www.parismetropole.fr/nos-chantiers/gouvernance/gouvernance-227/article/gouvernance.

Paris Métropole. 2013. *Paris Métropole in Brief*. Paris: Paris Métropole.

Paris Métropole. 2014. *Rapport d'activité 2014*. Paris: Paris Métropole. http://www.parismetropole.fr/nous-connaitre.

Pasotti, Eleonora. 2010. *Political Branding in Cities: The Decline of Machine Politics in Bogotá, Naples, and Chicago*. Cambridge: Cambridge University Press.

Patteeuw, Véronique. 2003. *Reading MVRDV*. Rotterdam: NAI Publishers.

Pavillon de l'Arsenal. 2013. *Paris la Métropole et ses Projets*. Dossier de Presse. Paris: Pavillon de l'Arsenal. http://www.pavillon-arsenal.com/img/exposition/50/cp/PAV_50_CP.pdf.

Peck, Jamie. 2010. *Constructions of Neoliberal Reason*. New York: Oxford University Press.

Peck, Jamie. 2011. "Geographies of Policy from Transfer-Diffusion to Mobility-Mutation." *Progress in Human Geography* 35 (6): 773–797.

Peck, Jamie, and Adam Tickell. 1994. "Searching for a New Institutional Fix: The After-Fordist Crisis and the Global-Local Disorder." In *Post-Fordism: A Reader*, ed. Ash Amin, 280–315. London: John Wiley and Sons.

Peck, Jamie, and Adam Tickell. 2002. "Neoliberalizing Space." *Antipode* 34 (3): 380–404.

Phelps, Nicholas A., and Andrew M. Wood. 2011. "The New Post-Suburban Politics?" *Urban Studies* 48 (12): 2591–2610.

Phillips, Peggy A. 1987. *Modern France: Theories and Realities of Urban Planning*. Lanham, MD: University Press of America.

Pierre, Jon, ed. 2000. *Debating Governance*. Oxford: Oxford University Press.

Pierre, Jon, ed. 2011. *The Politics of Urban Governance*. New York: Palgrave Macmillan.

Pike, Andy, and Jane Pollard. 2010. "Economic Geographies of Financialization." *Economic Geography* 86 (1): 29–51.

Pinson, Gilles. 2009. *Gouverner la ville par projet: Urbanisme et gouvernance des villes européennes*. Paris: Presses de Sciences Po.

Pinson, Gilles. 2010. "Des métropoles ingouvernables aux métropoles oligarchiques." *Territoires 2040* 1: 65–69. Paris: DATAR.

Pinson, Gilles, and Patrick Le Galès. 2005. "State Restructuring and Decentralization Dynamics in France: Politics Is the Driving Force." *Cahier Européen numéro 7*.

Prager, Jean-Claude, and Émile Quinet. 2013. *Les effets des infrastructures sur la répartition spatiale des populations et des emplois*. Commissariat General à la Stratégie et à la Prospective Département Développement durable.

Prefecture de la Région d'Île-de-France. 2013. *Contrat de développement territorial Paris-Saclay Territoire Sud*. http://www.ile-de-france.gouv.fr/Carrousel/Le-projet-CDT-Paris-Saclay-valide.

Prefecture de la Région d'Île-de-France. 2014. *Contrat de développement territorial Val de France/Gonesse/Bonneuil-en-France*. http://www.agglo-valdefrance.fr/agir/

lamenagement-et-lhabitat/contrat-de-developpement-territorial-val-de-francegonessebonneuil.

Préteceille, Edmond. 1986. "Collective Consumption, Urban Segregation, and Social Classes." *Society and Space* 4 (2): 145–154.

Préteceille, Edmond. 2006. "La ségrégation sociale a-t-elle augmenté?" *Sociétés Contemporaines* 2:69–93.

Préteceille, Edmond. 2007. "Is Gentrification a Useful Paradigm to Analyse Social Changes in the Paris Metropolis?" *Environment & Planning A* 39 (1): 10–31.

Property Investor Europe. 2013. "Grand Paris Expected to Yield €74bn Economic, Social Gains." *Property Investor Europe*, June 11. https://www.pie-mag.com/articles/5544/grand-paris-expected-to-yield-euro-74bn-economic-social-gains.

Quénelle, Benjamin. 2013. "Moscou s'inspire du Grand Paris." *Les Echos*, May 30. http://www.lesechos.fr/30/05/2013/LesEchos/21446-148-ECH_moscou-s-inspire-du-grand-paris.htm.

Raco, Mike. 2012. "The Privatisation of Urban Development and the London Olympics 2012." *City* 16 (4): 452–460.

Raco, Mike. 2014. "Delivering Flagship Projects in an Era of Regulatory Capitalism: State-Led Privatization and the London Olympics 2012." *International Journal of Urban and Regional Research* 38 (1): 176–197.

RATP (Régie Autonome des Transports Parisiens). 2013. "The Network." http://www.ratp.fr.

Rehberg, Vivian, and Christina Ricupero. 2008. Paris: City Report, *Frieze*. Issue 17. http://www.frieze.com/issue/article/paris.

Ren, Xufei. 2008. "Architecture as Branding: Mega-project Developments in Beijing." *Built Environment* 34 (4): 517–531.

Ren, Xufei. 2011. *Building Globalization: Transnational Architecture Production in Urban China*. Chicago: University of Chicago Press.

Renard, Vincent. 2008. La ville saisie par la finance. *Le Débat* 148:106–117.

République Française. 2009. *Le Grand Pari de l'agglomeration Parisienne*. Paris: Ministère de la Culture et de la Communication. http://www.legrandparis.culture.gouv.fr.

République Française. 2010. *Loi no. 2010-597 du 3 juin 2010 relative au Grand Paris*. Paris: Legifrance. http://www.mon-grandparis.fr/sites/default/files/loi_n2010-597_du_3_juin_2010_version_consolidee_au_20100606.pdf.

Revel, Judith. 2008. *Qui a peur de la banlieue?* Paris: Bayard.

Rey, Henri. 1996. *La Peur des banlieues*. Paris: Presses de Sciences Po.

Rhodes, R. A. W. 1997. *Understanding Governance: Policy Networks, Governance, Reflexivity and Accountability*. Berkshire: Open University Press.

Robinson, Jennifer. 2002. "Global and World Cities: A View from off the Map." *International Journal of Urban and Regional Research* 26 (3): 531–554.

Rogers, Richard. 1998. *Cities for a Small Planet*. Boulder, CO: Westview Press.

Rogers, Richard, and Mike Davies. 2010. Grand Paris 01 Rogers Stirk Harbour and Partners, LSE, ARUP. YouTube video, posted by citearchitecture, January 18. https://www.youtube.com/watch?v=o6_v-EiWdag.

Rogers Stirk Harbour + Partners, LSE and ARUP. 2009. *Paris Métropole: Designs for a Metropolitan Paris of the Future*. Executive Summary for Le Grand Pari(s) de l'Agglomération Parisienne. http://www.richardrogers.co.uk/render.aspx?siteID=1&navIDs=1,4,25,1690.

Rose, Nikolas. 1999. *Powers of Freedom: Reframing Political Thought*. Cambridge: Cambridge University Press.

Rose, Nikolas, and Peter Miller. 2008. *Governing the Present: Administering Economic, Social and Personal Life*. London: Polity.

Ross, Kristin. 1988. *The Emergence of Social Space: Rimbaud and the Paris Commune*. Minneapolis: University of Minnesota Press.

Ross, Kristin. 1996. *Fast Cars, Clean Bodies: Decolonization and the Reordering of French Culture*. Cambridge, MA: MIT Press.

Roy, Ananya. 2006. "Praxis in the Time of Empire." *Planning Theory* 5 (1): 7–29.

Roy, Ananya, and Aihwa Ong, eds. 2011. *Worlding Cities: Asian Experiments and the Art of Being Global*. New York: John Wiley & Sons.

Sachs, Susan. 2009. "Sarkozy's Daring Design Dreams for a New 'Grand Paris.'" *Christian Science Monitor*, March 19. http://www.csmonitor.com/World/2009/0319/p01s03-wogn.html.

Sarkozy, Nicolas. 2009. *Inauguration de l'exposition "Grand Pari(s)."* Video. http://www.legrandparis.culture.gouv.fr/videosdetail/153/Inauguration%20de%20l%27exposition.

Sarkozy, Nicolas. 2010. "Exclusive Interview with Nicolas Sarkozy President of the French Republic." *AA: L'Architecture d'Aujourd'Hui*, February, 42–58.

Sassen, Saskia. 2001. *The Global City: New York, London, Tokyo*. Princeton, NJ: Princeton University Press.

Schmid, Christian. 2012. "Henri Lefebvre, the Right to the City, and the New Metropolitan Mainstream." In *Cities for People, Not for Profit: Critical Urban Theory and the Right to the City*, ed. Neil Brenner, Peter Marcuse, and Margit Mayer, 42–62. New York: Routledge.

Scott, Allen J., John Agnew, Edward W. Soja, and Michael Storper. 2001. "Global City Regions." In *Global City-Regions: Trends, Theory, Policy: Trends, Theory, Policy*, ed. Allen Scott, 11–30. New York: Oxford University Press.

Scott, Allen J. 2008. "Resurgent Metropolis: Economy, Society and Urbanization in an Interconnected World." *International Journal of Urban and Regional Studies* 32 (3): 548–564.

Scott, James C. 1998. *Seeing Like a State: How Certain Schemes to Improve the Human Condition Have Failed*. New Haven, CT: Yale University Press.

Secchi, Bernardo, and Paola Viganò. 2010. Grand Paris 07 Studio09. YouTube video, posted by citearchitecture, January 19. https://www.youtube.com/watch?v=RzMWB2KyrAo.

Secchi, Bernardo, and Paola Viganò. 2011. *La Ville poreuse: Un Projet pour le grand Paris et la métropole de l'après-Kyoto*. Paris: Metis Presses.

Sennett, Richard. 1998. *The Corrosion of Character: The Personal Consequences of Work in the New Capitalism*. New York: W. W. Norton.

SGP (Société du Grand Paris). 2010. *Le Réseau de transport public du Grand Paris: Le dossier du maître ouvrage*. Paris: Société du Grand Paris. http://cpdp.debatpublic.fr/cpdp-grandparis.

SGP (Société du Grand Paris). 2012. *Le Grand Paris*. Paris: Société du Grand Paris. http://www.societedugrandparis.fr/wp-content/uploads/2014/05/booklet-anglais2.pdf.

SGP (Société du Grand Paris). 2014. *Grand Paris Express: Le métro du Grand Paris*. Paris: Société du Grand Paris. http://www.societedugrandparis.fr.

Shapiro, Michael. 1992. *Reading the Postmodern Polity: Political Theory as Textual Practice*. Minneapolis: University of Minnesota Press.

Sheller, Mimi, and John Urry. 2006. "The New Mobilities Paradigm." *Environment & Planning A* 38 (2): 207–226.

Schivelbusch, Wolfgang. 1986. *The Railway Journey: The Industrialization of Time and Space in the Nineteenth Century*. Berkeley: University of California Press.

Silverstein, Paul A. 2004. *Algeria in France: Transpolitics, Race, and Nation*. Bloomington: Indiana University Press.

Simmel, Georg. 1971 (1903). "The Metropolis and Mental Life." In *Simmel: On Individuality and Social Forms*, ed. Donald Levine, 324. Chicago: University of Chicago Press.

Sklair, Leslie. 2005. "The Transnational Capitalist Class and Contemporary Architecture in Globalizing Cities." *International Journal of Urban and Regional Research* 29 (3): 485–500.

Sklair, Leslie. 2011. "Iconic Architecture and Urban, National, and Global Identities." In *Cities and Sovereignty: Identity Politics in Urban Spaces*, ed. Diane Davis and Nora Libertun De Duren, 179–196. Bloomington: Indiana University Press.

Smith, Neil. 2002. "New Globalism, New Urbanism: Gentrification as Global Urban Strategy." *Antipode* 34 (3): 427–450.

Smith, Neil. 2008. *Uneven Development: Nature, Capital, and the Production of Space*. Athens: University of Georgia Press.

Soja, Edward W. 2000. *Postmetropolis: Critical Studies of Cities and Regions*. Malden, MA: Wiley-Blackwell.

Soja, Edward W. 2002. "Six Discourses on the Postmetropolis." In *The Blackwell City Reader*, ed. Gary Bridge and Sophie Watson, 188–196. Malden, MA: Wiley-Blackwell.

Soja, Edward W. 2005. "On the Concept of Global City Regions." *Art-E-Fact*. http://artefact.mi2.hr/_a04/lang_en/theory_soja_en.htm.

Stanek, Łukasz. 2011. *Henri Lefebvre on Space: Architecture, Urban Research, and the Production of Theory*. Minneapolis: University of Minnesota Press.

STIF (Syndicat des Transports d'Île-de-France). 2010. *Arc Express: Débat sur le métro de rocade*. http://www.orbival.fr/pdf/debatpublic/arc%20express%20cahier%20arc%20sud.pdf.

Stone, Clarence N. 1989. *Regime Politics*. Lawrence: University Press of Kansas.

Stone, Clarence N. 2005. "Looking Back to Look Forward: Reflections on Urban Regime Analysis." *Urban Affairs Review* 40 (3): 309–341.

Storper, Michael. 2014. "Governing the Large Metropolis." *Territory, Politics, Governance* 2 (2): 115–134.

Studio 09. 2009. *Le diagnostic prospectif de l'agglomération parisienne. La ville "poreuse": Chantier 2*. For the Consultation Internationale de Recherche et Développement sur le Grand Pari de l'Agglomération Parisienne. http://www.ateliergrandparis.fr/aigp/conseil/studio/STUDIOlc02.pdf.

Subra, Philippe. 2009. *Le Grand Paris*. Paris: Armand Colin.

Subra, Philippe. 2012. *Le Grand Paris: Géopolitique d'une ville mondiale*. Paris: Armand Colin.

Suzuki, Hiroaki, Robert Cervero, and Kanako Iuchi. 2013. *Transforming Cities with Transit: Transit and Land-Use Integration for Sustainable Urban Development*. Washington, DC: World Bank.

Swyngedouw, Erik. 2009. "The Zero-ground of Politics: Musings on the Post-political City." *New Geographies* 1 (1): 52–61.

Swyngedouw, Erik, Frank Moulaert, and Arantxa Rodriguez. 2002. "Neoliberal Urbanization in Europe: Large-Scale Urban Development Projects and the New Urban Policy." *Antipode* 34 (3): 542–577.

Tilly, Charles. 1975. *The Formation of National States in Western Europe*. Princeton, NJ: Princeton University Press.

Upmeyer, Bernd. 2013. "Editor's Introduction." *MONU* 19.

Urry, John. 2007. *Mobilities*. London: Polity.

Van der Haak, Bregtje. 2009. *Grand Paris: The President and the Architect*. DVD. Brooklyn: Icarus Films.

Veltz, Pierre. 2012. *Paris, France, monde: Repenser l'économie par le territoire*. Paris: Editions de l'Aube.

Veran, Cyrille. 2012. "Après le Grand Paris, le Grand Moscou." *Le Moniteur*, March 7. http://www.lemoniteur.fr/143-immobilier/article/actualite/877075-mipim-apres-le-grand-paris-le-grand-moscou.

Viganò, Paola. 2012. *Les territoires de l'urbanisme: Le projet comme producteur de connaissance*. Geneva: Metis Presses.

Virilio, Paul. 2006. *Speed and Politics*. Los Angeles, CA: Semiotext(e).

Wacquant, Loïc. 2007. "Territorial Stigmatization in the Age of Advanced Marginality." *Thesis Eleven* 91 (1): 66–77.

Wacquant, Loïc. 2008. *Urban Outcasts: A Comparative Sociology of Advanced Marginality*. Malden: Polity Press.

Wallis, Keith. 2011. "Chinese Help Wanted for 'Grand Paris.'" *South China Morning Post*, November 17.

Weber, Rachel. 2002. "Extracting Value from the City: Neoliberalism and Urban Redevelopment." *Antipode* 34:519–540.

Weber, Rachel. 2010. "Selling City Futures: The Financialization of Urban Redevelopment Policy." *Economic Geography* 86 (3): 251–274.

Wiel, Marc. 2009a. "Grand Paris: Qui sont les nouveaux professionnels de l'illusionnisme?" http://www.colos.info/images/doc/GrandParis-nouveaux_professionnels_illusionnisme.pdf.

Wiel, Marc. 2009b. *Le Grand Paris: Premier conflit né de la décentralisation*. Paris: L'Harmattan.

Williams, Timothy. 2011. "Ministry of Culture: Loosely Holding the Reins." *Le Grand Pari(S)yndey* (blog), September 15. http://www.twarch.com.au/blog.

World Bank. 2014. "Sustainable Development: Overview." http://www.worldbank.org/en/topic/sustainabledevelopment/overview#1.

Young, Douglas, and Roger Keil. 2010. "Reconnecting the Disconnected: The Politics of Infrastructure in the In-between City." *Cities* 27 (2): 87–95.

Urban and Industrial Environments
Series editor: Robert Gottlieb, Henry R. Luce Professor of Urban and Environmental Policy, Occidental College

Maureen Smith, *The U.S. Paper Industry and Sustainable Production: An Argument for Restructuring*

Keith Pezzoli, *Human Settlements and Planning for Ecological Sustainability: The Case of Mexico City*

Sarah Hammond Creighton, *Greening the Ivory Tower: Improving the Environmental Track Record of Universities, Colleges, and Other Institutions*

Jan Mazurek, *Making Microchips: Policy, Globalization, and Economic Restructuring in the Semiconductor Industry*

William A. Shutkin, *The Land That Could Be: Environmentalism and Democracy in the Twenty-First Century*

Richard Hofrichter, ed., *Reclaiming the Environmental Debate: The Politics of Health in a Toxic Culture*

Robert Gottlieb, *Environmentalism Unbound: Exploring New Pathways for Change*

Kenneth Geiser, *Materials Matter: Toward a Sustainable Materials Policy*

Thomas D. Beamish, *Silent Spill: The Organization of an Industrial Crisis*

Matthew Gandy, *Concrete and Clay: Reworking Nature in New York City*

David Naguib Pellow, *Garbage Wars: The Struggle for Environmental Justice in Chicago*

Julian Agyeman, Robert D. Bullard, and Bob Evans, eds., *Just Sustainabilities: Development in an Unequal World*

Barbara L. Allen, *Uneasy Alchemy: Citizens and Experts in Louisiana's Chemical Corridor Disputes*

Dara O'Rourke, *Community-Driven Regulation: Balancing Development and the Environment in Vietnam*

Brian K. Obach, *Labor and the Environmental Movement: The Quest for Common Ground*

Peggy F. Barlett and Geoffrey W. Chase, eds., *Sustainability on Campus: Stories and Strategies for Change*

Steve Lerner, *Diamond: A Struggle for Environmental Justice in Louisiana's Chemical Corridor*

Jason Corburn, *Street Science: Community Knowledge and Environmental Health Justice*

Peggy F. Barlett, ed., *Urban Place: Reconnecting with the Natural World*

David Naguib Pellow and Robert J. Brulle, eds., *Power, Justice, and the Environment: A Critical Appraisal of the Environmental Justice Movement*

Eran Ben-Joseph, *The Code of the City: Standards and the Hidden Language of Place Making*

Nancy J. Myers and Carolyn Raffensperger, eds., *Precautionary Tools for Reshaping Environmental Policy*

Kelly Sims Gallagher, *China Shifts Gears: Automakers, Oil, Pollution, and Development*

Kerry H. Whiteside, *Precautionary Politics: Principle and Practice in Confronting Environmental Risk*

Ronald Sandler and Phaedra C. Pezzullo, eds., *Environmental Justice and Environmentalism: The Social Justice Challenge to the Environmental Movement*

Julie Sze, *Noxious New York: The Racial Politics of Urban Health and Environmental Justice*

Robert D. Bullard, ed., *Growing Smarter: Achieving Livable Communities, Environmental Justice, and Regional Equity*

Ann Rappaport and Sarah Hammond Creighton, *Degrees That Matter: Climate Change and the University*

Michael Egan, *Barry Commoner and the Science of Survival: The Remaking of American Environmentalism*

David J. Hess, *Alternative Pathways in Science and Industry: Activism, Innovation, and the Environment in an Era of Globalization*

Peter F. Cannavò, *The Working Landscape: Founding, Preservation, and the Politics of Place*

Paul Stanton Kibel, ed., *Rivertown: Rethinking Urban Rivers*

Kevin P. Gallagher and Lyuba Zarsky, *The Enclave Economy: Foreign Investment and Sustainable Development in Mexico's Silicon Valley*

David N. Pellow, *Resisting Global Toxics: Transnational Movements for Environmental Justice*

Robert Gottlieb, *Reinventing Los Angeles: Nature and Community in the Global City*

David V. Carruthers, ed., *Environmental Justice in Latin America: Problems, Promise, and Practice*

Tom Angotti, *New York for Sale: Community Planning Confronts Global Real Estate*

Paloma Pavel, ed., *Breakthrough Communities: Sustainability and Justice in the Next American Metropolis*

Anastasia Loukaitou-Sideris and Renia Ehrenfeucht, *Sidewalks: Conflict and Negotiation over Public Space*

David J. Hess, *Localist Movements in a Global Economy: Sustainability, Justice, and Urban Development in the United States*

Julian Agyeman and Yelena Ogneva-Himmelberger, eds., *Environmental Justice and Sustainability in the Former Soviet Union*

Jason Corburn, *Toward the Healthy City: People, Places, and the Politics of Urban Planning*

JoAnn Carmin and Julian Agyeman, eds., *Environmental Inequalities Beyond Borders: Local Perspectives on Global Injustices*

Louise Mozingo, *Pastoral Capitalism: A History of Suburban Corporate Landscapes*

Gwen Ottinger and Benjamin Cohen, eds., *Technoscience and Environmental Justice: Expert Cultures in a Grassroots Movement*

Samantha MacBride, *Recycling Reconsidered: The Present Failure and Future Promise of Environmental Action in the United States*

Andrew Karvonen, *Politics of Urban Runoff: Nature, Technology, and the Sustainable City*

Daniel Schneider, *Hybrid Nature: Sewage Treatment and the Contradictions of the Industrial Ecosystem*

Catherine Tumber, *Small, Gritty, and Green: The Promise of America's Smaller Industrial Cities in a Low-Carbon World*

Sam Bass Warner and Andrew H. Whittemore, *American Urban Form: A Representative History*

John Pucher and Ralph Buehler, eds., *City Cycling*

Stephanie Foote and Elizabeth Mazzolini, eds., *Histories of the Dustheap: Waste, Material Cultures, Social Justice*

David J. Hess, *Good Green Jobs in a Global Economy: Making and Keeping New Industries in the United States*

Joseph F. C. DiMento and Clifford Ellis, *Changing Lanes: Visions and Histories of Urban Freeways*

Joanna Robinson, *Contested Water: The Struggle Against Water Privatization in the United States and Canada*

William B. Meyer, *The Environmental Advantages of Cities: Countering Commonsense Antiurbanism*

Rebecca L. Henn and Andrew J. Hoffman, eds., *Constructing Green: The Social Structures of Sustainability*

Peggy F. Barlett and Geoffrey W. Chase, eds., *Sustainability in Higher Education: Stories and Strategies for Transformation*

Isabelle Anguelovski, *Neighborhood as Refuge: Community Reconstruction, Place-Remaking, and Environmental Justice in the City*

Kelly Sims Gallagher, *The Global Diffusion of Clean Energy Technology: Lessons from China*

Vinit Mukhija and Anastasia Loukaitou-Sideris, eds., *The Informal American City: Beyond Taco Trucks and Day Labor*

Roxanne Warren, *Rail and the City: Shrinking Our Carbon Footprint and Reimagining Urban Space*

Marianne Krasny and Keith Tidball, *Civic Ecology: Adaptation and Transformation from the Ground Up*

Erik Swyngedouw, *Liquid Power: Contested Hydro-Modernities in Twentieth-Century Spain*

Julian Agyeman and Duncan McLaren, *Sharing Cities: Enhancing Equity, Rebuilding Community, and Cutting Resource Use*

Jessica Smartt Gullion, *Fracking the Neighborhood: Reluctant Activists and Natural Gas Drilling*

Nicholas Phelps, *Sequel to Suburbia: Glimpses of America's Post-Suburban Future*

Shannon Elizabeth Bell, *Fighting King Coal: The Barriers to Grassroots Environmental Justice Movement Participation in Central Appalachia*

Theresa Enright, *The Making of Grand Paris: Metropolitan Urbanism in the Twenty-First Century*

Index

Note: Page numbers followed by *f* or *t* denote figures or tables.

Agence Grumbach & Associés, 50, 52t, 56–58, 259n2
Airports, 13, 86, 112, 114–115, 119, 132, 151–152, 154, 243n1, 248n7
Air quality, 146
AJN-Jean Nouvel/AREP-Jean-Marie Duthilleul/Michel Cantal-Dupart, 50, 52t, 58
Allmendinger, Phil, 203, 216
Andi, Giulia, 50, 52t, 59–60, 79, 246n6
Arc Express, 111–118, 125, 248n9
Architectural Department of Moscow City Government, 228–229
Architecture
  aesthetics and, 2, 37–38, 66, 68, 71, 81–83, 89, 91–92, 104, 132, 205, 233, 238, 257n8
  Bibliothèque Nationale de France François Mitterrand and, 14
  Bilbao strategy and, 69
  capitalism and, 33–34, 67–68, 84–87, 89–90, 92, 247n12
  Centre Pompidou and, 14
  communication and, 66, 88–90
  competitions and, 25, 49, 68–69, 77, 81, 228, 230, 245n9 (*see also* Design)
  connected city and, 46, 48–49, 53, 55–56, 60, 63, 69, 85–87, 234
  consultation and, 2, 8, 26, 32–34, 68–69, 74, 79, 89, 93, 97, 146, 205, 225
  Corbusier and, 91
  cultural production and, 24, 64, 92
  designed city and, 81–83
  exhibitions and, 2, 25, 46–47, 50, 52t, 55, 63, 66–67, 70, 72–73, 76, 81–82, 87–90, 152, 159, 244n4, 245n9
  ex-*soixante-huitards* and, 70, 244n5
  financial crisis and, 70, 243n12
  flexible city and, 1, 83–85
  foreign, 229, 231, 259n2
  Gallo-Roman, 34–35
  gentrification and, 20–22, 69, 80, 85, 237–238 (*see also* Gentrification)
  governance and, 10, 23–24, 32, 74–77, 92, 234, 238
  grandeur and, 72–74
  Grand Moscow and, 225–233
  Grand Pari(s) design teams and, 49–62, 73, 88
  Grand Prix de l'urbanisme and, 58–59
  grand urbanism and, 22, 24, 25–26, 32–34, 62–64, 66–71, 89–92, 223–225, 233–234
  Greater Urbanism and, 21
  iconography and, 31, 228
  imagineering and, 34, 49, 68–71

Architecture (cont.)
  international networks and, 49–62, 232–233
  knowledge creation and, 25, 33, 37, 59, 63–64, 90–92, 224
  megaprojects and, 4, 14, 20–22, 67 (*see also* Megaprojects)
  metropolitanization and, 37, 196, 201, 205, 208, 212, 215–216, 219
  modernism and, 20, 40, 83, 92, 123, 128, 197, 201
  Museum of Architecture and Heritage and, 1, 50–51, 73
  policy initiatives and, 2, 64, 66–68, 70–71, 88–93
  Pritzker Prize and, 53, 55, 58
  Prost Plan and, 39, 105
  public funding and, 14, 23, 69, 156, 247n1
  public space and, 2, 39, 58, 71, 81–82, 131, 141, 167, 258n13
  rationalities of, 6, 66–68, 82, 89–92
  revolt and, 91–92
  Sarkozy and, 8, 15, 49–50, 63, 68, 70, 76, 88, 91–92, 248n6
  SDRIF and, 75, 110–112, 173, 177, 180–181, 186, 249n10
  spatial transformation and, 36, 205, 239–240
  starchitects and, 25, 69, 73, 89
  state productivism and, 66–71, 196
  suburbs and, 32–34, 37, 39, 46–64, 244n5, 245n9
  territorial politics and, 159, 165, 169, 187–188
  transit and, 54, 56, 60, 85–87, 97, 132, 138, 146–147, 154, 241n3
  unified city and, 77–80
  urban policy and, 63, 67–68, 71, 88–93, 224, 229, 232
  vision of, 66–93
Atelier Castro Denissof Casi, 50, 52t, 60–61
Atelier Christian de Portzamparc, 50, 52t, 55–56, 85–86, 138, 148, 205, 212
Aubervilliers, 43, 178
Auchan, 152, 154
Audrey Chernikhov Architectural Studio, 259n2
Auguste, Philippe, 34–35
Authoritarianism, 39, 70, 82, 126, 188–189, 216, 256n3
Autogestion, 174, 179, 195, 254n12
Automobiles, 54, 98, 100, 103, 125, 137–138, 145, 147, 243n3, 247n4
Automobility, 99–100
Ayrault, Jean-Marc, 149, 183, 256n21

Baeten, Guy, 223
Balibar, Étienne, 45
Balladur, Édouard, 180–182
Banlieues. *See* Suburbs
Barbier, Christophe, 65
Barthes, Roland, 129
Beauregard, Robert, 245n2
Bibliothèque Nationale de France François Mitterrand, 14
Bicycles, 54, 60, 98, 144, 247n4, 252n16
Bienvenüe, Fulgence, 104
Blanc, Christian
  Castro and, 80
  competitive urban network and, 16, 18, 87
  economic growth and, 16, 18
  as eleventh team, 88
  Sarkozy and, 16, 41, 88
  SDRIF criticism of, 112
  as secretary of state, 98, 134
  suburbs and, 39, 41, 80
  supermetro and, 87
  territorial politics and, 169, 181, 216
  transit and, 89, 98, 112, 114t, 116, 134, 149, 248n6, 248n8
  vision of, 12, 16, 65, 80, 243n10, 245n3, 246n9, 248n6

Index

Bobos, 89
Bombings, 144–145
Bonaparte, Napoleon, 130, 258
Bondy Blog, 47, 215
Bonneuil-en-France, 148, 151–154
Boulevards, 35, 37, 54, 108, 241n2
Bourgeoisie, 11, 38, 65, 83, 89, 139, 141
Branding (urban), 23, 69–70, 80, 137, 151, 175, 204, 217–218, 227–228, 242n5
Braouezec, Patrick, 178, 185
Brenner, Neil, 5–6, 17, 131, 166–167, 194–196
BRIC countries, 198, 257n4
Budget Ministry, 207
Buses, 54, 60, 86, 98, 108–109, 112, 137, 144, 150, 247n3

Caisse des Dépôts et Consignations, 213, 258n11
Cantal-Dupart, Michel, 50, 52t, 58, 78, 89, 154–155, 209, 244n5
Capitalism
  architecture and, 89–90, 92
  Clark on, 33
  connected city and, 13, 56, 87, 92, 208–209, 219–220
  flexible, 83–85
  grand urbanism and, 5–6, 20–24, 85, 92, 196–201, 211, 218–219, 221, 233–236, 238
  inequality of, 22–23, 143, 148, 238–239
  resistance to, 247n12
  state productivism and, 3, 19, 192–199, 214–220
  (sub)urbanization and, 5–6, 16, 22–24, 35, 37–38, 40–44, 48, 63, 85, 122, 129, 131, 133–137, 156, 177, 192–220, 223, 234–237, 246n10
  suburbs and, 33, 35, 38, 40, 44, 49–50
  territorial politics and, 167, 174
  transit and, 26, 97–101, 129–137, 156, 247nn12–13
  transnational capitalist class and, 17, 233
Castells, Manuel, 49–50, 221
Castro, Roland, 50, 52t, 60–61, 79–80, 83, 90, 244n5
CBRE Global Investors, 136
Center for Twentieth-Century Social History (CNRS), 47
Centralités magazine, 47
Centralization, 39, 167–168, 170, 183, 192, 218
Central Research and Project Institute of Urbanism, 259n2
Centre Pompidou, 14, 53
Chapon, Jean-Paul, 47
Charles de Gaulle Airport, 119, 151, 154, 243n1
Charles V, 35
Charon, Pierre, 181
Chemetov, Paul, 109–110
Chevènement law, 255n16
Chirac, Jacques, 18
Cité de l'Architecture et du Patrimoine. *See* Museum of Architecture and Heritage
City Calculator, 61–62
Clark, T. J., 33–34
Clichy-sous-Bois, 11, 45–46, 109, 258n12
Climate change, 51, 145, 245n10
Collective for the Gonesse Triangle (CPTG), 153–154
Commodification, 17, 80, 92, 131, 152–154, 195–196, 238, 252n16
Common sense, 24, 64, 67, 71, 128, 155, 236, 238
Communication, 8, 12, 35, 40, 43, 50, 66, 101, 113, 122, 198, 232
Communism, 18, 41, 75, 171, 178, 248n8

Compromise, 5, 15
  governance and, 5, 91, 171–172, 177, 185, 187–188, 195, 203, 209, 216
  grand urbanism and, 233–235, 239
  shared dream of Grand Paris and, 65–68, 77–78, 89–90, 215, 234
  transit issues and, 91, 103, 112–127, 133, 142, 146–148, 248n9, 249n12
Conservation, 146, 248n9, 255n17
Corbusier, Le, 91
COSTIF, 150, 155, 258n12
Cyberspace, 49, 52t, 55, 205

Davies, Mike, 50, 53, 63
Decay (urban), 16–17, 135
Decentralization
  autogestion and, 174, 179, 195, 254n12
  centralization and, 39, 167–168, 170, 183, 192, 218
  MAPTAM and, 183, 185–186
  metropolitanization and, 192, 202, 204, 218
  state productivism and, 175, 177, 192
  stronger departments from, 254n12
  suburbs and, 42
  territorial politics and, 42, 75, 110–111, 160, 162–163, 167–178, 181, 185, 192, 202, 204, 218, 227, 254n12
  transit and, 110–111
Défense, La, 43, 115–116, 135, 138, 180, 200, 213, 229
Défense Public Development Authority, La (EPAD), 43
de Gaulle, Charles, 40, 61, 119, 151, 154, 199, 243n1
Delanoë, Bertrand, 7, 76, 169, 171, 173, 178–179, 231, 247n4, 255n17
Deleuze, Gilles, 87
Delouvrier, Paul, 40–42, 45, 97, 105, 108, 110, 177

Democracy, 3–4, 19
  autonomy, 255n14
  grand urbanism and, 10, 66, 73–75, 82, 121–122, 195–197, 215–220, 221, 234, 237–240
  metropolitanization and, 193, 195–197, 215, 218, 256n3
  state productivism and, 3, 193, 195–197, 209, 215–218
  suburbs and, 48
  territorial politics and, 179–180, 182–185, 188, 255n14
  transit and, 121–123, 126
Densification, 58, 86, 115, 119, 139–141, 155, 200
de Portzamparc, Christian, 50, 52t, 55–56, 85–87, 89–90, 138, 148, 205, 212
de Selves, Justin, 38
Design
  aesthetics and, 2, 37–38, 66, 68, 71, 81–83, 89, 91–92, 104, 132, 205, 233, 238, 257n8
  competitions for, 49–62
  connected city and, 85–87
  designed city and, 81–83
  exhibitions and, 2, 25, 46–47, 50, 52t, 55, 63, 66–67, 70, 72–73, 76, 81–82, 87–90, 152, 159, 244n4, 245n9
  flexibility and, 48, 83–85, 87, 90, 128, 138, 148, 176, 179
  governable city and, 74–77
  Grand Moscow and, 225–233
  Grand Paris Express (GPE) and, 128, 133–137, 152
  grand urbanism and, 222–232, 238
  imagineering and, 34, 49, 68–71
  megaprojects and, 4, 14, 20–22 (*see also* Megaprojects)
  metropolitanization and, 191, 199–200, 205–207, 215
  modernism and, 20, 40, 83, 92, 123, 128, 197, 201

public funding and, 14, 23, 156, 247n1
public space and, 2, 39, 58, 71, 81–82, 131, 141, 167, 258n13
rational, 66–67
SDRIF and, 75, 110–112, 173, 177, 180–181, 186, 249n10
shared dream for Grand Paris and, 65–73, 77–78, 81–83, 86–92
suburbs and, 32–34, 37–38, 45, 49–56, 59–64
transit and, 103–104, 113, 117, 119, 128, 133–137, 152
unified city and, 77–80
utopian, 55, 65, 83
World's Fair and, 73
Deutsche, Rosalyn, 81–82
Deutsche Bank, 53
Dirigisme, 14, 160, 173–174, 176, 194, 197, 200, 214, 236
tactical, 208, 214, 236
Displacement, 83, 123, 138–141, 145
Dôme Arena, 152
Donzelot, Jacques, 108
Double Ring. *See Grand Huit*
Duflot, Cécile, 146, 200, 256n21
Dunham-Jones, Ellen, 10
Dupuy, Gabriel, 206
Duthilleul, Jean-Marie, 58

Easterling, Keller, 206–207
Echos, Les (newspaper), 226
Economist journal, 199, 246n4
Eiffel Tower, 73
Elden, Stuart, 175, 195–196
Elections, 75, 178, 181, 185, 242n5, 247n4
Elitism
corporate, 5
governance and, 167–171, 175, 192, 197, 209, 215–216, 219
grand urbanism and, 221, 224, 233, 248–249
intellectual, 25
metropolitanization and, 167–171, 175, 192, 197, 209, 215–216, 219
shared dreams of Grand Paris project and, 67–69, 72–73, 77, 84, 87
territorial politics and, 167–171, 175
transit and, 101, 126, 130–131, 153–154
transnational, 4, 17, 38
Environmental issues
air quality, 146
climate change, 51, 145, 245n10
conservation, 146, 248n9, 255n17
determinism and, 83, 244n5
economic context and, 222
governance and, 22, 165, 172–173, 177, 183, 186, 188, 207–208, 212–213, 257n5
Kyoto paradigm and, 1, 51–55, 146, 148, 245n10
metropolitanization and, 207–208, 212–213, 257n5
quality of life, 16
suburbs and, 50, 53, 56, 59, 244n5, 245n10
sustainability, 2 (*see also* Sustainability)
territorial politics and, 165, 172–173, 177, 183, 186, 188
transit and, 99–100, 124–125, 128, 142, 145–147, 150–151, 248nn7,9
Environment Île-de-France (IDFE), 147, 153
EPCIs (public authorities for intercommunal cooperation), 176, 186, 255n18
Equal Rights and Opportunities Law, 251n10
Euro currency, 17–18
Euro Disney, 42–43
Europa City, 152–154, 253n21

Évry, 41, 43
Exclusion, 11, 33–35, 38, 46–47, 71, 78, 81, 83, 87, 109, 121, 141, 144, 246n10

Fainstein, Susan, 69, 201
Farmer's General, 35
Federation of Real Estate and Financial Societies (FSIF), 212
Fifth Republic, 168
Figaro, Le (newspaper), 81
Fillon, Francois, 1
Financialization, 5–6, 19, 22–24, 34, 131, 136, 193, 195–197, 209–215, 218–219, 252n15, 258n9
  financial real-estate complex, 4
FIRE (financial, information and real estate) industries, 13, 17, 43
Flexibility, 48, 83–85, 87, 90, 128, 138, 148, 176, 179, 183
Flyvbjerg, Bent, 6, 14, 125–126, 132, 250nn2–3
Fol, Sylvie, 140
Fondation Cartier, 58
Fondation Mov'eoTec, 231
Fordism, 40, 49, 84–85, 166, 196–197, 253n1
Fortune 500 companies, 12–13
Foucault, Michel, 193, 242n4
Fourcaut, Annie, 47
Franco-Russian Chamber of Commerce (CCIFR), 230
French Revolution, 72, 76, 167

Gallez, Caroline, 140
Gardens, 58, 84
Garnier, Jean-Pierre, 89, 235, 247n12, 251nn8–9
Geipel, Finn, 50, 52t, 59–60, 79, 84, 246n6
Gens aises (wealthy inhabitants), 38
Gentrification
  banalization of, 15
  contemporary, 5, 20–22, 130–132, 237–238, 158n13
  generalized, 5, 20–22, 85, 195, 234
  metropolitanization and, 5, 20–24, 37, 130–137, 152–156, 191, 195, 219, 236–240
  resistance to, 153–154, 258n12
  Rogers on, 191
  state productivism and, 22, 37, 194–197, 209–214, 236–237
  Taksim Square and, 258n13
  transit and, 97–101, 122–123, 128–137, 154–156, 218–219, 223, 234–238
Ghettos, 44–45, 242n6, 252n13
Gilli, Frédéric, 43, 48, 74, 171
Gilroy, Paul, 15
Globalization, 3, 13, 20, 22
  competition and, 11, 16, 68, 87, 110, 115, 117, 133, 165, 173, 192
  metropolitanization and, 199, 212, 253n4
  suburbs and, 42–45, 56
  territorial politics and, 160–161, 164, 166–167, 189, 199, 253n4
Golubchicov, Oleg, 197
Gonesse, La, 148, 151–155, 208, 213, 258n12
Google Earth, 77
Governance
  autogestion and, 174, 179, 195, 254n12
  capitalist (sub)urbanization and, 197–215
  centralization and, 39, 167–168, 170, 183, 192, 218
  collaborative, 21, 50, 55, 62, 70, 73, 76, 81, 83, 85, 90, 119, 130, 165, 173, 176–180, 183–184, 193, 197, 200, 204, 207–209, 216, 230, 234, 244n6, 257n5
  concept of, 253n4
  cumul des mandats and, 254n9

Index

decentralization and, 42, 75, 110–111, 160, 162–163, 167–178, 181, 185, 192, 202, 204, 218, 227, 254n12
dirigisme and, 160, 173–174, 176, 197, 214, 236
elitism and, 167–171, 175, 192, 197, 209, 215–216, 219
environmental issues and, 22, 165, 172–173, 177, 183, 186, 188, 207–208, 212–213, 257n5
EPCIs and, 176, 186, 255n18
financial sector issues and, 209–215
globalization and, 160–161, 164, 166–167, 189, 199, 212, 253n4
governable city and, 74–77
Grand Moscow and, 225–233
ideologies and, 160, 167, 171–174, 177, 185, 188, 194–195, 205, 217
infrastructures and, 162, 167–169, 175–176, 181, 186, 194–198, 205–210, 214, 219
jurisdictional issues and, 75–76, 161, 163, 166, 206–207
labor and, 162, 199, 204
legal issues and, 159, 163, 181, 205, 211–214, 219, 229, 241n3
MAPTAM and, 183, 185–186
master plans and, 41, 49, 64, 68, 75, 110–111, 136, 175, 181, 186, 197, 201, 254n12, 257n5
megaprojects and, 4, 201–202, 204, 213
metropolitanization and, 161–166, 191–220 (*see also* Metropolitanization)
mille-feuille (thousand layers) of, 164–165, 172, 182, 196, 202
mobility and, 160, 162, 182, 202, 206, 209
neoliberalism and, 6 (*see also* Neoliberalism)
network thinking and, 206–207
Paris Chamber of Commerce and Industry (CCIP) and, 110, 112, 248n9, 257n6
Paris Métropole and, 7, 49, 52t, 75–76, 89, 160, 166, 172–173, 179–180, 182–185, 207, 244n6, 249n10, 255n18, 256n19
Plaine Commune and, 173, 178, 184–185
postindustrial resurgence and, 222
public development agencies (EPAs) and, 186, 200, 256n20
reform and, 24, 46, 67, 131, 151 (*see also* Reform)
Regional Councils and, 114, 171–172, 177–178, 231
regulation and, 5–6, 26 (*see also* Regulation)
return of the state and, 180–182, 205–209
soft spaces of, 203
taxes and, 181, 186, 200, 204, 211–212, 218
Territorial Development Contracts (contrats du devéloppement territorials [CDTs]) and, 179, 187, 193, 204–205, 208–209, 213
territorial politics and, 159–189 (*see also* Territorial politics)
Voynet law and, 200
zoning and, 40, 84, 222, 246n7
Governmentality, 129, 193, 236, 256n1
Grand Huit, 87, 111–112, 114t, 116
Grand Moscow, 225–233, 258n1
Grand Paris
ambitious vision of, 1–4
better future and, 15–17
Cantal-Dupart's criticisms of, 154–155
city walls and, 11, 36–42, 221, 237
clustering strategy and, 13, 43–44 87, 101, 116, 133–137, 140, 147–154, 156, 199, 202, 211, 213–214, 222–223, 251nn5–6

Grand Paris (cont.)
  concept of, 7–8
  consensus on, 25, 33, 122, 126, 145, 216–219, 234, 238–239,
  first announcement of, 1–2
  gentrification and, 5, 15 (*see also* Gentrification)
  as *grand projet*, 13–15
  identity and, 25, 31, 33–34, 46, 57, 62, 78–80, 159, 185, 228, 236, 244n6, 246n7
  imagineering and, 34, 49, 68–71
  international architectural teams and, 49–62
  megaprojects and, 4, 14, 20–22 (*see also* Megaprojects)
  as model global city, 11–13
  New Grand Paris, 89, 146–147, 181, 242n5
  as post(sub)urban network, 8–15
  shared dreams of, 65–93
  taking account of, 233–237
  as third modernization movement, 36–37
  utopianism and, 7, 19, 55, 65, 83, 89, 92, 135
  world city and, 6, 11–12, 16, 42–49, 101, 136, 146, 197
Grand Paris Act
  gentrification and, 234
  justification of spending by, 250n4
  legal framework of, 2
  metropolitanization and, 194, 204
  preamble of, 97
  state productivism and, 19–22, 191–197, 217–218
  territorial politics and, 173, 180
  transit and, 111, 133, 149
Grand Paris Express (GPE), 2
  accessibility issues and, 141–143, 150, 155, 251n10
  Cantal-Dupart's criticisms of, 154–155
  capitalism and, 129–156, 234
  clustering and, 119, 133–137, 251nn5–6
  competition and, 127, 129, 131, 133, 135, 140, 142–143, 146–148, 155
  compromise and, 118–119, 121–124, 235, 248n9
  conflicts over, 125–127, 132
  consensus and, 126, 145–146, 249n11
  densification and, 139–141, 155, 200
  design and, 128, 133–137, 152
  Equal Rights and Opportunities Law and, 251n10
  gentlemen's agreement on, 118
  inauguration ceremony of, 249n11
  investment and, 126, 128, 130–137, 142, 154, 156, 250n3, 251n5, 252n17, 252n19
  layout of, 119, 120f
  metropolitanization and, 14, 119, 126, 130, 132–133, 156, 200, 205, 207, 209, 234–235
  mobility and, 125–129, 133, 137–147, 150, 154–156, 251n10
  myths and, 127–148
  Olympic villages and, 132
  rent and, 125, 128, 131, 135–140, 155
  station design of, 257n8
  taxes and, 117–118, 132, 137, 139, 200
  Territorial Development Contracts (contrats du devéloppement territorials [CDTs]) and, 119, 131, 137, 148–151, 154–155, 249n10, 253n20
  territorial politics and, 159, 162, 180
Grand Pari(s): International Consultation on the Future of the Parisian Metropolis, 8, 32–34, 49–64, 66–93, 187, 201, 205, 212, 224, 229, 233, 239

Index 297

Grand Prix de l'urbanisme, 58–59
Grand projets, 13–15, 58, 67, 76, 111, 130, 133, 248n7
Grand Roissy, 151, 253n20
Grand urbanism
  architecture and, 22, 24, 25–26, 32–34, 62–64, 66–71, 89–92, 223–225, 233–234
  bigness and, 5, 10, 20–21, 183, 188, 218
  capitalism and, 5–6, 20–24, 85, 92, 196–201, 211, 218–219, 221, 233–236, 238
  collaborative governance and, 2, 130, 176–177, 197–201, 208–209, 216–220, 236
  collective consumption and, 19, 97, 154, 195–196, 199, 235
  competition and, 5, 20–25, 90, 137, 148, 187, 209, 218–219, 232–233
  financialization and, 4–5, 20, 22, 209–215, 236
  gentrification and, 5, 20–24, 37, 130–137, 152–156, 191, 195, 219, 236–240
  global city and, 5–6, 20–25, 126, 164, 187, 196–199, 209, 215, 217, 219, 232–233, 236–238, 246n10
  global practice of, 21–25, 69, 91, 221–225, 232–233, 236–239
  growth and, 5, 20–25, 63, 71, 92, 137, 148, 157, 199, 211, 218–219, 236–237
  infrastructure and, 6, 20–25, 68–69, 97, 101, 125, 195, 205–209, 219, 222–232, 234, 236, 239
  investment and, 4, 20–23, 92, 214, 221, 223, 227, 230–232, 237
  market values and, 4–6, 20–25, 92, 137, 218–219, 223, 236–237
  megaprojects and, 4, 14, 20–23, 129–133, 222–224, 237
  Moscow and, 225–233
  polycentrism and, 21, 71, 91, 223–234, 226
  project-based planning and, 20–25, 193, 201–209, 223, 236
  state role in, 20–25, 75, 132, 161–164, 187, 193–197, 200–205, 217, 223, 236
  sustainability and, 222, 229, 232, 234–235, 239
  transit and, 22–23, 228, 231–232, 236
Grassroots groups, 7, 74–75, 172, 175, 185
Gravier, Jean-François, 170
Greater Helsinki Vision, 223
Greater London, 53, 165, 254n11
Greenhouse gases, 51, 145, 245n10
Green paper, 182–183
Green Party, 118, 146, 172, 256n21
Green spaces, 2
  building modes and, 119
  economics and, 116
  gardens, 58, 84
  green parties and, 18
  nature-cities and, 229
  networked, 67, 250n13
  offices and, 82
  parks, 26, 37–38, 53, 82, 84, 98, 140, 150
  Saclay Plateau and, 248n9
  smart infrastructures and, 82, 257n8
  suburbs and, 41, 51, 58, 63
  territorial politics and, 177, 182–183
  transit and, 86, 116, 118–119, 140, 145–147, 150
Gromov, Boris, 227
Groupe Descartes, 50, 52t, 53–54, 74–75
Grumbach, Antoine, 56–57, 60, 62, 90–91, 191, 201, 229, 259n2
Guggenheim Museum, 68–69

Hackworth, Jason, 132, 135–136
Haine, La (film), 109
Hardt, Michael, 125

Harrison, John, 197, 218
Harvey, David, 5, 12, 15, 17, 37–38, 68, 131, 210, 238
Haughton, Graham, 203, 216
Haussmann, Georges Eugène, 14, 19, 37–41, 130, 210, 221, 246n7
Hazan, Eric, 34–35, 37, 221
Hidalgo, Anne, 76–77
Highways, 41, 61, 100, 111, 137, 150, 248n7, 254n12
Hollande, François, 8, 89, 92, 142, 146–147, 154, 181, 203, 242n5, 243n12
Housing
  affordable, 38, 70
  city greening and, 2
  decay and, 82
  densification of, 86
  global city regions and, 22
  infrastructural gaps and, 222
  metropolitanization and, 198, 200, 205, 207, 215
  peripheral, 226
  private investment and, 252n17
  revolt and, 91
  shortages in, 225
  single-family, 242n6
  suburbs and, 38–41, 44, 47, 53, 244n4
  sustainability and, 239
  state productivism and, 198
  territorial politics and, 10, 165, 176, 179, 182–184, 186–187, 254n12, 255n17, 256n21
  transit and, 98, 109, 113, 121, 127, 135, 139–145, 148–155, 249n10, 251n8, 252n17
  unit projections for, 249n10
  universal, 70
  unsafe, 251n8
Hoyler, Michael, 197, 218
Huchon, Jean-Paul, 114t, 117–118, 169, 172, 177, 181, 231, 255n17, 256n20

Île-de-France Institute of Planning and Development (IAURIF), 110
Île-de-France Mayoral Association, 2, 207
Île-de-France Transport Union (STIF), 105, 110, 113–115, 117, 162, 178, 186, 207–208, 247n3
Icade, 213
Identity
  geographic, 80
  metropolitanization and, 25, 33, 46, 228, 236, 244n6, 246n7
  republican, 80
  suburbs and, 31, 33–34, 46, 57, 62
  territorial politics and, 159, 185
  unified, 78–79
Ideologies
  aesthetics and, 2, 37–38, 66, 68, 71, 81–83, 89, 91–92, 104, 132, 205, 233, 238, 257n8
  compromise and, 5, 15, 66, 91, 103 (see also Compromise)
  consensus and, 25, 33, 49, 69, 82, 89, 118, 122, 126, 145, 180, 188, 192, 205, 216–219, 234, 238–239, 248n9, 249n12, 257n7
  governance and, 160, 167, 171–174, 177, 185, 188, 194–195, 205, 217
  knowledge production and, 37
  Marxist, 256n2
  metropolitanization and, 194–195, 205, 217, 233
  mobility and, 127–148
  myths and, 127–148
  neoliberalism and, 4 (see also Neoliberalism)
  partisan, 5, 76, 82, 111–112, 119, 121, 127, 129, 171–173, 179, 181, 188, 192, 217, 254n11
  representation vs. reality and, 245n2
  Soviet, 231
  suburbs and, 244n4, 246n10

Index

system of truths and, 127
territorial politics and, 160, 167,
  171–174, 177, 185, 188
transit and, 98–102, 122–123,
  126–148
urbanism and, 76
utopianism and, 7, 19, 55, 65, 83, 89,
  92, 135
Imagineering, 34, 49, 68–71
Immigrants, 15, 46, 109, 199
Infrastructure
  congealed social interests and, 102
  connected geographies and, 21
  as contested artifacts, 98, 102–103,
    121–124
  defining urban space and, 6, 21–24,
    38, 63, 98–99, 125, 127, 130, 135,
    140, 186, 196, 198, 206, 236, 239
  development myth of, 129–133
  economic stimulation and, 19, 23, 37,
    40–41, 86, 98–99, 130–137, 139, 198,
    205, 214, 219, 232
  governance and, 162, 167–169,
    175–176, 181, 186, 194–198,
    205–210, 214, 219
  grand urbanism and, 6, 20–25, 68–69,
    97, 101, 125, 195, 205–209, 219,
    222–232, 234, 236, 239
  green spaces and, 82, 257n8
  increased importance of, 18, 98,
    101–103, 186, 219
  megaprojects and, 22 (*see also*
    Megaprojects)
  metromobility and, 98–99
  metropolitanization and, 194–198,
    205–210, 214, 219
  networked, 2, 24, 98, 102, 126, 162,
    196, 205–208, 228, 239
  political, 6, 102, 236
  power relationships and, 23
  shared dreams of Grand Paris project
    and, 69, 80–87, 91
  smart, 82, 257n8

suburbs and, 37–41, 46, 49, 53–54, 60,
  63
territorial growth and, 10, 20
territorial politics and, 162, 167–169,
  175–176, 181, 186
transit and, 4, 11, 98–105, 108, 112,
  119–132, 135–143, 150–151, 156,
  248n7, 250n13, 257n6, 258n13
Institute du Monde Arabe, 58
Institute for Urban Development in the
  Île-de-France (IAU-IDF), 205
Institute National de la Statistique et
  des Études Économiques (INSEE), 8,
  12, 108–109, 138, 252n12
Interministerial Delegation for
  Development and Territorial
  Competitiveness (DIACT), 200
Interministerial Delegation for Regional
  Development and Territorial
  Planning (DATAR), 40, 199–200
International Workshop of Grand Paris
  (AIGP), 2, 90–91
  design team summaries and, 51
  Lemoine and, 228
  Mansat and, 90
  metropolitanization and, 207, 256n22
  suburbs and, 51
  territorial politics and, 179
  transit and, 91, 117, 140, 151, 153,
    249n10
Investment, 13
  architecture and, 92 (*see also*
    Architecture)
  capital flow and, 86
  competition and, 22
  direct, 118, 142
  Grand Paris Express (GPE) and,
    252n19
  grand projets and, 67
  grand urbanism and, 4, 20–23, 92,
    214, 221, 223, 227, 230–232, 237
  infrastructural, 80
  long-term, 258n11

Investment (cont.)
  metropolitanization and, 193–195, 199, 201, 205, 211–216, 257n6, 258n11
  Plaine-Saint-Denis and, 43
  priority sites and, 23
  private, 4, 20, 136, 201, 214
  public, 14, 23, 41, 118, 130, 156, 214, 216, 247n1, 252n17
  real estate investment trusts (REITs) and, 27, 211–213
  Saclay and, 149–151
  shifting patterns of, 85
  state productivism and, 193–195, 199
  suburbs and, 35, 41, 43
  surplus, 35
  territorial politics and, 169–170, 173–175, 178, 188
  transit and, 87, 100, 102, 117–118, 126, 128, 130–137, 142, 154, 156, 250n3, 251n5, 252n17, 252n19
Isin, Engin, 159

James, Kery, 47
Jameson, Fredric, 92
Jobert, Bruno, 18, 243n11
Jurisdictional issues, 75–76, 161–163, 166, 206–207

Kantor, Paul, 22, 164, 172, 192
Kearns, Gerry, 76
Keynesianism, 123, 131, 170, 197, 223
Klouche, Djamel, 50, 55
Kozlov, Sergei, 231
Kyoto paradigm, 1, 51, 52t, 55, 58, 146, 148, 245n10

Labor, 243n11
  division of, 44, 116
  employment and, 10–11, 22, 43, 46–47, 70, 98, 108, 115, 121, 127, 135, 138–140, 142, 160, 165, 176, 183, 187, 218, 226, 228, 251n5

  governance and, 162, 199, 204
  intellectual, 91
  job loss and, 43
  red belt and, 41–42
  suburbs and, 43–44
  transit and, 116, 135, 137, 139, 145
  unions and, 84, 105, 178, 228
Lacoste, Gérard, 249n12, 251n6
Land ownership, 131, 211
l'AUC, 50, 52t, 55, 84, 86, 147, 229, 259n2
Law on the Modernization of Territorial Public Action and the Affirmation of Metropolitan Areas (MAPTAM), 183, 185–186
Lefebvre, Henri, 5, 26, 32, 128–129, 175, 194–196, 210, 218, 238, 256nn2–3
Lefèvre, Christian, 50, 166, 199
Le Galès, Patrick, 164, 167–169, 194, 197, 253n4
Legal issues
  governance and, 159, 163, 181, 205, 211–214, 219, 229, 241n3
  Grand Paris Act and, 2, 97, 111, 133, 149, 173, 180, 194, 204, 234, 250n4
  redevelopment and, 2, 241n3
  suburbs and, 39, 49
  taxes and, 181, 186
Lemoine, Bertrand, 228
Léonhardt, Frédéric, 147, 253n22
Leroy, Maurice, 1, 19, 118, 181
Libération newspaper, 81
LIN-Finn Geipel + Giulia Andi, 50, 52t, 59–60, 79, 86, 246n6
Lion, Yves, 50, 53, 85, 259n2
Livingstone, Ken, 53
London, 19
  aesthetics of, 82
  as financialization model, 250n4, 252n15
  Greater London authority and, 53, 165, 254n11

Livingstone and, 53
Olympics and, 223, 250n4
rivalry with, 11–12, 187, 242n7, 250n4
transit and, 104, 224
Underground of, 104
as world city, 12
London School of Economics, 52t, 53
Louis XIII, 35
Lynch, Kevin, 78

Maas, Winy, 50, 61
Macroeconomics, 18, 42, 214
Maillage, 250n13
Mairie de Paris, 33, 159, 160, 165
Mansat, Pierre, 90, 179–180
Marxism, 256n2
Maspero, François, 31
Massey, Doreen, 6, 12, 142
Master Plan of the Île-de-France Region (SDRIF), 75, 110–112, 173, 177, 180–181, 186, 249n10
Master Plan of Urban Development, 41
McFarlane, Colin, 6, 23, 102
Media, 47, 61, 73, 81, 113, 181
Medvedev, Dimitri, 226–227
Megalopolis magazine, 47
Megaprojects
  development myth of, 129–133
  gentrification and, 69
  governance and, 4
  grand urbanism and, 4, 14, 20–23, 129–133, 222–224, 237
  iron law of, 132
  metropolitanization and, 201–202, 204, 213, 223
  regional transformation and, 14, 237
  restructuring and, 20
  site-specific, 88, 222
  transit and, 21–22, 99, 122–123, 125, 129–133, 147, 153, 234, 250nn2–3
Merlin, Pierre, 40–41, 97, 103, 147, 249n12

Merrifield, Andy, 38, 130
Metromobility, 26
  concept of, 14, 98–103
  contemporary dynamics of, 113
  ever-changing complexity of, 121
  Grand Paris Express (GPE) and, 125–127, 137, 155
  network effects and, 101, 249n12
  politics of, 100–103, 125
  transit debates and, 98–104, 113, 121–124
Metronews newspaper, 47
Métropole du Grand Paris (MGP), 2
  formation of, 182–187
  institutional big bang, 199
  state productivism and, 191–193, 199
  territorial politics and, 174, 183, 185–187, 256n24
Metropolitanization, 4–5, 10
  architecture and, 37, 196, 201, 205, 208, 212, 215–216, 219
  capitalism and, 192–220, 246n10
  centralization and, 167–168, 170, 183
  collaboration and, 176–180
  connected city and, 85–87
  consensus and, 25, 33, 49, 69, 82, 89, 118, 122, 126, 145, 180, 188, 192, 205, 216–219, 234, 238–239, 248n9, 249n12, 257n7
  decentralization and, 192, 202, 204, 218
  democracy and, 193, 195–197, 215–218, 256n3
  design and, 81–83, 191, 199–200, 205–207, 215
  elitism and, 167–171, 175, 192, 197, 209, 215–216, 219
  environmental issues and, 207–208, 212–213, 257n5
  flexible city and, 83–85
  gentrification and, 24, 191, 195
  globalization and, 160–161, 164, 166–167, 189, 199, 212, 253n4

Index

Metropolitanization (cont.)
  governance challenges of, 74–77, 161–166
  grand city and, 72–74
  Grand Paris Act and, 194, 204
  Grand Paris Express (GPE) and, 200
  housing and, 198, 200, 205, 207, 215
  identity and, 25, 31, 33–34, 46, 57, 62, 78–80, 159, 185, 228, 236, 244n6, 246n7
  ideologies and, 194–195, 205, 217, 233
  infrastructures and, 194–198, 205–210, 214, 219
  International Workshop of Grand Paris (AIGP) and, 207, 256n22
  investment and, 193–195, 199, 201, 205, 211–216, 257n6, 258n11
  MAPTAM and, 183, 185–186
  megaprojects and, 201–202, 204, 213, 223
  mobility and, 25 (*see also* Mobility)
  multidimensionality of, 166–172
  neoliberalism and, 192–193, 196–197, 201, 205, 216–217, 220
  Paris Métropole and, 7–8, 207, 244n6
  postindustrial resurgence and, 222
  Public Authority of Paris-Saclay (EPPS) and, 198
  reform and, 105, 180–182, 191–193, 197, 199–203, 208–210, 216
  regulation and, 192–193, 195, 202, 208, 217, 219
  re-presenting the metropolis and, 72–87
  Sarkozy and, 203
  SDRIF and, 75, 110–112, 173, 177, 180–181, 186, 249n10
  Society of Grand Paris (SGP) and, 207–208
  spatial issues and, 42–43, 191–197, 201, 205–206, 208, 210, 215, 219–220, 258n13

  state productivism and, 191–199
  sustainability and, 207, 213
  Territorial Development Contracts (contrats du devéloppement territorials [CDTs]) and, 193, 204–205, 208–209, 213
  territorial politics and, 160–161, 166–191
  tourism and, 80, 209
  transit and, 126 (*see also* Transit)
  unified city and, 77–80
  urbanism and, 17, 24, 37–38, 47, 62, 193–209, 211, 214–219
  Voynet law and, 200
  works of representation and, 62–64
Metropolitan Plan for Sustainable Development (PADD), 186
Miller, Peter, 253n2
Ministry in Charge of Grand Paris, 207
Ministry of Cities, 181
Ministry of Culture, 50–51
Ministry of Development for the Capital Region, 181
Ministry of Housing, Territorial Equality and Rurality, 198–200
Ministry of Territorial Equality and Housing, 256n21
Ministry of the Economy, 207
Mitterrand, François, 14, 45, 76, 174
Mobility
  access to public transport and, 11, 23, 54, 59–60, 85–86, 108–110, 155
  equivocal, 137–141
  as essential element of modern city, 22–23, 85–87, 100–101
  governance and, 160, 162, 182, 202, 206, 209
  Grand Paris Express (GPE) and, 125–129, 133, 137–147, 150, 154–156, 251n10
  grand urbanism and, 22–23, 228, 231–232, 236
  ideologies and, 127–148

Index

infrastructure and, 22–23
metromobility and, 14, 26, 98–104, 113, 121–127, 137, 155
metropolitan identity and, 25
myths and, 127–148
network effects and, 101, 249n12
political economic patterns and, 97–98
suburbs and, 41, 54, 58–60, 85–87
territorial politics and, 160, 162, 182
transit and, 97–103, 107–113, 121–129, 133, 137–147, 150, 154–156, 247n2, 251n10, 252n11
Modernization, 12, 14–15, 222
framing of, 33–34
governance and, 183, 210, 257n7
Haussmann and, 37–41
modernist agenda and, 20, 40, 83, 92, 123, 128, 197, 201
postwar, 138
suburbs and, 36–41
transit and, 99, 130, 138
Monde, Le (newspaper), 81, 255n17
Mongin, Pierre, 103
MONU magazine, 21
Moscow Architectural Institute, 259n2
Moscow City Agglomeration, 229
Moscow City Duma, 227
Musée du quai Branly, 58
Museum of Architecture and Heritage (Cité de l'Architecture et du Patrimoine), 1, 50–51, 73
MVRDV, 50, 52t, 61–62, 243n9
Myth, 127–148

Nanterre, 43, 212–213, 258n12
Napoleon, Louis, 104
Napoléon III, 37
National Commission on Public Debate (CNDP), 112–113, 116–118, 121–122, 248n7, 248n9
National Interest Operations (OINs), 180, 200, 252n17

National Society of France Railways (SNCF), 58, 108, 144, 207–208, 253n20
National Stadium, Beijing, 69
Negri, Antonio, 125
Neoliberalism, 24, 26
à la française, 18–20, 24, 234–235, 243n11
competition and, 4, 17–20, 33, 146–147, 177, 196–197, 234–235
economic growth and, 4, 18–20, 33, 146, 222, 236–237
global city and, 17–20
metropolitanization and, 192–193, 196–197, 201, 205, 216–217, 220, 236–237
paternalism and,
projects and, 67–68, 193, 201–205
as regime of capital accumulation, 17
republicanism and, 18, 243n11
roll-out, 131
territorial politics and, 160, 177, 188
transit and, 123, 127, 129, 131, 146
urbanism and, 17, 222, 231, 234–235, 238
utopianism and, 19
Network thinking, 206–207
New Moscow, 227
New Towns (*villes nouvelles*), 41, 53
New York, 11–12, 69, 82, 187
Nouvel, Jean, 50, 52t, 58, 59, 78–80, 84, 86, 89–90

Objectif Grand Paris magazine, 47
Obsolescence, 16–17, 34, 86, 135
Office for Metropolitan Architecture (OMA), 229
Offner, Jean-Marc, 10, 97–98, 143, 146, 206, 241n3
Olson, Mancur, 165
Olympics, 59, 132, 223, 242, 250n4, 259n4

OMA, 259n2
Oosterlynck, Stijn, 203, 216
ORBITALE (Regional Organization of Congestion-free Transport of the Inner Basin Ring), 110–111
ORBIVAL, 110–111
Orfeuil, Jean-Pierre, 249n12
Orsay, 43, 150
Orueta, Fernando, 69
Ostozhenka Architects, 259n2

Panerai, Philippe, 10, 35, 108–109, 241n3
Paris. *See also* Grand Paris
  boulevards of, 35, 37, 54, 108, 241n2
  city walls of, 11, 34–42, 221, 237
  core of, 2, 11, 35–36, 42–43, 47–48, 59, 61, 79–80, 86, 112, 143, 147, 186,
  designation of City of, 241n2
  Gallo-Roman architecture and, 34–35 (*see also* Architecture)
  Greater, 5, 7, 12, 31, 43–47, 58–62, 88, 103, 161, 167, 172–173, 181, 198, 213, 230, 233, 237, 246n8, 258n11
  identity and, 25, 31, 33–34, 46, 57, 62, 78–80, 159, 185, 228, 236, 244n6, 246n7
  periphery of, 11 (*see also* Suburbs)
  preeminence of capital region and, 169–170
  territorial politics and, 169–170 (*see also* Territorial politics)
  urban-suburban divides and, 42, 170–171, 233
  vision of the future and, 1–4, 7, 12, 15–17, 22, 31–34, 49–66, 77, 92, 93, 112, 148, 233
  as world city, 11–13, 16, 42–49, 146, 197
Paris, the Metropolis and Its Projects (exhibition), 76–77
Paris Chamber of Commerce and Industry (CCIP), 110, 112, 248n9, 257n6
Paris Commune, 38, 243n2
Paris est sa banlieue (blog), 47
Parisian Autonomous Transport Operator (RATP), 103, 105, 108, 162, 207–208, 247n3
Paris Je T'aime (film), 109
Paris Métropole, 7–8, 75–76, 89, 160, 166, 172–173, 179–180, 182–185, 207, 244n6, 255n18
  architectural consultation and, 89
  CDTs and, 249n10
  Delanoë and, 7, 76
  metropolitanization and, 7–8, 207, 244n6
  SDRIF and, 75
  territorial politics and, 160, 166, 172–173, 179–185, 255n18, 256n19
Paris Prefecture, 151, 207
Parks, 26, 37–38, 53, 82, 84, 98, 140, 150
Paternalism, 243n11
Pavillon de l'Arsenal, 46, 76
Peck, Jamie, 131, 197, 231–232
Pedestrians, 60, 98, 146
Piano, Renzo, 53
Pierre, Jon, 163
Pinson, Gilles, 168–169, 201–202, 257n7
Plaine Commune, 173, 178, 184–185
Plaine-Saint-Denis, 43
Plan Abu Dhabi, 223
Plan for the Development and General Organization of the Paris Region (PADOG), 40, 105
PlaNYC, 223
Policy mobility, 224–233
Politique de la ville, 202, 212, 255n14
Polycentrism, 2, 21, 24, 40–41, 44–45, 48, 53–54, 62, 68, 71, 85, 87, 91, 99,

Index

101, 105, 127, 139, 147, 156, 159, 179, 183–185, 226
Delouvrier and, 41–42, 45, 105
hierarchical, 44–45, 85
governance and, 159, 173, 179, 183–185, 223
grand urbanism and, 21, 71, 91, 223–234, 226
Moscow, 226–228
networked metropolis and, 2, 24, 62, 99, 173, 234
Populism, 67, 69, 77, 104, 123, 209, 215, 238, 246n4
Postpolitics, 69, 126, 217
Potsdamer Platz, 69
Poverty, 11, 46–47, 127, 255n14
Pritzker Prize, 53, 55, 58
Productivism
architecture and, 5, 196, 201, 205, 208, 216
capitalism and, 192–197
decentralization and, 192
democracy and, 193, 195–197
design and, 191, 199
gentrification and, 22
Grand Paris Act and, 194
housing and, 198
hyperproductivism and, 196
investment and, 193–195, 199
Métropole du Grand Paris (MGP) and, 191–193, 199
metropolitanization and, 191–199
Public Authority of Paris-Saclay (EPPS) and, 198
reform and, 105, 191–193, 197, 199
regulation and, 192–193, 195
spatial issues and, 82, 191–197
state-backed, 3, 19, 27, 191–199, 216, 218–219, 234–236, 256n3
state mode of production (SMP) and, 194–197, 205, 209, 216, 218–219, 232, 256n3

Territorial Development Contracts (contrats du devéloppement territorials [CDTs]) and, 193
urbanism and, 193–214
"Prospective Diagnostics of Parisian Agglomeration, The" (design theme), 51
Prost Plan, 39, 105
Public action, 8, 143, 183, 216, 235
Public Authority of Paris-Saclay (EPPS), 2
metropolitanization and, 198
state productivism and, 198
transit and, 149–150
Public debate
compromise and, 5, 15, 66, 91, 103 (see also Compromise)
consensus and, 25, 33, 49, 69, 82, 89, 118, 122, 126, 145, 180, 188, 192, 205, 216–219, 234, 238–239, 248n9, 249n12, 257n7
suburbs and, 47
transit and, 99, 112–122, 125–126, 144
Public development agencies (EPAs), 186, 200, 256n20
Public Development Authority for La Défense Seine Arche (EPADESA), 180, 228–229, 259n2
Public funding, 14, 23, 156, 247n1
Public-private partnerships (PPPs), 211–212, 230
Public space, 2, 39, 58, 71, 81–82, 131, 141, 167, 258n13
Public Transport Network of Grand Paris (RTPGP), 112–118, 248n9. See also Grand Huit

Quality of life, 16, 19, 38, 98, 100, 110, 127, 138, 154, 215, 222, 226–227

Racing Métro Arena 92, 212
Racism, 44, 127, 140, 144–145, 252

Raffarin, Jean-Pierre, 178
Rail. *See* Transit
Real estate investment trusts (REITs), 27, 211–213 (*See also Sociétés d'investissement immobilier cotées*)
Recreation, 48, 98
Reform (urban)
  Blanc and, 18
  economic, 84, 93, 246n4
  gentrifying, 17
  Haussmann and, 14, 19, 37–41, 130, 210, 221, 246n7
  hyperbolic, 72
  infrastructural, 91
  institutional, 66, 75, 170, 172
  metropolitanization and, 105, 180–182, 191–193, 197, 199–203, 208–210, 216
  neoliberalism and, 18
  paternalism and, 243n11
  pension, 246n4
  populist consensus for, 69
  post–World War II, 83
  project-based, 73, 191, 197, 202, 209, 221, 236
  Sarkozy and, 66, 72
  Second Empire and, 14, 37, 83, 130
  state productivism and, 105, 191–193, 197, 199
  suburbs and, 37, 46–47, 244n6
  territorial, 24, 46, 67, 131, 151, 164–166, 169–172, 175, 178, 180–182, 188
  transit and, 118, 130–131, 135, 151, 155
  urbanism and, 3, 221–238
  utopianism and, 89
Regional Council of the Île-de-France, 1–2, 114, 171–172, 177–178, 231
Regional Development Agency (ARD), 178, 207
Regional Express Network (RER), 41, 98, 105–111, 116, 118, 143–144, 150

Regional planning, 39, 46, 173, 177, 221, 223
Regulation
  deregulation and, 83, 161, 175, 199, 222, 243n11, 246n7
  environmental, 147, 245n10
  future-proofing and, 83
  Little Big Bang and, 175
  metropolitanization and, 192–193, 195, 202, 208, 217, 219
  mode of, 5
  nation-state and, 26–27
  private, 6
  state productivism and, 192–193, 195
  suburbs and, 37
  territorial politics and, 160, 175, 253n5, 254n8
  transit and, 132, 147
  zoning and, 40, 84, 222, 246n7
Renard, Vincent, 210, 214
Rent
  gaps and, 16, 135–136, 211, 219, 234
  Grand Paris Express (GPE) and, 125, 128, 131, 135–140, 155
  ground, 128, 238
  production of, 4–5, 16, 99, 122, 131, 136–137, 237, 250n1
  territorial politics and, 168
  transit and, 99, 122, 125, 128, 131, 135–140, 155
Rentability, 16, 90, 137, 176, 213
Republicanism, 4, 16, 18, 20, 80, 141–142, 167, 194, 219, 235, 243n11
RFF, 207–208
Rhizome (urban), 52, 56–57, 87, 134
Rocard, Michel, 177
Rodeos, 109
Rogers, Richard, 50, 191
Rogers Stirk Harbour + Partners, 46, 50, 52t, 53, 74–75
Rose, Nikolas, 253n2
Ross, Kristen, 43, 99, 137–138

Index

Russian Academy of Architecture and Building Science, 259n2
Rutherford, Jonathan, 6, 23, 102

Saclay, 259n2
  governance and, 180, 198, 208, 258n12
  Public Authority of Paris-Saclay (EPPS), 2, 149–150, 198, 229
  as Silicon Valley of Paris, 116, 149, 248n9
  technology clusters and, 43
  transit and, 116, 119, 135, 148–151, 155, 248n9, 252n17
Saint Simonian ideal, 82
Sarkozy, Nicolas
  architecture and, 8, 15, 49–50, 63, 68, 70, 76, 88, 91–92, 248n6
  banlieue uprisings and, 1, 82, 83
  Blanc and, 88, 248n6
  declining polls of, 246n4
  global economy and, 12, 19
  Grand Paris vision of, 1, 3, 8, 11–16, 65
  Greater London Council and, 254n11
  Haussmann and, 37, 41
  Hollande and, 242n5, 243n12
  ideal city values and, 16
  metropolitanization and, 203
  poll ratings of, 246n4
  reform and, 66, 72
  social service cuts and, 18
  suburbs and, 1, 8, 11, 36–37, 41, 49–50, 63, 82–83, 242n6
  territorial politics and, 159, 172, 179–182
  transit and, 97, 111, 114t, 133, 152
  UMP party and, 75, 248n6
  utopianism and, 65
Sassen, Saskia, 6, 12, 21–22, 44, 50, 164
Schema de développement territorial (SDT), 149–150
Secchi, Bernardo, 50, 52t, 58–59, 79

Second Empire, 14, 24, 36, 83, 130, 210
Segregation, 45, 85–86, 109–110, 126, 151, 155–156, 187, 208, 226
Shantytowns (*bidonvilles*), 40
Sharanov, Andrei, 226–227
Silicon Valleys, 116, 149, 151, 223, 227, 231, 248n9
Silverstein, Paul, 145, 252n14
Simmel, Georg, 31
Skolkovo Foundation, 231
Sobyanin, Sergey, 227
Socialist Party, 8, 111, 171, 174, 183, 184t
Sociétés d'investissement immobilier cotées (SIIC), 212
Society of Grand Paris (SGP), 2, 16
  grand urbanism and, 226, 229, 231, 259n2
  metropolitanization and, 207–208
  Russians and, 226
  Scientific Committee of, 224
  territorial politics and, 162, 173, 181
  transit and, 111–119, 121, 137, 141, 146, 249n10, 249n12, 251n10
Soja, Edward, 10, 49, 84, 245n11
Starchitects, 25, 69, 73, 89
State mode of production (SMP), 194–197, 205, 209, 216, 218–219, 232, 256n3
State-Region Planning Agreements (CPERs), 111, 176–177
State rescaling, 5–6, 23–25, 164, 166–167, 188, 192–195, 201, 208–209, 214, 235–236
Stigmas (territorial), 11, 45, 109
Studio 09, 50, 52t, 58–59, 79, 86, 147
Studio Associato Secchi-Viganò, 229, 259n2
Subra, Philippe, 110, 176, 248n8
Suburbs
  architecture and, 32–34, 37, 39, 46–64, 244n5, 245n9
  banlieue concept and, 242n6

Suburbs (cont.)
banlieusards and, 46–47
Blanc and, 39, 41
capitalism and, 33, 35, 38, 40, 44, 49–50
as dangerous, 10–11
decentralization and, 42
Delouvrier and, 40–42, 45, 97, 105, 108, 110, 177
democracy and, 48
derelict sites and, 53–54
design and, 32–34, 37–38, 45, 49–56, 59–64
effective solidarity and, 35, 38–39, 58
environmental issues and, 50, 53, 56, 59, 244n5, 245n10
gentrification and, 155 (*see also* Gentrification)
ghettos and, 44–45, 242n6, 252n13
globalization and, 42, 44–45, 56
green spaces and, 41, 51, 58, 63
housing and, 38–41, 44, 47, 53, 244n4
identity and, 31, 33–34, 46, 57, 62
ideologies and, 244n4, 246n10
immigrants and, 15, 46, 109
infrastructures and, 37–41, 46, 49, 53–54, 60, 63
inner (*petit couronne*), 11, 40–44, 104–105, 110–111, 114, 116, 119, 171, 182, 186, 247n4, 256n24, 257n6
international architectural teams and, 49–62
International Workshop of Grand Paris (AIGP) and, 51
investment and, 35, 41, 43
job loss and, 43
labor and, 43–44
mobility and, 41, 54, 58–60, 85–87
neoliberalism and, 33
New Towns and, 41, 53
outer (*grand couronne*), 40, 43, 114, 138–139, 166, 171, 186, 247n4

poverty and, 46–47
Prost Plan and, 39, 105
proximity of extremes and, 45–46
Sarkozy and, 1, 8, 11, 36–37, 41, 49–50, 63, 82–83, 242n6
spatial politics and, 34–36, 38, 42, 45, 49, 56, 59
sustainability and, 53, 56, 59, 63
tourism and, 42, 47
transit and, 108–109, 111, 115
uprisings in, 1, 15, 45, 62, 72, 83, 86–87, 109, 258n13
urbanism and, 32–33, 36–42, 46–48, 53, 56, 58–64
urban-suburban divides and, 170–171
vision of the future and, 31–34
world city concept and, 42–49
Super-bobos, 89
Sustainability, 2
critique of, 2–3, 19, 85, 128, 145–148, 222, 239
flexibility and, 145–148
grand urbanism and, 222, 229, 232, 234–235, 239
housing and, 239
metropolitanization and, 207, 213
Metropolitan Plan for Sustainable Development (PADD) and, 186
quality of life and, 19
suburbs and, 53, 56, 59, 63
territorial politics and, 165, 188
transit and, 128, 145–148

Taxes
CDTs and, 204
corporate tax breaks and, 18
governance and, 181, 186, 200, 204, 211–212, 218
legal issues and, 181, 186
local initiatives and, 116
property, 200
territorial politics and, 181, 186

Index

transit and, 116–118, 132, 137, 139
value capture, 137–139
Technological Review (MIT journal), 149
Territorial Development Contracts (contrats du devéloppement territorials [CDTs])
  development myth and, 131
  governance and, 179, 187, 193, 204–205, 208–209, 213
  Grand Paris Express (GPE) and, 119, 131, 137, 148–151, 154–155, 249n10, 253n20
  housing and, 249n10
  metropolitanization and, 193, 204–205, 208–209, 213
  Paris Métropole and, 249n10
  raising land values and, 26
  state productivism and, 193
  taxes and, 204
  territorial politics and, 179, 187
  transit and, 26–27, 119, 131, 137, 148–151, 154–155, 249n10, 253n20
Territorial politics
  architecture and, 159, 165, 169, 187–188
  Blanc and, 169, 181, 216
  capitalism and, 167, 174
  central authorities and, 167–169
  centralization and, 167–168, 170, 183
  challenges of, 161–166
  Chevènement law and, 255n16
  collaboration and, 176–180
  decentralization and, 42, 75, 110–111, 160, 162–163, 167–178, 181, 185, 192, 202, 204, 218, 227, 254n12
  democracy and, 185, 188, 255n14
  elitism and, 167–171, 175
  environmental issues and, 165, 172–173, 177, 183, 186, 188
  EPCIs and, 176, 186, 255n18
  globalization and, 160–161, 164, 166–167, 189, 199, 253n4
  Grand Paris Act and, 173, 180
  Grand Paris Express (GPE) and, 159, 162, 180
  green spaces and, 177, 182–183
  housing and, 10, 165, 176, 179, 182–184, 186–187, 254n12, 255n17, 256n21
  identity and, 159, 185
  infrastructures and, 162, 167–169, 175–176, 181, 186
  International Workshop of Grand Paris (AIGP) and, 179
  investment and, 169–170, 173–175, 178, 188
  jurisdictional issues and, 75–76, 161–163, 166, 206–207
  MAPTAM and, 183, 185–186
  Métropole du Grand Paris (MGP) and, 174, 183, 185–187, 256n24
  metropolitanization and, 160–161, 166–191
  Metropolitan Plan for Sustainable Development (PADD) and, 186
  mille-feuille (thousand layers) of, 164–165, 172, 182, 196, 202
  mobility and, 160, 162, 182
  multidimensionality of, 166–172
  neoliberalism and, 160, 177, 188
  Paris Métropole and, 160, 166, 172–173, 179–185, 255n18, 256n19
  path-dependent processes and, 17–18
  Plaine Commune and, 173, 178, 184–185
  preeminence of capital region and, 11, 34–35, 169–170
  public development agencies (EPAs) and, 186, 200, 256n20
  reform and, 24, 46, 67, 131, 151, 164–166, 169–172, 175, 178, 180–182, 188
  Regional councils and, 114, 171–172, 177–178, 231
  regionalism and, 167, 238

Territorial politics (cont.)
  regulation and, 160, 175, 253n5, 254n8
  rent and, 168
  RER (Regional Express Network) and, 41, 98, 105–111, 116, 118, 143–144, 150
  return of the state and, 180–182
  Society of Grand Paris (SGP) and, 162, 173, 181
  sustainability and, 165, 188
  taxes and, 181, 186
  Territorial Development Contracts (contrats du devéloppement territorials [CDTs]) and, 179, 187
  tourism and, 187
  urbanism and, 161, 164, 177, 186–187
Terrorism, 69, 252n14
Théret, Bruno, 18, 243n11
Thiers, 35
Third Republic, 104
Tokyo, 11–12, 187, 223–224
Tourism, 13, 17
  campaigns for, 246n8
  competition and, 42, 87, 101
  London and, 242n7
  metropolitanization and, 80, 209
  rebranding urban spaces and, 69, 80, 152
  shifting regional economy and, 42–43
  suburbs and, 42, 47, 243n1
  territorial politics and, 187
  transit and, 101, 104, 116, 149, 152, 248n7
Trams, 54, 98, 116, 137, 229, 248n5
Transit, 4
  accessibility issues and, 11, 23, 54, 59–60, 85–86, 108–110, 141–143, 150, 155, 251n10
  airports and, 13, 86, 112, 114–115, 119, 132, 151–152, 154, 243n1, 248n7
  Arc Express and, 111–118, 125, 248n9
  architecture and, 54–61, 68, 85–89, 92, 97, 132, 138, 146–147, 154, 241n3
  automobiles and, 54, 98, 100, 103, 125, 137–138, 145, 147, 243n3, 247n4
  beyond Grand Paris and, 222–223
  bicycles and, 54, 60, 98, 144, 247n4, 252n16
  Blanc and, 89, 98, 112, 114t, 116, 134, 149, 248n6, 248n8
  boulevards and, 35, 37, 54, 108, 241n2
  buses and, 54, 60, 86, 98, 108–109, 112, 137, 144, 150, 247n3
  Cantal-Dupart's criticisms of, 154–155
  clusters and, 116, 133–137, 150, 251nn5–6
  commuting and, 54, 97, 100, 104–105, 108–109, 114, 117, 121–122, 129, 138–141, 144–145, 147, 243n3, 246n9, 247n4
  competition and, 99–101, 110–123, 127, 129, 131, 133, 135, 140, 142–143, 146–148, 155
  compromise and, 91, 103, 112–127, 133, 142, 146–148, 248n9, 249n12
  conflicts over, 98, 102–105, 109, 111–112, 121–127, 132
  crisis of representation and, 108–109
  decentralization and, 110–111
  defining urban space and, 6, 21–24, 38, 63, 98–99, 125, 127, 130, 135, 140, 186, 196, 198, 206, 236, 239
  democracy and, 121–123, 126
  densification and, 115, 119, 139–141, 155
  design and, 103–104, 113, 117, 119, 128, 133–137, 152
  development myth of, 129–133
  environmental issues and, 99–100, 124–125, 128, 142, 145–147, 150–151, 248nn7,9
  Equal Rights and Opportunities Law and, 251n10

Index

as essential element of modern city, 100–101
gentrification and, 97–101, 122–123, 128–137, 154–156, 218–219, 223, 234–238
Grand Moscow and, 229
Grand Paris Act and, 111, 133, 149
Grand Paris Express (GPE) and, 2 (*see also* Grand Paris Express [GPE])
Great Eight and, 87, 111–112, 114t, 116
green spaces and, 86, 116, 118–119, 140, 145–147, 150
highways and, 41, 61, 100, 111, 137, 150, 248n7, 254n12
housing and, 98, 109, 113, 121, 127, 135, 139–145, 148–155, 249n10, 251n8, 252n17
IAURIF and, 110
ideologies and, 98–102, 122–123, 126–148, 160, 167, 171–174, 177, 185, 188
International Workshop of Grand Paris (AIGP) and, 91, 117, 140, 151, 153, 249n10
investment and, 87, 100, 102, 117–118, 126, 128, 130–137, 142, 154, 156, 250n3, 251n5, 252n17, 252n19
labor and, 116, 135, 137, 139, 145
London Underground and, 104
maillage and, 250n13
megaprojects and, 21–22, 99, 122–123, 125, 129–133, 147, 153, 234, 250nn2–3
mobility and, 97–103, 107–113, 121–129, 133, 137–147, 150, 154–156, 247n2, 251n10, 252n11
neoliberalism and, 123, 127, 129, 131, 146
network effects and, 101, 249n12
ORBITALE and, 110–111
ORBIVAL and, 110–111

PADOG and, 40, 105
Parisian Autonomous Transport Operator (RATP) and, 103, 105, 108, 162, 207–208, 247n3
Paris Métropole and, 7, 49, 52t, 75–76, 89, 160, 166, 172–173, 179–180, 182–185, 207, 244n6, 249n10, 255n18, 256n19
pedestrians and, 60, 98, 146
Public Authority of Paris-Saclay (EPPS) and, 149–150
public debates over, 99, 112–126, 144
public transit myth of, 141–145
rail and, 13, 41, 57, 60, 86, 97–101, 104–111, 116, 137, 144, 147, 228–229, 236, 248n9, 251n7
Regional Express Network (RER) and, 41, 98, 105–111, 116, 118, 143–144, 150
regulation and, 132, 147
rent and, 99, 122, 125, 128, 131, 135–140, 155
RTPGP and, 87, 111–118, 248n9
Sarkozy and, 97, 111, 114t, 133, 152
SNCF and, 58, 108, 144, 207–208, 253n20
Society of Grand Paris (SGP) and, 111–119, 121, 137, 141, 146, 249n10, 249n12, 251n10
spatial issues and, 98, 108–109, 119, 121, 125, 128, 133, 142–143, 148, 156, 252n12
STIF and, 105, 110, 113–115, 117, 162, 178, 186, 207–208, 247n3
suburbs and, 108–109, 111, 115
sustainability and, 128, 145–148
taxes and, 116–118, 132, 137, 139
Territorial Development Contracts (contrats du devéloppement territorials [CDTs]) and, 26–27, 119, 131, 137, 148–151, 154–155, 249n10, 253n20
territorial politics and, 116

Transit (cont.)
  terrorism and, 252n14
  tourism and, 101, 104, 116, 149, 152, 248n7
  trams and, 54, 98, 116, 137, 229, 248n5
  underground, 102, 104, 108, 110, 114, 116, 141, 147, 150, 248n9
  urbanism and, 97–104, 109, 119, 123, 125–132, 136–138, 146–148, 151–152
  value-added territory and, 116, 139–140
  Vigipirate security plan and, 144–145
  world city and, 101, 136, 146
Transit-oriented development (TOD), 127, 129, 139, 155
Transmission (policy), 66, 224–233
Transport Ministry, 207

Unibail, 214
Union for a Popular Movement (UMP), 70, 75, 111, 171, 181, 184t, 185, 248n6
Union of Architects of Russia, 228
Unions, 84, 105, 178, 228
Urban Age project, 53
Urban development projects (UDPs), 250n1
Urbanism
  architecture and, 5 (*see also* Architecture)
  beyond Grand Paris, 221–225
  Blanc and, 87
  capitalism and, 5, 195–215, 236–237 (*see also* Capitalism)
  connected city and, 85–87
  consensus and, 25, 33, 49, 69, 82, 89, 118, 122, 126, 145, 180, 188, 192, 205, 216–219, 234, 238–9, 248n9, 249n12, 257n7
  contemporary, 10, 32, 59, 61, 88–89, 99, 127–128, 137, 160
  densification and, 58, 86, 115, 119, 139–141, 155, 200
  designed city and, 81–83
  displacement and, 83, 123, 138, 140
  flexible city and, 83–85
  gentrification and, 5, 15, 17 (*see also* Gentrification)
  globalization and, 3, 13, 20, 22, 42, 44–45, 56, 160–161, 164, 166–167, 189, 199, 212, 253n4
  governable city and, 74–77
  Grand Moscow and, 225–233
  Grand Paris, 1–4 (*see also* Grand Paris)
  Haussmann and, 14, 19, 37–41, 130, 210, 221, 246n7
  hegemonic tenets of, 3
  identity and, 25, 31, 33–34, 46, 57, 62, 78–80, 159, 185, 228, 236, 244n6, 246n7
  ideologies and, 37, 76, 81–82, 98–99, 101–102, 126–127, 129–148, 177, 195, 205, 217, 233
  megaprojects and, 4, 14, 20–22 (*see also* Megaprojects)
  metropolitanization and, 193–209, 211, 214–219
  mobility and, 97 (*see also* Mobility)
  mode of regulation and, 5
  modernization and, 12, 14–15, 36–39, 99, 130, 138, 183, 210, 222, 257n7
  neoliberalism and, 17, 222, 231, 234–235, 238
  networked, 2, 63, 119, 123, 161, 198, 205–209
  property and, 36–40
  Prost Plan and, 39, 105
  regional planning and, 39, 46, 173, 177, 221, 223
  SDRIF and, 75, 110–112, 173, 177, 180–181, 186, 249n10
  SGP and, 226, 229, 231 (*see also* Society of Grand Paris [SGP])

Index

solidarity and, 1, 18, 24, 26, 35, 39, 58, 90, 93, 118, 121, 142, 155, 177, 180–181, 187, 204, 219, 234–235, 244n5, 248n8
suburbs and, 32–33, 36–42, 46–48, 53, 56, 58–64
territorial politics and, 161, 164, 177, 186–187
transit and, 97–104, 109, 119, 123, 125–132, 136–138, 146–148, 151–152
unified city and, 77–80
works of representation and, 62–64
world city and, 6, 11–12, 16, 42–49, 101, 136, 146, 197
Utopianism, 7, 19, 55, 65, 83, 89, 92, 135

Val-de-France, 148, 151–154, 213
Val d'Oise, 151, 153, 253n20, 254n10
Vélib bicycle-sharing program, 144, 247n4
Veltz, Pierre, 188, 198, 254n6
Viganò, Paola, 50, 58–59, 79
Vigipirate security plan, 144–145
Villetaneuse, 43, 178
Vinci Construction, 212, 231
Violence, 55, 78, 110, 144–145, 154, 235, 243n2
Voynet law, 200

Weber, Rachel, 258n9
Why Invest in Paris (Ernst & Young/Jones Lang Lasalle), 136
Wiel, Marc, 88, 128–129, 139, 141, 145, 249n12
Williamson, June, 10
Wilmotte & Associés, 259n2
Wilmotte, Michel, 229
World Bank, 146
World city (*ville monde*), 6
  economic growth and, 16
  imagineering and, 34, 49, 68–71

Paris as model of, 11–13, 42–49
productivism and, 197
transit and, 101, 136, 146
World Expo, 259n4
World's Fair, 73, 104
World Trade Center, 69

Zoning, 40, 84, 222, 246n7

www.ingramcontent.com/pod-product-compliance
Lightning Source LLC
Chambersburg PA
CBHW021345300426
44114CB00012B/1083